HIS TRUTH IS
MARCHING ON

By Jon Meacham

HIS TRUTH IS MARCHING ON

JOHN LEWIS *and*
the POWER *of* HOPE

JON MEACHAM

Afterword by John Lewis

 RANDOM HOUSE NEW YORK

Published in the United States by Random House, an imprint and
division of Penguin Random House LLC, New York.

RANDOM HOUSE and the HOUSE colophon are registered trademarks
of Penguin Random House LLC.

Originally published in hardcover in the United States by Random
House, an imprint and division of Penguin Random House LLC,
in 2020.

Grateful acknowledgment is made to The Heirs to the Estate of Martin
Luther King, Jr., c/o Writers House, as agent for the proprietor for
permission to reprint "Paul's Letter to the American Christians" by Dr.
Martin Luther King, Jr., copyright © 1965 by Dr. Martin Luther King, Jr.,
and copyright renewed 1993 by Coretta Scott King. Reprinted by
arrangement with The Heirs to the Estate of Martin Luther King, Jr.,
c/o Writers House as agent for the proprietor.

LIBRARY OF CONGRESS CATALOGING-IN-PUBLICATION DATA
Names: Meacham, Jon, author.
Title: His truth is marching on: John Lewis and the power of hope / Jon
Meacham; Afterword by John Lewis.
Description: First edition. | New York: Random House, [2020] |
Includes bibliographical references and index.
Identifiers: LCCN 2020024320 (print) | LCCN 2020024321 (ebook) |
ISBN 9781984855046 (trade) | ISBN 9781984855039 (ebook)
Subjects: LCSH: Lewis, John | African American civil rights workers—
Biography. | Civil rights workers—United States—Biography. | United
States. Congress. House—Biography. | Legislators—United States—
Biography. | Protest movements—United States.
Classification: LCC E840.8.L43 M43 2020 (print) | LCC E840.8.L43
(ebook) | DDC 328.73/092 [B]—dc23
LC record available at https://lccn.loc.gov/2020024320
LC ebook record available at https://lccn.loc.gov/2020024321

Printed in the United States of America on acid-free paper

randomhousebooks.com

2 4 6 8 9 7 5 3 1

Book design by Simon M. Sullivan

FOR ALL WHO TOIL AND FIGHT AND LIVE AND DIE
TO REALIZE THE TRUE MEANING OF AMERICA'S CREED

Also I heard the voice of the Lord, saying, "Whom shall I send, and who will go for us?" Then said I, Here *am* I; send me.

—THE BOOK OF ISAIAH

CONTENTS

HIS TRUTH IS
MARCHING ON

Ku Klux Klansmen on a stroll through downtown Montgomery, Alabama, in November 1956; they were promoting a nighttime cross-burning rally amid the boycott to end segregated bus service.

THE LAST MARCH

We were beaten. Tear-gassed. Bullwhipped. On this bridge,
some of us gave a little blood to help redeem the soul of
America.

—JOHN LEWIS, on the Edmund Pettus Bridge, commemorating
the Bloody Sunday march of 1965

H IS STEPS WERE SLOW, careful, precarious. But John Lewis
knew the way, and his gaze was steady, even peaceful, as he
took in the old steel ramparts above his head and the brown
asphalt under his feet. It was a Sunday in March 2020, on the Edmund Pettus Bridge in Selma, Alabama, not unlike that first, fabled
Sunday, fifty-five years before. Then as now, the breeze was cool, the
late-winter sun soft, and the water below silent and swirling. The civil
rights hero and longtime U.S. congressman from Atlanta was back
again, walking the old path, his mind a mix of past and present. Once
stocky from endless church suppers and innumerable political picnics
and banquets, he was now frail and thin—shockingly so to friends ac-
customed to his familiar girth, a thickness of body that had made him
so reassuringly solid, so central, so orienting, so much *John Lewis*. The
weight loss was not a matter of choice, but of affliction—the worst
kind of affliction, the result of cancer that had attacked his pancreas.
Yet here he was, just weeks after his eightieth birthday, smaller but
unbowed, standing once more above the Alabama River.

He led his fellow pilgrims up the bridge. They sang, inevitably, a
few verses of "We Shall Overcome." Lewis knew the song was important, just as days like these were important. They brought the story to
life. As the years passed, he worried that the civil rights movement
was receding into myth and legend. The battles of more than a half
century ago could seem as distant as Agincourt or Antietam. The last
chapter of Lewis's life, then, was about history and hope, remem-

brance and renewal. His message was consistent: "If the young people of the South—young black people, young women, young men—could change the world then," he'd say, "then we can do it again, now." There were these pilgrimages to Selma, to Montgomery, and to Birmingham, the commemorations, and, day in and day out, the fact of *being* John Lewis, a man whose physical scars mirrored the wars of a nation. Quietly charismatic, forever courtly, implacably serene, he was charming about his effect on others. "People come up to me in airports, they walk into the office, and they say, 'I'm going to cry; I'm going to pass out.' And I say, 'Please don't pass out; I'm not a doctor.'" He was, rather, a preacher and a prophet, a man of faith and of action.

Surrounded by civil rights veterans and members of Congress on that day in 2020, Lewis was handed a microphone. His frame may have been diminished, but his voice was not. That voice was still big and booming and passionate—a surprise, often, to audiences who saw Lewis as a quiet man. He was quiet, though, only until he had something to say. And when he had something to say, he said it with the preacherly cadences he'd honed delivering sermons to a flock of chickens on his family's tenant farm in Pike County, Alabama—a place, Lewis recalled, so small it was nearly impossible to find on a map.

"It is good to be in Selma, Alabama, one more time," he said to the crowd, pausing between phrases, letting the words sink in. "On this bridge just a few short years ago a few of the children of God started on a journey." He'd been one of them—just twenty-five years old and already, from the age of twenty, a bloodied soldier of the movement. They'd been there, he recalled, because of his teacher in nonviolence, the Reverend James M. Lawson, who stood there still, in 2020, at the age of ninety-one. They'd been there because of Martin Luther King, Jr., and Ralph D. Abernathy, and Lewis's fellow student activist Diane Nash. And they'd been there, Lewis told the other pilgrims, because of "the saints of old."

There could be no more profound inspiration. In his *Ad Martyras,* Tertullian, the second-century Church Father, wrote that to face prison and death for the faith was a noble fate. The real prison was sin and injustice; to love in the face of hate was the deepest call of the Lord Himself. Prison, Tertullian wrote, "is full of darkness, but you yourselves are light; it has bonds, but God has made you free." To Tertullian, the blood of the martyrs was the seed of the church.

To John Lewis, the truth of his life—a truth he had lived out on that bridge in 1965—was of a piece with the demands of the gospel to which he had dedicated his life since he was a child. He was moved by love, not by hate. He was as important to the founding of a modern and multiethnic twentieth- and twenty-first century America as Thomas Jefferson and James Madison and Samuel Adams were to the creation of the republic in the eighteenth century. This is not hyperbole. It is fact—observable, discernible, undeniable fact.

On this anniversary, Ralph and Juanita Abernathy's daughter Juandalynn took the microphone from Lewis and broke into a hymn of the movement:

> *Oh freedom, oh freedom, oh freedom over me*
> *And before I'd be a slave, I'll be buried in my grave,*
> *And go home to my Lord and be free.*

> *No more mourning, no more mourning, no more mourning over me*
> *And before I'd be a slave, I'll be buried in my grave,*
> *And go home to my Lord and be free.*

Listening intently, his eyes and ears taking everything in, Lewis simply said, "God bless you."

He'd heard the song before. He'd seen the sights before. He'd walked this pavement before. On Sunday, March 7, 1965, in a planned march from Selma to Montgomery to protest the systematic exclusion of African Americans from the voting booth—in violation of the Fifteenth Amendment to the Constitution, still flagrantly ignored in the American South a century on—Lewis and his friend Hosea Williams were stopped by Alabama authorities at the foot of the bridge. Some on horseback, all wielding weapons, the white officers charged the column of nonviolent marchers. "Get 'em!" one white woman cried out. "*Get* the niggers!" Lewis was beaten and, lying on the pavement, was ready to die.

Yet he survived, and the images of the attack that Sunday helped push President Lyndon B. Johnson to call for, and pass, federal legislation guaranteeing voting rights. Taken together with sit-ins to integrate lunch counters and other public facilities and Freedom Rides to integrate interstate travel, the Selma march, Lewis recalled, "injected something very special into the soul and the heart and the veins of America. It said, in effect, that we must humanize our social and political and economic structure. When people saw what happened on that bridge, there was a sense of revulsion all over America." Revulsion, then redemption: Is there anything more American? "Redemption—redemption is everything," Lewis said. "It is what we pray for. It is what we march for."

In the middle of the last century, Lewis marched into the line of fire to summon a nation to be what it had long said it would be but had failed to become. Arrested forty-five times over the course of his life, Lewis suffered a fractured skull and was repeatedly beaten and tear-gassed. He led by example more than by words. He was a peaceful soldier in the cause of a religiously inspired understanding of humanity and of America. And he bent history to his will—though he would insist the important thing was not his will, but God's.

The world was one way before John Lewis came out of Pike County and into the maelstrom of history, and it was another way when he was done. Though, to be strictly accurate, he was never done. "In the final analysis, we are one people, one family, one house—not just the house of black and white, but the house of the South, the house of America," Lewis said. "We can move ahead, we can move forward, we can create a multiracial community, a truly democratic society. I think we're on our way there. There may be some setbacks. But we are going to get there. We have to be hopeful. Never give up, never give in, keep moving on." Devoted to the ideal of a soul's pilgrimage from sin to redemption, from the wilderness of the world to the Kingdom of God, Lewis walked with faith that tomorrow could be better than today, and that tomorrow was but prelude to a yet more glorious day after that.

To put complicated matters simply: John Robert Lewis embodied the traits of a saint in the classical Christian sense of the term. A complex concept, sanctity has at various times been applied to all believers or to a special few. In Greek, the language of the New Testament, sainthood is derived from *hagíazo,* which means "to set apart" or "make holy." (The Latin is *sanctus.*) Generations of believers have held that some human lives are in such harmony with the ideals of God that they should be singled out. One need not embrace Catholic practice and doctrine to benefit from the contemplation of men and women who, in the words of an old hymn, "toiled and fought and lived and died for the Lord they loved and knew." One test of a saint, closely tied to the test of a martyr, is the willingness to suffer and die for others. Which Lewis was willing to do—again and again and again.

This may sound sentimental and overly grand, and if one were saying it about virtually anyone other than Lewis, it likely would be. To see John Lewis as a saint and a hero, however, is not nostalgic, nor does such an understanding flow from a kind of easy-listening historical sensibility in which the civil rights movement is white America's safe and redemptive drama. It comes, rather, from the straightforward story of what Lewis did, how he lived, and why. He accomplished something on the battlefields of twentieth-century America, in the skirmishes in our streets and in our cities and in our hearts, that links him with the saints of ancient ages, with the revolutionaries of the eighteenth century, and with the abolitionists and Union soldiers of the nineteenth. In Abraham Lincoln's First Inaugural, the new president appealed, eloquently but theoretically, to "the better angels of our nature." John Lewis *is* a better angel. The American present and future may in many ways hinge on the extent to which the rest of us can draw lessons from his example.

That is, to be sure, the most difficult of tasks. Our Constitution was founded on a dark yet realistic view of human nature: that we are fallen, frail, and fallible. The aim of the new republic was not perfection, an impossibility on this side of Paradise, but, as Gouverneur Morris put it in the preamble to the Constitution, a Union that would prove "more perfect." Experience teaches us that injustice is endemic to political life. "The tragedy of man," the twentieth-century Protestant theologian Reinhold Niebuhr observed, "is that he can conceive self-perfection but cannot achieve it." And the tragedy of America is that we can imagine justice but cannot finally realize it.

Such an acceptance of the inevitability of falling short—that we will never fully be all we ought to be—is comforting for many. By allowing for failure, history is reassuring, for failure can thus be seen as inherent and excusable. If living with injustice is part of the nature of things, then perhaps we need not put ourselves through the most anguishing of trials to fight it. We can become too quick to be satisfied with a bit of progress, unconsciously limiting our vision by focusing on the incremental rather than on the transformative. As Martin Luther King, Jr., put it in a phrase drawn from the abolitionist Theodore Parker, "The arc of the moral universe is long, but it bends toward justice." *Bends,* not *swerves*—but what we can miss in this cold-eyed understanding of history is that the arc won't even bend without devoted Americans pressing for the swerve.

That's why Lewis is so vital. He rejected the tragedy of life and history, dismissed the suffocating limits of pragmatism, and instead embraced the possibilities of realizing a joyful ideal. He seemed to walk with Jesus Himself, who called on his followers to give everything to the cause of the poor and the downtrodden and the oppressed. The injunction of the gospel is to take up one's cross, not to take it as it comes; to lose one's life in the service of others, not to keep one's options open.

"The finest task of achieving justice," Niebuhr wrote, "will be done neither by the Utopians who dream dreams of perfect brotherhood nor yet by the cynics who believe that the self-interest of nations cannot be overcome. It must be done by the realists who understand that nations are selfish and will be so till the end of history, but that none of us, no matter how selfish we may be, can be only selfish."

Fair enough—but without the Utopians the experiment fails, for without a peak to scale we would remain in the valley, milling about. Lewis was a prophet of the mountaintop, a signpost in the wilderness. In pointing toward the perfect, he insisted that a moderate course was no course at all, only a continuation of the wrong. He understood sin, but he chose to see the depravity of the world as something to be fought, not to be accepted. His inspiration came from the New Testament: *"Blessed are the meek; for they shall inherit the earth. . . . Blessed are they who are persecuted for righteousness' sake; for theirs is the kingdom of heaven."* As Lewis recalled, the struggle within time and space was about "Heaven *and* earth. This was the social gospel in action. This was love in action, what we came to call in our workshops soul force."

In December 1975, in a story headlined SAINTS AMONG US, *Time* magazine listed Lewis, along with Mother Teresa (a portrait of whom appeared on the issue's cover), Dorothy Day, and others as "Messengers of Love and Hope: Living Saints." The term, the magazine wrote, "is heavy with meanings, not all of them congenial to modern man. . . . To many, 'saint' is a medieval word, redolent of incense, conjuring up halos and glowing, distant images of spiritual glory in some great cathedral's stained-glass windows. To others, the word is still useful, if prosaic, shorthand to describe someone who willingly suffers something that seems beyond the call of duty: a son or daughter, for instance, who spends years caring for a senile and demanding parent. Somewhere between the two is the vision of the contemporary saint as a person of persistently heroic virtue and courage whose life is a model for others—a Mother Teresa, perhaps, or a Mahatma Gandhi."

Or a John Lewis. "A saint has to be a misfit," the historian of religion Martin Marty told *Time*. "A person who embodies what his culture considers typical or normal cannot be exemplary." It was neither typical nor normal to sit at segregated lunch counters in Nashville, or to walk into segregated bus stations in Rock Hill, Montgomery, Birmingham, and Jackson, or to march across that bridge in Selma.

Lewis was not perfect, but that's not the test of a saint. Diane Nash, who loved him, said she didn't think of him in saintly terms. "He was human," she recalled. "He was my friend, my brother." Saints, however, *are* human. That's what makes them saints rather than saviors. Yes, he could be prideful and stubborn, and down the decades some found his message antiquated, trite, and incommensurate with enduring racial, economic, and criminal justice inequities. "*Time* magazine called John Lewis 'a saint,'" Joseph Lowery, a King lieutenant who

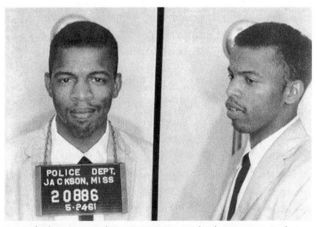

Lewis after his arrest in Jackson, Mississippi, on Wednesday, May 24, 1961, during the Freedom Rides. He'd be sent to Parchman Farm, the notorious penitentiary William Faulkner once described as "destination doom."

became president of the Southern Christian Leadership Conference, said after Lewis had defeated Julian Bond, an old and intimate friend of Lewis's, in a tumultuous 1986 congressional campaign. "I never heard anybody in the black community say that.... John Lewis gives the appearance of humility. I don't know whether he's humble or not, but white folk think he's humble. And white people tend to like humble black folk."

A blunt, biting, and fair point, but Lewis need not have all the answers to all our questions to be a figure of inspiration and illumination. "Next to Holy Scripture there certainly is no more useful book for Christians than that of the lives of the saints, especially when unadulterated and authentic," Martin Luther wrote. "For in these stories, one is greatly pleased to find how they sincerely believed in God's Word, confessed it with their lips, praised it by their living, and honored and confirmed it by their suffering and dying."

Was John Lewis a saint in the classical sense of the term? "I would say yes," James Lawson said long years after Nashville. "He clearly tried to be one who followed Jesus. That was a very important mantra for me in teaching nonviolence: to let the 'Kingdom' about which Jesus prayed when he said 'Thy Kingdom come'—a kingdom governed by the Sermon on the Mount—begin in every person. And John made that Christian understanding the center of his life. In the nonviolent movement—which he followed in different forms through all the years—and in his personal life, John always lived that faith. I would say that without reservation or hesitation." Lewis, then, made the Christian ideal real.

For many Americans, especially non-Christians, the thought that Christian morality can be a useful guide to much of anything is risible, particularly since so many white evangelicals from 2016 forward chose to throw in their lot with a solipsistic American president who bullies, boasts, and sneers. Yet Lewis's life suggests that religiously inspired activism may hold one of the best hopes for those who aim to make the life of the nation more just.

At times in its history, Christianity has been an instrument of repression. In our living memory, however, it has also been deployed as a means of liberation and progress. "All men," Homer wrote, "have need of the gods," and the secular wish to banish religion from the public square is perennial but doomed—one might as well try to eliminate economics, geography, or partisanship as forces that shape our politics. The more productive task is to manage and marshal the effects of religious feeling on the broader republic. "In ages of faith the final aim of life is placed beyond life," Alexis de Tocqueville wrote in his *Democracy in America* in the Age of Jackson. "The men of these ages, therefore, . . . learn by insensible degrees to repress a multitude of petty, passing desires." This was the vision, a religious vision, that elevated America in the mid-1960s.

The story of the civil rights movement is often rendered as a struggle between nonviolence and violence, between the demand for "Freedom Now" and the cry for "Black Power." John Lewis and Martin Luther King preached and practiced nonviolence, believing strongly that the vote was the most formidable of weapons. There were, however, other important voices in the arena. Malcolm X, for instance, argued that black Americans had a moral obligation to use "any means necessary" to achieve what the Founders had thought of as the rights of man. Those means included the right of self-defense, and the right of self-defense included the right to engage in violence to defend against white-supremacist terror. Yet the ethos articulated by Malcolm X was not, as many white critics would have it, about burning America down. It was, instead, about urging African Americans to draw on the traditions of the American Revolution to battle state-sanctioned white supremacy in order to claim their rightful place as citizens. George Washington and Patrick Henry had resorted to arms to win their liberty—so, Malcolm X argued, why shouldn't African Americans be able to draw on that example in the face of fear, intimidation, and brutality?

Remedying four centuries of slavery, of segregation, and of inequality of opportunity is no simple matter. The witness of a Lewis and of a King and a Malcolm and a host of others was—and is—necessary to reform a nation in which racist ideas still prevail. Experience tells us that the task is staggeringly difficult. Lewis approached the work one way; many others choose different routes. In the fourth century, arguing against Christians who wanted to remove an altar to the pagan deity Victory, the Roman writer Symmachus noted, "We cannot attain to so great a mystery by one way."

Nor can America attain racial, economic, and political justice in only one way. This book is about John Lewis and his vision, which was also the vision of Martin Luther King, and which changed, in a limited but real sense, how America saw itself. When the nation sees differently, it enhances its capacity to act differently. From Seneca Falls to Selma to Stonewall, America has gradually expanded who's included when the country speaks of "We the People."

Now as then, the tradition of faith that drove Lewis is too often used not to pursue justice but to amass power. Now as then, many white Americans profess to believe the gospel. And now as then, too many are content to accede to religious teachings more in principle than in practice. My aim is to show how John Lewis did both—and if he did both, then perhaps more of us can, too.

No sect, no nation, has a monopoly on virtue. Still, history teaches us that the religious element was essential to the movement. Lewis shared King's view: "The more I thought about human nature the more I saw how our tragic inclination for sin causes us to use our minds to rationalize our actions," King observed in recalling the Montgomery bus boycott. "Reason, devoid of the purifying power of faith, can never free itself from distortions and rationalizations." The American past also tells us that one way to transcend our selfishness and greed is the way of Lewis, which was also the way of Jesus. "We say we are a believing nation, yet when we are wronged, the people demand revenge," Lewis said. "If we truly believe, then what is the role of forgiveness, mercy, and compassion in public life?"

In Judeo-Christian terms, the world was created whole and perfect, but Adam and Eve's defiance brought corruption and disorder. The work of the ensuing eons has been to seek deliverance from evil, to find light in the darkness, to establish justice amid injustice. In the Hebrew scriptures, the story of Israel is one in which the people of God are exiled and persecuted and yet forever seek renewal. In the theology of Christianity, human souls dwell in what Augustine of Hippo called the "City of Man" as they live in hope to bring about the reign of the "City of God." Progress is therefore possible; hope, rational, for progress and hope are based on the evidence of history. "The education of the human race, represented by the people of God, has advanced, like that of an individual, through certain epochs, or, as it were, ages," Augustine wrote, "so that it might gradually rise from earthly to heavenly things, and from the visible to the invisible."

The quest to rise from despair and injustice to restoration and redemption—not only beyond time and space, but within time and space—is the fundamental drama of the Hebrew Bible and, down the ages, of the Christian West.

The means of restoration include faith and works—works of charity and of justice that offer glimpses of the all-enveloping love of God. To Lewis, the pursuit of justice, of the full equality of all people, was the object of life. And to him, redemption required suffering. "He had a remarkable degree of toughness, of inner courage, of commitment," his fellow activist Diane Nash recalled. "I always had the impression that he was just never going to let anybody turn him around. We didn't expect him to be a martyr. But we always knew, and he certainly knew, that it was a possibility." He never flinched from that terrible reality. Indeed, he sought it out.

He never gave up on what he and King thought of as the Beloved Community, which was not the more perfect union of the American Founders. The Beloved Community was something different, something wholly perfect. It was, as Lewis said, "nothing less than the Christian concept of the Kingdom of God on earth. According to this concept, all human existence throughout history, from ancient Eastern and Western societies up through the present day, has strived toward community, toward coming together. That movement is as inexorable, as irresistible, as the flow of a river toward the sea."

From Homer's *Iliad* forward, we have told the stories of warriors, generals, and statesmen. Combat is dramatic and compelling; the imagination has long thrilled to Mark Antony's exhortation to "Cry 'Havoc!' and let slip the dogs of war" in Shakespeare's *Julius Caesar*. The American civil rights movement in the middle of the twentieth century is a war epic about a struggle between two opposing forces—but it is an epic with essential distinctions from standard tales of war, strategy, and statecraft. The heroes of this story laid down no fire, but rather walked into fire. The heroes of this story drew no blood, but rather shed their own. The heroes of this story sought no spoils, but rather asked only that the founding words of the national experiment be logically applied to all. Montgomery, Nashville, Rock Hill, Birmingham, Selma: These Southern cities were the scenes of battles as real as Bunker Hill, New Orleans, Gettysburg, the Argonne, Normandy.

"Sometimes I hear people saying nothing has changed, but for someone to grow up the way I grew up in the cotton fields of Alabama to now be serving in the United States Congress makes me want to tell them come and walk in my shoes," Lewis said at the fiftieth anniversary of the March on Washington in 2013. "Come walk in the shoes of those who were attacked by police dogs, fire hoses and nightsticks, arrested and taken to jail." Yet as often as Lewis was asked to look back, to tell the old stories and, in a sense, sing the old songs, he was always looking ahead, past the foot of the bridge and along the highway to come. He lived in hope.

If the Framers were about limits, Lewis was about horizons. The men who wrote the Constitution believed that human appetites and ambitions were the controlling forces of history. Lewis believed hope shaped history—the hope that Lincoln's better angels could prevail if men and women heeded the still, small voice of conscience that suggested the country, and the world, would be better off if Jefferson's assertion of human equality were truly universal.

Lewis would risk all in service to that mission. "There was never any question in John's mind about whether he was doing the right thing," his college roommate, movement comrade, and fellow Freedom Rider Bernard LaFayette, Jr., recalled. "That was so unusual for someone so young. He was always on the front line, wherever the front line was. He had no reservations about that. And as his friend, I got concerned. To be honest with you, I was afraid for him. They always went for his head, and I worried about him—about his physical safety, about his life. But I was the one who worried about him. He didn't worry about himself. I am surprised that he survived."

Standing in Selma in 2020, Lewis mused to his fellow pilgrims about what had come to pass and what lay ahead. "We took a little walk to try to dramatize the need for the rights of all of our people to be able to participate in the democratic process," he said. "In an orderly, peaceful, nonviolent fashion, we were walking, not saying a word. We were beaten. Tear-gassed. Bullwhipped. On this bridge, some of us gave a little blood to help redeem the soul of America. Our country is a better country, we are a better people, but we still have a distance to travel, to go, before we get there. I want to thank each and every one of you for being here"—and with this his voice rose almost to a shout, which in the Bible signifies a great call to action, often re-demptive, miraculous action—"for not giving up, for not giving in, for keeping the faith, for keeping your eyes on the prize. You're wonder-ful. You're beautiful. All of you look so good."

A voice from the crowd called out, "We love you, John."

"I—I love you, too," he said. He paused. The breeze blew. The clouds shifted. "We have a lot of work to do," Lewis said. "So don't get weary! Keep the faith!" Falling into the vernacular of the old days, he called for forward motion, for marching feet: "Keep picking 'em up," he cried, "and puttin' 'em down." It was, after all, what he'd always done.

STREET SCENE - TROY, ALA.

CHAPTER ONE

A HARD LIFE,
A SERIOUS LIFE

Troy, Alabama: Beginnings to 1957

Work and put your trust in God, and God's gonna take care
of his children. God's *gonna* take care of his children.

—Oft-repeated counsel from
WILLIE MAE CARTER LEWIS, John's mother

Costly grace . . . is costly because it costs a man his life, and it
is grace because it gives a man the only true life.

—DIETRICH BONHOEFFER

F OR JOHN LEWIS, slavery wasn't an abstraction. It was as real to
him as his great-grandfather, Frank Carter, who lived until his
great-grandson was seven. Light-skinned, hardworking, and
self-confident, Carter, whom Lewis called "Grandpapa," had been
born into enslavement in Pike County, Alabama, in 1862. The family
has long believed that a white man was likely Frank Carter's father—
Carter and his own son, whose name was Dink, were, Lewis recalled,
"light, very fair, and their hair was different, what we could call good
hair"—but the subject was shrouded in secrecy and silence. This much
is clear: The trajectory of the infant Frank Carter's life was fundamentally changed on Thursday, January 1, 1863, when President Lincoln declared the enslaved in the seceded Confederate States of
America were now free, and by the ratification, in December 1865, of
the Thirteenth Amendment to the Constitution, which abolished
slavery "within the United States, or any place subject to their juris-
diction."

Coming of age in Reconstruction and under Jim Crow, Carter was
driven and skilled in the world available to him. Yet the "new birth of
freedom" of which Lincoln had spoken at Gettysburg in 1863 had
failed to come fully into being after the Confederate surrender at Appomattox in 1865. Within eight months of the war's end, Alabama's
legislature had instituted a Black Code to curtail the rights of African
Americans and give the old ways new form and new force. In 1866,
the federal government, driven by Republicans in Congress, sought to

bring interracial democracy to the South. The reactionary Black Code was repealed; new constitutions were written; black people were by and large allowed to vote; and African American candidates were elected to federal, state, and local office.

White reaction was fierce. The Ku Klux Klan was founded in these postbellum years—a Confederate general named Edmund Pettus was a grand dragon—and, by 1901, when Frank Carter was nearly forty, white Alabama had reverted as much as it could to an antebellum order by legalizing segregation, circumscribing suffrage, and banning interracial marriage. At the dawn of a new century, then, the old color line had been redrawn and reinforced.

Alabama's 1901 constitution establishing white supremacy had been debated in Montgomery from May to September of that year, ending in time for the cotton harvest. Fifty miles away from the state capital, Frank Carter leased his land from J. S. "Big Josh" Copeland, a major figure in Troy, the Pike County seat. Carter worked his way to an unusual level of sharecropping called "standing rent," which meant he paid Copeland to lease the land but did not owe the landlord any of his yield beyond the rent. Diligent, resourceful, and determined, Lewis's great-grandfather did the best he could under the constraints of his time. "He couldn't read or write," his great-grandson said, "but he could do financial transactions in his head faster than the man on the other side of the desk could work them out with a pen and paper." Carter took great pride in just about everything he did. "He would sit in his rocking chair on his porch," John Lewis recalled, "and he acted like he was the king."

In a way, he was—at least of the piece of Pike County that came to be known as Carter's Quarters. It was there, in 1914, that his granddaughter Willie Mae was born to Frank's son Dink. In 1932, she married Edward Lewis, who had been born (along with his twin sister, Edna) in 1909 in Roberta, Georgia. Eddie's mother, Lula, had come to Carter's Quarters after a separation from her husband, Henry. Willie Mae and Eddie met at Macedonia Baptist Church and fell in love. He called her "Sugarfoot"; she called him "Shorty."

They were to have ten children: Ora, Edward, Sammy, Grant, Freddie, Adolph, William, Ethel, Rosa (also called Mae)—and John Robert Lewis, who was born in a shotgun shack in Carter's Quarters on a cold Wednesday, February 21, 1940. Readers of *The Montgomery Adver-*

tiser that day saw headlines about the German sinking of three British ships and Democratic anxiety about President Franklin D. Roosevelt's silence on whether he'd seek a third term. Closer to home, *The Troy Messenger* reported on a local man's suicide—he had jumped from the nineteenth floor of a downtown Montgomery hotel—and announced an upcoming fiddling contest in the County Activities building that would include Harpo Kidwell, "national champion harmonica king." The Troy paper also published a biblical "Thought for the Day," drawn from First Peter: "Beloved, think it not strange concerning the fiery trial which is to try you."

It was a harrowing era to be black, Southern, and American. In June 1940, when John Lewis was four months old, Jesse Thornton, a twenty-six-year-old churchgoing African American man who lived twenty miles away from Troy, in Luverne, Alabama, was standing outside a black barbershop when a white Luverne police officer walked by. Thornton allegedly failed to address the policeman with the honorific "Mister." Thornton wasn't thinking, or at least wasn't thinking the way a black man was supposed to think under a regime of white supremacy. He was lynched, his corpse dumped in a nearby swamp.

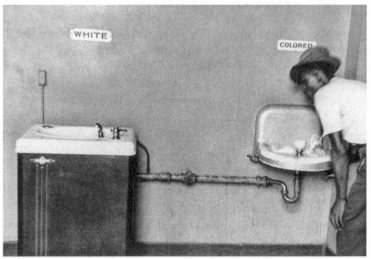

Born three-quarters of a century after Appomattox, Lewis grew up in a universe governed by Jim Crow laws designed to maintain segregation and ensure white supremacy. "From my earliest memories," he recalled, "I was fundamentally disturbed by the unbridled meanness of the world around me."

Thornton's body was found several days later floating in the Patsaliga River, mauled and gnawed by vultures and buzzards. According to the Luverne newspaper, "the cause of his death is a mystery that will probably never be solved." In a typewritten report on the incident, Charles A. J. McPherson, the secretary of the Birmingham branch of the NAACP, wrote, "These lynchings are organized and hushed up too in Hitler fashion and who knows how often? ? ?"

Mrs. Recy Taylor, who was kidnapped and raped by white men in 1944 in Abbeville, Alabama, and who courageously spoke out about the crime.

Terror could strike African Americans at any time—and justice was bitterly elusive. On the evening of Sunday, September 3, 1944, in Abbeville, Alabama—about fifty miles from the Lewises' Troy—a twenty-four-year-old African American woman, Recy Taylor, was walking home after services at the Rock Hill Holiness Church. She had a husband and a two-year-old baby. In the darkness, seven white men kidnapped her at gunpoint; six of them gang-raped her. "I'm begging them to leave me alone—don't shoot me—I got to go home and see about my baby," Mrs. Taylor recalled. "They wouldn't let me go. I can't help but tell the truth of what they done to me." The NAACP in Montgomery heard about the case and asked one of its members, a woman who happened to have family in Abbeville, to go over and investigate. Rosa Parks accepted the assignment, learned the details of the attack, and helped organize a campaign for justice for Mrs. Taylor, who bravely spoke up about the crime. But there would be no justice: All-white grand juries twice refused to indict the well-known assailants.

There seemed no hope. An omitted "Mister" might get you dumped in a swamp on an otherwise unremarkable summer day; walking home from church could lead to horrific sexual violence. "We know that if we protest we will be called 'bad niggers,'" the novelist Richard Wright wrote in his 1941 book *Twelve Million Black Voices.* "The Lords of the Land will preach the doctrine of 'white supremacy' to the poor whites who are eager to form mobs. In the midst of general hysteria they will seize one of us—it does not matter who, the innocent or guilty—and, as a token, a naked and bleeding body will be dragged through the dusty streets." That was the way of the world into which John Lewis was born.

His first memory was of his mother's garden. "There was a little gate, and when you opened the gate, there was a large bucket that filled with rain, and we used it to water the vegetables and the flowers and the plants," Lewis recalled. "I loved to make things grow, to pour out that water. I somehow always knew that water was good. I would always love raising things."

His family called him "Robert"; "John" did not become his common name until he moved to Nashville as a seminary student and joined the civil rights movement. There is a bit of the biblical in this. Several figures in the great story of God's people were renamed as they began a different, more public phase of their lives. In the Hebrew scriptures, the Lord transformed "Abram" into "Abraham" and "Sarai" into "Sarah." In the New Testament, Jesus announced that the disciple known as Simon would henceforth be "Peter, and upon this rock I will build my church."

Lewis's was not a family of revolutionaries. "Change, as I learned back when I was growing up, was not something my parents were ever very comfortable with," Lewis recalled. "Theirs was, as the Bible says, a straight and narrow way." His father, Eddie, had started out as a sharecropper, working the land for J. S. Copeland, Jr., or "Little Josh." (His in-laws had been tenants of "Big Josh.") Young John Lewis never saw the landlord—he was, Lewis recalled, "a figure like Santa Claus or the tooth fairy—not quite real." Copeland's impact on the Lewises, however, was all too real, and evident. For proof, Lewis needed look no further than his mother's hands.

He always remembered those hands, particularly Willie Mae Lewis's fingers—fingers split and hardened by years in the cotton fields. Her son honored her endurance, even marveled at it. Yet he also recoiled from a way of life that put struggling people out under the Southern sun, hunched over and compelled, season after season, decade after decade, to eke out a living while fingers bled and muscles

Clockwise from top left: Lewis's great-grandfather, Frank Carter, who was born into slavery; Lewis's mother, Willie Mae Carter Lewis; and John Robert Lewis, at age eleven. His first memory was of his mother's garden: "I loved to make things grow," he recalled.

ached. Later in life, he was horrified to realize that his parents had made $1.40 for every four hundred pounds of cotton—and it took a person about two days to pick that four hundred pounds.

The young Lewis had an instinctive aversion to the inequities of the world. "Working for nothing, that's what I would tell my mother we were doing," Lewis recalled in 1998 of the tenant farming and cotton picking of his youth. "I know it upset her and my father. . . . I carried my load, I did my duties, but I also spoke my mind, and even today my mother shakes her head at what an irritating habit that was."

He may have irritated her, but he was also learning from her, even if he didn't quite realize it at the time. Her spirit, he remembered, was unbreakable. It propelled her through the years, and long afterward Lewis came to see that the character of the woman whose fingers worked and worked and worked foreshadowed what drove her son to march and march and march.

Lewis's father was ambitious for his family and, in 1944, after saving $300, he bought 110 acres of his own about half a mile from Copeland's plantation at Carter's Quarters. The seller was A. M. Hickman, a white grocer from Troy. "It was good to get to have something you could call yours," Mrs. Lewis recalled to her son. "Working for somebody else all your days, and then to have a little something you could call your own, it was *bound* to make you feel good." The work was still hard, of course. The family raised cotton, corn, peanuts, and chickens, and the task of picking the cotton remained brutal.

Lewis recalled riding to the new place, sitting next to a radio and to Riley, the family's dog. The house was small—just three rooms, counting the kitchen. There were cracks between the floorboards, no electricity, and water came from a well by the porch near an old pecan tree (whose nuts, alas, were inedible; "even the hogs," Lewis recalled, "wouldn't eat them"). Pages from Sears, Roebuck catalogs were available for toilet paper in the outhouse. But, Lewis remembered, "If no catalogs were on hand, there were always some dried corncobs around—which, let me tell you, was incentive enough to keep those catalogs in stock." It was a life of extremes—the fireplace in the house provided overwhelming heat if you were near it, but cold set in just a few feet away. Same with the outhouse: "In the winter, it was bitter cold, with the wind cutting through the cracks between the wood planks that made up the walls," Lewis recalled. "You might as well have been outside for all the good those walls did. In the summer, it was the smell that did you in, with the heat turning that little hut into a tiny oven."

A good bit of life centered on church. Like those of their neighbors, the Lewis farm was so isolated that families were expected at services about once a month. "That's an indication of how rural this area was—traveling a distance of merely a few miles over those rough roads, roads that turned into impassable quagmires with just a little bit of rain, was a difficult task," Lewis recalled. "And these were people who worked their fingers to the bone week in and week out. Making it to church every Sunday would have been simply another load in already overloaded lives. But once or twice a month, that was a joy." Dunn's Chapel AME met on the first Sunday of each month; Macedonia Baptist, where Willie Mae had met Eddie, on the third Sunday. Dressed carefully in their little-worn Sunday clothes, the Lewises would climb into a mule-drawn wagon for the journey.

The services followed a familiar pattern. There was the singing—a cappella—of hymns such as "Leaning on the Everlasting Arms," "Father, I Stretch Out My Hand to Thee," and "Amazing Grace." A prayer from a congregant would follow. Then came the sermon, the offering, and the dismissal. To the young Lewis, the rhythms of the church were fascinating, fulfilling, and transporting. The stories of enslavement and deliverance and, above all, of radical love, carried him far beyond those muddy roads. He was at one with his fellow believers. In a harsh and segregated world—Lewis remembered seeing only two white people in his childhood, the mailman and a single traveling salesman—the church was comforting and restorative.

He loved the singing and the sermons—so much so that he seems to have always seen himself as a preacher. Given a Bible at age four, he listened to his mother read the first chapter of Genesis: "In the beginning, God created the heaven and the earth." Soon he could read on his own, and a phrase from the Gospel of John echoed in his mind and heart: "Behold the Lamb of God, which taketh away the sin of the world."

That these two verses were so vivid to Lewis was telling, for they are themselves intertwined. The New Testament quotation—the words of John the Baptist as he greeted Jesus—is from the prologue of John's gospel, a conscious echo of the opening words of Genesis. "In the beginning was the Word," John wrote, "and the Word was with God, and the Word was God"—a Christian effort to assign Jesus a place as the eternal Son of God, forever present in the Lord's cosmos but only latterly revealed. "And the Word was made flesh, and dwelt among us," John's gospel says, "full of grace and truth." From the beginning of his engagement with scripture, then, Lewis was drawn to the sweep and scope of the Christian story—the story of a created order disrupted by sin and redeemed by Jesus. For a youngster of great imagination and quickening faith, there could be no more moving saga than the biblical epic of fall and resurrection, of exile and deliverance—themes that shaped and suffused Lewis's life from his earliest days.

His burgeoning vocation intersected with his chief chore on the farm: the care of the family's poultry. "We had a lot of chickens," Lewis recalled. His interest in the ministry informed his daily duty. "Somehow, it got together, and I literally started preaching to the chickens," he said. "They became members of this sort of invisible church or

Willie Mae Carter had met Eddie Lewis at Macedonia Baptist, and their son John came to love the rituals and rhythms of the church here and at Dunn's Chapel AME.

maybe you want to call it a real church. . . . I remember my first act of nonviolent protest was when my parents would kill one of the chickens and I would refuse to eat the chicken. . . . I thought that it was so wrong." There were pastoral mishaps. "When I was about five or six years old, I wanted to save the soul of a chicken," and he accidentally drowned it during an attempted baptism. Lewis noted the irony. "In the process of trying to save this chicken," he said, smiling at the memory, "I lost the chicken." But not quite: There was resurrection, too, for the now-saved chicken managed to revive in the sun. "The little thing stirred," Lewis recalled, "then stood up and waddled back toward the coop."

When one of his feathered charges did die, Lewis would conduct a full funeral, complete with readings from scripture and a eulogy. The tale of his congregation of chickens is a staple of the Lewis story. It's oft told, not least by him. And for good reason, for it's a charming tableau: the serious young farm boy presiding over an unruly flock, attentive to detail, concerned for the well-being of others, and insistently offering the gospel to an audience disinclined to heed it. Lewis himself long saw his work in the coop as formative. He learned the art of *agape,* of self-giving love, among those chickens—and he learned that the more difficult the task, the better he liked it.

"I don't think there's any way to estimate how much that experience of tending those nesting hens taught me about discipline and responsibility, and, of course, patience," Lewis recalled. "It was not a struggle, not at all. It was something I *wanted* to do. The kinship I felt with these other living creatures, the closeness, the compassion, is a feeling I carried with me out into the world from that point on. It might have been a feeling I was born with, I don't know, but the first time I recall being aware of it was with those chickens."

The chickens offered him hours of happiness on the farm, but picking cotton—the main business that kept the family going—was nothing but painful and dispiriting. After Lewis worked the fields, his fingers—and those of his family—would be raw and bloody. He made his views clear. "Nobody," he'd say, "should have to work like this."

School soon joined church as a relief from field work. Lewis walked a half mile in his elementary years to Dunn's Chapel, for classes in a two-room schoolhouse next to the AME church. There was a big handmade Alabama state flag on the wall: He thought it "majestic." He loved going to school. "Public speaking, or playacting of any sort, terrified me—ironic, considering my performances at home with my chickens," he recalled. "Still, despite my discomfort, some of my sweetest memories are of standing in front of my classmates, having finished reciting a poem or reading a short essay, and hearing the teacher tell me I'd done a good job. . . . By the time I was done, I didn't want it to be over. I could feel that connection with my classmates, I guess, just as with my birds." He was delighted, too, to discover biographies of Booker T. Washington, George Washington Carver, Joe Louis, and Mary McLeod Bethune—"black people out there who had made their mark on the world."

After sixth grade, Lewis and his classmates were bused eight miles to Banks Junior High School off Route 29. Their buses were battered castoffs from the white schools. The roads over which they rode were "left literally, deliberately, unpaved," Lewis recalled. "During the winter months we would run in ditches on the way to school, because of the rain and the red mud and the clay in that part of Alabama. During evenings, returning from school, we would be late returning home because the bus would break down, we'd get stuck in the mud."

With its hand-me-down books and buses, the segregated school was a vivid expression of the Jim Crow order. "We saw the signs that said COLORED ONLY. WHITE ONLY. COLORED WAITING," Lewis recalled. "In a little five and ten [cent] store was a silver fountain, a clean fountain for white people to come and drink water, but in another corner of the store there was a little spigot, a rusty spigot, that said COLORED DRINKING."

The contrasting images of the sparkling silver fountain and of the rusty spigot burned themselves into his consciousness. "From my earliest memories, I was fundamentally disturbed by the unbridled meanness of the world around me," Lewis recalled. "Though I was not yet familiar with the words of the Declaration of Independence, I could feel in my bones that segregation was wrong, and I felt I had an obligation to change it." Nearly half a century earlier, in 1903, W.E.B. Du Bois had captured something of what Lewis was experiencing. "One ever feels his two-ness—an American, a Negro; two souls, two thoughts, two unreconciled strivings; two warring ideals in one dark body, whose dogged strength alone keeps it from being torn asunder," Du Bois wrote in *The Souls of Black Folk*. "The history of the American Negro is the history of this strife—this longing to attain self-conscious manhood, to merge his double self into a better and truer self.... He would not Africanize America, for America has too much to teach the world and Africa. He would not bleach his Negro soul in a flood of white Americanism, for he knows that Negro blood has a message for the world. He simply wishes to make it possible for a man to be both a Negro and an American, without being cursed and spit upon by his fellows, without having the doors of Opportunity closed roughly in his face."

A founder of the NAACP, W.E.B. Du Bois wrote landmark books, including The Souls of Black Folk *and* Black Reconstruction in America.

Lewis felt those doors were shut to him. He saw the nice white schools—"very sleek, very modern, with nice playground equipment outside"—from the windows of his dilapidated buses. He knew the fancy schools and the shiny playgrounds were not for him. In their landmark work on segregation's effects on black children—work that would drive the 1954 Supreme Court decision in *Brown v. Board of Education*—Kenneth Clark and Mamie Clark proved the sociological and psychological impact of Jim Crow schools on children like Lewis. "It is clear that the Negro child, by the age of five, is aware of the fact that to be colored in contemporary American society is a mark of inferior status," Clark and Clark wrote in studies that spanned 1939 to 1950. "A child accepts as early as six, seven or eight the negative stereotypes about his own group."

Moreover, as Chief Justice Earl Warren wrote in the *Brown* decision, "Segregation of white and colored children in public schools has a detrimental effect upon the colored children. The impact is greater when it has the sanction of the law; for the policy of separating the races is usually interpreted as denoting the inferiority of the Negro group. A sense of inferiority affects the motivation of a child to learn. Segregation with the sanction of the law, therefore, has a tendency to [retard] the educational and mental development of Negro children and to deprive them of some of the benefits they would receive in a racial[ly] integrated school system."

Such was the clinical conclusion of formal academic studies and of opinions of the court. On the most human of levels, far from the marble halls of the Supreme Court, an afternoon's daydream in Pike County proved the point that was being debated at the highest levels. Lewis and his cousin Della Mae, both about nine years old, were musing about the world around them—a world, Lewis recalled, that saw him "as inferior, a reject, a substandard creation." They decided to act. The two "grabbed a handsaw out of the barn" and went in search of "the biggest, tallest pine tree we could find, because we were going to build ourselves a bus," Lewis recalled. "We were going to saw down a tree, and somehow we were going to make it into a bus. And then we were going to roll right out of Alabama, leave the place behind for good and forever."

It was the most revealing of fantasies. Lewis did leave the South, albeit briefly, the year he turned eleven. It was 1951, and a Carter uncle—Otis, a grandson of Frank Carter—took his nephew up north for the summer, to Buffalo, New York, to visit relatives. "It was another world," Lewis recalled, "a whole other world." The car ride was

Writing for a unanimous U.S. Supreme Court in May 1954, Chief Justice Earl
Warren declared that schools segregated by color were unconstitutional. Lewis, who was
fourteen, recalled, "I wanted to jump for joy." Fifty miles away from Troy, The
Montgomery Advertiser *reassured its white readers. "Alabama's segregation
system," the capital's paper wrote, "is not to be suddenly upended."*

a kind of pageant of segregation. There would be no place to stop and
eat until they reached safer territory—which meant more than seven
hundred miles away in Ohio. Willie Mae filled the car with food to
sustain them—"fried chicken," Lewis recalled. "And biscuits. And
pound cake. And sandwiches. And sweet potato pie."

Lewis was dazzled by upstate New York. He couldn't believe that
blacks and whites mixed together, shopped in the same stores, lived in
the same neighborhoods. He rode an escalator in a department
store—and he'd never even heard of an escalator before, much less
seen one. A small thing, perhaps, but it loomed large for the eleven-
year-old. The dynamism, bigness, busyness, and integration of the
world he experienced in Buffalo offered concrete evidence that things
could be different than they were in Troy. One detail stuck with him:
White families lived next door to his Buffalo kin—"on *both* sides."

But, as it does, summer ended, and he returned home. He got everything he could out of Pike County Training School, the local black
high school, and always appreciated the library there run by Coreen
Harvey. "She was beautiful—she looked a lot like Lena Horne—and

she was regal in a firm but soft-spoken way," Lewis recalled. "'My dear children,' she would say, putting her finger against her lips to shush the loud ones, 'read. Read *everything*.'" At the all-white public library, he applied for a library card. The request was denied.

He was fourteen when news came of the *Brown v. Board of Education* decision to desegregate public schools. "I wanted to jump for joy," he recalled. The unanimous opinion was read by Chief Justice Earl Warren in Washington at midday on Monday, May 17, 1954, and *The Montgomery Advertiser* reported the ruling the next morning. ALABAMA LEADERS TO 'WAIT AND SEE' ON SUPREME COURT DECISION, the paper headlined, and the *Advertiser* reassured its white readers: "Alabama's segregation system is not to be suddenly upended and rent," the paper wrote. "Reform will not come at a bound." Still, the *Brown* decision was a landmark, the *Advertiser* noted, and came at a time when Jim Crow seemed ever less reasonable. "More and more our churches, in the South the same as the North, have become aggressive in attacking segregation, being ever more uneasy of conscience in the preposterous effort to reconcile segregation with the teachings of Christ Jesus," the paper said. "Other forces have been weakening the foundations of segregation, and not least of these is the fact that each new generation has a more liberal viewpoint towards segregation than the one before."

The coverage in *The Troy Messenger* was not as moderate in tone and substance. On the day after the decision led the paper, the *Messenger*'s main story was about a French attack on rebelling Communists in Vietnam. The implications of the court's epic opinion were discussed under the headline SOUTH FACES PROBLEMS OF SEGREGATION. The news shared space with Margaret Truman's denial of a romance with Robert B. Meyner, the bachelor governor of New Jersey, and the birth of quadruplets in Baltimore. An editorial in the Troy paper signaled trouble ahead. "While the Supreme Court may have the right to rule that Negroes may not be denied access to any public school, they cannot say what Negroes, as free citizens MUST do," the *Messenger* said. "To take that view would be contrary to Democracy itself. . . . What is there to prevent separate schools from being operated with attendance at either optional, either by white or Negro, as long as the student has a legal freedom of choice?"

These gathering forces of reaction in the white South were, at the time, lost on Lewis. In his naïveté, he looked for instant results. "Every day after I read about the *Brown* decision," he recalled, "I kept expecting that one day when I climbed onto my school bus I might see some white students on board or maybe a new friend might just sit down beside me." That never happened. He sometimes looked to the church for guidance, but found none. The preacher at Macedonia, who came out from Montgomery to preach once a month, focused on the hereafter, not the here, Lewis recalled, "how the soul must be saved by and by for that pie in the sky after you die, but hardly a word about *this* life, about *this* world, about some sense of salvation and righteousness right *here,* between the cradle and the grave."

Even as a youngster, Lewis interpreted the gospel differently. "It seemed to me," he recalled, "that the Lord had to be concerned with the way we lived our lives right here on earth, that everything we did or didn't do in our lives had to be more than just a means of making our way to heaven." These weren't your typical teenage thoughts. Looking back, Lewis understood that he had grown up more quickly than most. "In most ways it was a hard life, a serious life, and I was a serious child," he recalled. "When it comes down to it, I don't really feel I ever had a childhood. I feel childhood just passed me by."

The tributaries of his young life—the religious fervor, the conscientious concern for others, the thrill of education, the resentment of segregation at home, the glimpse of freedom up north, the hope of change—met to form a larger, faster-moving river of identity, imagination, and action when a soon-to-be-familiar voice came to Pike County over the airwaves, on WRMA from Montgomery, in the middle of the 1950s.

He heard him before he saw him. Lewis first encountered Martin Luther King, Jr., on the radio—the big, bulky radio that Eddie Lewis had brought with the family when they moved the half mile between the sharecropper's shotgun shack and the three-room house he'd bought from A. M. Hickman. The sermon that so moved Lewis was "Paul's Letter to the American Christians," an imaginative address from Saint Paul that King delivered in 1956. "You have a dual citizenry," King said in Paul's voice. "You live both in time and eternity; both in heaven and earth. Therefore, your ultimate allegiance is not to the government, not to the state, not to nation, not to any man-made institution. The Christian owes his ultimate allegiance to God, and if any earthly institution conflicts with God's will it is your Christian duty to take a stand against it. You must never allow the transitory evanescent demands of man-made institutions to take precedence over the eternal demands of the Almighty God."

This was what Lewis had been thinking, if inchoately. King continued: "I understand that there are Christians among you who try to justify segregation on the basis of the Bible. They argue that the Negro is inferior by nature because of Noah's curse upon the children of Ham. Oh my friends, this is blasphemy. This is against everything that the Christian religion stands for. I must say to you as I have said to so many Christians before, that in Christ 'there is neither Jew nor Gentile, there is neither bond nor free, there is neither male nor female, for we are all one in Christ Jesus.'"

Then, for the first time, Lewis was introduced to a vision of nonviolent, religiously inspired protest, to a way of seeing the world in terms of bringing the temporal into tune with the timeless. King, Lewis saw, "was not concerned about the streets of heaven and the pearly gates and the streets paved with milk and honey. He was more concerned about the streets of Montgomery and the way that black people and poor people were being treated in Montgomery." King rolled on:

> In your struggle for justice, let your oppressor know that you are not attempting to defeat or humiliate him, or even to pay him back for injustices that he has heaped upon you. Let him know that you are merely seeking justice for him as well as yourself. Let him know that the festering sore of segregation debilitates the white man as well as the Negro. With this attitude you will be able to keep your struggle on high Christian standards.... Honesty impels me to admit that such a stand will require willingness to suffer and sacrifice. So don't despair if you are condemned and persecuted for righteousness' sake. Whenever you take a stand for truth and justice, you are liable to scorn. Often you will be called an impractical idealist or a dangerous radical. Sometimes it might mean going to jail. If such is the case you must honorably grace the jail with your presence. It might even mean physical death. But if physical death is the price that some must pay to free their children

from a permanent life of psychological death, then nothing could be more Christian.

Lewis was left nearly breathless. "When I heard King, it was as though a light turned on in my heart," he recalled. "When I heard his voice, I felt he was talking directly to me. From that moment on, I decided I wanted to be just like him."

Nobody would have said that such a wish would be easy to grant. King and Lewis came from different spheres of the African American South. A prince of the black church, King had been educated at Morehouse College, Crozer Theological Seminary, and Boston University. Lewis was a sharecropper, King a student of Saint Augustine. Yet they held a religious faith in common, and God, in this instance, transcended class. King, Lewis recalled, was "a Moses, using organized religion and the emotionalism within the Negro church as an instrument, as a vehicle, toward freedom." In Washington, Thurgood Marshall, the counsel for the NAACP, was focused on the courts. In Montgomery, King was deploying Christ. It was this invocation of the Lord that so moved the young Lewis, listening in Troy.

The roots of King's worldview can be traced to the Bible up through the work of Walter Rauschenbusch, a Rochester, New York, minister and scholar who preached the "Social Gospel" of Christian-inspired reform, love, and action on earth. Rauschenbusch published *Christianity and the Social Crisis* in 1907; King read the book in the early 1950s, and Lewis came to it a few years later. (Six decades afterward, asked which thinker had been most important to him, Lewis, without hesitation, replied, "Walter Rauschenbusch.")

To Rauschenbusch, the stakes of Christian duty were clear. "In a few years," he wrote, "all our restless and angry hearts will be quiet in death, but those who come after us will live in the world which our sins have blighted or which our love of right has redeemed." In a moving chapter entitled "The Social Aims of Jesus," Rauschenbusch observed, "Whoever uncouples the religious and the social life has not understood Jesus."

In a passage inspired by Rauschenbusch, King was to write, "The gospel at its best deals with the whole man, not only his soul but his body, not only his spiritual well-being, but his material well-being. Any religion that professes to be concerned about the souls of men

and is not concerned about the slums that damn them, the economic conditions that strangle them and the social conditions that cripple them is a spiritually moribund religion awaiting burial."

To Rauschenbusch's way of thinking, the Christian story promised a radical reformation of existing injustices, and the message of John the Baptist was instructive. When John was asked what had to be done to thrive in the coming messianic age, he replied, "He that hath two coats, let him share with him that hath none; and he that hath food, let him do likewise." Preparing for the Kingdom of God meant making the world as like unto that Kingdom as possible, and the Kingdom was to be a new reality of restoration, redemption, renewal, and resurrection. The Gospel of Luke explicitly cited Isaiah's cry about making gentle the life of the world in telling the story of the Baptist and of Jesus:

The theologian Walter Rauschenbusch, a defender of the Social Gospel, was a key influence on King and Lewis.

> The voice of him that crieth in the wilderness, Prepare ye the way of the Lord, make straight in the desert a highway for our God.
> Every valley shall be exalted, and every mountain and hill shall be made low: and the crooked shall be made straight, and the rough places plain:
> And the glory of the Lord shall be revealed, and all flesh shall see it together: for the mouth of the Lord hath spoken it.

To King and, soon, to Lewis, the mission of the believer was to exalt valleys, lower mountains, straighten the crooked, and smooth the rough. "I couldn't accept the way things were, I just couldn't," Lewis recalled. "I loved my parents mightily, but I could not live the way they did, taking the world as it was presented to them and doing the best they could with it." He had begun to see that the world into which he'd been born required the revolutionary energy that had driven the apostles and saints of ancient days—the apostles and saints who had, following Jesus's instructions, taken up their own crosses to follow him.

Blood and death, pain and loss, sacrifice and the hope of redemption: Lewis was coming of age in the most intense of eras, an era that made this young black man in the South something of a child of wartime. George H. W. Bush—who joined the U.S. Navy on his eighteenth birthday, married when he was twenty, and had his first child by the time he was twenty-two—once explained the urgency of his generation of World War II veterans as a result of "heightened awareness," a sense that everything mattered, that life was to be lived, in Bush's phrase, "on the edge." "It was a time of uncertainty," Bush recalled, "when every evening brought dramatic radio broadcasts—Edward R. Murrow from London, William L. Shirer from Berlin—reporting a war we knew was headed our way."

John Lewis was even younger when he was touched by history, and he didn't have to leave rural Alabama to feel the same forces that had transformed the lives of Americans who had been old enough to sign up and ship out to fight Imperial Japan and Nazi Germany. His enemies were all about him, and the news from the front didn't have to come across the seas. It just came from Montgomery.

Or from Mississippi. The *Brown* decision had been handed down in May 1954. In August 1955, Emmett Till was murdered in the Delta. Till was almost exactly John's age—Till was fourteen, Lewis fifteen—when white men killed him for allegedly making overtures and saying "Bye, baby" to a white woman in Money, Mississippi. (In a book published in 2017, the woman, Carolyn Bryant Donham, recanted to the historian Timothy B. Tyson, saying that Till had never "grabbed her around the waist and uttered obscenities," adding, "Nothing that boy did could ever justify what happened to him.") Till was beaten, shot, and hurled into the Tallahatchie River. "The body," *Time* reported, "was swollen and decomposing, the skull smashed by blows and pierced by a bullet, and a heavy cotton-gin fan was lashed to the neck." Moses Wright, Till's great-uncle, bravely testified against the killers, but to no avail in a trial with an all-white jury.

"I remember that so well," Lewis recalled. "It was so terrifying. I remember the pictures"—Till's mother had allowed photographers to record the grievous wounds her son had suffered—"and how terrible

In 1955 fourteen-year-old Emmett Till, pictured here with his mother, was lynched for allegedly making overtures to a white woman in the Mississippi Delta. Long afterward, the woman recanted the story. "He could have been me," Lewis recalled. "That could have been me, beaten, tortured, dead at the bottom of a river."

it was." The killing stayed in his mind for the rest of his life. "I was fifteen, black, at the edge of my own manhood, just like him," Lewis recalled. "He could have been me. *That* could have been me, beaten, tortured, dead at the bottom of a river." For neither the first nor the last time, Lewis felt he was in enemy country—in his *own* country.

Rosa Parks was ready. Inculcated in nonviolent protest at the Highlander Folk School in Monteagle, Tennessee, in the summer of 1955, Parks, the NAACP activist and investigator, who also worked as a seamstress at a downtown Montgomery department store, was arrested after declining to surrender her seat on a segregated Cleveland Avenue Montgomery city bus on Thursday, December 1, 1955.

By Monday, December 5, Martin Luther King, Jr., was addressing a mass meeting called to consider a boycott of the buses. "We are here this evening—for serious business," King told the huge crowd. "We are here in a general sense, because first and foremost—we are American citizens—and we are determined to apply our citizenship—to the fullness of its means. . . . We are here—we are here because we are tired now. . . . And we are determined here in Montgomery—to work

Rosa Parks is booked on charges of violating Jim Crow laws on a Montgomery city bus in December 1955. To Lewis, who closely followed the news in his grandfather's copies of the Montgomery newspaper, the ensuing boycott was an inspiration.

and fight until justice runs down like water, and righteousness like a mighty stream!"

In Troy, John Lewis avidly followed the news from Montgomery. "I can still say without question that the Montgomery bus boycott changed my life more than any other event before or since," Lewis recalled. He read accounts in the editions of *The Montgomery Advertiser* that his grandfather, who could afford a subscription, passed along to Lewis's parents, who could not. To Lewis, the boycott was faith in action, the gospel moving from the pulpit to the streets, from theory to reality, from word to deed.

The newspaper was soon filled with other news from another battle in the war against segregation. This time the dateline was Tuscaloosa, the home of the University of Alabama. As in Montgomery, it was a woman who was doing the brave work of resistance. A native of Shiloh, Alabama, Autherine Lucy had been admitted to the university four years before, in 1952, but only because officials had not realized she was black. After prolonged litigation, Lucy was readmitted and began attending classes in the winter of 1956. Angry whites quickly lashed out. "A cross had been burned and the milling students had

Former first lady and longtime human rights advocate Eleanor Roosevelt meets with Rosa Parks and Autherine Lucy, the first black student to attend the University of Alabama, at a rally for civil rights at New York's Madison Square Garden in 1956.

become a mob," *Newsweek* wrote. "Boys peddled eggs and tomatoes for 10 cents each; the price for miniature Confederate flags rose from 15 to 25 cents. . . . Pistols, rifles, and shotguns were bought. You could taste tension in the air." The crowd chanted, "Hey, hey, ho, ho. Autherine must go." A car she was riding in was pelted with eggs and stones. Within weeks, university trustees voted to expel *her*.

The disaster at Tuscaloosa was very much in the air when, in February 1956, Lewis preached his first sermon to a congregation other than that of his chickens. Taking the pulpit at Macedonia for what was called his "trial sermon"—a key step to becoming licensed as a minister— Lewis told the story of the birth of Samuel to Hannah, who had had difficulty conceiving and promised the Lord that she would repay the gift of a son by dedicating him to God's service. Entitled "A Praying Mother," the sermon was about duty and justice, for Samuel grew up to become a righteous judge who anointed Saul the king of Israel. In other words, Samuel was a figure of holiness who sought—with varying degrees of success—to keep his nation faithful to the Lord. "Do not be afraid," Samuel said in his farewell to Israel. "For the Lord will not forsake his people, for his great name's sake, because it has pleased the

Lord to make you a people for himself." *Do not be afraid:* It was a text the morning's preacher at Macedonia took to heart. *The Montgomery Advertiser* published a photo of Lewis afterward, dubbing him Pike County's "boy preacher."

That same month, a kinsman of Lewis's, Dr. Thomas Brewer, was shot to death in Columbus, Georgia. A voting rights advocate and member of the NAACP, Brewer was asking a white store owner to testify about an incident of police brutality when the owner, Lucio Flowers, opened fire. Brewer was shot seven times, but a grand jury freed Flowers. Describing the episode in his memoirs, Lewis, who said he was "jolted" by the killing, was surprised by his own pacific reaction to the violence. "Curiously, at least to many people with whom I have shared my feelings about racism at that time—and my feelings have in essence not changed at all since then—I did *not* feel anger or ill will toward white people in general. I did not really know any white people. And I refused to believe that all white people acted or felt like the ones I read about. I know it might sound simplistic, but then some of the most basic truths in this world are just that when you boil them down—basic." That truth would be tested time and again down the years. In the winter of Lewis's last year in high school, Ku Klux Klansmen kidnapped and murdered a Montgomery man, Willie Edwards, Jr., forcing him at gunpoint to leap to his death from the Tyler Goodwin Bridge over the Alabama River.

So much was happening—some of it good (the bus boycott), but most of it bad (the lynchings, the expulsion of Autherine Lucy, the broader failure to implement *Brown*). As he neared college age—his parents had never finished high school—Lewis was determined to find a way for the good to overcome the evil. His dream was to walk the

Martin Luther King, Jr., outside Dexter Avenue Baptist Church. The Alabama state capitol, the site of Jefferson Davis's inauguration as president of the Confederacy, is in the background.

"I can still say without question," Lewis recalled, *"that the Montgomery bus boycott changed my life more than any other event before or since."* To him, the broad decision of black people in the city to walk and carpool rather than ride segregated buses was the gospel in action.

path Dr. King had traveled by going to the elite Morehouse in Atlanta, but Lewis had neither the grades nor the family finances to make that happen. One day Lewis's mother—providentially, he came to believe—arrived home from her job at a Baptist-owned orphanage in Troy with a brochure for a school he'd never heard of in a city he'd never been to: American Baptist Theological Seminary in Nashville, Tennessee. A tiny institution founded in 1924 to train black ministers, American Baptist was tuition free: Students worked on campus to pay their way.

Lewis's parents were proud but wary as he packed for Nashville. They were of a generation that kept largely to themselves, and they knew even then, at the beginning of their son's journey, that he was taking a different path. "It's not hard to understand at all the mixture of fear and concern they both felt as they watched me walk out into the world as a young man and join a movement aimed, in essence, at turning the world they knew upside down," Lewis recalled. The preaching they understood—they'd called him "Preacher" for a long while now, since the chickens—but they wanted him to save souls among his people, not the soul of a whole nation. "When I'd come home and preach civil rights," he recalled, "my mother would say: 'Preach the Bible, preach the Scripture.' She'd talk about my 'call,' and I'd say, 'Mama, if I'm called by God, why can't *I* do what He tells me to do?'"

Such true discipleship was the hardest of choices. "Whoever comes to me and doesn't hate father and mother, spouse and children, and brothers and sisters—yes, even one's own life—cannot be my disciple," Jesus says in Luke. "Whoever doesn't carry their own cross and follow me cannot be my disciple." In Greek, the word for "hate," *miseo,* is best understood as "loving less" rather than as viewing something with hostility. Dietrich Bonhoeffer, the German theologian martyred by the Nazi regime, had written of the difficulty of following one's conscience in terms of costly grace versus cheap grace. "Costly grace is the gospel which must be *sought* again and again and again, the gift which must be asked for, the door at which a man must *knock,*" Bonhoeffer wrote. "Such grace is *costly* because it calls us to follow, and it is *grace* because it calls us to follow *Jesus Christ.* It is costly because it costs a man his life, and it is grace because it gives a man the only true life." Costly grace was the grace that Lewis was seeking for his own life. Of Bonhoeffer, Lewis recalled, "His writing, his thinking—it took you places that you had to be willing to go."

With $100—a gift of his uncle Otis Carter—a footlocker of clothes, and a Bible, Lewis left Troy in the fall of 1957. His father took him to the Greyhound station. The journey north was only about three hundred miles, but the young man in the back of the bus was moving toward more than a new city—he was riding into an entirely different future.

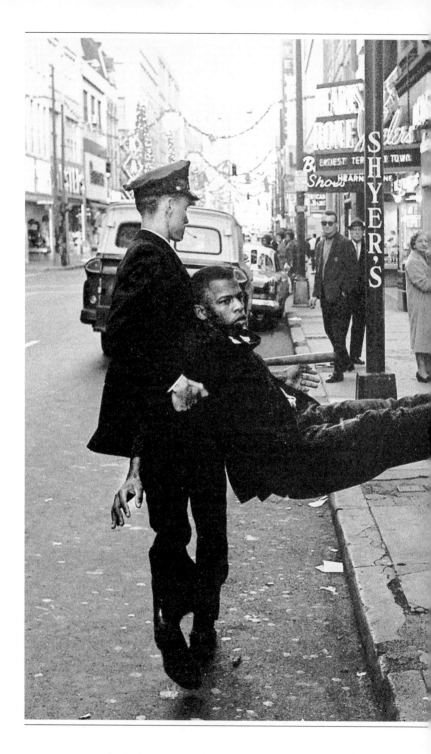

CHAPTER TWO

THE SPIRIT
OF HISTORY

Nashville, Tennessee: 1957-60

PREVIOUS PAGES: *Following the code of nonviolence, Lewis is taken to a police paddy wagon during a protest against a segregated restaurant in downtown Nashville.*

The universe of philosophy and religion was opened to me,
and I took to it like a fish to water.

—JOHN LEWIS, on his studies at American Baptist Theological
Seminary in Nashville

However large the number of individual white men who do
and who will identify themselves completely with the Negro
cause, the white race in America will not admit the Negro to
equal rights if he is not forced to do so.

—REINHOLD NIEBUHR, *Moral Man and Immoral Society*

SEMINARY WAS LIBERATING. "By going to school in Nashville,
Tennessee—many, many miles away from my parents and from
rural Alabama—I felt freer to find a way to get involved," Lewis
recalled. Still, American Baptist (known as ABT) did not look like a
center of revolution. Bucolic in its way, the campus was made up of a
few redbrick buildings, tall trees, a view of the Cumberland River,
and, beyond the river, of downtown Nashville. For Lewis, it was a
seven-dollar cab ride from the bus station on Commerce Street to the
ABT campus. Students—there were about ninety of them, seventy
men and twenty women—thought of their citadel as "the Holy Hill,"
and they lived much of their lives in and around Griggs Hall, where
Lewis took up residence in Room 202 in September 1957.

The primary activity—the only activity, really—was summed up in
a question James Bevel, a charismatic fellow student, put to the new-
comer from Troy on their first meeting: "Can you *preach,* boy?" It was
all that mattered. Preaching was also free, and Lewis didn't have
money for much else. In exchange for washing pots and pans in the
dining hall kitchen, he was paid $42.50 a month. Thirty-seven dollars
went back to the school, which left him with a disposable income of
$5.50 a month, and even that had to cover his books.

He was a diligent student. "John always had a kind of seriousness
about him," Bernard LaFayette, who roomed with Lewis and would

join him in the movement, recalled. "He was very committed to his academic work, very devoted. We all studied, but John *really* studied." Late nights would be taken up with dorm cooking—boiled eggs and toast were favorites—and singing and improvised bits of preaching. "We were small in number," LaFayette recalled, "but mighty in spirit." It was a tight-knit community. One spring, around Easter and Mother's Day, LaFayette's mother sent her son two new suits. He and Lewis wore the same size then, and he gave one to Lewis, who, a year ahead, shared his old books and tutored LaFayette. "So many of us were close even before the movement," LaFayette recalled, "and the movement sealed those bonds." James Bevel, LaFayette recalled, was in charge of "clowning." "It was preachers' clowning, but clowning all the same," LaFayette said. "Bevel would go up on the top floor of Griggs at night and call out to the other students, in the voice of the Lord, 'Go preach *my* Word.' They would look up and around and try to figure out if the Lord was calling unto them. But it wasn't the Lord—it was Bevel. So we had jokes—but they were preachers' jokes, which you might not appreciate if you weren't a preacher."

The ABT students listened to one another, to the radio sermons of the Reverend C. L. Franklin of Detroit (the father of Aretha), to Dr. Caesar Arthur Walter Clark, Sr., of Dallas, an evangelist who held well-attended revivals on the road, and to Martin Luther King, Jr., out of Montgomery. Lewis was totally enamored with King, and his reverence put some of his fellow future preachers off. "Lewis," Bevel said one day, "why you always preaching this *social* gospel and not the *Gospel* gospel?"

Until these years, the culture at ABT had tended to favor a focus on the City of God rather than on the City of Man. You were supposed to preach about how to get to Heaven, not how to change history. The pulpit wasn't for politics. "The American [Baptist] Seminary is doing the job that needs to be done," the seminary's executive secretary, L. S. Sedberry, had written in 1950, "training Negro ministers, without raising the issue of race or stirring up the prejudices and animosities of either whites or Negroes."

Lewis disagreed. "I think we need to be less concerned with getting people up to those streets paved with gold," he'd say to his classmates, "and more concerned about what people are dealing with right down here on the streets of Nashville."

"John," another student said, "you gotta stop preaching the gospel according to Martin Luther *King* and start preaching the Gospel of Jesus *Christ*."

To Lewis, that was a false choice. The words of Jesus had to be put into action. Lewis loved an 1859 quotation from Horace Mann, the great nineteenth-century educator: "Be ashamed to die until you have won some victory for humanity."

The teacher who introduced Lewis to Mann was John Lewis Powell, dean of students and professor of missions at ABT. Powell also explained the philosophical views of Hegel, views that Lewis said "seemed so completely and absolutely *right* to me." "Professor Powell would run around the classroom—actually *run*—scribbling ideas along the length of the blackboard, spelling out the dynamics of thesis and antithesis and the process of synthesis," Lewis recalled. "Segregation, he would explain, is a thesis. Its antithesis would be the struggle to destroy segregation. Out of that struggle would come the synthesis: integration. Birth, death, and rebirth."

To Lewis, the classes with Powell were a revelation. "The Holy Hill" was changing his life. "It was at this time that I began believing in what I call the Spirit of History," Lewis said. "Others might call it Fate. Or Destiny. Or a Guiding Hand. Whatever it is called, I came to believe that this force is on the side of what is good, of what is right and just."

The autumn of 1957 was hectic. As the seventeen-year-old Lewis was enlarging his understanding in this first semester of college, he was also following the news out of Little Rock, Arkansas, where the governor, Orval Faubus, was attempting to prevent the integration of Central High School. Faubus's resistance compelled President Dwight D. Eisenhower to intervene with federal troops. For a time the nation was fascinated by images of angry white mobs attacking peaceable black students. Headlines in *The Tennessean,* Nashville's morning newspaper, chronicled the story: U.S. TROOPS RING SCHOOL: END MOB RULE, EISENHOWER TELLS LITTLE ROCK. It was Autherine Lucy all over again, and Lewis prayed for the young black people in the line of fire in Little Rock.

He was, however, moved to do more than pray. He had joined a youth chapter of the NAACP in Nashville and explored organizing one on the ABT campus, but the school's president, Dr. Maynard P.

*Elizabeth Eckford under siege on the first day of court-ordered integration at
Central High School in Little Rock, Arkansas, in September 1957—Lewis's first
semester at American Baptist in Nashville.*

Turner, Jr., resisted. "We didn't succeed in that effort," Lewis recalled,
"because this little school was gently supported by the Southern Baptist Convention, which was, for the most part during that period, all
white."

Lewis refused to surrender. Inspired by Autherine Lucy and by the
students at Little Rock, Lewis asked himself what he could do in the
service of integration—and he now saw integration as a key step toward
bringing the world into closer tune with the gospel. The answer came
to him after much thought. He would become the Autherine Lucy of
Pike County and integrate Troy State College back home in Alabama.
He loved his classmates at ABT, he loved his professors, he loved the
preaching and the philosophy and the convivial late hours at Griggs
Hall. But duty was summoning him to take up a cross.

To integrate Troy State was no small matter. Lewis knew that. So he
reached out for help—from his distant hero, Dr. King. At Christmas
1957 he wrote King and received a reply from Fred Gray, King's Mont-

gomery lawyer. By early summer 1958—Lewis was already home from Nashville for the vacation—King had sent him a bus ticket to come up to Montgomery. "I was overwhelmed," Lewis recalled. "I was actually going to meet Martin Luther King, Jr. I kept telling myself to be calm, that Fate was moving now, that I was in the hands of that Spirit of History. But I was still nervous. I had only just turned eighteen. I was a baby, really. And now I had an appointment with destiny." And as William Jennings Bryan once observed, "Destiny is not a matter of chance; it is a matter of choice. It is not a thing to be waited for; it is a thing to be achieved."

Lewis rode a Greyhound from Troy and called at Gray's office at 113 Monroe Street in Montgomery. The lawyer greeted him and drove them both over to First Baptist Church, where the Reverend Ralph D. Abernathy, perhaps King's closest colleague, was waiting with King. In the pastor's study, the two men looked Lewis over.

"Are you the boy from Troy?" King asked. "I just want to meet the boy from Troy."

Lewis could barely speak. "I was mesmerized, just listening, trying to take it all in," Lewis recalled.

Abernathy asked, "Who is this young man who wants to desegregate Troy State?"

The two ministers quizzed Lewis on his background and his motivations. "They talked and talked," Fred Gray recalled. They were probing, seeking to understand how serious the young man was—and whether he truly understood what would be in store if he took this step. There would be a lawsuit, appeals—and opposition that would almost certainly turn violent.

"You know, John," King said, "if you do this, something could happen to you. It's not just you who could be hurt, John. Your parents could be harassed. . . . Your home could be attacked. The farm could be burned."

Lewis was willing. "If you really want to do it," King said, "we will see you through." Nothing about it would be easy. "The pressure that white people could bring to bear on the families of those involved in the civil rights movement could be immense," Gray recalled. "But I was willing to file the lawsuit, and the Southern Christian Leadership Council was willing to finance it, if young Lewis wanted to go through with it."

King sent Lewis off with a charge. "He told me I needed to go home and talk this through with my family," Lewis remembered. "Being a minor, I would need my parents' permission to file a lawsuit. He explained it all, and when he was done, we stood and shook hands."

It had been the most important afternoon of Lewis's young life. The voice on the radio had become a real human being, sitting in the same room, talking of vital things. King had given Lewis a sense of peace—or at least had ratified the younger man's natural calm. The bus ride home to Troy was a quiet but intense joy. "Total darkness swallowed the fields outside and I was lost in a swirl of feelings," Lewis recalled. "No thoughts, really. Just sweet, delicious feelings."

Yet this mission—his integration of Troy State—was not to be. Lewis's parents tried to be supportive, and they initially agreed to sign on to the lawsuit. But they could not shake an enveloping sense of gloom and danger. What if they lost the farm? What if Eddie Lewis were fired from his school bus route? What about bombings, or shootings, or lynchings? There were a lot of Lewises, not just John. They'd all be targets.

In the end, Willie Mae and Eddie Lewis just couldn't do it. They told their son no—his battle at Troy State couldn't be their battle, too. "I was heartbroken," Lewis recalled, "but I didn't argue." Lewis wrote King to give him the news. "That was a hard letter to write," Lewis said. But it had to be done, and he did it. He would go back to Nashville, back to ABT, back to life at Griggs Hall. The Spirit of History, he guessed, must have other plans for him. Or at least he hoped so.

For Lewis, typical college pastimes were few and far between. "There were girls, and I can't say I wasn't interested," he recalled. "In fact, I had my first girlfriend, if you can call it that, my freshman year." She was Helen Johnson. Johnson had moved from Helena, Arkansas, to Indianapolis as a girl and, hoping to become a missionary, had won a scholarship to ABT. "We spent a lot of time together, walking down by the river, talking," Lewis recalled. "I was very taken with her, just a case of classic puppy love." In his memoirs, he wrote that it was not a passionate connection—and neither were most of his relationships with other women as a young man. Of Helen Johnson, he said, "I was more a little brother than a boyfriend. Helen felt very protective of me—a response I would encounter from women during all the years of my young adulthood. I always looked and acted younger than I was, and women tended to mother me, to shield me, to keep the big, bad wolves away."

He never drank much (he didn't have his first beer until 1961) and didn't learn to drive until middle age. Women, wine, and fast cars—the joys of more than a few young American men—weren't consuming concerns. But Lewis came alive on the dance floor, played a mean game of Scrabble, loved to deploy a dry wit to spar with friends, and had a deep, if infrequent, laugh. "John's smile—it's very genuine, and very merry," Diane Nash recalled. "And always with a twinkle in his eye. He can seem so serious, but then there's that smile."

In the fall of 1958, Lewis was looking forward to seeing Dr. King again, this time at a Nashville meeting of King's Southern Christian Leadership Conference. Everything changed, though, when King, who was in New York to promote *Stride Toward Freedom,* his account of the 1955 Montgomery bus boycott, was assaulted at a Harlem book signing by a deranged woman who plunged a seven-inch ivory-handled letter opener into his chest, nearly killing him. "That's all right," King had said in the moments after the attack, the knife in his chest. "That's all right. Everything is going to be all right." But he couldn't know that. "And that blade had gone through, and the X-rays revealed that the tip of the blade was on the edge of my aorta, the main artery," King would recall in a sermon on the eve of his assassination in Memphis, Tennessee, in April 1968. "And once that's punctured, you're drowned in your own blood—that's the end of you." A United Press International story reported that one of King's attending doctors had said that a sneeze could have killed him in those dangerous hours.

With King recovering, Coretta Scott King filled in for her husband in Nashville. Describing a January 1956 bombing of their house in Montgomery during the bus boycott—she and Yolanda, the Kings' eldest child, had been inside but had been unhurt—Mrs. King said that she had "found there was something greater than myself to rely on—that was my strong religious faith, which has carried me through this difficult period. The experiences at Montgomery have strengthened my determination and dedication to work for the cause of freedom and human equality of my people and all people."

She also sang in Nashville, drawing on spirituals such as "Steal

Diane Nash and the Reverend Kelly Miller Smith, essential figures in Lewis's early movement days.

Away to Jesus." As he had been with the husband, Lewis was also moved by the wife. "Watching Coretta Scott King that day, I felt even more certain that this thing that was swelling around me, this movement, was not going to be stopped," Lewis recalled. "Not by a madwoman wielding a letter opener. Not by men throwing bombs in the night. Not by a government committed to keeping an entire people apart from the country to which they belonged."

The precise nature of what Lewis referred to as "this movement" was becoming clearer, but quietly, and far from the headlines and the corridors of power. He was a regular at services led by the Reverend Kelly Miller Smith, pastor of the First Baptist Church in Nashville. A white-run First Baptist had been founded in 1824. Black congregants (who numbered about half of the worshippers) were exhorted to know their place. "He truly honors his master who conducts himself towards him with all due deference," a white minister would preach to them. They formed their own congregation after emancipation and the Civil War, and the church Lewis attended in the late 1950s had been built on Eighth Avenue North, near the state capitol.

Under the Reverend Smith, First Baptist was the Nashville outpost of the movement that had begun at King's Dexter Avenue Baptist in Montgomery. "Nashville, at the time, was considered a sort of citadel of education in the South with all of the colleges and all of the universities there, and many, many churches," Lewis recalled. "Sort of progressive and liberal." Such things were relative, of course, even in the black community. "Since integration and segregation were political and social," L. S. Sedberry, ABT's executive secretary, wrote in 1958, "these problems should not be permitted to interfere with the

Christ-appointed task of making disciples and teaching them all things."

Kelly Smith had a different view. One early autumn Sunday in 1958, Lewis was in the pews at First Baptist when the pastor announced a visitor in their midst: the Reverend James Morris Lawson, Jr., a field secretary for the Fellowship of Reconciliation, a nonviolent pacifist organization founded during World War I. Its members and leaders had included Jane Addams and Norman Thomas; its message was the possibility of bringing an unruly world into good order through acts of conscience. As Lawson was to put it, "Nonviolent revolution is always a real, serious revolution. It seeks to transform human life in both private and public forms . . . involves the whole man in his whole existence . . . maintains balance between tearing down and building up, destroying and planting." More than six decades later, standing on the Pettus Bridge in Selma, Alabama, Lewis would look at Lawson—now white-maned, and in his early

Theologian, teacher, and guiding force behind the nonviolent philosophy of King, Lewis, Nash, and others, the Reverend James M. Lawson is arrested in Nashville.

nineties—and say simply, "My leader, my teacher, my brother. Bless you. Our teacher. If it hadn't been for you, young man, where would we be? Where would we be?"

Born in Uniontown, Pennsylvania, in 1928, James Lawson grew up in Ohio and was educated at Baldwin-Wallace College and Boston University. The son of a Methodist minister, Lawson became one, too, and was imprisoned for refusing to register for the military draft during the Korean War. Lawson spent thirteen months behind bars. After his release, he traveled to India as a Methodist missionary. There he dove deeply into the nonviolent example of Gandhi, who had used passive resistance to help liberate India from the British Empire. Lawson returned to the United States and was studying at Oberlin College in Ohio when he met a visiting Martin Luther King, Jr. On learning of Lawson's experience in India, King implored him to move to the South. "Don't wait!" King said. "Come now! You're badly needed. We don't have anyone like you!"

So it was that the experience of Gandhi in the Raj intersected with the spirit of the black church in the Old Confederacy. Lawson heeded King's words and was in Nashville by the beginning of 1958. "Jim came south, almost like a missionary," Lewis recalled. "A nonviolent teacher, a warrior, to spread the good news."

That good news was a hybrid of the gospel and of Gandhi. "It was the Sermon on the Mount, rather than a doctrine of passive resistance, that initially inspired the Negroes of Montgomery to dignified social action," Martin Luther King recalled. "It was Jesus of Nazareth that stirred the Negroes to protest with the creative weapon of love. As the days unfolded, however, the inspiration of Mahatma Gandhi began to exert its influence. I had come to see early that the Christian doctrine of love operating through the Gandhian method of nonviolence was one of the most potent weapons available to the Negro in his struggle for freedom." In sum, "Christ furnished the spirit and motivation, while Gandhi furnished the method."

King had encountered the Gandhi doctrines in a sermon delivered one Sunday afternoon in Philadelphia by Mordecai Johnson, the president of Howard University. In a talk in a seminary class, King had included Gandhi with Jesus as "individuals who greatly reveal the working of the Spirit of God." The Gandhian example had long been a source of interest and inspiration to African American reformers. The influential theologian Howard Thurman, who served as dean of the chapels at both Howard and Boston University, had met Gandhi on a 1935–36 pilgrimage. Engaged by the prospects of nonviolence, Thurman later published *Jesus and the Disinherited,* arguing for the liberating power of Christianity—a book that King turned to amid the Montgomery bus boycott. It became Jim Lawson's task to weave the threads of faith, philosophy, and justice together into a larger tapestry, and it was a task that he took up during Tuesday night workshops in the basement of the redbrick Clark Memorial United Methodist Church in Nashville.

Lawson had heard something of the young Lewis. In a brief conversation, Kelly Miller Smith had told Lawson, "John Lewis ought to be outstanding. He grew up on racism and segregation in Troy, and he's ready and eager to take it on." In the workshops, Lewis stood out. "He was marked because John Lewis, as I remember him, had no questions," Lawson recalled. "He has written and said that I saved his life. But I maintain that I did not save his life. I maintain that John was totally prepared to hear the ideas that were rooted in Jesus and in nonviolent struggle. He grabbed the ideas, and the ideas grabbed him. His was a gentle but extremely strong voice."

Lewis met Diane Nash in the workshops. Born in 1938, she was bright, engaging, brave, and beautiful (growing up in Chicago, she'd competed in the local Miss America pageant in 1956). Nash had transferred from Howard University in Washington to Fisk University in Nashville, where Jim Crow had a profound impact on her. "Segregation was dehumanizing, demoralizing, depressing—and of course that was its purpose," she recalled. "To me and to John and to many people, obeying a rule of segregation was agreeing that we were lesser people."

Like Nash, Lewis was more than a willing pupil. Lawson had the same kind of effect on him that King did. "It was John Lewis who convinced me to go to Jim Lawson's workshops," Bernard LaFayette recalled. "I had several jobs—I was a janitor, I worked in the kitchen, and I was the assistant librarian—so I was really busy. 'Man,' I told John, 'I don't have time for anything else.' I could barely do all of that and get my schoolwork done. But he just kept aggravating me—he was so determined, so convincing—and so I went just to shut him up. And when I went, it stuck. He was absolutely right."

Nearly a dozen years older than Lewis, Lawson and King were more elder brothers than father figures, and they were far more learned and polished than "the boy from Troy." It was not quite hero worship, though. Lewis did not seek a pulpit like King's or a portfolio like Lawson's. He never forgot that the mortals around him were just that—mortals—and that he was serving a cause with divine origins and purposes. His joy in finding a King and a Lawson (and, later, a Robert Kennedy) was about his seeking the best means to channel his sense of justice into redemptive action. Lewis knew the gospel story of James and John's request to sit at the right and left hands of Jesus in the Kingdom of God, a plea for power and place that the Lord turned back on his apostles, telling them that he who would rule must serve—a reminder of the radical nature of the New Testament, in which the earthly order of things would one day be overturned.

King and Lawson gave Lewis an intellectual framework, but Lewis's motivation was by all accounts innate. Taken together, his experiences with King and Lawson may have played the same kind of role that the voice of God played in the calling of the prophet Isaiah. "Also I heard the voice of the Lord, saying, 'Whom shall I send, and who will go for us?' Then said I, Here *am* I; send me."

Lawson's Tuesday night workshops gave Lewis armor for the missions he was to seek. "It changed my life forever, set me on a path, committed to the way of peace, to the way of love, and I have not looked back since," Lewis recalled, continuing:

> We studied the whole idea of passive resistance. We studied the way to love. That if someone beat you, or spit on you, or poured hot water or hot coffee on you, you looked straight ahead and never ever dreamed of hitting that person back or being violent toward that person. And we accepted it, most of us accepted it, as a way of life, as a way of living. Made us much better human beings. We had what we called role-playing, or what some people would call social drama. Someone pretending that they were beating you or hitting you. And there were young people who would light a cigarette and then blow smoke in the faces of, in the eyes of, some of those people, preparing them for whatever could happen or might happen. . . .
>
> Hate is too heavy a burden to bear. If you start hating peo-

ple, you have to decide who you are going to hate tomorrow, who you are going to hate next week? Just love everybody. And on one occasion I heard Dr. King said, "Just love the hell out of everybody, it's the better way. It's the best way."

They read Henry David Thoreau and Reinhold Niebuhr, Mo Ti, and Lao-tzu. As Thoreau wrote in his 1849 essay "Civil Disobedience," "Unjust laws exist; shall we be content to obey them, or shall we endeavor to amend them, and obey them until we have succeeded, or shall we transgress them at once?" Thoreau's answer was clear: Conscience should trump conformity. Why, he asked, do governments "always crucify Christ, and excommunicate Copernicus and Luther, and pronounce Washington and Franklin rebels?" In the essay's closing lines, Thoreau wondered, "Is a democracy, such as we know it, the last improvement possible in government? Is it not possible to take a step further towards recognizing and organizing the rights of man? There will never be a really free and enlightened State, until the State comes to recognize the individual as a higher and independent power, from which all its own power and authority are derived, and treats him accordingly."

The Protestant theologian Reinhold Niebuhr saw history and politics in tragic terms; Lewis, driven by faith that the "Beloved Community" of love and justice could in fact come to pass, declined to accept Niebuhr's bleaker worldview.

In Niebuhr's 1932 book *Moral Man and Immoral Society,* he acknowledged that sin made great reform enormously difficult. To Niebuhr, to count on the goodness of human nature to bring about justice was wishful thinking. Nonviolence, though, offered an encouraging path forward, for it forced society to judge itself in a religious as well as a political light. "It is hopeless for the Negro to expect complete emancipation from the menial social and economic position into which the white man has forced him, merely by trusting in the moral sense of the white race," Niebuhr wrote. "It is equally hopeless to attempt emancipation through violent rebellion."

Something had to be done to dramatize injustice. Talking and preaching about it wasn't enough. To Niebuhr, nonviolence was "a particularly strategic instrument for an oppressed group which is hopelessly in the minority and has no possibility of developing sufficient power to set against its oppressors." Nonviolence grew out of the kind of religious sensibility that was essential for such a large-scale task. "There is no problem of political life to which religious imagination can make a larger contribution than this problem of developing nonviolent resistance," Niebuhr wrote. "The discovery of elements of common human frailty in the foe, and . . . the appreciation of all human life as possessing transcendent worth, creates attitudes which transcend social conflict and thus mitigate its cruelties."

The question confronting the small group at Clark Memorial was not the right to revolt. The issue, rather, was the means of revolution. In the Declaration of Independence, Jefferson had granted the justice of humankind's instinct to resist tyranny. What they needed to decide was *how.* And Lawson believed unreservedly in the power not of traditional arms but in nonviolence.

Founded at an April 1960 conference at Shaw University in Raleigh, North Carolina, the Student Nonviolent Coordinating Committee, or SNCC (pronounced "Snick"), was the product of labors undertaken by Ella Baker, a key NAACP and SCLC organizer. A descendant of slaves, Baker was born in Norfolk, Virginia, in 1903, and grew up in Littleton, North Carolina. Though less well known than the men of the movement—a common reality of the day despite the innumerable contributions of women engaged in the fight for justice—she was central to the struggle. "You didn't see me on televi-

An architect of the Student Nonviolent Coordinating Committee (SNCC), Ella Baker argued that the movement was "much bigger than a hamburger or even a giant-sized Coke"—it was about "a destined date with freedom."

sion, you didn't see news stories about me," Baker told the authors of *Moving the Mountain: Women Working for Social Change.* "The kind of role that I tried to play was to pick up pieces or put together pieces out of which I hoped organization might come. My theory is, strong people don't need strong leaders." Revered and essential, she was known as "Fundi," the Swahili word for one who hands down a craft from one generation to another.

The spring 1960 conference in North Carolina, Baker remarked, "made it crystal clear that current sit-ins and other demonstrations are concerned with something much bigger than a hamburger or even a giant-sized Coke. Whatever may be the difference in approach to their goal, the Negro and white students, North and South, are seeking to rid America of the scourge of racial segregation and discrimination—not only at lunch counters, but in every aspect of life. . . . By and large, this feeling that they have a destined date with freedom was not limited to a drive for personal freedom, or even freedom for the Negro in the South. Repeatedly it was emphasized that the movement was concerned with the moral implications of racial discrimination for the 'whole world' and the 'Human Race.'"

As it set to work, SNCC adopted a Lawson-drafted statement of principles—the principles Lawson had begun imparting to Lewis and others in Nashville in the fall of 1958:

We affirm the philosophical or religious ideal of nonviolence as the foundation of our purpose, the presupposition of our faith, and the manner of our action. Nonviolence as it grows from Judaic-Christian traditions seeks a social order of justice permeated by love. Integration of human endeavor represents the crucial first step towards such a society.

Through nonviolence, courage displaces fear; love transforms hate. Acceptance dissipates prejudice; hope ends despair. Peace dominates war; faith reconciles doubt. Mutual regard cancels enmity. Justice for all overthrows injustice. The redemptive community supersedes systems of gross social immorality.

Love is the central motif of nonviolence. Love is the force by which God binds man to Himself and man to man. Such love goes to the extreme; it remains loving and forgiving even in the midst of hostility. It matches the capacity of evil to inflict suffering with an even more enduring capacity to absorb evil, all the while persisting in love.

By appealing to conscience and standing on the moral nature of human existence, nonviolence nurtures the atmosphere in which reconciliation and peace become actual possibilities.

It was the most radical of worldviews. Like the Sermon on the Mount, like the Passion of Jesus, nonviolence challenged power, force, and self. The Nietzschean will to power has claimed far more adherents than the biblical admonition, first found in Leviticus, to love one's neighbor as oneself. The past—and the present—is in many ways the story of how we have hated those neighbors and have loved ourselves and our own kind with decisive ferocity.

Yet Lawson's message to Lewis, and in turn Lewis's message to America in the twentieth and twenty-first centuries, turned history on its head. Love, not power, should have pride of place; generosity, not greed; kindness, not cruelty. Nonviolence had its tactical uses, but it was not only a tactic. It was an enveloping philosophy, a compelling cosmology, a transforming reality. "We are talking about *love* here," Lewis recalled. "Not romantic love. Not the love of one individual for another. Not loving something that is lovely to you. This is broader, deeper, more all-encompassing love. It is a love that accepts and embraces the hateful and the hurtful. It is a love that recognizes the spark of the divine in each of us, even in those who would raise their hand against us, those we might call our enemy." Lewis's nonviolent witness took place in a democratic context, but his vision transcended the familiar understanding of the progressive impulse in America.

The idea of progress, if not its reality, had been with us from the beginning. "I always consider the settlement of America with Reverence and Wonder," John Adams wrote in 1765, "as the Opening of a grand scene and Design in Providence, for the Illumination of the Ignorant and the Emancipation of the slavish Part of Mankind all over the Earth." Thomas Jefferson believed, too, in a nation where the future was brighter than the past. In great old age, he wrote of a "march of civilization" that had passed "over us like a cloud of light, increasing our knowledge and improving our condition. . . . And where this progress will stop no one can say." When Frederick Douglass observed—in the wake of the 1857 *Dred Scott* decision—that he knew "of no soil better adapted to the growth of reform than American soil," he was working within a political tradition of amendment and adjustment.

Lewis had even larger ideas. To him—and to Lawson, and to King—the goal of America was not simply a more perfect Union but a wholly new order as manifested in the gospel proposition of the Kingdom of God. Working from a phrase of the American philosopher Josiah Royce, Lewis, King, and Lawson believed in the Beloved Community, which was one in which Jesus, in King's words, has "made love the mark of sovereignty. Here we are left with no doubt as to Jesus' meaning. The Kingdom of God will be a society in which men and women live as children of God should live. It will be a kingdom controlled by the law of love."

The Kingdom of God was understood theologically but realized practically, in the Beloved Community. "The dream is one of equality of opportunity," King said, "of privilege and property widely distributed; a dream of a land where men will not take necessities from the many to give luxuries to the few; a dream of a land where men do not argue that the color of a man's skin determines the content of his character; a dream of a place where all our gifts and resources are held not for ourselves alone but as instruments of service for the rest of humanity; the dream of a country where every man will respect the dignity and worth of all human personality, and men will dare to live together as brothers."

It was the noblest of missions, and it all washed over Lewis in that basement on Phillips Avenue off Fourteenth Avenue North in Nashville. Lawson was about transforming ideas into action. Lewis was eager to take what he was learning and put it to work. But before he could march into nonviolent combat, he needed more preparation. He'd get it in an unlikely setting: on a small mountain farm ninety miles away near the town of Monteagle on the Cumberland Plateau.

It was called the Highlander Folk School. Founded by the organizer Myles Horton, a native of Savannah, Tennessee, in 1932, it was intended to be a center to train labor leaders. Norman Thomas and Niebuhr, a teacher of Horton's at Union Theological Seminary, were signatories on the institution's first fundraising appeal. "The southern mountaineers who are being drawn into the coal and textile industries are completely lacking in understanding of the problems of industry and the necessities of labor organization," the letter announced. In talking about practical action, Horton liked to quote an observa-

From left: King, Pete Seeger, Charis Horton, Rosa Parks, and Ralph Abernathy at the Highlander Folk School on the Cumberland Plateau.

tion of his grandfather's: "You can hitch your wagon to the stars, but you can't haul corn or hay in it if its wheels aren't on the ground."

Highlander hosted decades of workshops and classes designed to create effective change, first in labor relations and later in terms of civil rights and other social justice causes. Horton and his colleagues believed in action over theory, and Highlander was suffused with an ethic of love for one's fellow man. As a child Horton had picked up a volume of Cumberland Presbyterian theology and, on discovering the doctrine of predestination, went to his mother to say he couldn't accept the idea that everything was foreordained. "Don't bother about that, that's not important, that's just preachers' talk," his mother replied. "The only thing that's important is you've got to love your neighbor."

At Highlander, Horton created one of the few integrated facilities in the Jim Crow South. Blacks and whites ate together, swam together, square-danced together. The setting was simple and idyllic, with white frame buildings set in a clearing bordered by woods. "It looked like a small college campus," Andrew Young, a key lieutenant of King's, recalled. (Young also remembered "Highlander's version of the cocktail hour—drinking a martini out of a Vienna sausage can, complete with an olive.")

In 1955, before the Montgomery bus boycott, Rosa Parks traveled to Tennessee for a session on the mountain. The experience helped change her life. "At Highlander, I found out for the first time in my adult life that this could be a unified society, that there was such a thing as people of different races and backgrounds meeting together in workshops, and living together in peace and harmony," Parks recalled. "It was a place I was very reluctant to leave. I gained there the strength to persevere in my work for freedom, not just for blacks, but for all oppressed people."

Parks came to Highlander. Martin Luther King came to Highlander. Pete Seeger came to Highlander ("We Shall Overcome," a combination of sundry protest songs, reached its modern form there). Eleanor Roosevelt came to Highlander.

And, in 1958, John Lewis came to Highlander. Horton's vision complemented Jim Lawson's. "I think that people aren't fully free until they're in a struggle for justice," Horton recalled. "And that means for everyone. It's a struggle of such importance that they are willing, if necessary, to die for it. I think that's what you have to do before you're really free. Then you've got something to live for." Lewis absorbed such lessons, sang songs, and found solace among like-minded reformers for whom a religious ethic was not a Sunday obligation but a life force.

The person who most impressed Lewis at Highlander was Septima Clark, the school's director of workshops. Born in South Carolina in 1898, the daughter of a former slave, Clark was a pioneer in citizenship education. "Her specialty was working with grassroots people—sharecroppers, common folk, black men and women who had little or no schooling—teaching them basic literacy as a first step toward becoming voters," Lewis recalled. "What I loved about Clark was her down-to-earth, no-nonsense approach and the fact that the people she aimed at were the same ones Gandhi went after, the same ones I identified with, having grown up poor and barefoot and black."

Clark was the guiding force behind a wide-ranging grassroots movement to prepare people for the suffrage. "Day by day we silently pour the concrete of love into the furious, violent ocean of hate," read a workbook for a Georgia Citizenship School under Clark's direction. "Someday that concrete will build a foundation that will support a bridge to span the channel and open lines of communication to all peoples." To Clark, democracy was the heart of the matter. "The Supreme Court building, where the Justices decide legal disagreements, is the symbol of law. The Capitol, where our Senators and Representatives make the laws, is the symbol of free, representative government. The White House, where the President lives and his Cabinet meets, is the symbol of our country in world affairs. We accept the results of elections and abide by the rulings of the courts."

Lawson, who had taken Lewis and his group to Highlander, turned to pragmatic training back in Nashville. "He showed us how to curl our bodies so that our internal organs would escape direct blows," Lewis recalled. "It was not enough, he would say, simply to endure a beating. It was not enough to resist the urge to strike back at an assailant. 'That urge can't *be* there,' he would tell us. 'You have to do more than just not hit back. You have to have no *desire* to hit back. You have to *love* that person who's hitting you.'"

It was the most difficult of lessons. But Lewis was determined to make Lawson's words real—to *embody* the truth of nonviolence. In the winter of 1959–60—he was still a teenager until the third week of February 1960—he'd face the first test of his resolve.

The store's motto was straightforward: "Harvey's Has It!" Founded in 1942 on Church Street in downtown Nashville, about halfway between the Tennessee state capitol and the Grand Ole Opry's Ryman Auditorium, Harvey's Department Store was home to the segregated Monkey Bar lunch counter. On Saturday, November 28, 1959, much of Nashville's attention was fixed eastward, on Knoxville, where the annual University of Tennessee–Vanderbilt football game was taking place. (Vanderbilt would win, 14–0.) Lewis, Diane Nash, and a group of their fellow students from the basement sessions at Clark Memorial weren't following the game. They'd chosen the date with care: This was the Saturday after Thanksgiving, a busy shopping day. "I came to town to do my Christmas shopping," a woman had told a reporter for *The Tennessean* on Friday. "But I think everybody else had the same idea." Under the headline EARLY SHOPPERS FILL CITY, STORES, the paper wrote, "A solid mass of cars jammed the streets and the sidewalks were filled to overflowing as shoppers flocked in to take advantage of after-Thanksgiving sales. A freezing wind whistled around the corners and everyone from babies in strollers to grandmothers were bundled up in heavy coats and bright scarves."

In this busy moment, braving cold temperatures—it had snowed overnight—Lewis, Nash, and their friends walked into Harvey's, bought a few small items, and presented themselves as paying customers to order a bite of food. "I was nervous," Lewis recalled. "We were all nervous. We didn't know what to expect. All my life I'd heard, seen and obeyed the rules. You can't use that library. You can't drink at that fountain. You can't go in that bathroom. You can't eat in that restaurant. I hated those rules, but I'd always obeyed them. Until now."

This first foray to Harvey's was a Gandhian reconnaissance mission. Diane Nash was with Lewis, as was the Mississippi-born Marion Barry. They dressed in their Sunday clothes—"coats and ties," Lewis remembered, and "skirts and blouses"—and took seats at the lunch counter.

"I'm sorry," a waitress told them. "We can't serve you here." As

Lewis recalled, "She was very nice about it, not nasty at all. I'm sure she thought we were students from someplace up north, someplace where blacks were allowed to eat in a restaurant like this. We just didn't know any better."

"May we speak to the manager?" Diane Nash asked.

The waitress was puzzled. The polite request—part of the Lawson training—was something different, something new. A challenge, but a gentle, entirely calm one.

A manager, Greenfield Pitts, arrived. "It is our policy," he said, "not to serve colored people here. This is the policy of our store."

That was that. Lewis and his colleagues left the premises. The test had been successful. Part of the nonviolent strategy was to establish that institutions were in fact segregated, which then set the stage for fuller action. "I came back to my dorm room that afternoon elated, just about ready to burst," Lewis recalled. The next weekend they repeated the exercise at the Cain-Sloan Department Store, with the same results.

Then, on Wednesday, February 3, 1960, Lewis borrowed his dormitory mother's copy of *The Tennessean* newspaper and read reports from Greensboro, North Carolina, that four freshmen from North Carolina A&T had gone to the downtown Woolworth's lunch counter there and asked to be served. The story wasn't all that unusual. There had been quiet sit-ins for several years in different cities.

A telephone call from minister to minister, however, helped changed the calculus. On Wednesday, February 3, the Methodist clergyman Douglas Moore in Durham, North Carolina, reached out to Jim Lawson. "What can the students in Nashville do to support the students of North Carolina?" was Moore's question, and, in Lewis's recollection, the query was like the Lord's in Isaiah: "Whom shall I send?" "That was the question that we needed," Lewis recalled, "and we were ready." Greensboro had struck first. Nashville would now move, too, and express solidarity with their fellow demonstrators in North Carolina by sitting-in in Tennessee.

Hundreds of students participated. They marched quietly into Kress's, Woolworth's, McClellan's. "We took our seats in a very orderly, peaceful fashion," Lewis recalled. "The students were dressed like they were on the way to church or going to a big social affair. But they had their books, and we stayed there at the lunch counter studying and preparing our homework, because we were denied service. The manager ordered that the lunch counters be closed, that the restaurants be closed, and we'd just sit there and we continued to sit all day long. The first day nothing, in terms of violence or any disorder, nothing happened. This continued for a few more days, and it continued day in and day out."

Saturday, February 27, 1960, was a beautiful day in Nashville—cold but sunny. In the morning, the Reverend Will Campbell, a white minister and supporter of the movement—Lewis had first met him at Highlander—told the students who were about to head downtown that he'd heard some disconcerting news. "He said that if we go down on this particular day he understood that the police would stand to

Devoted to nonviolence—James Lawson wrote its founding manifesto—SNCC was created in 1960; Lewis would become its chairman in 1963.

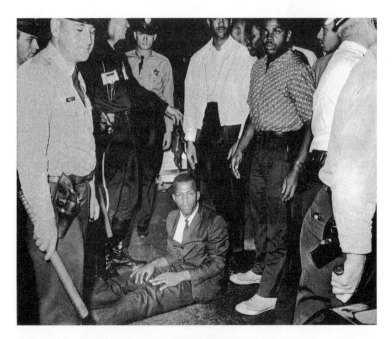

the side and let a group of white hoodlums and thugs come in and beat people up and then we would be arrested," Lewis recalled. "And we should make a decision about whether we wanted to go or not. . . . We made a decision to go."

Woolworth's was Lewis's assigned store that day. "Go home, nigger!" was the cry that greeted Lewis from a group of young white men. "Get back to Africa!" The white toughs wanted a fight, but they weren't getting the kind of fight they understood. "What's the matter? You *chicken*?" they said as Lewis and his compatriots silently pressed on to take their seats. Lewis was hit in the ribs and knocked to the floor. There was pulling, punching, and jabbing; some burned the students with lit cigarettes—both on their backs and in their hair. A young reporter, David Halberstam, described the scene in a piece headlined "A Good City Gone Ugly": "For more than an hour the hate kept building up, the hoodlums becoming increasingly bold. . . . The Negroes never moved. First it was the usual name calling, then spitting, then cuffing; now bolder, punching, banging their heads against the counters, hitting them, stuffing cigarette butts down the backs of their collars."

Then, just as Campbell had anticipated, the city police arrived. "As the young men who had beaten us looked on and cheered," Lewis recalled, "we were told that we were under arrest for 'disorderly conduct.'" The students met their fate not stoically but joyfully, singing "We Shall Overcome" as they were marched into the paddy wagon for the trip to the city jail. "That was the first time that I was arrested, and growing up in the rural South it was not the thing to do—to go to jail," Lewis said. "It would bring shame and disgrace on the family. But for me, I tell you, it was like being involved in a holy crusade. It became a badge of honor." He recalled the moment in religious terms; he was not humiliated but exalted, not captive but free:

> That paddy wagon—crowded, cramped, dirty, with wire cage windows and doors—seemed like a chariot to me, a freedom vehicle carrying me across a threshold. I had wondered all along, as anyone would, how I would handle the reality of what I had studied and trained and prepared for for so long, what it would be like to actually face pain and rage and the power of uniformed authority.

Now I knew. Now I had crossed over, I had stepped through the door into total, unquestioning commitment. This wasn't just about that moment or that day. This was about forever. It was like deliverance. I had, as they say in Christian circles when a person accepts Jesus Christ into his heart, come home. But this was not Jesus I had come home to. It was the purity and utter certainty of the nonviolent path.

He wasn't alone, and he drew strength from both the ethos of non-violence and from his friends, who were numerous, many of them from ABT. "It would not be an overstatement to say that the entire student body and many of the faculty members of the American Theological Seminary participated in some form or another," a history of ABT noted.

An ABT graduate, the Reverend Douglas Frazier, composed a poem that captured the spirit of Lewis's days:

They threw us all in jail last night
Because we stood for what is right
They drug us from this all white place
Because we're members of the Negro race. . . .

In the Nashville jail that February Saturday, the students refused to pay bail. "If the authorities chose to release us, fine," Lewis recalled. "But we were not about to *pay* our way out. We were not about to co-operate in any way with a system that allowed the discrimination we were protesting. Instead, we sang. We sang, and we chanted: 'Jail without bail!'" Six hours later they were released to the president of Fisk University, Stephen J. Wright, pending trial.

The students were represented by Z. Alexander Looby, a member of the Nashville City Council and a lawyer for the NAACP. The judge found Lewis and eighty other defendants—it had been a mass arrest—guilty of disturbing the peace and gave them a choice of paying a $50 fine or serving thirty-three and one-third days in the workhouse. Three thousand people had come to the courthouse in Nashville to show their support; the crowd sang "The Battle Hymn of the Republic" and "The Star-Spangled Banner," and the court officers used a loudspeaker system to call the cases.

"We feel that if we pay these fines," Diane Nash said for the group, "we would be contributing to and supporting the injustice and immoral practices that have been performed in the arrest and conviction of the defendants."

They would take the workhouse. By now the sit-ins were national news; it was the first time such nonviolent demonstrations had taken place on such a scale. On Sunday, February 28, *The Washington Post* put the story at the top of the front page. "We're going to fill their jails," a Fisk student said as he was being put in the paddy wagon. "That's a promise." In a companion piece, the *Post* reported Georgia senator Richard B. Russell, Jr.'s fury at the burgeoning movement. The segregationist lawmaker, the paper said, believed that the demonstrations were "deliberate efforts to provoke race riots in the South to whip up Northern sentiment for civil rights legislation."

In Nashville, the city's mayor, Ben West, arranged for the defendants to be released from their sentence. Still, the waves kept coming: The sit-ins went on. On Wednesday, March 2, Harrison E. Salisbury of *The New York Times* gave the country a glimpse of what Jim Lawson had been teaching Lewis and the other students. "A Negro minister called today for a sustained policy of nonviolence and Christian forbearance to end racial discrimination," Salisbury wrote. The *Times* then quoted a list of instructions the students had carried with them into the downtown stores—a list written not by Lawson but by Lewis:

Don't strike back or curse back if abused.
Don't laugh out [loud].
Don't hold conversations with floor workers.
Don't leave your seats until your leader has given you instruction to do so.
Don't block entrances to the stores and aisles.
[Be] friendly and courteous at all times.
Sit straight and always face the counter.
Report all serious incidents to your leader.
Refer all information to your leader in a polite manner.
Remember the teachings of Jesus Christ, Mohandas K. Gandhi and Martin Luther King.
Remember love and nonviolence, may God bless each of you.

Soon a full economic boycott of downtown was a new fact of life for Nashville's merchants. The mayor was struggling to find a middle way when attackers hurled dynamite at Alexander Looby's house near Meharry Medical College early on the morning of Tuesday, April 19, 1960. Looby and his wife were asleep and were unharmed, but the blast destroyed their living room picture window and blew out 147 windows at the nearby Meharry hospital. Lewis got the news almost immediately, and, with Bernard LaFayette, went over to Clark Memorial where they met Lawson and C. T. Vivian, among others. They quickly decided to organize a noonday march on city hall and sent Mayor West a telegram announcing their plans.

Within hours, about five thousand people had gathered and set out for city hall. "It was not a noisy march," Lewis recalled. "It was very orderly and people marched in twos." When the mayor came out, he answered questions composed by Lewis and his allies that morning at Clark. Diane Nash was the interlocutor.

Would the mayor use "the prestige of your office to appeal to the citizens to stop racial discrimination?" Nash asked.

"I appeal to all citizens," West replied, "to end discrimination, to have no bigotry, no bias, no hatred."

"Do you mean that to include lunch counters?"

The mayor stumbled a bit, but Nash kept after him, repeating, "Then, Mayor, do you recommend that the lunch counters be desegregated?"

"Yes," West said, and that was that.

Nonviolence had worked. Not without pain, and not without cost. There were bruises and burns to attest to that. And Jim Lawson, who had been enrolled as a graduate student at Vanderbilt's Divinity School, was expelled by the university's chancellor and conservative governing board; half the Divinity faculty temporarily resigned in protest, and twenty other professors from around the university threatened to do so as well. To the students of the sit-ins, the message of the Lawson expulsion was clear. The white establishment, Lewis and his compatriots believed, wanted to decapitate the movement by targeting Lawson. "Cut off the head, the thinking went," Lewis recalled, "and the body would fall." It didn't work; Lawson remained a vital part of the movement.

Under his tutelage, the young people of Nashville had done something remarkable, both with the sit-ins and the march on city hall, and they were just getting started. "There is more power in socially organized masses on the march than there is in guns in the hands of a few desperate men," King later wrote. "Our enemies would prefer to deal with a small armed group rather than with a huge, unarmed but resolute mass of people.... All history teaches us that like a turbulent ocean beating great cliffs into fragments of rock, the determined movement of people incessantly demanding their rights always disintegrates the old order."

They were so young. "I wonder for the first time what it can be like to be making, in the adolescent dark, such decisions as this generation of students has made," James Baldwin wrote in the summer of 1960. "They are in battle with more things than can be named. Not only must they summon up the force to face the law and the lawless—who are not, right now in [the South], easily distinguishable—or the prospect of jail or the possibility of being maimed or killed; they are also dealing with problems yet more real, more dangerous and more personal than these: who they are, what they want, how they are to achieve what they want and how they are to reconcile their responsibilities to their parents with their responsibilities to themselves."

To skeptics and to the merely curious, Baldwin expressed a deep truth. "Americans keep wondering what has 'got into' the students," Baldwin wrote. "What has 'got into' them is their history in this country. They are not the first Negroes to face mobs: they are merely the first Negroes to frighten the mob more than the mob frightens them.... They cannot be diverted. It seems to me that they are the only people in this country now who really believe in freedom. Insofar as they can make it real for themselves, they will make it real for all of us. The question with which they present the nation is whether or not we really want to be free."

It was only a beginning. "The lunch counter 'sit-in,'" the Southern Regional Council's Harold Fleming told the *Times's* Claude Sitton, "demonstrates something that the white community has been reluctant to face: the mounting determination of Negroes to be rid of all segregated barriers." To a writer for *The Nation,* Fleming added, "Just as the Supreme Court decision was the legal turning point, the sit-ins are the psychological turning point in race relations in the South. This is the first step to real change—when the whites realize that the Negroes just aren't having it anymore."

The Reverend Kelly Miller Smith linked the students with the Savior and the saints. "'Father, forgive them . . . ,'" Smith cried out from the First Baptist pulpit, evoking some of the last words of Jesus from the cross, continuing:

> The students sat at the lunch counters alone to eat and, when refused service, to wait and pray. And as they sat there on that southern Mount of Olives, the Roman soldiers, garbed in the uniforms of Nashville policemen and wielding night sticks, came and led the praying children away. As they walked down the streets, through a red light, and toward Golgotha, the segregationist mob shouted jeers, pushed and shoved them, and spat in their faces, but the suffering students never said a mumbling word. Once the martyr mounts the Cross, wears the crown of thorns, and feels the pierce of the sword in his side there is no turning back.
>
> And there is no turning back for those who follow in the martyr's steps. All we can do is to hold fast to what we believe, suffer what we must suffer if we would win, and as we face our enemy let us say, "Father, forgive them."

King had arrived the evening after the march to city hall to pay tribute to those who hadn't turned back. "I came to Nashville not to bring inspiration, but to gain inspiration from the great movement that has taken place in this community," he told a crowd at the Fisk University gym. "No lie can live forever. Let us not despair. The universe is with us. Walk together, children. Do not get weary."

Lewis didn't need the exhortation. Far from depleting him, the sit-ins, the arrest, the time in jail, even the Looby bombing, had energized him. "Going into the movement in those first days, I felt it was a baptism for me," Lewis recalled. "If it hadn't been for Nashville, for Jim Lawson, Kelly Miller Smith, and so many others, I don't know what would have happened to a poor young soul like me." The Beloved Community had not yet come to pass, but now

Lewis had seen what could be done to right wrongs, to act in love, to suffer yet to prevail. And there was a lot more for that poor young soul to do.

He couldn't breathe. On Thursday, November 10, 1960—just two days after John F. Kennedy defeated Richard Nixon for the presidency by the tiniest of popular vote margins—Lewis and James Bevel found themselves trapped in a Krystal hamburger restaurant on Fifth Avenue North in downtown Nashville. They'd been at First Baptist when they'd gotten word that three of their fellow students— Bernard LaFayette, Elmyra Gray, and Maryann Morgan—had been attacked at the Krystal, a Chattanooga-based chain founded in 1932 that specialized in small square burgers. At about two-thirty that afternoon, the three students had bought their food and sat down. "They told us the place was closed"—it self-evidently was not—"and we would have to leave," LaFayette told *The Tennessean.* The students wouldn't get up, and a waitress poured detergent down their backs, hosed them, and turned up the air-conditioning to try to freeze them out. "It was just the one waitress that did it all," Morgan recalled. "She went wild. The others just stood around and laughed." Lewis and Bevel went over about ninety minutes later and tried to speak to the general manager.

It did not go well. "He told us we would have to leave because they were going to fumigate the place," Lewis told reporters. Lewis and Bevel refused to leave, and the manager locked the front door, sent his staff out the back, and, as he followed them, turned on an exterminating fumigator filled with insecticide. There was no place to go, no escape. Bevel began to preach, quoting the book of Daniel: *"And whoever falleth not down and worshipeth, shall the same hour be cast into the midst of a burning fiery furnace."* The lines came from the story of Nebuchadnezzar, who erected a false god, demanded that his subjects venerate it, and cast Shadrach, Meshach, and Abednego into the furnace when they refused. The biblical episode had a happy ending: The fires failed to harm the three, and the king was awed. "Then Nebuchadnezzar spake," Daniel wrote, "and said, Blessed *be* the God of Shadrach, Meshach, and Abednego, who hath sent his angel, and delivered his servants that trusted in him."

In November 1960, Lewis and James Bevel were locked in a Krystal restaurant on Fifth Avenue North; the manager turned on a fumigator filled with insecticide, prompting Bevel to preach an impromptu sermon on Shadrach, Meshach, and Abednego, who had been cast into a furnace in the Book of Daniel.

Lewis and Bevel needed an angel—quickly. "We were both coughing, gasping for air," Lewis recalled. "We're going to suffocate, I thought. We're going to die. Could that man have really left us here to die?"

Then the city fire department arrived outside; passersby had mistaken the billowing insecticide for smoke and called for help. The manager who had trapped Lewis and Bevel unlocked the front door, sending a rush of cool autumn air into the restaurant. "That could

Part of the initial Nashville strategy was to integrate both downtown lunch counters and still-segregated movie theaters; here, demonstrators, including James Lawson, attempt to buy tickets at the Tennessee Theatre.

have been the end," he recalled. "It really could have. We really thought we could pass out. We could die. I was not eager to die, but I was at peace with the prospect of it. The prospect of death."

He was not yet twenty-one years old.

Life for Lewis was now a rush of events, an ever-rolling stream of strategy sessions, protests, arrests, mass meetings, interviews—all to be followed by more strategy sessions, more protests, more arrests, more mass meetings. In February 1961 he marked his twenty-first birthday in the Nashville jail after being arrested for "standing in," or peacefully picketing, the city's segregated movie theaters. *Swiss Family Robinson* was showing at the Loew's; *Gold of the Seven Saints* was at the Paramount; *The World of Suzie Wong* was at the Tennessee Theatre, which billed itself as the "Showplace of the South."

There was more bloodshed as white counter-protesters struck outside the theaters—cracked ribs, a head wound. The minister Will Campbell, who had gotten the heads-up about the planned violence against the sit-ins the year before, spoke to Lewis and the other students at First Baptist in February 1961, wondering whether the nonviolent demonstrations were worth the risk of physical harm. As Lewis recalled the evening meeting,

> I listened to the debate that night. I considered everything that was said. And I heard nothing fundamental enough to shift the sureness I had felt inside about what we were doing. I did not have a shred of doubt about what our next step should be.
>
> "We're gonna march," I said, when Will Campbell asked my opinion.
>
> He turned away and went on with the discussion. Someone else asked what I thought about something that was said, and my answer was the same.
>
> "We're gonna march," I said, as simply and softly as before.
>
> At that point, Campbell lost his temper with me. . . .
>
> "There's apt to be some serious violence if there's another demonstration," he continued. "You agree with that, and still you say, 'We're gonna march.'
>
> "What it comes down to," he went on, "is that this is just a matter of pride with you. This is about your own stubbornness, your own sin."
>
> The room was absolutely silent. Everyone turned to me.
>
> I looked straight at Will.
>
> "Okay," I said. "I'm a sinner."
>
> The room remained still.
>
> "But," I added, "we're gonna march."
>
> And that was that.

Campbell wasn't crazy. He was raising reasonable concerns about safety in a violent time. And he wasn't alone. Thurgood Marshall, the NAACP counsel, often expressed worries when it came to the movement's forward-leaning battles. Nonviolent provocations in dangerous places—especially in the deeper South of Alabama and Mississippi—were, Marshall believed, dangerously fraught. "It's a waste," Lewis recalled Marshall saying. "You'll get people hurt, he told us. You'll get people killed."

The older Marshall believed in the courts while the younger Lewis and his colleagues held that perilous direct action was essential. It's impossible to understand Lewis without taking him at his word that he was not thinking, or acting, in traditionally political or even rational terms. As improbable as it may seem, self-preservation was not a decisive factor in his vision of the world and of his place in it.

Watching him at Highlander, Myles Horton had realized that Lewis and the student movement were not about reform in the usual sense, but about redemption in an ultimate sense—redemption of the whole world through an embrace of the gospel and its implications. "The SNCC people—John Lewis . . . and then some of the others— said, 'We can't stop. We've got to carry on. If we give up now, then it's over. They can't stop us, and we've got to be willing to pay whatever price,'" Horton recalled. "At that time, they made a commitment to die if necessary. John Lewis almost did when they beat him to a pulp, but that's when they declared their independence, that's when they became free. If you aren't afraid to die for your cause, then nobody can get at you. . . . That's what liberation is, being willing to die for what you believe in."

Did age play a role in shaping that understanding? Certainly, for the young had less to lose than the middle-aged and the old. Fewer families, fewer spouses, fewer children. That's not to say that the young had *nothing* to lose. They did—chiefly their lives and the possibilities of family, spouses, children. But the remarkable young people of the movement understood the risks, and took them. "The nonviolent movement of the early 1960s was indeed a spiritual movement," Diane Nash recalled. "Faith was what we used. For many of us, it was also a matter of logic. Had we, in the 1960s South, responded with violence, I fully believe that we would have been mowed down by gunfire. We wanted to create not just the end of segregation, but in the process we wanted to have a community of increased tolerance and love and understanding. If you had violence, it would have just escalated. We knew that segregation was tough. It had been in place for one hundred years—and we knew that if we wanted to get rid of it, we had to be willing to go to jail, to suffer—and, yes, to die. John understood that."

When demonstrations turned violent, Lewis would come into meetings with bandages on his head. "People would show up for a while, and some were serious; some wanted to see if there were any cute girls or good-looking guys there," Nash recalled. "John was always there. He was determined, dependable. It was always clear to me, even when we were so young, that as long as he was living he was going to stand against segregation. That was so clear."

What makes Lewis so fascinating is that he was *in* the world but not really *of* it. He was more conversant with, and comfortable in, the prospective Kingdom of God (or Beloved Community) than he was in Carter's Quarters, or "the Holy Hill" of ABT, or Clark Memorial, or the Fifth Avenue Krystal. Once such a commitment was made, there was little left to be said. There was only work to be done, witness to be borne, love to give.

CHAPTER THREE

SOUL FORCE

The Freedom Rides: 1961

This is the most important decision in my life, to decide to
give up all if necessary for the Freedom Ride, that Justice
and Freedom might come to the Deep South.

—JOHN LEWIS, applying for the 1961 Freedom Rides

L EWIS FIRST READ about what was then called "Freedom Ride,
1961" in *The Student Voice,* a SNCC publication, in March 1961.
According to the announcement, which was published on page
seven of the eight-page newsletter, the Freedom Ride was to be "a
dramatic move to complete the integration of bus service and accommodations in the Deep South." Interested parties were to write to
Gordon R. Carey, field director of the Congress of Racial Equality
(CORE), in New York.

The previous December, in *Boynton v. Virginia,* the Supreme Court
had ruled that compelling interstate travelers to use segregated bus
station facilities—including waiting rooms, food service, and
restrooms—was unconstitutional. (The decision complemented *Morgan v. Virginia,* a 1946 ruling that had, in theory, outlawed segregation
on interstate buses.) The opinions were heartening, but the reality
was different. As was their wont, many Southern states had chosen to
ignore the high court and maintained Jim Crow's grip on interstate
travel. Now CORE wanted to force the issue in the same way the
students of Nashville had brought change to lunch counters in 1960.

Lewis had been thinking along these lines since at least Christmas
1959, when he and Bernard LaFayette had taken seats directly behind
the driver on a bus heading south out of Nashville. Lewis was going to
Troy; LaFayette to Tampa, Florida. The driver ordered them to get up
and go to the back of the bus, but they refused. The driver slammed
back his own seat, crushing the passengers, and threatened to call the
Klan. Lewis and LaFayette stood—or sat—their ground, and the episode passed without further violence. It was sufficiently scary, though,
that the two joked that this might be their last ride—ever.

Afterward, the two wrote to Fred Shuttlesworth, the minister and co-founder of the Southern Christian Leadership Council, to propose a trip to the heavily segregated Birmingham to test *Morgan* and *Boynton*. Shuttlesworth's reply was disappointing. "Though appreciative of their bravery, Shuttlesworth urged the Nashville insurgents to find some other way to serve the cause," the historian Raymond Arsenault wrote in his definitive account of the Freedom Rides. "Birmingham, he warned, was a racial powder keg that would explode if local white supremacists were unduly provoked, especially by outsiders."

CORE was willing to go where Shuttlesworth had not been. "I couldn't believe it," Lewis recalled of the Freedom Rides announcement. "Somehow, the Spirit of History was putting its hands on my life again." He applied to become a Freedom Rider, writing, "At this time, human dignity is the most important thing in my life. This is the most important decision in my life, to decide to give up all if necessary for the Freedom Ride, that Justice and Freedom might come to the Deep South."

The conventions of life, never particularly important to Lewis, were falling away. He'd had to postpone his senior sermon at ABT—a rite of passage—because he was in jail for protesting at the Loew's movie theater downtown, and he was now missing his commence-

"I couldn't believe how much blood there was," Lewis recalled of the beatings he, Jim Zwerg (pictured here with Lewis), and others endured during the Freedom Rides at Montgomery on Saturday, May 20, 1961.

ment exercises to go to Washington for the Freedom Rides back into hostile country. If he'd had a traditional youth, he could have said, with Saint Paul, that he had become a man and had put away childish things. But he'd never really been a child in the sense of being carefree and unburdened. From his chickens to civil rights, he'd always had cares and burdens. His spirit and his sphere of action were mature, expansive, even universal.

The text for Lewis's senior sermon came from Matthew. "Think not that I am come to send peace on earth," Jesus says. "I came not to send peace, but a sword." In context, Jesus means that strife must come before serenity, darkness before light. "The sword was not a blade but a spiritual sword," Lewis recalled. "We were going to tear down the old world—patiently, and nonviolently. But that was what we were going to do."

He'd never been to Washington before. The plan was for the Freedom Riders to gather in the capital, board the buses in integrated pairs, and strike out for New Orleans. On Sunday, April 30, 1961, Lewis arrived in Washington's Greyhound station on New York Avenue NW after an overnight ride from Tennessee. He checked into the Quaker Fellowship House at 945 L Street NW and joined the dozen other Freedom Riders for a few days of training. The Riders, CORE's James Farmer recalled, would "sit at a simulated counter asking for coffee. Somebody else refused them service, and then we'd have others come in as white hoodlums to beat 'em up and knock them off the counter and club 'em around and kick 'em in the ribs and stomp 'em, and they were quite realistic, I must say. I thought they bent over backwards to be realistic. I was aching all over."

The tension was thick, so on the evening before boarding the buses south the group went out to dinner, a Chinese feast at Yenching Palace in Cleveland Park, a gracious neighborhood in northwest Washington. Lewis had never had Chinese food before—hadn't, really, ever gone out for a fancy dinner before. He long remembered the delicious food being passed around the (integrated) table in big silver dishes. Mordantly, someone joked that this might well be their "Last Supper."

A few others were at dinner that night—including a young New Yorker who was studying at Howard University, Stokely Carmichael. Born in Trinidad in 1941, Carmichael moved to Harlem when he was eleven, tested into the highly competitive Bronx High School of Science, and had matriculated at Howard. "When I first heard about the Negroes sitting-in at lunch counters down South," he'd recall, "I thought they were just a bunch of publicity hounds. But one night when I saw those kids on TV, getting back up on the lunch counter stools after being knocked off them, sugar in their eyes, ketchup in their hair—well, something happened to me. Suddenly I was burning." Charming and eloquent, Carmichael joined SNCC. "That evening was my first meeting of John Lewis, and like everyone else in SNCC, I was overwhelmed by his courage, his quiet determination, his conviction in the rightness of the cause," Carmichael recalled. "He was a seminary student . . . always soft-spoken, and dressed in a suit in the cut of a Martin Luther King." To Carmichael, the Freedom Rides were self-evidently important. "In any sane, even half-civilized society it would have been completely innocuous, hardly worth a second thought or meriting any comment at all," he recalled. But the segregated South was neither fully sane nor fully civilized.

The next morning—Thursday, May 4, 1961—a few print reporters met the Riders as they boarded the Greyhound and Trailways buses. PILGRIMAGE OFF ON RACIAL TEST, *The Washington Post* headline said over a short story on page B4. "We had been told to expect some things in parts of Georgia, some things in parts of Alabama, in Mississippi, in Louisiana," Lewis recalled—and "some things" included jail. In an Associated Press story that was published in *The Montgomery Advertiser* under the headline MIXED GROUP'S TOUR TO CHALLENGE SEGREGATION, MONTGOMERY INCLUDED, James Farmer was quoted saying "If there is arrest, we will accept that arrest, and if there is violence we will accept that violence without responding in kind."

To be ready, the Riders had packed toothbrushes, toothpaste, and a few books to tide them over behind bars. Lewis had his toiletries in his knapsack and three books: a Bible, a volume about Gandhi, and one by Thomas Merton. "Christian nonviolence is not built on a presupposed division, but on the basic unity of man," Merton wrote. "The great historical event, the coming of the Kingdom, is made clear and is 'realized' in proportion as Christians themselves live the life of the Kingdom in the circumstances of their own place and time."

As the buses' engines roared to life, Lewis was making those abstract words real. The Riders had sung "We Shall Not Be Moved" as they boarded. He took a window seat. His partner, a white pacifist named Albert Bigelow, sat next to him on the aisle. A Harvard-educated Quaker convert and a former naval officer from Cos Cob, Connecticut, Bigelow had skippered a small craft, *The Golden Rule,* in an attempt to disrupt nuclear weapons testing in the Pacific's Marshall Islands in 1958.

Virginia was quiet—remarkably so. They rolled on into North Carolina, where the only real action came when one of the black Riders asked for a shoeshine in a station barbershop. A barber, Grady H. Williams, swore out a warrant charging Joe Perkins, a twenty-seven-year-old CORE staffer, with trespassing. Perkins was arrested and jailed after refusing to post a fifty-dollar bond, but the judge, citing *Boynton* as the law of the land, threw the case out. So far, the journey had been smooth, days of riding punctuated by church meetings at night.

At Shiloh Baptist Church in Greensboro, Jim Farmer preached a powerful sermon. "Life is not so dear and sweet that we must passively accept Jim Crow and segregation," he told the crowd. "If our parents had gone to jail we wouldn't have to go through the ordeal now. Our nation cannot afford segregation. Overseas it gives Uncle Sam a black eye. Future generations will thank us for what we have done."

Farmer's words were well received over the weekend. The Freedom Riders pressed on, heading southward. Tuesday, May 9, 1961, brought them to Rock Hill, South Carolina.

The Ku Klux Klan had been a dominant force in Rock Hill's York County as early as 1868, not long after the former Confederate cavalry commander Nathan Bedford Forrest had been elected "Grand Wizard of the Invisible Empire" at the Maxwell House Hotel in Nashville. Reconstruction in Rock Hill and its environs, the New Deal Writers' Program found, had been "a time of terror. . . . This section became a hotbed of Ku Klux activities." By 1871, scholars say, 1,800 of the 2,300 adult white males in York County—or 78 percent—were Klansmen, and they were believed to have been responsible for eleven murders and six hundred other attacks. President Grant declared martial law in the York region as part of his war on vigilante violence in 1871.

The sit-in movement had already come to Rock Hill the year before, and students from Friendship Junior College who had attempted to integrate a lunch counter had been sentenced to a month of hard labor. In that period, *The New York Times* reported, a "robed but unmasked Ku Klux Klansman paraded on Main Street," and an anonymous bomb threat forced the evacuation of a dormitory at Friendship.

Rock Hill, then, was not the most congenial of climates for the Freedom Riders. Among the young whites waiting for the Greyhound that Tuesday was Elwin Wilson, then in his early twenties. "I was once the meanest man that ever was in Rock Hill," Wilson would say. Andrew Dys, a reporter for *The Herald* in Rock Hill, interviewed Wilson nearly half a century later. An admitted Ku Klux Klansman, Wilson told Dys that he'd "marched against integration and went to rallies that beat hatred into the air along with ash from burning crosses. He threw cantaloupes and watermelons at blacks and beat up blacks who dared to be seen where he was. . . . 'I've done some bad things,' Wilson said. 'I thought it was cool. . . . I hated blacks. Hated 'em.' "*

He was at the Rock Hill Greyhound station on the Tuesday in May when Bigelow and Lewis got off the bus together and headed for the terminal waiting room door marked WHITE. Wilson and his friends were smoking cigarettes and standing by the station's pinball machines. Lewis remembered their ducktail haircuts and leather jackets—and their first words to him.

"Other side, nigger," one said, gesturing to the COLORED door.

"I have a right to go in there," Lewis replied, "on the grounds of the Supreme Court decision in the *Boynton* case." He wasn't nervous, he recalled, and he spoke "carefully and clearly." But he also knew what was coming. "I don't think either of these guys had ever heard of the *Boynton* case. Not that it would have mattered."

"Shit on that," one of Wilson's gang said.

Then it came. The white gang, Lewis recalled, "beat us and hit us." Repeatedly struck in the face and kicked in his sides as he fell to the ground, Lewis remembered the taste of blood in his mouth. Lewis and

---

* In 2009, after the election and inauguration of Barack Obama, Elwin Wilson publicly disclosed his role in the Rock Hill violence and sought Lewis's forgiveness, which Lewis, putting his principles into practice, freely gave. The two men met on a number of occasions afterward to bear witness to the power of reconciliation.

Bigelow never hit back. They absorbed the blows—blows in part inflicted by Elwin Wilson. It was an elemental attack. Asked what he'd used in the assault, Wilson replied, "My fists. I sure remember I didn't shake hands."

A Rock Hill policeman watched the beating and then stepped over. "All right, boys," he told Wilson and the other whites. "Y'all've done about enough now. Get on home."

Lewis struggled to his feet, "woozy and feeling stabs of sharp pain above both eyes and in my ribs. My lower lip was bleeding pretty heavily." He and Bigelow declined to press charges. "We're not here to cause trouble," Lewis told the police. "We're here so that people will love each other." The haters were the symptom, not the problem. "No child is born in hate," Lewis recalled. "All children are born in hope, love, and innocence. It is a troubled world that teaches these vicious values." The Rock Hill police captain accepted the decision not to move forward with charges.

Lewis needed a doctor, but he refused to leave the station before having a cup of coffee in the now-integrated café. At Friendship Junior College a bit later, he was bandaged up but serene—no need for a hospital, he said. He was doing what he was supposed to do.

Lewis was not in doubt about his pursuit of the Beloved Community. But he was still wondering about how, exactly, he was to serve the cause, and he'd applied for an overseas mission in Africa with the American Friends Service Committee. The day of the Rock Hill attack, the committee telegrammed him to ask if he'd come to Philadelphia for interviews and medical tests. (The Quakers had tracked him down by calling Nashville and getting an update on his whereabouts.) Lewis caught a flight from nearby Charlotte to Philadelphia, met with the committee, and was offered an assignment not in Africa, as he'd wished, but in India. He was thrilled to accept and returned to Nashville on the evening of Saturday, May 13, 1961. He'd go to church with his friends on Sunday—it was Mother's Day—and then drive down to Birmingham to rejoin the Freedom Ride.

Lewis landed at Nashville's Berry Field just as good news broke. The city's theaters had given in and pledged to integrate the movie houses. A pleased Lewis would join other Nashville students for a Sunday picnic celebration before heading to Alabama. Nashville was lovely that day; it was sunny and warm, with a high temperature in the

*Inside First Baptist Church in Montgomery, where Lewis and
1,500 others spent the night of Sunday, May 21, 1961, as hostile
white crowds stood outside.*

eighties. James Bevel was preaching—of course—and Lewis was savoring the respite when word came from Anniston, Alabama, that
Klansmen had firebombed the Greyhound that Lewis was supposed
to have been on. "I felt shock," Lewis recalled. "I felt guilt. That was
my bus, my group. . . . There were no details—no reports about injuries or deaths. I could only imagine, and imagination coupled with
fear is a torturous thing."

The bus had arrived at the Anniston station, in eastern Alabama,
en route from Atlanta to Birmingham, at about one in the afternoon.
A Klan-led mob attacked the Greyhound, slashing its rear tires, and
the driver rushed to pull back out of the station. But the back tires
gave out about six miles later. The bus came to a stop, putting the pas

A bandaged Lewis regroups with fellow Freedom Riders after the violence and chaos at Montgomery and the overnight siege at First Baptist.

sengers directly in harm's way as the Anniston mob gave chase. "The bus just couldn't roll," Lewis recalled. The Klansmen roared up behind the parked bus, surrounded it, smashed the windows, and tossed in a Molotov cocktail. "Burn them alive!" the mob had screamed. "Fry the goddamned niggers!"

"Oh my God, they're going to burn us up!" Genevieve Hughes, a Freedom Rider, cried out. In the chaos, the passengers managed to get off the Greyhound—both through the doors and the broken windows—just as the fuel tank exploded. Horrific and haunting, the images of the burning bus in Anniston flashed across the nation on the photo wire services.

The disastrous Sunday wasn't yet over. The Greyhound was in

flames in Anniston; the Freedom Riders' Trailways bus was in Birmingham, where another mob assaulted this second group with fists, feet, lead pipes, and clubs. One Rider sustained permanent brain damage. Another required fifty-three stitches in his head. "One passenger was knocked down at my feet by twelve of the hoodlums, and his face was beaten and kicked until it was a bloody pulp," Howard K. Smith reported that day for CBS. There was lawlessness in the land, Smith said, for "the riots have not been spontaneous outbursts of anger but carefully planned and susceptible to having been easily prevented or stopped had there been a wish to do so." There was, Smith added, only one person in the country who could bring order to the chaos. The "laws of the land and purposes of the nation badly need a basic restatement, perhaps by the one American assured of intent mass hearing at any time, the President."

The president, however, wasn't especially interested—at least not at the moment. "Nobody needs to convince me any longer that we have to solve the problem, not let it drift on gradualism," JFK had told Martin Luther King in an earlier conversation about civil rights in 1961. "But how do you go about it? If we go into a long fight in Congress, it will bottleneck everything else and still get no bill."

JFK had signaled his sympathy for the cause in the closing weeks of the 1960 presidential campaign. On Sunday, October 16, 1960, Martin Luther King, Jr., had been arrested during a sit-in at Rich's department store in Atlanta—he was attempting to desegregate the store's Magnolia Room restaurant—and he was sentenced to four months of hard labor at Georgia's Reidsville penitentiary. Coretta King, who was six months pregnant, was terrified that her husband might not come out of prison alive. "They are going to kill him," Mrs. King told Harris Wofford, a Notre Dame law professor and Kennedy adviser. "I know they are going to kill him." Wofford reached out to Kennedy brother-in-law Sargent Shriver with an idea. Would JFK call Mrs. King to express his concern? Shriver called the candidate, who was in Chicago.

"Why don't you telephone Mrs. King and give her your sympathy?" Shriver recalled saying to Kennedy. "Negroes don't expect everything will change tomorrow, no matter who's elected. But they do want to know whether you care. If you telephone Mrs. King, they will know you understand and will help. You will reach their hearts and give support to a pregnant woman who is afraid her husband will be killed."

"That's a good idea," JFK replied after a pause. "Why not? Do you have her number? Get her on the phone."

It all happened quickly. The candidate was soon speaking with Mrs. King. "I know this must be very hard for you," Kennedy told her. "I understand you are expecting a baby, and I just wanted you to know that I was thinking about you and Dr. King."

Robert Kennedy was initially furious with Wofford and Shriver. "You bomb throwers better not do anything more in this campaign," RFK said. Then Robert Kennedy thought again, and he decided to intervene in King's case, calling the judge to suggest bail. It worked; King was soon released. RFK briefed Lyndon B. Johnson of Texas, the vice presidential nominee, about the campaign's outreach. "Tell Jack that we'll ride it through down here some way," LBJ said, "but at least he's on the side of right."

The maneuvers paid off politically. Martin Luther King, Sr., known as "Daddy King," had endorsed Richard Nixon—the elder King had said he couldn't support a Roman Catholic—but now reversed course. "Because this man [JFK] was willing to wipe the tears from my daughter[-in-law]'s eyes," Daddy King said, "I've got a suitcase of votes, and I'm going to take them to Mr. Kennedy and dump them in his lap." Flyers heralding the Kennedy-King episode were widely distributed at black churches and in black neighborhoods. In such a close-run election, it's possible that the Kennedys' intervention was crucial to the outcome.

But that was then, and this was now. The prevailing white view of the movement tended to range from the temporizing to the ambivalent to the hostile. "Historians of the twenty-first century," Arthur Schlesinger, Jr., wrote, "will no doubt struggle to explain how nine-tenths of the American people, priding themselves every day on their kindliness, their generosity, their historic consecration to the rights of man, could so long have connived in the systematic dehumanization of the remaining tenth—and could have done so without not just a second but hardly a first thought."

To Schlesinger, the historian and adviser to both Kennedys, "The answer to this mystery lay in the belief, welling up from the depths of the white unconscious, in the inherent and necessary inferiority of those of a darker color." The persistence of that conviction had long undergirded a segregated order. American presidents largely chose to view Jim Crow through the prism of states' rights. "It is not the disposition or within the province of the Federal Government to interfere with the regulation by Southern States of their domestic affairs," William Howard Taft declared in his inaugural address in 1909, and, as Schlesinger noted, "By such means white America virtuously succeeded in cutting the Negro out of conscience and even, except for servants, entertainers, and athletes, out of sight."

On Saturday, May 6, 1961—two days after the Freedom Rides began—Robert Kennedy was in Athens, Georgia, to deliver a Law Day address at the University of Georgia. The attorney general was nervous. His hands trembled as he rose to speak. It was an educated audience, a world away from the pinball machines of the Rock Hill Greyhound station. It was, however, still the Deep South.

RFK linked the domestic struggle over civil rights with the Cold War. "From the Congo to Cuba, from South Vietnam to Algiers, in India, Brazil and Iran, men, women, and children are straightening their backs and listening—to the evil promises of Communist tyranny, and the honorable promises of Anglo-American liberty," Kennedy said. "And those people will decide not only their own future, but ours; how the cause of freedom fares around the world. That will be their decision."

America had to live by the rule of law rather than the rule of force. By supporting integration of the schools, for instance, Kennedy said, "We are maintaining the orders of the court. We are doing nothing more and nothing less. And if any one of you were in my position you would do likewise, for it would be required by your oath of office. You might not want to do it. You might not like to do it. But you would do it because it would be required. . . . You may ask, will we enforce the civil rights statutes? And the answer is yes, we will."

With the images of burning buses and beatings coming out of Alabama in the middle of the Freedom Rides, the Kennedy administration faced a clear test of how to translate those sentiments into action.

The bravery of the Riders gave some liberals great heart. In these months Eleanor Roosevelt was working hard to finish her final book, *Tomorrow Is Now.* She came down to breakfast one morning humming happily. "I had the most wonderful dream last night, Maureen," Mrs. Roosevelt remarked to her secretary Maureen Corr. "I dreamt I was marching and singing and sitting in with the students in the South." Mrs. Roosevelt could imagine no place she would rather be.

John Kennedy, for his part, would have preferred to see the whole thing go away. The president was furious about the Mother's Day bombing in Anniston and assaults in Birmingham—and his anger was directed not just at the attackers but at the Freedom Riders. "Tell them to call it off!" JFK told Harris Wofford. "Stop them! Get your friends off those buses!"

Kennedy couldn't know it, but CORE's James Farmer was thinking along the same lines. Things, Farmer believed, had gotten too dangerous. It was a miracle no one had been killed, but it was only a matter of time. Maybe Rock Hill, Anniston, and Birmingham had been enough to make the point. The governor of Alabama, John Patterson, declared the Freedom Riders, not the white mobs, were at fault—and in the line of fire. "The citizens of the state are so enraged," Patterson said, "that I cannot guarantee protection for this bunch of rabble-rousers."

The president and the attorney general decided to send an emissary to Alabama: the Tennessee-born newspaperman John Seigenthaler, who was now serving as a special assistant to RFK. The Kennedys' charge to Seigenthaler was clear: "Fly down immediately to Birmingham and get [the Freedom Riders] out of there this afternoon." Seigenthaler grabbed some clothes and headed south. For harried hours on Monday, May 15, the Riders divided their time between the bus station and, finally, the airport, where they'd been put on a plane after Farmer and others decided the Rides should end. There was a bomb scare on the flight, but at last, at 10:38 P.M. on Monday, the Freedom Riders were flown to New Orleans.

The crisis, it seemed, was over. Seigenthaler went to bed that night convinced he was the hero of the hour. "I thought I was the greatest thing that the administration could possibly have found," Seigenthaler recalled. "I'd been given this assignment by the president, by the attorney general. In one afternoon, I'd worked it out." In Nashville, John Lewis and Diane Nash had other ideas.

During meetings at Kelly Miller Smith's First Baptist Church, Lewis, Nash, and others opposed the withdrawal. They weren't naïve.

As Nash recalled, they received calls from Alabama urging them to stay in Nashville. "Don't come," they were told. "It's a bloodbath. Be assured, someone will be killed if you do come." But they couldn't stay away. "Mob violence," Nash said, "must not stop men's striving toward right."

Lewis agreed with Nash. "Retreat is one thing; surrender is another," Lewis recalled. "Backing down in a situation like that means that other values matter more than the issues or principles that are at stake—values such as personal safety." They weren't thinking pragmatically or even rationally, for their thought was shaped not by the fears of the world they knew but by the hopes of the one they were seeking.

In New Orleans, Seigenthaler was jolted awake by a ringing telephone at five o'clock in the morning. It was Robert Kennedy.

"Who the hell," the attorney general said, "is Diane Nash?"

"Bob, she's a young student," Seigenthaler replied. "I don't know her well, but I have seen her many times during the sit-ins, and she's a Fisk student."

"Well, she's sending more Freedom Riders down [to Alabama] from Nashville, and would you please get on the telephone and tell her she's got to stop this. She can't do this, she's going to get somebody killed."

Seigenthaler tracked Nash down and made his case. "I began rationally and reasonably explaining to her why sending more Freedom Riders down was a mistake, that I had seen people in the hospital, and people who had escaped with serious injuries and that as Emmett Till had died in Mississippi, certainly it was not unlikely that some of her friends were going to die if she sent them down."

"Of course we can't [stop now]," Nash said. "A great deal of planning has gone on the last couple of days, to take up these rides, and we simply can't let violence overcome nonviolence." As Seigenthaler recalled decades later, "She was preaching to me, everything Jim Lawson had preached to her and her colleagues, and reason and rationality turned quickly to frustration and heat. I think back on that and her voice stayed at one decibel throughout that conversation, and I can, almost in my head right now, hear my voice go up and up and up, and finally at the top of my voice, in a hotel room by myself, [I said], 'Young woman, do you understand, you are going to get somebody killed?' And she said, 'Do you understand, we all signed our wills last night, we know somebody will die, but we are not going to let nonviolence be overcome by violence.'"

They were going to press on.

O n the evening the Nashville students decided to reinforce the Freedom Rides, the older civil rights leaders in town were worried. "The adults did not want us to continue the Freedom Rides after Anniston, after Birmingham," Bernard LaFayette recalled. "They knew it was dangerous, but they gave us a check—we needed the money for tickets and food. When we got it, we realized we couldn't cash it. It needed two signatures, and one of the men who had to sign it was working on the railroad. So here we were, at ten o'clock at night, with no money. We said, 'Who would have money on a Sunday night?' So we went to the numbers man in Nashville—a numbers man always has cash. So he took it even though the adults had thought they had bought some time, and the older folks were stunned when they woke up and the Riders were actually gone."

On Wednesday, May 17, 1961, Lewis and nine other relief Freedom Riders left Nashville for Birmingham on a Greyhound. At the Birmingham city limits, police boarded the bus and arrested two of the Riders—one black, and one white—and told the driver to drive on to the Greyhound station. Once there, the police held the Freedom Riders on board for three hours. An angry crowd gathered outside. Police taped newspapers over the windows, throwing the interior of the bus into what Lewis thought was a "strange [and] eerie" gloom. The driver scheduled to take the bus out of Birmingham to Montgomery had bailed because of the dangers. In limbo, Lewis and other Riders were escorted into the station.

Before long the Birmingham commissioner of public safety, Theophilus Eugene Connor, arrived at the station. "I had seen pictures of him, and even his pictures conveyed a nastiness, a meanness," Lewis recalled. "He didn't like the idea of people coming together as human beings. I think it created a madness in him."

B orn in 1897 in Selma, Alabama, Connor lost his mother early on and never finished high school. As a radio sportscaster for the minor-league Birmingham Barons baseball team, he earned a lifelong

Furious at President Truman for his civil rights program, Strom Thurmond of South Carolina bolted the Democratic Party in 1948 and launched a Dixiecrat bid for the White House.

nickname: "Bull," in honor of his gift for banter. In 1934, "partly for the fun of it and partly to see how many friends I had," Connor successfully sought a seat in the state legislature and won his citywide office three years later. He was a devoted defender of Jim Crow, once opposing an integrated meeting in Birmingham in 1938 that included Eleanor Roosevelt and Supreme Court justice Hugo Black. "Negroes and whites," he said, "would not segregate together" on his watch. A decade later, Connor was a delegate to the 1948 Democratic National Convention. "It is part of the Communist program to stir up strife between white and Negro people and keep it stirred up," Connor said. "It is my hope that, as one of your delegates, I can help roll back the attempt of meddlers, agitators and Communist stooges, to force down our throats, through our own Democratic Party, the bitter dose they are now offering us under the false name of Civil Liberties."

At the national convention in Philadelphia, Connor joined South Carolina governor Strom Thurmond and other Dixiecrats in bolting from the party to protest President Truman's civil rights initiatives. (The president would soon order the desegregation of the U.S. military.) And it was Commissioner Connor who welcomed the States' Rights Democratic Party when the breakaway segregationists met at Birmingham's Municipal Auditorium to nominate Thurmond for president. "I want to tell you, ladies and gentlemen," Thurmond declared in accepting the nomination, "that there's not enough troops in

Thurmond was officially nominated as the States' Rights Democratic Party candidate for president at a convention in Birmingham's Municipal Auditorium in the summer of 1948.

the army to force the Southern people to break down segregation and admit the nigra into our theaters, into our swimming pools, into our homes, and into our churches."

Connor stood strong through the years, reflecting in many ways the will of his constituents. "Bull is the law in Birmingham, like it or not," a businessman said, and Birmingham could be brutal. "Ball parks and taxicabs are segregated," *The New York Times* reported in the spring of 1960 in a piece entitled "Fear and Hatred Grip Birmingham." "So are libraries. A book featuring black rabbits and white rabbits was banned. A drive is on to forbid 'Negro music' on 'white' radio stations. . . . A year ago a Negro girl and a white girl, both elementary pupils, quarreled on their way to school. A white man emerged from a near-by house with a bull whip and flogged the Negro girl." On the issue of race, the *Times* wrote, "every channel of communication, every medium of mutual interest, every reasoned approach, every inch of middle ground has been fragmented by the emotional dynamite of racism, reinforced by the whip, the razor, the gun, the bomb, the torch, the club, the knife, the mob, the police and many branches of the state's apparatus."

To a meeting of the White Citizens' Council in his native Selma a week after the *Times*'s "Fear and Hatred" piece, Connor was unapologetic. Speaking to an audience of several hundred at Baker Elementary School, Connor moved the microphone to the side as he took the podium. "I don't need this thing," he said in what *The Birmingham News* called "a booming voice," "because I feel so strongly about what I'm going to say they can hear me all over the state." To him, disaster was at hand if blacks were allowed to press forward with the civil rights movement. "They want to use our parks, and they want to send their children to white schools," Connor said. "They want Negro bus drivers and Negro teachers in white schools. They want to desegregate hotels, motels, restaurants, buses, taxis. The truth is, ladies and gentlemen—they don't want racial equality at all. The Negroes want black supremacy."

He worried, too, about the calls for voting rights, warning that black leaders in Birmingham were "daily encouraging more Negro voting." This could not stand. "I'll tell you right now, unless the South makes up its mind to stand up and fight this plague—and it is a plague—we are going to find Negroes who can't read or write . . . enforcing our laws," he said. "You may as well face it now—this is the way it will be if it is left up to Russia and those so-called Northern Democrats such as Eleanor Roosevelt." Connor spoke in the most familiar of Alabama vernaculars: that of football. "Yes, we are on the one-yard line," Connor said. "Our backs are to the wall. Do we let them go over for a touchdown, or do we raise the Confederate flag as did our forefathers and tell them . . . 'You shall not pass!'" The white crowd ate it up.

Two weeks before the Nashville Freedom Riders reached Birmingham in 1961, Connor had been reelected in a landslide, winning 61 percent of the vote. "By golly," he said, "we swamped 'em this time."

After the Mother's Day 1961 violence—violence he'd allowed to take place—Connor said, "We are not going to stand for this in Birmingham. And if necessary we will fill the jail full—and we don't care whose toes we step on.... Our people of Birmingham are a peaceful people and we never have any trouble here unless some people come into our city looking for trouble. And I've never seen anyone yet look for trouble who wasn't able to find it."

In the waning hours of the afternoon of Wednesday, May 17, 1961, Connor approached Lewis. It was the first time Lewis had seen Connor in the flesh. The Riders, Lewis recalled Connor's saying, "were being taken to jail. We were not being arrested, but we were being placed in protective custody for our own safety, for our own well-being."

In the Birmingham City Jail, which Lewis remembered as a "dungeon" with "no mattresses or beds, nothing to sit on at all, just a concrete floor," he and the remaining Riders went on a hunger strike. They sang freedom songs, not least because they knew it drove Connor to distraction. And they waited—something at which they were getting better and better. Waiting for a bus, waiting for a beating, waiting for the police, waiting for a judge. Waiting.

That evening, the nation had a chance to glimpse what they'd been facing when Howard K. Smith anchored a CBS News documentary, *Who Speaks for Birmingham?* "After ten minutes of undeterred savagery," Smith said, the mob of whites "had, as if on signal, dispersed and had gone further down the street, where I saw some of them discussing their achievement of the day right under the windows of the police commissioner's office." ("Witnessing the savage beatings in Birmingham," Smith recalled, "was my worst experience since the opening of the concentration camps at the end of WWII.")*

By eleven-thirty P.M. on the night of the CBS broadcast, Connor had taken matters into his own hands. He didn't want to wait anymore on the governor, or on Washington, or on the bus companies. Birmingham was his town—had been for a long time—and he wanted

---

* Smith would lose his job at CBS when he attempted to quote Edmund Burke ("the only thing necessary for the triumph of evil is for good men to do nothing") at the conclusion of the documentary. Anxious about alienating the network's Southern affiliates, CBS cut the quotation. Smith soon moved to ABC News.

"Bull is the law in Birmingham, like it or not," a
businessman said in 1960, describing the hold Bull Connor,
the safety commissioner, had on the city.

these people gone. Standing in front of the cells, the commissioner, who had brought along two *Birmingham News* reporters, announced that the Freedom Riders were going home—right then. "You people came in here from Tennessee on a bus," Connor said. "I'm taking you back to Tennessee in five minutes under police protection."

A ride in the dark of the Alabama night with Bull Connor and his deputies was not high on Lewis's list of desirable outcomes. "We didn't go in a voluntary way," Lewis recalled. "We went limp, so they literally picked us up and put us in the car, and we started back up the highway toward the Tennessee state line."

Lewis rode in the car Connor was driving. There was some—not much, but some—actual human communication. "He tried being friendly, making small talk as we drove through dark empty streets and out of the city, headed north toward Tennessee," Lewis recalled. One of the Riders, Catherine Burks-Brooks, told Connor he should join them for breakfast in the Fisk cafeteria once they reached Nashville. Happy to, Connor replied.

But Connor wasn't going that far. About 120 miles from Birmingham, the caravan reached tiny Ardmore, Alabama. "This is where you'll be gettin' out," Connor said. "There is the Tennessee line. Cross it and save this state and yourself a lot of trouble." The police left the Riders and their bags by the desolate roadside in the depths of night. "We were frightened," Lewis recalled. "We didn't know anyone in Ardmore, Alabama, or Ardmore, Tennessee." What they did know was that this was the kind of place where the Klan was strong, fearless, and likely ready to finish what the toughs in Rock Hill and Birmingham had started.

Connor pointed toward nearby railroad tracks and said "a bus will be coming along or a train will be coming along and you can make your way back to the city of Nashville." But it sure didn't feel like anything, or anyone, was coming, save for night riders. The small group set off down the tracks, looking for help, and found an elderly black couple—Lewis, who never learned their names, thought they were at least in their seventies—living in a ramshackle house about a mile away. The man of the house resisted at first—helping people like Lewis could get you killed—but his wife insisted. In that time and place, taking in this small band of Freedom Riders was an act of profound bravery, a radical thing to do. Lewis used their telephone to call Diane Nash, who agreed to send a car for them. Their hostess, meanwhile, gave the Riders hot water to use to clean up, and her husband, at daybreak, bought breakfast supplies at several different stores to avoid, as Lewis put it, "making a single, suspiciously large purchase at one." He came back with bread, baloney, cheese, and eggs. To the famished students, it was a feast.

"What do you want to do?" Nash had asked Lewis on the phone. "Do you want to come back to Nashville or do you want to go back to Birmingham and continue the ride?"

"We will continue the ride," Lewis replied. Back to Birmingham they would go.

Another of Diane Nash's calls that night was to Washington, to Howard University and Stokely Carmichael. "Hey, you watching this mess?" she asked.

"Whad'you think?" Carmichael replied.

She told him straight out. "Diane was a persuasive young woman," Carmichael recalled. Her argument: "It was not just ugly bad, it was ominous. If the Freedom Rides were stopped because of violence, and only because of violence, then the nonviolent movement was over. . . . Give the racists this victory and it sends the clear signal that at the first sign of resistance, all they have to do is mobilize massive violence, the movement will collapse, and the government won't do a thing. We can't let that happen." Carmichael agreed; the students of Washington, D.C., would send help.

Back in Alabama, Lewis and his fellow Riders returned to Birmingham. It was now Friday, May 19, and they huddled at Fred Shuttlesworth's house for a few hours before gathering at the Birmingham Greyhound station. Once again there was no driver, and a white mob was on hand. At an estimated three thousand people, it was the largest crowd Lewis had yet seen, and he thought it "loud and angry."

For eighteen hours, the Riders took refuge in the Birmingham station as the mob laid siege outside. "No bus driver would drive, because the bus drivers were literally afraid of what could happen," Lewis said. "The Klan had surrounded the bus station. They were throwing stink bombs. There were police officials there trying to keep the Klan from getting to us inside of this so-called white waiting room. They had the police dogs." The scheduled white driver, Joe Caverno, whom the *New York Herald Tribune* described as a "stocky, powerful man," refused the route, saying, "I have only one life to give, and I'm not going to give it to the NAACP, not to CORE." Working from Washington, Robert Kennedy demanded that "Mr. Greyhound" find a driver, and the bus company finally prevailed on Caverno to do the driving.

At last, at eight-thirty on the morning of Saturday, May 20, 1961, the Freedom Riders left Birmingham. As they reached Montgomery's Greyhound station on South Court Street—it was now 10:23 A.M.—the police escorts and a highway patrol plane that had seen them out of Birmingham and along the highway disappeared. The bus, and the Riders, were alone. The Montgomery commissioner of public safety—Bull Connor's opposite number—was L. B. Sullivan. "Not since Reconstruction have our customs been in such jeopardy," a defiant Sullivan had told a White Citizens' Council "Salute to Law and Order" the year before. "We can, will and must resist outside forces hell-bent on our destruction." To laughs and applause, Commissioner Sullivan had added, "Spring is here, and birds are singing, but with the help of our law-enforcement people, the *blackbirds* aren't gonna sing on the Capitol steps."

Or on South Court Street. "At the bus station it was just eerie, just a strange feeling," Lewis recalled. "It was so quiet, so peaceful—nothing." Stuart H. Loory, a reporter for the *New York Herald Tribune*, asked Lewis to explain the goal of the journey.

"We just got out of Birmingham," Lewis replied. "We got to Montgomery." Loory noted that Lewis's "words trailed off as his gaze fixed over the shoulder of this reporter. . . . Mr. Lewis had spotted the mob approaching." Lewis never finished the sentence.

"Get those niggers!" the crowd cried.

"The moment we started down the steps off of that bus," Lewis recalled, "an angry mob—they grew into about two to three thousand people—came out of nowhere: men, women, children with baseball bats, clubs, chains and they literally—there was no police official around—they just started beating people."

Lewis knew what to do. "Do not run," he said to his friends. "Let's stand here together."

In the Montgomery mayhem, Lewis was struck over the head with a wooden Coca-Cola crate and knocked unconscious. "I could feel my knees collapsing and then nothing," he said. "Everything turned white for an instant, then black."

John Seigenthaler arrived and tried to help the Freedom Rider Susan Wilbur, who was being assaulted, but he was clubbed in the back of the head with a lead pipe. The special assistant to the attorney general fell to the pavement. Like Lewis, he was unconscious. Seigenthaler was out for almost half an hour.

John Doar, the chief lawyer in the Department of Justice's civil rights division, was watching from a window in the nearby Federal Building. "Oh, there are fists, punching," Doar reported to Washington by phone. "There are no cops. It's terrible. There's not a cop in sight. People are yelling, 'Get 'em, get 'em.' It's awful."

Lewis's pain was such that he wondered if he could go on. "I literally thought it was the last march. It was the last Freedom Ride," Lewis recalled. "It was a very bloody event. It was a very nasty mob." After he regained consciousness on the pavement, he became aware of the state attorney general, MacDonald Gallion, standing over him reading an injunction against "entry into and travel within the state of Alabama and engaging in the so-called 'Freedom Ride' and other acts or conduct calculated to promote breaches of the peace."

"I hardly listened to those words," Lewis recalled. "My head was spinning, both with thoughts about the carnage that had occurred and with pain. I was bleeding pretty badly from the back of my head. I couldn't believe how much blood there was."

The Riders found safe harbor for the rest of the day and overnight in different houses around town. "I was sickened today," a white Montgomery man told Calvin Trillin, then of *Time,* after the Saturday, May 20, beatings. "For the first time, I was ashamed of being from this town. But this is not sympathy for those nuts. I hate them."

But "those nuts"—the Freedom Riders—weren't going anywhere. On Sunday, May 21, Lewis joined the congregation at Montgomery's First Baptist, where Ralph Abernathy was still pastor. Martin Luther King flew in from Chicago, and by late afternoon a mass meeting was under way. There was preaching and singing; the congregation cooled off with Ross-Clayton Funeral Home fans; Lewis remembered joining in during "Ain't Gonna Let Nobody Turn Me 'Round."

The Reverend B. D. Lambert offered a prayer. "This is a great moment in history," Lambert said. "We thank Thee, Lord, for the protection Thou has given us. You have blessed us in so many ways that we have not the words to describe them. You are too wise to make a mistake and too powerful to fail. Bless our enemy and we thank Our Father for these fine young people."

Outside the church, the white crowds grew in number and in hostility. There were Confederate flags, Rebel yells, Molotov cocktails like the one that had destroyed the bus in Anniston, a brick crashing through a stained-glass window, and whiffs of tear gas. In Abernathy's basement office—where Lewis had first met King in the Troy State conversations, conversations that seemed a lifetime ago—King was in communication with Robert Kennedy, who in turn was negotiating with Alabama governor John Patterson through the fraught hours of the night. "John, John," the attorney general was heard to say to the governor. "What do you mean you're being invaded? Who's invading you, John? You know better than that."

RFK had arranged for hurriedly deputized federal marshals to help restore order. Several were Alabama federal employees, including ATF agents, leading Byron White, the Kennedy intimate, deputy attorney general, and future Supreme Court justice, to say, "I wonder

Lewis and King at a press conference in Montgomery announcing that the Freedom Rides would go on—straight into the heart of Mississippi.

which side they'll take on." Murray Kempton, the New York columnist, thought the marshals "seemed a home guard of family men suddenly called up for an invasion." But they did their duty, standing as strong as they could against a mob that kept moving ever closer to First Baptist's doors. The church, Kempton wrote, "had become a postage stamp beachhead."

"Fear not," King told the congregation, "we've come too far to turn back." On the telephone, RFK tried mordant humor to ease the tension. "As long as you're in church, Reverend," Kennedy said, "and our men are down there, you might as well say a prayer for us." But it wasn't the time for jokes. There was a real fear, King said, that "we're going to have a bloody confrontation."

The congregation sang the words composed by Julia Ward Howe in Willard's Hotel amid the Civil War, the "Battle Hymn of the Republic":

Mine eyes have seen the glory of the coming of the Lord;
He is trampling out the vintage where the grapes of wrath are stored;
He hath loosed the fateful lightning of His terrible swift sword;
His truth is marching on.

Glory! Glory! Hallelujah!
Glory! Glory! Hallelujah!
Glory! Glory! Hallelujah!
His truth is marching on. . . .

In the beauty of the lilies Christ was born across the sea,
With a glory in His bosom that transfigures you and me;
As He died to make men holy, let us die to make men free!
While God is marching on.

The National Guard arrived, but nobody was sure whether they would protect or persecute. When the congregants tried to leave the church, they found their way blocked. "Their rifles were pointed our way," Lewis recalled. "They looked like the enemy."

Lewis and the rest of the 1,500-odd people in the church were trapped. "So now we settled in for the night," he recalled. "The children were taken back down to the basement to sleep. The elderly were given the cushioned pews. And the rest of us slept as best we could on the floor."

By four-thirty on the morning of Monday, May 22, 1961, the siege had broken. "Out on the pavement, hemmed in by the National Guard, a woman was wondering how she would be able to call her boss," Murray Kempton wrote. "These are proud, brave and faithful people and some of them even found time to worry about the wives of pillars of the White Citizens Councils who were in danger of having to cook their own breakfasts this morning."

Lewis was taken to the home of Dr. Richard Harris, an African American pharmacist, Tuskegee airman, and friend of the movement. (Harris served the strait-laced Lewis his first beer.) On that Monday, Lewis testified in a hearing before U.S. District Judge Frank M. Johnson, Jr.

Everyone was exhausted. But Lewis and the Riders weren't done. It was time, they decided, to press on to Mississippi. The state's governor, Ross Barnett, wired a warning to Robert Kennedy: "You will do a great disservice to the agitators and the people of the United States if you do not advise the agitators to stay out of Mississippi."

Figures like Barnett hadn't gotten the point—and neither, really, had Robert Kennedy. The point of the Freedom Rides—the point of everything Lewis was undertaking—was not to conform or give in or be reasonable, but to persist in the cause of repealing unjust laws and coldhearted customs. On the morning of Wednesday, May 24, as Lewis boarded a bus from Montgomery to Jackson, Mississippi, RFK issued a statement on Department of Justice stationery: "A mob asks no questions. . . . A cooling off period is needed."

James Farmer's response spoke for many ("We've been cooling off for a hundred years") as did John Patterson's ("the first time the federal government has displayed any common sense in some days"). At a press conference where Lewis sat to King's left, King said, "Freedom Riders must develop the quiet courage of dying for a cause. We would not like to see anyone die. . . . We all love life, and there are no martyrs here—but we are well aware that we may have some casualties. . . . I'm sure these students are willing to face death if necessary."

For Lewis, it was time to move forward. The next big stop: Jackson, Mississippi. "I'd never been to Mississippi before," Lewis recalled. "All my life I had heard unbelievably horrible things about the place, stories of murders and lynchings, bodies dumped in rivers, brutality and hatred worse than anything I'd ever heard of growing up in Alabama or attending college in Tennessee." Along the route, the Freedom Rider Frank Holloway recalled, "At the outskirts of small Mississippi towns, people outside their houses and stores shook their fists and threw rocks at us." In Jackson, the writer Theodore H. White once asked "a particularly intelligent state official whether it didn't gnaw at him or bother him in any way at all that Negroes could find no place in the downtown heart of his city where they might sit and eat like human beings."

"Not one goddamned bit," the man replied.

At the Jackson, Mississippi, bus station, Lewis walked into the whites-only restroom, stood at a urinal, and was quickly arrested. Convicted of breaching the peace, he was sentenced to sixty days in jail. He spent a couple of weeks at the Hinds County prison farm and then, in the darkness of night on Thursday, June 15, 1961, Lewis and his brethren were herded into a windowless truck.

They were being taken to Parchman Farm, the Mississippi state penitentiary, a place William Faulkner once summed up in a single phrase: "destination doom."

"We have bad niggers here," Parchman's superintendent, Fred Jones, a Sunflower County planter, told the prisoners after they were unloaded from the trailer at the 21,000-acre prison complex in the Mississippi Delta. "Niggers on death row that'll beat you up and cut you as soon as look at you." The guards wielded shotguns and stood against a barbed wire fence that stretched farther than Lewis could see in the gloaming of early morning. "Sing your goddamned Freedom Songs *now*," Jones said. "Won't do you a bit of good *here*."

They remained at the prison for nearly a month. "Parchman was not a blessed place, that I can tell you," Lewis said. His recollections of their captivity seem to come from a premodern world:

> We were led into a cement building where deputies with cattle prods stood by while we were ordered to strip naked. For two and a half hours we stood wearing nothing, while we waited for . . . well, we didn't know *what* we were waiting for. I could see that this was an attempt to break us down, to humiliate and dehumanize us, to rob us of our identity and self-worth. . . . When we were finally led, two by two, into a shower room guarded by a sergeant with a rifle, I thought of the concentration camps in Germany. This was 1961 in America, yet here we were, treated like animals for using the wrong bathroom. . . .
>
> Again we waited naked, this time for an hour and a half. . . .
>
> On one occasion a fire hose was brought in and we were blasted with jets of water. Giant fans were then set up and turned on full blast, freezing us in our flooded cells.
>
> On especially hot days—and there were many, this being summer in Mississippi—the windows were kept closed and we baked in the airless heat. Ceiling lights were kept on around the clock, making it difficult to sleep. One of the women, who were kept in another building, miscarried while a prison guard watched and did nothing.

In Parchman, Lewis came to a decision. His place was here, on the battlefield of his homeland, not in India. He wrote the American Friends Service Committee to withdraw from the overseas program into which he'd just been accepted. "The people who were together at

Parchman Farm, where Lewis and his fellow Freedom Riders were incarcerated, "was not a blessed place, that I can tell you," he recalled. "Sing your goddamned Freedom Songs now," the superintendent told them. "Won't do you a bit of good here."

Parchman—we grew up in that time there together," Lewis recalled. "We grew tougher, we grew wiser." Each Freedom Rider was assigned to give a lecture based on his college major. "We did a lot of teaching and praying and singing there. We became better souls, more committed to the way of peace and the way of love."

Bernard LaFayette remembered that the prisoners had to walk past the state's death chamber on the way to the showers. They were conscious of biblical parallels, particularly the story, related in Acts, of the imprisonment of Paul and Silas, who were stripped, beaten, flogged, and jailed for preaching the gospel. "About midnight Paul and Silas were praying and singing hymns to God, and the other prisoners were listening to them," the author of Acts wrote. "Suddenly there was such

Lewis would be arrested forty times during the civil rights movement, and on five additional occasions as a member of Congress. He saw suffering as redemptive—and essential.

a violent earthquake that the foundations of the prison were shaken. At once all the prison doors flew open, and everyone's chains came loose." Lewis and his friends remembered a spiritual:

Paul and Silas bound in jail,
Had no money for . . . their bail.

"It was like we had been called or chosen to try to bring justice to the world," Lewis recalled. "We didn't have a choice—we had been ordained by God Almighty to do this work. It was the right place to be at that time—to redeem the larger society."

There was no earthquake, but Lewis and the others were released from Parchman on Friday, July 7. King met them in Jackson, telling the white South, "We will wear you down by our capacity to suffer." It was, America was learning, more than just words. "Do to us what you will and we will still love you," King would add on the circuit. "We will meet your physical force with soul force. You may bomb our homes and spit on our children and we will still love you." Nineteen sixty-one, King was to say, was "a year of the victory of the nonviolent method: though blood flowed, not one drop was drawn by a Negro from his adversary."

For Lewis, the ordinary was extraordinary, and a familiar pattern of life prevailed in the fall of 1961. It was back-to-school season, and he enrolled at Fisk University in Nashville. "I was hungry for a secular liberal arts education to supplement the Bible-focused education I had received at American Baptist," he recalled. For the rest of the year and through 1962, Lewis went to class and moved around the country. "I could have made better grades if I had focused entirely on school—especially in German; Lord, I had trouble with German. But I didn't do that. It all mattered to me, school *and* the movement."

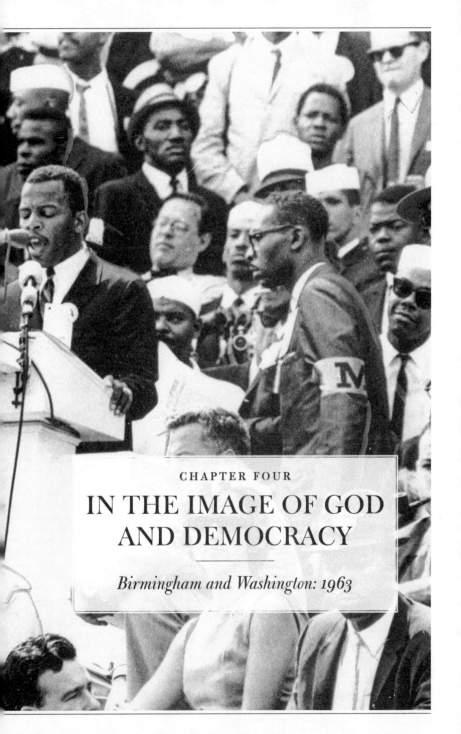

CHAPTER FOUR

IN THE IMAGE OF GOD
AND DEMOCRACY

Birmingham and Washington: 1963

PREVIOUS PAGES: *As chairman of SNCC, Lewis addresses the March on Washington for Jobs and Freedom, Wednesday, August 28, 1963.*

Altogether, it was a moving feeling within me that I was
sitting there demanding a God-given right, and my soul
became satisfied that I was right in what I was doing.

—JOHN LEWIS, in a 1960 NBC documentary used to train
the youth of Birmingham in 1963

Nigguhs hate whites, and whites hate nigguhs.
Everybody knows that deep down.

—Governor GEORGE C. WALLACE of Alabama

TWO YEARS LATER, in the late winter and spring of 1963, Birmingham was back at center stage. In a concerted campaign against segregation, King and his lieutenants launched an all-out nonviolent siege of the city, at times deploying children and teenagers on the front lines to dramatize the evils of Jim Crow and the viciousness of white resistance to change. Bull Connor rose—or stooped, really—to the occasion, playing his role to a kind of tragic perfection. These were the days and weeks of fire hoses and snarling police dogs, of brutality and misery. The hoses that Connor directed to be aimed at the children were so powerful, *The New York Times* noted, that "the water skinned bark off trees in parks and along sidewalks." Len Holt, a civil rights lawyer, watched as "bricks were torn loose from the walls," and Fred Shuttlesworth was taken away by ambulance after being blasted. ("I waited a week to see Shuttlesworth get hit with a hose," Connor said. "I'm sorry I missed it. I wish they'd carried him away in a hearse.") One African American father, asked how he felt about his twelve-year-old son's arrest, told a reporter, "It's fine with me. His father's been a slave all his life." In a contentious White House meeting with representatives of the liberal group Americans for Democratic Action in the first week of May 1963, President Kennedy, under pressure for being too slow on civil rights, remarked, "And as it is today, Bull Connor's in charge, and this is just what Bull Connor wants. . . . Bull Connor just eats this up. . . . I think

In an address to the nation on Tuesday, June 11, 1963, President Kennedy described civil rights as a "moral crisis." Medgar Evers would be assassinated later that night in Jackson, Mississippi.

it is a national crisis." The images and stories out of Alabama were having their effect. "I am not asking for patience," Kennedy said. "I can well understand why the Negroes of Birmingham are tired of being asked to be patient."

The nonviolent troops in the Birmingham of 1963 had been trained for their trial by Lewis and the Nashville movement of 1960–61. In a television documentary that first aired on Tuesday, December 20, 1960, anchorman Chet Huntley had narrated the NBC *White Paper: Sit-In,* which reconstructed the campaign to integrate the city's lunch counters in spare but revealing detail. *The New York Times*'s television critic, Jack Gould, praised the program lavishly, calling the broadcast "one of the network's superior accomplishments, a vivid and exciting social document that contained well-organized factual data and enjoyed brilliant pictorial composition." In Birmingham, the young people who were taking to the streets and the stores in their own long battle watched the NBC film, studying the movement's work and witness in Nashville.

In the documentary, Lewis is shown walking quietly down a Nashville street, in company with fellow students. He's wearing a narrow, striped tie, a jacket, and a checked overcoat. There is a sign

"Snarling German shepherds loosed on teenaged boys and girls, the animals' teeth tearing at slacks and shirts," Lewis recalled of Bull Connor's attacks in Birmingham in the spring of 1963. "It was absolutely unbelievable."

outside one store, McLellan's: BAKED MEAT LOAF DINNER: TWO VEGETABLES—ROLL AND BUTTER, 49 CENTS. "It was on February the thirteenth we had the very first sit-in in Nashville," Lewis says. "And I took my seat at the counter. I asked the waitress for a hamburger and a Coke."

The filmmakers cut to a heavy-set, middle-aged white waitress in eyeglasses and a white uniform, staring straight at the camera. "I said, 'I'm sorry, our management does not allow us to serve niggers in here.' "

Angeline Butler, a young Fisk student from South Carolina, picks up the narration. "These sorts of comments—they touch to your soul and they make you realize that it's all the more important to do something about it. . . . I think on this day many of us didn't realize just how important our movement would grow to be."

Lewis's voice returns. He is on camera, sitting alone, impossibly young, his Alabama accent thick. "Altogether, it was a moving feeling within me that I was sitting there demanding a God-given right, and my soul became satisfied that I was right in what I was doing," he says. "At the same time, there was something deep down within me, moving me, that I could no longer be satisfied or go along with an evil system—that I had to be maladjusted to it and in spite of all of this I had to keep loving the people who denied me service, who stared at me."

Angeline Butler is brought back into the story. "On the morning of the twenty-seventh, this was to be our first real violent day. It was the first time when we could really test our own convictions as far as nonviolent means were concerned. Five ministers said to us, 'If you go downtown today, you're going to be arrested. Please don't go downtown because we're not prepared, we should have [the] community behind us.' "

Of course, they went anyway. A white tough's voice plays over images from an integrated group of students at a counter: "I saw a bunch of coloreds sittin' on the stools. They looked like a bunch of idiots sitting up there waiting for people to try to throw 'em off—they looked like they were just tryin' to egg on a fight."

As the white crowd grabbed the quiet demonstrators and hurled them to the floor, Butler says, "None of us looked back and yet we could see everything that was going on through the long mirror."

The NBC film moves to Nashville special city judge John Harris's courtroom, where the demonstrators—not the white mob—are on trial. The judge gives the sit-in students a choice: a fifty-dollar fine or jail time. "Each of them chose jail," Chet Huntley said over the footage. "Their attitude reflected the words of Reverend Martin Luther King, who in a speech made in Nashville at the time, said, 'We will meet the capacity to inflict suffering with the capacity to endure suffering. We will say, Do what you will to us, but we will wear you down.'" The scene closes with students, now free from jail, marching anew, singing softly: "Deep in our hearts, we know that we shall overcome some day."

Lewis's example, then, informed the mission of the young people of Birmingham who were facing Bull Connor's police force in 1963. In Nashville, Lewis and his team would cut out images of Birmingham from the newspapers and post them with announcements about meetings and marches. "Snarling German shepherds loosed on teenaged boys and girls," he recalled, "the animals' teeth tearing at slacks and shirts. . . . It was absolutely unbelievable." Except that it was all too believable, as Lewis knew better than almost anyone.

The fury of the segregationist South was now focused not only on black communities and their allies in the streets and in the stores but on the Kennedys, who had failed, in the prevailing white view, to shut down the civil rights movement altogether. "I hope that every drop of blood that's spilled he tastes in his throat," the mayor of Birmingham said of Robert Kennedy, "and I hope he chokes on it." Of King, the mayor said, "This nigger has got the blessing of the Attorney General and the White House."

The administration was being criticized by whites for being too permissive and by the movement for being too incremental. "In his broadest attack to date on President Kennedy's civil rights record," *The New York Times* wrote in a front-page story on Monday, June 10, 1963, Martin Luther King "charged the President with a failure of leadership and with not having lived up to his campaign promises." Perhaps, King added, it was time for "a march on Washington, even sit-ins in Congress."

It was a hectic moment. "We were like a bunch of firemen," a Justice Department official said, "trying to put out a big fire at the same time we were trying to set up a permanent code of safety regulations to abolish fire." Over that weekend, President Kennedy had flown to Hawaii to address the National Conference of Mayors. He spent the night at Pearl Harbor, attended a Trinity Sunday mass, and spoke to the leaders of America's cities. "Justice cannot await too many meet-

The Ku Klux Klan burns a cross near Tuscaloosa, Alabama, on the eve of Governor George C. Wallace's attempted defiance of federal orders to allow black students into the state university.

ings," he said. "It cannot await the action of the Congress or even the courts. We face a moment of moral and constitutional crisis, and men of generosity and vision must make themselves heard in every part of the land."

Voices of reason, though, were few and far between. The same edition of the *Times* featured a large front-page photograph of national guardsmen arriving by helicopter at the University of Alabama to support what the paper called "the planned defiance of Federal court desegregation orders" by the state's new governor, George Corley Wallace. Inside the paper, on the jump page for the stories about King, about Alabama, and about Kennedy, there was a United Press International photograph of a huge burning cross aflame in a field outside Tuscaloosa. Hooded Klansmen stand in the foreground.

In Hawaii President Kennedy was telling the nation's mayors, "It is clear to me that the time for token moves and talk is past, that these rights are going to be won, and that our responsibility, yours and mine,

"Segregation forever!" Wallace declared in his inaugural address as Alabama governor in January 1963. He made a show of standing in the door of the University of Alabama to prevent its integration—but failed.

is to see that they are won in a peaceful and constructive manner." Back home in Alabama, Governor Wallace, addressing the state on television, deplored the coming federal enforcement of the integration order. "In my opinion," Wallace said of the Kennedy administration, "this is a military dictatorship."

A native of Barbour County, Alabama—not far from Lewis's Pike County—Wallace had not always been a race-baiter. Just after World War II, as a young man, he expressed progressive thoughts. "You know, we just can't keep the colored folks down like we been doin' around here for years and years," Wallace told a Sunday school teacher at his church. "We got to quit. We got to start treatin' 'em right. They just like everybody else." He veered between hard-line segregation and a (relatively) more moderate stance for the next decade or so. In 1958, in his race for governor against John Patterson, Wallace denounced the Ku Klux Klan while Patterson ran right. Wallace's attack on the Klan, an old ally of Wallace's told the writer Marshall Frady, was heartfelt. "He had a genuine aversion to the Klan," the ally said. "He just, in some vague way, didn't trust them. Anything that's basically uncontrollable makes him feel a little uneasy; he'd rather just stay away from it, whether it's for him or against him." Yet he lost, and he hated it. "John Patterson out-nigguhed me," Wallace was reputed to have remarked to a group of pols at Montgomery's Jefferson Davis Hotel after he lost. "And boys, I'm not goin' to be out-nigguhed again." (Wallace denied this oft-repeated anecdote ever afterward.) "He used to be anything but a racist," an old political associate recalled, "but with all his chattering, he managed to talk himself into it."

Campaigning in 1962, Wallace had denounced Judge Frank M. Johnson, the Montgomery-based federal judge who had ruled in favor of integration during the bus boycott, the Freedom Rides, and in voting cases, as "a low-down, carpetbaggin', scalawaggin', race-mixin' liar." A Wallace aide recalled the first time his candidate used the line:

> The crowd liked to went wild. People started advising him he ought not to be talking about a federal judge that-away, it wasn't *dignified,* but we told him to stay with it. Got to where, later in the campaign, ever time he started coming up on that line, the folks'd start punching and poking each other and grinning and all, waiting for him to get to it. Once he put in "pool-mixin'" just to see how that would sound. He liked to work around with things like that, and we'd watch the crowd reaction. There'd be a bunch of farmers standing around at some little crossroads, and you knew he'd scored with something when you saw them just kinda quietly nod their heads. Or even better, when you'd see those hands coming out of those coverall pockets to clap, out from behind those coverall bibs, you knew he'd reached them. Those folks don't take their hands out from behind them bibs for much they hear. It's got to be something special. So when we'd get back in the car with George and start out for the next place, we'd tell him where the hands had come out of the pockets and say, "You wanna stick with that one, now."

Elected governor in 1962, Wallace was inaugurated on Monday, January 14, 1963. He stood where Jefferson Davis had taken the oath as president of the Confederate States of America; Dexter Avenue Baptist Church, King's old pulpit, sat nearby. "In the name of the greatest people that have ever trod this earth," Wallace said, "I draw the line in the dust and toss the gauntlet before the feet of tyranny and I say . . . segregation today . . . segregation tomorrow . . . segregation forever."

On Tuesday, June 11, Wallace made a show of resisting the federal order to integrate the University of Alabama—of, as the phrase went, standing in the schoolhouse door. He'd made his plans clear to Robert Kennedy, who had paid a call on the governor in Montgomery earlier in the spring. In anticipation of Kennedy's visit, Wallace had asked the United Daughters of the Confederacy to put a wreath over the star that marked where Jefferson Davis had taken the oath. "He didn't like the idea of Bobby maybe steppin' on it," a Wallace friend said.

In an awkward session in the governor's office, Kennedy said, "You think it would be so horrifying to have a Negro attend the University of Alabama, governor?"

"Well, I think it's horrifying for the federal courts and the central government to rewrite all the law and force upon the people that which they don't want, yes," Wallace replied. "I will never myself submit voluntarily to any integration of any school system in Alabama. And I feel it's in the best interests of the country and Alabama, and everybody concerned, that these matters ought to be—attempts ought to be—at least, delayed. In fact, there is *no* time in my judgment when we will be ready for it—in my lifetime, at least. Certainly not at this time." When the showdown came, Wallace symbolically resisted, then gave way to federal authority.

On the evening of the day of the standoff in Tuscaloosa, President Kennedy at last addressed the nation on civil rights. "No one can deny the complexity of the problems involved in assuring to all of our citizens their full rights as Americans," Kennedy had said at Vanderbilt University in mid-May. "But no one can gainsay the fact that the determination to secure these rights is in the highest traditions of American freedom."

He had not given much notice for his June 11 plan to speak, and his special counsel and speechwriter, Theodore Sorensen, worked on the text right up until airtime—7 P.M. Eastern. "For the first time," Kennedy joked afterward, "I thought I was going to have to go off the cuff."* In his remarks, Kennedy said, "Now the time has come for the

---

* The president did in fact have to extemporize the latter part of the speech—rare for Oval Office addresses.

James Baldwin and Medgar Evers in conference. Of the nonviolent, student-led movement, Baldwin had observed, "They are not the first Negroes to face mobs: they are merely the first Negroes to frighten the mob more than the mob frightens them."

nation to fulfill its promise. . . . We face a moral crisis as a country and as a people. It cannot be met by repressive police action. It cannot be left to increased demonstrations in the streets. It cannot be quieted by token moves or talk. It is a time to act. . . . Those who do nothing are inviting shame as well as violence. Those who act boldly are recognizing right as well as reality."

Late that night, Medgar Evers, the Mississippi field secretary of the NAACP, was shot to death in Jackson by a Klansman armed with .30-06 rifle. After parking his 1962 sedan in his driveway, Evers had "turned to walk into a side entrance opening into a carport" when the sniper's bullet "struck him just below the right shoulder blade," *The New York Times* reported. "The slug crashed through a front window of the home, penetrated an interior wall, ricocheted off a refrigerator and struck a coffee pot. The battered bullet was found beneath a watermelon on a kitchen cabinet. Mr. Evers staggered to the doorway, his keys in his hand, and collapsed near the steps. His wife, Myrlie, and three children rushed to the door." Cries of "Daddy! Daddy! Daddy!" woke the neighbors. Evers, thirty-seven, was pronounced dead at Jackson's University Hospital.

"It was hard to keep up with events and emotions at the pace they were tumbling that week," Lewis recalled. What the sit-ins and Freedom Rides had set in motion was gaining ferocious, even dizzying, speed, and the forces of fear and hate were taking their stand against hope and love. For Lewis, though, love remained the constant and essential element in the unfolding drama of liberty versus captivity. The sniper's bullets had to be met not with blows but with gentle resistance; the dogs and fire hoses not with arms but with understanding.

In the movement of that time and place there was no better exemplar of nonviolence than Lewis, and that same week, in Atlanta, he was elected chairman of SNCC, the Ella Baker and James Lawson–inspired manifestation of nonviolent activism. Lewis won by acclamation, and the announcement of the news highlighted his record. "Lewis, 23, has been arrested 24 times since he became involved in the civil rights movement in November, 1959," SNCC's *Student Voice* reported. "Seventeen of these occurred in Nashville alone. He was also savagely beaten in Montgomery, Alabama, when he and other Nashville students continued the Freedom Ride into Mississippi after a Greyhound was burned in Anniston, Alabama."

In Atlanta, Lewis stood in silent tribute to Medgar Evers when the train bearing Evers's body to Washington—a veteran, he would be buried at Arlington National Cemetery—came through the city. The victory at Tuscaloosa, the speech from the White House, the martyrdom of Medgar Evers: "Again, as I had already felt so many times in my life, I sensed a power at work that was much larger than any of us," Lewis recalled. "I truly believed it was the Spirit of History at work."

Lewis's life in Atlanta was centered on SNCC headquarters at 6 Raymond Street NW, only a few miles away from King's Ebenezer Baptist Church. (King had left Montgomery in 1960 to join his father as co-pastor at "Daddy King's" Atlanta church.) In his memoirs, Lewis described his Atlanta apartment during his leadership of SNCC: "It was sparsely furnished, with just the basics: a bed, a couple of extra mattresses for whoever might be passing through, and there was *always* somebody passing through who needed a place to stay and would grab one of the mattresses or put a sleeping bag down on the floor; no sofa, just a couple of chairs from Goodwill or the Salvation Army; bookshelves fashioned with planks and cinder blocks; a refrigerator with nothing inside but some cold cuts and condiments—there was no time and no real desire for cooking."

He could be strangely childlike—he did not drive, had no girl-friends to speak of, and eschewed liquor and hell-raising. Preternaturally serious, he seemed gifted with the weight of wisdom. "I'm not impetuous," Lewis recalled. "But once I make a decision, I stay the course. I was that way when I was eight, and I'm that way today. . . . I am not without passion; in fact, I have a very strong sense of passion. But my passion plays itself out in a deep, patient way. When I care about something, when I commit to it, I am prepared to take the long, hard road, knowing it may not happen today or tomorrow, but ultimately, eventually, it *will* happen."

He remained at a remove from his family. "During that period, my mother would say, 'You went to Nashville to get an education, but you're involved in that mess.' That's the way she talked about the movement—'that mess.' Later, I think I convinced her that it was a call—it was the will of God Almighty." Mae Lewis Tyner, a younger sister of Lewis's, remembered their mother praying for "Robert." "She'd be in the kitchen, washing the dishes, and just praying for him," Mae Tyner recalled. Their father covered his worry with resolute optimism. "Bob's going to be all right," Eddie Lewis would say. As John Lewis recalled, "My father was supportive, but he was very quiet, very quiet. He'd be asked, 'Is that your son? Is that Robert?' And he never denied me. I think he took a great deal of pride in what I was doing in the movement. But he was not an expressive person."

Music was one of John Lewis's few pleasures. "Some of the deepest, most delicious moments of my life," Lewis recalled, "were getting out of jail in a place like Americus, or Hattiesburg, or Selma—especially Selma—and finding my way to the nearest Freedom House, taking a good long shower, putting on a pair of jeans and a fresh shirt and going to some little Dew Drop Inn, some little side-of-the-road juke joint where I'd order a hamburger or a cheese sandwich and a cold soda and walk over to that jukebox and stand there with a quarter in my hand, and look over every song on that box because this choice had to be *just* right . . . and then I would finally drop that quarter in and punch up Marvin Gaye or Curtis Mayfield or Aretha, and I would sit down with my sandwich, and I would let that music wash over me, just wash right *through* me."

Women tended to see him in the way Helen Johnson had back at ABT in the late 1950s: as someone to be protected rather than seduced. The actress Shirley MacLaine recalled a party in Atlanta during the movement. "One of the guys on the floor caught my eye and began to sway and bump his hips toward me," MacLaine said. "He had a rotund body with a great roly-poly fanny. He was John Lewis. . . . There was nothing militant about John; he was all love and soul and just to be with him made you smile inside, even though you knew he'd never make it because he was too sweet."

"Make it," Lewis later explained, meant "making a move" in "a sexual way." He thought MacLaine had read him accurately. "And she was right," he recalled. "I wasn't one to make a move. I was not a predator. But I did respond occasionally. It happened a few times when I was spending time in one place, sharing a lot of strong feelings with someone about life. . . . I didn't go out sowing my seeds throughout the South. I wasn't trying to replenish the earth. But I was certainly not a virgin when I married my wife."

Not long after the Evers assassination, Evers's widow, Myrlie, and the Evers children visited the White House to see President Kennedy. As the family left, Arthur Schlesinger, Jr., remarked to the president, "What a terrible business."

"Yes," JFK replied. "I don't understand the South. I'm coming to believe that Thaddeus Stevens was right. I had always been taught to regard him as a man of vicious bias. But, when I see this sort of thing, I begin to wonder how else you can treat them."

It was a reasonable thing to wonder. Stevens, a Civil War–era congressman from Pennsylvania, had been among the most radical of Radical Republicans. He had fought for the Thirteenth Amendment, abolishing slavery throughout the nation, and had argued for the harshest of post–Civil War measures against the rebellious Confederate states. "The purpose and avowed object of the enemy 'to found an empire whose corner-stone should be slavery,' rendered its perpetuity or revival dangerous to human liberty," Stevens said. "Surely these things are sufficient to justify the exercise of the extreme rights of war—'to execute, to imprison, to confiscate.'"

The South of the 1960s was born in the 1860s, both during the Civil War and during Reconstruction. As Stevens noted in his quotation of Confederate vice president Alexander Stephens, the war had been fought to secure slavery as the "corner-stone" of the breakaway nation. In an 1868 book, *The Lost Cause Regained,* the Virginia Confederate and journalist Edward Alfred Pollard wrote that white supremacy "has not been 'lost' immeasurably or irrevocably, but is yet in a condition to be 'regained' by the South on ultimate issues of the political contest." Racial subjugation through the defense of states' rights, Pollard added, was the "true hope of the South."

It was a hope that was largely realized for nearly a century after Robert E. Lee surrendered to Ulysses S. Grant on Palm Sunday 1865. "White men alone must manage the South," President Andrew Johnson had declared that year, and in 1867 he wrote that blacks were incapable of self-government. "No independent government of any form has ever been successful in their hands," Johnson said in his annual message. "On the contrary, wherever they have been left to their own devices they have shown a constant tendency to relapse into barbarism." As the historian Eric Foner noted, this was "probably the most blatantly racist pronouncement ever to appear in an official state paper of an American president."

By 1896, the Supreme Court had codified Jim Crow, sanctioning the principle of "separate but equal" in *Plessy v. Ferguson.* Justice John Marshall Harlan dissented, writing, "The white race deems itself to be the dominant race in this country. And so it is, in prestige, in achievements, in education, in wealth, and in power.... But in the view of the Constitution, in the eye of the law, there is in this country no superior, dominant, ruling class of citizens. There is no caste here. Our Constitution is color-blind.... In respect of civil rights, all citizens are equal before the law. The humblest is the peer of the most powerful."

Such was the American ideal. The American reality, of course, was starkly different. "Criticism, analysis, detachment, all those activities and attitudes so necessary to the healthy development of any civilization . . . took on the aspect of high and aggravated treason," W. J. Cash wrote of the white South during Reconstruction in his 1941 *The Mind of the South.* This willful suspension of reason in favor of tribal feeling shaped everything and foreclosed reform.

The *Brown v. Board of Education* decision in 1954 had given rise to the Citizens' Councils in the South, organizations devoted to defending white supremacy with more polish than the Klan brought to the fight. Founded in the Mississippi Delta, the Citizens' Councils promoted states' rights in the face of the Warren Court and subsequent (though sporadic) federal enforcement efforts.

In her novel *Go Set a Watchman,* Harper Lee cast Atticus Finch as a member of the Citizens' Council in her fictional Maycomb. Written before Lee's 1960 Pulitzer Prize–winning *To Kill a Mockingbird, Watchman* remained unpublished for nearly sixty years. Atticus is heroic in *Mockingbird;* in *Watchman,* he is a conventional white racist. In one scene, he sits and listens to a speaker, a Mr. O'Hanlon, who had been "born and bred in the South, went to school there, married a Southern lady, lived all his life there, and his main interest today was to uphold the Southern Way of Life and no niggers and no Supreme Court was going to tell him or anybody else what to do . . . essential inferiority . . . kinky woolly heads . . . still in the trees . . . greasy smelly . . . marry your daughters . . . mongrelize the race . . . mongrelize . . . *mongrelize* . . . save the South."

That was fiction, but barely. In 1961, prison officials at Parchman had given Lewis and his fellow Freedom Riders a book entitled *Race and Reason,* by Carleton Putnam, a Princeton graduate and onetime head of Delta Airlines. "The whole matter can really be put in a nutshell: a gullible, trusting nation has been misled by various minority groups . . . into believing that Negroes have an inborn capacity for Western civilization equal to the white race," Putnam wrote. "Thus it is not the South which is committing a moral crime against the Negro in maintaining segregation, but the North which is committing a moral crime against the South in forcing integration."

There were, then, all sorts and conditions of white views—and few were aligned with the movement itself. During the crisis over integration at the University of Mississippi in the fall of 1962, Robert Kennedy told Arthur Schlesinger that Governor Ross Barnett's performance and the public's support of the governor's defiance had given the attorney general a better sense of how Adolf Hitler had come to power. "Everyone in Mississippi is accepting what that fellow is doing," RFK told Schlesinger. "There are no protests anywhere—from the bar or from professional men or from the professors. I wouldn't have believed it."

From the Birmingham jail, King, who had been arrested on Good Friday 1963, wrote an epistle to a group of ministers that illuminated the forces in play. "I have almost reached the regrettable conclusion that the Negro's great stumbling block in his stride toward freedom," King wrote, "is not the White Citizens' Counciler or the Ku Klux Klanner, but the white moderate who is more devoted to 'order' than to justice; who prefers a negative peace which is the absence of tension to a positive peace which is the presence of justice; who constantly says: 'I agree with you in the goal you seek, but I cannot agree with your methods'; who paternalistically believes he can set the timetable for another man's freedom; who lives by a mythical concept of time and who constantly advises the Negro to wait for a 'more convenient season.'"

King cited Jesus, Amos, Paul, Martin Luther, John Bunyan, Abraham Lincoln, and Thomas Jefferson, noting that they, too, were seen as extremists in their time. "So the question is not whether we will be extremists," King wrote, "but what kind of extremists we will be. Will we be extremists for hate or for love? Will we be extremists for the preservation of injustice or for the extension of justice?"

Privileged classes, King noted, rarely surrender power voluntarily. The point of the present struggle was to make the America of the middle of the twentieth century an exception that might, alas, prove the rule—but at least the exception would bring a measure of justice to the nation. Soon, in the summer of 1963, the March on Washington would offer King and Lewis the largest of stages from which to reach the possibly persuadable.

A major March on Washington was not a new idea. The dean of civil rights activists, A. Philip Randolph, the founder of the Brotherhood of Sleeping Car Porters, had broached the idea in 1941 out of frustration with the Roosevelt administration's reluctance to integrate the defense industries. HOW TO BLAST THE BOTTLE-NECKS OF RACE PREJUDICE IN NATIONAL DEFENSE was the unflinching headline on a January 1941 Randolph press release announcing the planned march. "The virtue and rightness of a cause are not alone the condition and cause of its acceptance," Randolph said. "Power and pressure are at the foundation of the march of social justice and reform." Yet FDR (and even Mrs. Roosevelt, who was more sympathetic to the African American cause) worried that a large demonstration might turn violent and alienate Southern Democrats, a key part of the president's base. In a difficult meeting in the Oval

Office, FDR told Randolph that a president did not negotiate with "a gun at his head." Randolph reaffirmed his pledge to summon one hundred thousand marchers to the capital. New York City mayor Fiorello La Guardia then brokered a compromise. FDR would sign an executive order desegregating defense employment, at least in part, in exchange for Randolph's cancellation of the march. Randolph agreed.

Nearly a quarter century later, in 1963, plans for a march in Washington were under way anew, and a different American president wanted the same thing FDR had wanted: an end to those plans. At ten-thirty on the morning of Saturday, June 22, the president met with King, Lewis, and other leaders at the White House before helicoptering to Camp David and then, that evening, returning to Andrews Air Force Base for a flight to Germany, where he would deliver his bold "Ich bin ein Berliner" speech at the Berlin Wall. Kennedy appeared preoccupied, greeting each caller with a simple "Hello." ("No names," Lewis recalled.) The president's agenda was clear: Call off the proposed march on Washington and focus on passing his civil rights bill. "We want success in Congress," Kennedy said, "not just a big show at the Capitol." Echoing FDR's concerns of a generation before, Kennedy added, "Some of these people [in the Congress] are looking for an excuse to be against us. I don't want to give any of them a chance to say, 'Yes, I'm for the bill, but I'm damned if I will vote for it at the point of a gun.' It seemed to me a great mistake to announce a march on Washington before the bill was even in committee. The only effect is to create an atmosphere of intimidation—and this may give some members of Congress an out."

"The Negroes are already in the streets," Philip Randolph told Kennedy. (Lewis admired Randolph a great deal. "In spite of his age," Lewis recalled, "he was very young and ready to go and demand all of the things that black people needed and wanted at that time.") "If they are bound to be in the streets in any case," Randolph went on, "is it not better that they be led by organizations dedicated to civil rights and disciplined by struggle rather than to leave them to other leaders who care neither about civil rights nor about non-violence?"

It was Lewis's first visit to the White House, his first session with an American president. To him the scene in the Cabinet Room was surreal, but then nearly everything about his life had been surreal. "President Kennedy's body language was very clear," Lewis recalled.

"He twisted in his chair. His face told us that he thought a march on Washington would be chaos."

"Well, I worry that there will be problems," Kennedy said. There might be violence, he said, and Congress could resent the pressure of a mass march at its doorstep. Why have a huge demonstration, the president wondered, when the focus should be on passing the civil rights bill?

King weighed in. "It is not a matter of either/or, but of both/and," King said. "Take the question of the march on Washington. This could serve as a means through which people with legitimate discontents could channel their grievance, under disciplined, non-violent leadership. It could also serve as a means of dramatizing the issue and mobilizing support in parts of the country which don't know the problems at first hand. I think it will serve a purpose. It may seem ill-timed. Frankly, I have never engaged in any direct action movement which did not seem ill-timed. Some people thought [the Children's Crusade at] Birmingham ill-timed."

The coolly ironic president couldn't resist the opening. "Including the attorney general," JFK joked. Going on in a fatalistically humorous vein, he said, "I don't think you should all be totally harsh on Bull Connor." Schlesinger reported "an audible intake of breath around the cabinet table" before Kennedy delivered his punch line: "After all, he has done more for civil rights than almost anybody else."

Lewis listened as the president picked up the thread of the conversation. "This is a very serious fight," Kennedy said. "The Vice-President and I know what it will mean if we fail. I have just seen a new poll—national approval of the administration has fallen from 60 percent to 47 percent. We're in this up to the neck."

As Kennedy prepared to leave the meeting to his brother and to Vice President Johnson, he said, "I may lose the next election because of this. I don't care."

But he did care—immensely. Realizing that he couldn't stop the march, the president, through his brother, sought to control it. John Douglas, an assistant to Robert Kennedy, worked with the civil rights organizers, settling on the Lincoln Memorial, not the Capitol, as the site. A Kennedy advance man was stationed behind the memorial with a power switch that could cut off the microphones at the podium that faced the vista of the Mall. John Reilly, a Justice Department official and Kennedy friend, was standing by to blast a recording of Mahalia Jackson's "He's Got the Whole World in His Hands" through the sound system if any of the speeches turned too inflammatory. Everything was to take place midweek, on a Wednesday, and in daylight hours.

Lewis had worked on his own speech for a week or so, beginning by dictating thoughts to a SNCC staffer, Nancy Stern, in Atlanta. "I thought it was a very simple, very elementary statement," he recalled. The night before the march, at the Statler Hilton, Julian Bond, SNCC's communications director, put out copies of Lewis's speech. Bayard Rustin, the march's chief organizer, called Lewis down for a meeting. The Roman Catholic archbishop of Washington, among others, was upset by some of the language in the prepared remarks. Lewis and his SNCC colleagues pushed back. "We really argued about the speech," Lewis recalled, and the dispute carried over onto the day of the march itself.

In a small room inside the Lincoln Memorial, Lewis and the other leaders—including Randolph and King—went back and forth. Out front the program had begun. The draft was tough on the Kennedy bill, and Roy Wilkins of the NAACP confronted Lewis, telling him that the remarks would set back the cause of the legislation. "Mr. Wilkins," Lewis replied, "you don't understand. I'm not just speaking for myself. I'm speaking for my colleagues in SNCC, and for the people in the Delta and in the Black Belt. You haven't *been* there, Mr. Wilkins. You don't *understand.*"

Things were deteriorating. Then Randolph made a direct appeal to Lewis's spirit of generosity. "John," Randolph said. Lewis thought the old man "might cry." "We've come this far together. Let us *stay* together."

"How could I say no?" Lewis recalled. "It would be like saying no to Mother Teresa."

Lewis tweaked his speech. He cut a frontal assault on the administration: "In good conscience, we cannot support wholeheartedly the administration's civil rights bill, for it is too little and too late." He lost a direct assertion of good versus evil: "For the first time in one hundred years this nation is being awakened to the fact that segregation is evil and that it must be destroyed in all forms." He forewent this cry: "The revolution is at hand, and we must free ourselves of the chains of political and economic slavery. The nonviolent revolution is saying, 'We will not wait for the courts to act, for we have been waiting for hundreds of years. We will not wait for the President, the Justice Department, nor Congress, but we will take matters into our own hands and create a source of power, outside of any national structure, that could and would assure us a victory.'" He also agreed to drop this: "The revolution is a serious one. Mr. Kennedy is trying to take the revolution out of the streets and put it into the courts. Listen, Mr. Kennedy. Listen, Mr. Congressman. Listen, fellow citizens. The black masses are on the march for jobs and freedom, and we must say to the politicians that there won't be a 'cooling-off' period"—a shot at Robert Kennedy's call during the Freedom Rides. And gone was this line: "We will march through the South, through the heart of Dixie, the way Sherman did. We shall pursue our own 'scorched earth' policy and burn Jim Crow to the ground—nonviolently." ("John," King had said to him in the harried moments before the speech, "that doesn't sound like you.")

Time was short. On the steps of the memorial, in his deep baritone, Randolph introduced Lewis. "I now have the pleasure to present to this great audience young John Lewis, national chairman, Student Nonviolent Coordinating Committee. Brother John Lewis."

His amended notes in hand, Lewis approached the lectern. He wore a dark suit, a dark tie, and his march credential around his neck. He shook Rustin's hand, then took a few steps more and shook Randolph's. Unfolding the papers of his speech, Lewis looked down at his feet, braced himself, wet his lips, faced the seven microphones on the rostrum, bobbed his head once more, and began. He would sway slightly as he went along, his body emphasizing certain points.

"We march today for jobs and freedom, but we have nothing to be proud of, for hundreds and thousands of our brothers are not here, for they are receiving starvation wages or no wages at all," he said. Spectators milled about him on the steps of the memorial, but his voice was steady, clear, certain.

> While we stand here, there are sharecroppers in the Delta of Mississippi who are out in the fields working for less than three dollars a day, twelve hours a day. While we stand here, there are students in jail on trumped-up charges. . . . We come here today with a great sense of misgiving.

He was speaking well—he was preaching, and he knew his business when it came to preaching—but an organizer reached over at this point and adjusted four of the microphones to bring them down a bit in front of Lewis.

He didn't miss a beat. "It is true that we support the administration's civil rights bill," he said. "We support it with great reservation, however. Unless Title III is put in this bill, there's nothing to protect the young children and old women who must face police dogs and fire hoses in the South while they engage in peaceful demonstration."*

The crowd reacted for the first time at this line, clapping its approval.

> In its present form this bill will not protect the citizens of Danville, Virginia, who must live in constant fear of a police state.† It will not protect the hundreds and thousands of people that have been arrested on trumped-up charges. What about the three young men, SNCC field secretaries in Americus, Georgia, who face the death penalty for engaging in peaceful protest?‡ As it stands now, the voting section of this bill will not help the thousands of people who want to vote. It will not help the citizens of Mississippi, of Alabama and Georgia who are unqualified to vote for lack of sixth-grade education. "One Man, One Vote" is the African cry. It is ours too. It must be ours.

More applause; he took the moment to check his text. The sprawling setting and the echoing acoustics of the Mall made it difficult to form a sustained intimate connection between preacher and congregants, but if the crowd wasn't electric, it was attentive and appreciative.

> We must have legislation that will protect the Mississippi sharecropper who is put off of his farm because he dares regis-

---

* Title III was a provision that prohibited state and local governments from denying access to public property and facilities.

† Danville, Virginia, was the scene of terrible violence amid desegregation efforts.

‡ Americus, Georgia, had been another front in the struggle; the three SNCC staffers who had been arrested were Donald Harris, Ralph Allen, and John Perdew.

ter to vote. We need a bill that will provide for the homeless and starving people of this nation. We need a bill that will ensure the equality of a maid who earns five dollars a week in the home of a family whose total income is $100,000 dollars a year. We must have a good FEPC bill.*

Again, applause. A pattern had emerged: The audience was responding to specifics, to detailed calls for action.

"My friends, let us not forget that we are involved in a serious social revolution," he cried, his voice rising with emotion.

By and large, American politics is dominated by politicians who build their career on immoral compromise and allow themselves an open forum of political, economic and social exploitation. There are exceptions, of course. We salute those. But what political leader can stand up and say, "My party is a party of principles"? For the party of Kennedy is also the party of Eastland.

Applause at the mention of the segregationist Mississippi senator James Eastland, who was—like Kennedy—a Democrat.

The party of Javits is also the party of Goldwater.

Applause again at the mentions of Jacob Javits, the liberal Republican senator from New York, and Barry Goldwater, the conservative Republican senator from Arizona.

Where is our party? Where is the political party that will make it unnecessary to march on Washington? Where is the political party that will make it unnecessary to march in the streets of Birmingham? Where is the political party that will protect the citizens of Albany, Georgia? . . .

To those who have said, "Be patient and wait," we must say that we cannot be patient. We do not want our freedom gradually, but we want to be free now.

---

* FEPC was the acronym for the Fair Employment Practices Committee, which FDR had created as part of his agreement with Randolph in 1941.

He drew out the *"gradually,"* stretching the word with a rising voice and punching the air with his right hand as he called for freedom *"now."* The audience went along with him, following his cadences, and gave him his most sustained cheers. There was something more elemental in the clapping at this juncture; Lewis had hit a deeper nerve.

Without glancing at his pages, he continued, holding eye contact with the masses before him.

> We are tired. We are tired of being beaten by policemen. We are tired of seeing our people locked up in jail over and over again, and then you holler "Be patient." How long can we be patient? We want our freedom and we want it now.

He touched his left ear briefly, a small human gesture as he made the turn to his crescendo.

"We do not want to go to jail, but we will go to jail if this is the price we must pay for love, brotherhood and true peace," Lewis said, almost quietly.

> I appeal to all of you to get in this great revolution that is sweeping this nation. Get in and stay in the streets of every city, every village and hamlet of this nation until true freedom comes, until the revolution of 1776 is complete. We must get in this revolution and complete the revolution. For in the Delta of Mississippi, in Southwest Georgia, in the Black Belt of Alabama, in Harlem, in Chicago, Detroit, Philadelphia, and all over this nation the black masses are on the march for jobs and freedom.
>
> They're talking about slow down and stop. We will not stop. All of the forces of Eastland, Barnett, Wallace, and Thurmond will not stop this revolution.

Slowly, the crowd reacted, their approval of his words rising in calls and cheers.

> If we do not get meaningful legislation out of this Congress, the time will come when we will not confine our march into Washington. We will march through the South, through the

streets of Jackson, through the streets of Danville, through the streets of Cambridge,* through the streets of Birmingham.

At the roll call of flashpoints, the crowd applauded.

> But we will march with the spirit of love and with the spirit of dignity that we have shown here today.
> By the forces of our demands, our determination, and our numbers, we shall send a desegregated South into a thousand pieces, and put them together in the image of God and Democracy. We must say wake up America, wake up! For we cannot stop, and we will not and cannot be patient.

The remarks clocked in at about seven and a half minutes. Toward the end, Bayard Rustin, cigarette in hand, had leaned in and whispered something to Lewis. "I think he was saying, 'Close it out, John,'" Lewis recalled. "He was keeping the trains moving."

Read and watched now, Lewis's speech is one of tempered passion. "Unlike popular opinion that Dr. King's 'I Have a Dream' sermon was *the* speech of the March on Washington," Harry Belafonte recalled, "that was not the case. The case was that John Lewis delivered a kind of Gettysburg Address. It was one of the most brilliant speeches I had ever heard. He spoke for the young, for the future of America." In his closing remarks, King spoke from a mountaintop, a prophet bringing word from on high. Lewis spoke more simply, from the valley, among the people whose burdens he knew because they were his burdens, too.

A fter the speeches, a delegation of civil rights leaders called on President Kennedy at the White House. "He's damn good," the president had said after watching King. To King, Kennedy, with a nod, remarked, "'I have a dream.'" ("He nodded again. It was an appreciation, an acknowledgment," the Kennedy biographer Richard Reeves wrote. "King was a star, too.")

To Lewis, Kennedy said only, "I heard you speak." Lewis was quiet.

---

* Cambridge, Maryland, on the Eastern Shore, was roiled by demonstrations, particularly focused on housing.

The president's "face gave no hint of how he felt about my speech, but I could guess," Lewis recalled. Even with the changes he'd made at the last minute, Lewis had spoken bluntly about the limitations of politics ("Where is our party?"), and the president, who believed he was risking everything for his civil rights legislation, was hardly thrilled with the suggestion that the administration's efforts fell short in any way.

The group posed for photographs in the Oval Office. Lewis was obscured in the background, which was not uncommon in such moments. His SNCC colleague James Forman long urged Lewis to be more aggressive on occasions like this. "You've got to get out *front*," Forman told him. "Don't let King get all the credit. Don't stand back like that. Get out *front*."

Lewis demurred. "I've never been the kind of person who naturally attracts the limelight," Lewis recalled. "I'm not a handsome guy. I'm not flamboyant. I'm not what you would call elegant. I'm short and stocky. My skin is dark, not fair—a feature that was still considered a drawback by many black people in the early sixties. For some or all of these reasons, I simply have never been the kind of guy who draws attention."

This was not strictly true. Lewis had become a national figure, or at least a figure familiar to the journalists who had covered the South since the Nashville sit-ins in the winter of 1960. Part of the movement's strategy, one ably executed by Julian Bond, was to keep the students' nonviolent work constantly in the news. With his election as SNCC chairman, Lewis was now someone who met with presidents, vice presidents, and attorneys general, as well as with the grandest leaders of the movement, from Randolph to King.

It was true that Lewis's humility remained intact as he rose to fame. His lack of polish, his quiet conviction, and his unassuming physical presence created, oddly but undeniably, a kind of charisma, understood as a special grace that set him apart as a figure of note and of inspiration. In the moral universe of the Kingdom of God—and of the Beloved Community—reversal is the rule. It's fitting, then, that the rough-edged John Lewis would be the means by which a smooth path should be carved through the wilderness of the world.

The history of the twentieth century would be nobler if we could say that the March on Washington was in real time what it has become in retrospect: a clear turning point that brought white America to the recognition that, as King had said, it was time to include all, not just some, in the Jeffersonian creed of liberty.

But our story is not so noble, nor is it so straightforward. Sixty percent of Americans polled disapproved of the march (only 23 percent approved), a split similar to the prevailing view of the Freedom Rides in 1961. By May 1964, fully 74 percent thought demonstrations "hurt" the cause of civil rights, with only 16 percent saying demonstrations would help.

Whites thought the march too radical; the more strident black activists found it too timid. "It's just like when you've got some coffee that's too black, which means it's too strong," Malcolm X said of the march. "What do you do? You integrate it with cream, you make it weak. But if you pour too much cream in it, you won't even know you ever had coffee. It used to be hot, it becomes cool. It used to be strong, it becomes weak. It used to wake you up, now it puts you to sleep. This is what they did to the March on Washington. . . . It ceased to be angry, it ceased to be hot, it ceased to be uncompromising. Why, it even ceased to be a march. It became a picnic, a circus. Nothing but a circus, with clowns and all."

Accounts of the forced editing of Lewis's speech had leaked out, and Malcolm seized on that, too. "They told those Negroes what time to hit town, how to come, where to stop, what signs to carry, what song to sing, what speech they could make and what speech they couldn't make; and then told them to get out of town by sundown."

Lewis, though, believed in what he had said. In any event, his métier, the source of his power—and power it was—was less about words than it was about deeds. Words were plentiful. Words were easy. Words came and went. In writing for *The New York Times* on the day of the march, James Reston thought King's "peroration . . . was an anguished echo from all the old American reformers. Roger Williams calling for religious liberty, Sam Adams calling for political liberty, old man Thoreau denouncing coercion, William Lloyd Garrison demanding emancipation, and Eugene V. Debs crying for economic equality—Dr. King echoed them all."

Echo was the key here. The speeches of Wednesday, August 28, 1963, live in our memory, and rightly so. They would not have been delivered at that time and in that place and in that context for that audience, however, if the young African Americans of the South had not left the security of enclaves like Griggs Hall on ABT's "Holy Hill" and marched into the fires of hate and of history. The Cabinet Room, the Lincoln Memorial, the Oval Office—the reality unfolding at the pinnacle of American power had been shaped by the lunch counters of Nashville, the bus stations of Rock Hill and of Montgomery and Jackson, and the streets of Birmingham.

In the summer of 1963, reflecting on the civil rights bill, Kennedy remarked to a friend, "Sometimes you look at what you've done and the only thing you ask yourself is—what took you so long to do it?"

"John," Robert Kennedy told Lewis that same summer, "the people, the young people of SNCC, have educated me. You have changed me. Now I understand."

CHAPTER FIVE

WE ARE GOING TO MAKE YOU WISH YOU WAS DEAD

*Freedom Summer and
Atlantic City: 1963–64*

PREVIOUS PAGES: *The Democrats met in Atlantic City in August 1964 to nominate Lyndon Johnson for president in the campaign against Barry Goldwater.*

> During the past ten years, Mississippi as a society reached a condition which can only be described, in an analogous but exact sense of the word, as insane.
>
> —WALKER PERCY, 1965

> If they want Goldwater, they can have Goldwater.
>
> —LYNDON JOHNSON, over the Mississippi Freedom Democratic Party's battle to be seated at the 1964 convention

---

H E WAS BACK HOME in Pike County, on a brief visit with his parents and his uncle Otis Carter—who had so generously given him $100 when he'd left Troy for American Baptist six years earlier—when he heard the news from Birmingham. Sunday, September 15, 1963, had been Youth Day at the Sixteenth Street Baptist Church. Mrs. Ella C. Demand had just finished teaching the day's Sunday school lesson (its title: "The Love That Forgives") when the church was dynamited by Ku Klux Klansmen, killing four young girls: Addie Mae Collins, Cynthia Wesley, Carole Robertson, and Carol Denise McNair. "Short of a mass holocaust," *The Washington Post* wrote, "the bombing of the Negro church . . . must be considered a maximum tragic failure in race relations."

Lewis needed to get to Birmingham. To bomb a church, on a Sun-

From left: Carol Denise McNair, Carole Robertson, Addie Mae Collins, and Cynthia Wesley were killed by a Klansman's bomb at the Sixteenth Street Baptist Church in Birmingham on Youth Day, Sunday, September 15, 1963.

Lewis rushed from Troy to Birmingham when he heard the news of the Sixteenth Street bombing. He is pictured here across the street from the church with, from left, Jimmy Hicks, Julian Bond, and Jeremiah X.

day morning, was to strike at the heart of everything the movement—and decent people everywhere—held dear. Otis Carter didn't want his high-profile nephew catching a bus out of Troy or Montgomery, so he drove Lewis to Dothan, sixty miles in the other direction, to catch a Greyhound into Birmingham. "He thought that the Klan might recognize me closer to home," Lewis recalled. Dothan was an inconvenient but sound alternative.

Late in the afternoon, Lewis was in Birmingham, outside the church's sanctuary on Sixteenth Street. The church's pastor, the Reverend John H. Cross, used a megaphone to urge calm in the chaos. "'The Lord is our shepherd,'" he called out, quoting Psalm 23, "'We shall not want.'"

Lewis's eyes moved from the rubble of the side of the brick sanctuary to the stunned people who stood, staring. "I looked at . . . these black men and women of Birmingham, who had lived through so much, and I knew that they had to be asking themselves, How much *more*? What *else*? What's *next*? . . . Four children killed on a Sunday morning in church, in God's house. What *could* be next?" The dynamite had blown out the face of Jesus in one of the Sixteenth Street Baptist Church's stained-glass windows.

King preached later in the week at a funeral for three of the four girls. "God still has a way of wringing good out of evil," King said from the Sixteenth Street pulpit. "And history has proven over and over again that unmerited suffering is redemptive. The innocent blood of these little girls may well serve as a redemptive force that will bring new light to this dark city. . . . And so I stand here to say this afternoon to all assembled here, that in spite of the darkness of this hour, we must not despair. We must not become bitter, nor must we harbor the desire to retaliate with violence. No, we must not lose faith in our white brothers. Somehow we must believe that the most misguided among them can learn to respect the dignity and the worth of all human personality."

Listening, Lewis was nearly overwhelmed. "So many tears," he recalled. "So much grief. It was almost too much." Yet King's sermon, for Lewis, and apparently for enough of the gathered mourners who crowded the sanctuary and stood silently outside, filling the street in tribute, reassured amid the pain. "There were many who felt bitter, many who felt let down," Lewis recalled. "There were some who were ready to take up guns, who were saying, 'We *told* you this nonviolence would not work.' But most shared Dr. King's attitude. . . . Dr. King had an uncanny ability to comfort and calm when you would have thought it impossible, when people were so upset."

The bombing gave the debate over nonviolence new resonance. What good were the Lawson-taught troops doing, it was asked, when they were fighting with love and the haters were using dynamite? "That was always a question during the movement," Lewis recalled. "After the church bombing—after so many violent episodes, and there were so many, in so many different places, all over the South—people would say, 'How can nonviolence defeat violence? The Klansmen don't go to funerals, *We're* the ones who go to funerals.' But we couldn't give up. Violence was not an option for us—not if we wanted to prevail, not if we wanted the Beloved Community."

On a television program in New York, James Baldwin and Reinhold Niebuhr exchanged views. "We are in a revolutionary situation," Niebuhr told Baldwin, "and all through history, it was a despised minority—the proletarians, the peasants, the poor—who recaptured the heights and depths of faith." On nonviolence, Niebuhr said, "People ask me, since I am such a strong anti-pacifist, how I can have this admiration for a pacifist? Well, I have a simple answer. . . . King's doctrine of nonviolent resistance is not pacifism. Pacifism of really the classical kind is where you are concerned with your own purity and not responsibility. And the great ethical divide is between people who want to be pure and those who want to be responsible. And I think King has shown this difference."

Eight days after the bombing at Sixteenth Street, Lewis went to Selma, on the Alabama River, to work on sit-ins and voter registration. The first and third Mondays of the month were known as "Freedom Mondays" there. Those were the only days Dallas County officials opened the registrar's office in the courthouse for voter registration. As the African Americans gathered to try to register, county police and state troopers made mass arrests in and around the city. Lewis was rounded up almost immediately.

That was when he saw the electric prods. "I knew what those things could do, how they burn, and how the men who used them enjoyed aiming for the genital area," Lewis recalled. "I was quick enough to dodge, but others weren't so lucky. I could hear sharp cries of pain here and there as we were loaded onto" a bus bound for the jail.

He and others were sentenced to the Selma prison farm. "Our men's cell looked like a chicken coop, not much different from the one I had kept my birds in as a boy, only larger," Lewis recalled. "It was a coop made for humans. Just a long hall with filthy mattresses on the floor. No tables. No chairs. One commode, one sink." It reminded him, inevitably, of Parchman.

O n Friday, November 22, 1963, Lewis was in Nashville, about to leave Fisk for the city's airport, Berry Field, to take off on a weekend speaking trip through Michigan, Illinois, and Ohio, when the first bulletins from Dallas came over the radio just after 12:30 P.M. Central time. The president had been shot. "I felt sick," Lewis recalled. "I didn't know what to do."

He kept to his schedule and went to the airport, where, half an hour after the initial bulletin, he heard that the president was dead. He called Julian Bond in Atlanta, and they decided that Lewis would follow through on his weekend plans. "I felt lost—faint, really," Lewis recalled. "I just wanted to go back to my apartment and forget about everything for a while. I've often felt like this at times of great crisis in my life. . . . I want to be home."

He got back to Atlanta on Sunday evening, the night before Kennedy's funeral in Washington. Alone with his thoughts, Lewis watched the daylong ceremonies on television in that spare apartment. The caisson, the royals and generals and statesmen in formation, the touching salute from John F. Kennedy, Jr. (the day of his father's funeral was his third birthday), the burial at Arlington: the pageant of images, set to the sound of drums and the verses of the Navy Hymn and the notes of Taps, transported Lewis back into the recent past. "I felt as if I was watching them all—Medgar Evers, the little girls in Birmingham, and now this," Lewis recalled. "So much sorrow."

Lewis's reaction to Kennedy's death is telling. "He was the first American president to say that the issue of civil rights and social justice was a moral issue," Lewis recalled. "He represented our hope, our idealism, our dreams about what America could become. . . . When he died, a light went out in America and the nation has never quite been the same since."

Sentiment did color Lewis's recollections about Kennedy. In a statement on the fiftieth anniversary of the assassination, Lewis painted a glowing picture of that last meeting in the White House on the afternoon of the March on Washington: "I can still see him standing in the door of the Oval Office beaming, waiting to greet us. He shook the hand of each person saying, 'You did a good job. You did a good job.' And when he got to Dr. King he said, 'And you had a dream.'" But the president *hadn't* told Lewis that he'd done "a good job"—JFK had merely said, "I heard your speech." Over the decades, Lewis remembered the hour, and the man, more and more warmly. Such is human nature, particularly when that nature is inclined to the kind and the hopeful rather than to the cutting and the harsh.

Kennedy was a complicated figure. Depending on the moment, John Kennedy could be calculating and idealistic, hard-nosed and far-seeing. People like Lewis and the other leaders of the movement saw both sides of him, often in the same conversation or the same situation. In a pre-presidential JFK biography, James MacGregor Burns wrote, "Kennedy could bring bravery and wisdom; whether he would bring passion and power would depend on his making a commitment not only of mind, but of heart, that until now he has never been required to make."

Through all the length of days, Lewis chose to believe that Kennedy's June 11, 1963, speech marked that commitment of heart. It was not mindless romanticism, but a choice to see a complex man at the pinnacle of power as a human being, and to judge him whole, and with love. Watching in Atlanta that sad November Monday, Lewis could pay no higher tribute to the fallen president than to see him in the same light as Medgar Evers and Carol Denise McNair and Carole Robertson and Cynthia Wesley and Addie Mae Collins.

However frustrating Kennedy could be, tacking this way and that, JFK was a known quantity. The movement had invested much blood and toil to educate the thirty-fifth president and his brother. Now the fate of the freedom they sought had shifted to another pair of hands: those of Lyndon Baines Johnson.

"I had several preconceived notions about Johnson, as most black people did," Lewis recalled. "He was a Southerner, a Texan, which made him immediately suspect. He'd been raised on Jim Crow, and he had blocked his share of civil rights legislation during his time in Congress. I did not anticipate his being a friend of the movement, but I kept those thoughts to myself when the press began calling for comments. I was guarded, I didn't say much. . . . Give him time, I said, and see what he will do."

In truth, Johnson was in the midst of a great conversion. A native Texan, LBJ had long appeased his racist constituents. In 1948, when he was running for the Senate, Johnson attacked Truman's push for civil rights in the year of the Dixiecrat rebellion. "This civil rights program, about which you have heard so much, is a farce and a sham—an effort to set up a police state in the guise of liberty," Johnson said in rhetoric that closely tracked that of Strom Thurmond.

Though LBJ had declined (along with Tennessee senators Albert Gore, Sr., and Estes Kefauver) to sign the 1956 Southern Manifesto that pledged resistance to the Warren Court's school-integration decisions, he had also weakened civil rights bills in the Senate. "I wasn't a crusader," LBJ recalled. "I represented a southern state, and if I got out too far ahead of my voters they'd have sent me right back to Johnson City where I couldn't have done anything for anybody, white or Negro."

As vice president, his vision broadened. Part of this, of course, was politically motivated. If Johnson wanted to succeed Kennedy in 1968, the vice president needed to convince the liberal Northern element of the Democratic Party that he was no unreconstructed Southerner.

Whatever his motivations, though, the effect was real. In the first week of June 1963, in a telephone call with Kennedy counsel and speechwriter Ted Sorensen, Johnson had pressed Sorensen on the need for President Kennedy to make an explicit statement of support for civil rights—ideally in the South. Kennedy, Johnson told Sorensen, should say something like this: "We're all Americans. We got a Golden Rule, 'Do unto others as you would have them do unto you.' Now I'm leader of this country. When I order men into battle I order the men without regard to color. They carry our flag into foxholes. The Negro can do that, the Mexican can do it, others can do it. We've got to do the same thing when we drive down the highway at places they eat. I'm going to have to ask you all to do this thing. I'm going to have to ask the Congress to say that we'll all be treated without regard to our race."

Kennedy's death shifted the trajectory of Johnson's life and, if Johnson had anything to say about it—and he would—the trajectory of the life of the nation as well. "Lyndon acts as if there is never going to be a tomorrow," his wife, Lady Bird, once observed. He set out with all speed. "Now I represent the whole country," Johnson said, "and I can do what the whole country thinks is right. Or ought to."

On the night of Kennedy's assassination, back in Washington at the Johnsons' Spring Valley house, the new president lay in bed dictating orders to a circle of subordinates. "Well, I'm going to tell you," LBJ said, "I'm going to pass the civil rights bill and not change one word of it. I'm not going to cavil, and I'm not going to compromise. I'm going to fix it so everyone can vote, so everyone can get all the education they can get."

On Sunday, November 24, Johnson spoke with the Urban League's Whitney Young about what the president should say to Congress. "I think you've just got to . . . point out that . . . with the death of President Kennedy . . . that hate anywhere that goes unchecked doesn't stop just for the week," Young told the president. "And the killing at Birmingham [at Sixteenth Street Baptist Church]—the people feel that they can react with violence when they dissent."

"I dictated a whole page on hate—hate international—hate domestically," Johnson replied. "It's a cancer that just eats out our national existence." Before Congress, Johnson called for passage of the civil rights bill. "John Kennedy's death commands what his life conveyed—

that America must move forward," LBJ said. "Let us turn away from the fanatics of the far left and the far right, from the apostles of bitterness and bigotry, from those defiant of law, and those who pour venom into our Nation's bloodstream."

In a call with the president on the day of the Kennedy funeral, King said, "We know what a difficult period this is."

"It's just an impossible period," Johnson said. "We've got a budget coming up that's . . . practically already made and we've got a civil rights bill. . . . We've just got to not let up on any of 'em and keep going. . . . I'll have to have you-all's help. I never needed it more'n I do now."

Under Lewis, SNCC held a previously scheduled conference on "Food and Jobs" in Washington the weekend after the assassination and the funeral. James Baldwin opened the proceedings in the Andrew Rankin Memorial Chapel at Howard. "Kennedy was killed," Baldwin said, "because he broke the long-standing agreement between the North and South—that you do with your Negroes what you want to do, and we'll do with ours what we want to do." Bayard Rustin addressed the movement's broader agenda to bring economic opportunity to a wider swath of the nation. "When the day comes that the white unemployed adopt the spirit and tactics of the civil rights movement," Rustin said, "we are on our way to a revolution in this country." In closing the conference, Lewis made it clear that he intended to carry on as he had set out: bearing witness not to conform to reality but to create a new reality.

"We, as students, we who represent, as we like to say, the masses, we must not sell out," Lewis said. "We must stand up and stand up for what is right. . . . We cannot depend on or expect President Johnson or Congress to do it, but we must help them do it."

The right to vote—promised in the Fifteenth Amendment but denied before and since—was top of mind as 1963 drew to a close. "There will be no revolution until we see Negro faces in all positions that help to mold public opinion, help to shape policy for America," James Lawson had written at the time of the founding of SNCC. "One federal judge in Mississippi will do more to bring revolution than sending 600 marshals to Alabama. We must never allow the President to substitute marshals for putting people into positions where they can affect public policy." As early as 1961, King had said,

"*The central front, however, we feel is that of suffrage.* If we in the south can win the right to vote it will place in our hands more than an abstract right. It will give us the concrete tool with which we ourselves can correct injustice." It fell to Lewis to make the abstract real.

He spent Christmas 1963 in jail in Atlanta for a sit-in at a segregated Toddle House restaurant; he was also arrested and had his lip split open by a policeman's nightstick while demonstrating at a Morrison's cafeteria on West End Avenue in Nashville in late April and early May 1964. His major focus, though, was on the coming summer, in Mississippi. "Before the Negro people get the right to vote," Lewis said, "there will have to be a massive confrontation, and it will probably come this summer. . . . We are going to Mississippi full force."

The announcement came in *The Student Voice* in early March 1964: MISS. SUMMER PROJECT SET. The mission: "a summer Peace Corps type operation for Mississippi." Much of October had been taken up with a "Freedom Vote" in the state, a nonviolent protest in which more than eighty thousand black people symbolically "voted" in Mississippi's gubernatorial election. The winner of the actual race, Paul B. Johnson, Jr., who succeeded Ross Barnett, had said that "NAACP" really stood for "niggers, alligators, apes, coons, and possums."

In Mississippi, SNCC set up headquarters in Greenwood in the Delta, and, in the state capital, at 1017 Lynch Street (the "irony of *that* name . . . was lost on no one," Lewis recalled), a storefront next to the Streamline Bar in a black section of Jackson. With the Harvard-educated Bob Moses, the architect of what became Freedom Summer, Lewis surveyed a sorry scene. Only 5 percent of the state's blacks were registered to vote; racial violence was rampant; white supremacy was entrenched.

In April 1964, at a meeting of the American Society of Newspaper Editors in Washington, Lewis laid out the plans for the summer. "Any person who in any way interferes with the right of a Negro to vote in Mississippi commits a crime against the Federal Government," he said. "The Federal Government must decide whether it wants to let southern Negroes register. It must make that choice this summer, or make us all witness to the lynching of democracy."

The world they were entering was in many ways unhinged. The

prospect of Freedom Summer—the plans called for waves of nonviolent students, black and white, to come into the state to help with registration—prompted the Klan, Lewis recalled, to burn crosses in sixty-four of the state's eighty-two counties. *The Freedom Fighter,* a KKK publication, attacked the "Kennedy brats, the black Warren Court, and the Nationally Associated American Communist Party," as well as "the too dumb to learn, filthy, diseased, evil-minded Negro." Other groups took shape, too. The Society for the Preservation of the White Race and Americans for the Preservation of the White Race were reportedly formed by "whites dissatisfied with the Ku Klux Klan and white Citizens' Councils." Governor Paul Johnson, meanwhile, signed a law giving himself personal control over an expanded state police force. "Mississippi is now a bona fide police state," Lewis said, "and the governor has a private army to suppress civil rights efforts."

"No ex-Mississippian is entitled to write of the tragedy which has overtaken his former state with any sense of moral superiority," Walker Percy observed in *Harper's* in the spring of 1965. "For he cannot be certain in the first place that if he had stayed he would not have kept silent—or worse. And he strongly suspects that he would not have been counted among the handful, an editor here, a professor there, a clergyman yonder, who not only did not keep silent but fought hard."

White Mississippi was governed by hate and fear—and, as Edmund Burke wrote in the eighteenth century, "No passion so effectually robs the mind of all its powers of acting and reasoning as *fear.*" As Percy saw it, "Once the final break is made between language and reality, arguments generate their own force and lay out their own logical rules. The current syllogism goes something like this: (1) There is no ill-feeling in Mississippi between the races; the Negroes like things the way they are; if you don't believe it, I'll call my cook out of the kitchen and you can ask her. (2) The trouble is caused by outside agitators who are communist-inspired. (3) Therefore, the real issue is between atheistic communism and patriotic, God-fearing Mississippians. Once such a system cuts the outside wires and begins to rely on its own feedback, anything becomes possible."

Mayhem and murder had become not only possible but real. On Sunday, June 21, 1964—Father's Day—three Freedom Summer workers, Michael Schwerner, Andrew Goodman, and James Chaney, disappeared after being arrested and jailed in Philadelphia, Mississippi, in Neshoba County. Schwerner and Goodman were white; Chaney was black. Lewis joined the seemingly fruitless search for their bodies. With friends from SNCC, he "walked around in the hot, sticky dusk,

The burned station wagon in which Freedom Summer activists Michael Schwerner, Andrew Goodman, and James Chaney were last seen; their bodies were later found buried at a dam site in Neshoba County.

bugs buzzing around, out in the middle of nowhere, poking at scrub grass and bushes and dirt. It was really pretty useless, not to mention dangerous. . . . Rivers were dragged, woods were scoured, dirt was turned . . . and bodies were found. Old bodies, unidentified corpses, the decomposed remains of black people long given up as 'missing.' . . . It was ugly, sickening, horrifying. Here was proof—as if it was needed—that those woods and rivers in the heart of this state had long been a killing field, a dumping ground for the Klan."

By the first week of August, the bodies of the three martyred activists were found at a dam site in Neshoba County, buried deep. Each had been shot; Chaney had been horribly beaten as well. In the face of such violence, nonviolence seemed inadequate, antiquated, unseasonable. Lewis was crushed by the murders and listened at James Chaney's funeral as David Dennis of CORE cried out in understandable bitterness, "If you go back home and sit down and take what these white men in Mississippi are doing to us . . . if you take it and don't do something about it . . . then God *damn* your souls!" With a shout, he went on, "Stand up! Don't bow *down* anymore. Hold your heads up. We want our freedom now, I don't want to go to another memorial. I'm *tired* of funerals." To the writer Bruce Watson, the funeral was twofold. "On Friday, August 7," Watson wrote, "both James Chaney and nonviolence were laid to rest in Mississippi."

Still, Lewis kept his faith. It wasn't easy—it was, in fact, the hardest thing in the world. David Dennis was rational, *human,* in the sense that he reacted the way virtually any human being would. Lewis was the irrational one. He was the oddity. How could you not act on the instinct for self-defense? How could you not despair of a path that led lambs to slaughter? How could you hold to a creed that appeared to produce more pain than progress? The only way to explain Lewis's persistent nonviolence, his unending commitment to answering hate with love and death with life, is to take him at his word.

"We truly believed that we were on God's side, and in spite of everything—the beatings, the bombings, the burnings—God's truth would prevail," Lewis recalled. The anguish and the duration of the struggle was, in a way, a vindication of the premise of the struggle itself—that this was the ultimate battle to bring light to darkness no matter how often darkness prevailed.

Lewis held fast. "To me, 'doing something' meant to keep on keeping on," he recalled. "To others, however, it meant changing directions, taking another tack. Out of frustration, bitterness, outright hostility to the system, to the government, to white people in general, every day the more radical arm of the movement was swelling a little more." As early as 1962, Lewis recalled, "You heard the term 'revolution' more than the word 'integration.' The spirit of redemptive love was being pushed aside by a spirit of rage."

Robert F. Williams of Monroe, North Carolina, had been an early advocate of armed resistance to Jim Crow. "Since the federal government will not bring a halt to lynching in the South," Williams had said, "and since the so-called courts lynch our people legally, if it's necessary to stop lynching with lynching, then we must be willing to resort to that method." On Saturday, October 5, 1957, in Monroe—the seat of Union County—Williams, who had received a charter from the National Rifle Association, led a successful skirmish against the Klan. Williams complained that his Black Armed Guard was undercovered in the press. "It's as if they were afraid to let other Negroes know what we have done here," he said. "We have proved that a hooded man who thinks a white life is superior to a black life is not so ready to risk his white life when a black man stands up to him." In 1962, Williams published a tract, *Negroes with Guns.*

The Kennedys had worried that Williams might be the beginning of a trend. "On the other side, [there are] the Negroes who are tough and mean and have guns, who have been bitter for a long period of time, who are worked up about this, and figure one of the best services they can perform is to shoot some of them," RFK had told the president in May 1963. "So if you have an incident, and the incident, an-

Robert F. Williams (shown here with his wife, Mabel Williams) was an advocate of armed resistance to the armed forces of white supremacy. A former NAACP official in North Carolina, he published Negroes with Guns *in 1962.*

other bombing for instance, something like that, or a fire, and it attracted large numbers of Negroes, the situation might very well get out of hand. . . . The Negroes saying that they have been abused for all these years, and they are going to have to start following the ideas of the Black Muslims, not go along with the white people. If they feel, on the other hand, that the federal government is their friend, and is intervening for them, is going to work for them, this could head some of that off."

That same month, Alex Haley had published an interview with Malcolm X in *Playboy* magazine. "Within the past five years, the militant American Negro has become an increasingly active combatant in the struggle for civil rights," Haley wrote. "Espousing the goals of unqualified equality and integration, many of these outspoken insurgents have participated in freedom rides and protest marches against their segregationist foes. Today, they face opposition from not one, but two inimical exponents of racism and segregation: the white supremacists and the Black Muslims." The Black Muslims, under the leadership of Elijah Muhammad, saw blacks as "divine" and whites as the "devil."

Malcolm X had been born Malcolm Little in Omaha, Nebraska, in 1925, the son of a Baptist minister who supported the black nationalism of Marcus Garvey. When Malcolm was small, the family's house was burned and the Reverend Little was likely murdered by the white supremacist group Black Legion. Convicted of burglary in Boston in 1946, Malcolm spent about seven years in prison. While incarcerated, he studied and joined the Nation of Islam, taking the name Malcolm X.

He at first disdained nonviolence. "We don't deserve to be recognized and respected as men," he said, "as long as our women can be brutalized . . . and nothing being done about it, but we sit around singing 'We shall overcome.'" King's view of self-defense was subtler than his critics would have it. "The question was not whether one should use his gun when his home was attacked," King said, "but whether it was tactically wise to use a gun while *participating in an organized demonstration.*"

The debate was real. Speaking of the segregated Southern states as "outlaw communities," the historian Howard Zinn wrote, "The use of ordinary methods of nonviolent direct action in these outlaw communities is met in the same way a totalitarian state crushes opposition—by open brutality, overwhelming force." In Mississippi, Zinn noted, the white authorities had created a "Thompson Tank," named for Jackson mayor Allen C. Thompson—an armored vehicle that featured multiple machine guns. "In situations like this, there is increased talk among Negroes of 'self-defense'; Malcolm X's exhortation to Negroes to arm themselves and shoot back when attacked is hard to counter in the light of the murder of Medgar Evers, the bombing in Birmingham, the endless instances of brutality by police."

Zinn, who dedicated his 1964 book on SNCC to Ella Baker, saw that the battle over nonviolence versus violence would go on. "There is one powerful justification for asking Negroes in the Deep South to stick to nonviolence in the face of the terrible measures used against them by private and official forces in the Black Belt; that is, that they live in a nation where the power of the federal government can disarm and neutralize those who would take away their constitutional liberties," Zinn wrote. "*But thus far the federal government has not done this.* Hence there is a renewed debate among Negroes and in civil rights groups about nonviolence."

The tensions of the time had been evident in an April 1961 debate between Malcolm and James Baldwin. "I think that this is, in my opinion, why we disagree with the sit-in movement," Malcolm said. "If they are willing to wait for another hundred years for the white man to change his mind to accept them as a human being, then they're wrong. But if they're willing to lay down their life tonight, or in the morning, in order that we can have what is ours by right tonight, or in the morning, then it's a good move. But as long as they're willing to wait for the white man to make up his mind that they are qualified to be respected as human beings, then I'm afraid that all of their waiting and their planning is for naught."

Baldwin demurred. "I don't agree that the sit-in . . . is necessarily passive," he said. "I think it demands a tremendous amount of power, both in one's personal life and in terms of political or polemical activity, sometimes to sit down and do nothing, or seem to do nothing."

"The black man in America," Malcolm said, "is the only one who is encouraged to be nonviolent. . . . Never do you find white people encouraging other whites to be nonviolent. Whites idolize fighters. . . . Everyone loves a fighter. They respect a fighter. But at the same time that they admire these fighters, they encourage the so-called Negro in America to get his desires fulfilled with a sit-in stroke or a passive approach or a love-your-enemy approach or pray for those who despitefully use you. This is insane."

Malcolm drew on recent American history to illustrate his point. "Take Pearl Harbor," he said. "When the Japanese attacked Pearl Harbor, the American white man didn't say, 'Pray for the Japanese, and let them now bomb Manhattan or Staten Island.' No, they said, 'Praise the lord, [and] pass the ammunition.' . . . The only people who are told to forget the injustices that have been done to them are the black people."

Why, Malcolm continued, should a black man "wait for the Supreme Court to give him what a white man has when he's born? Why should he wait for the Congress or the Senate or the president to tell him that he should have this, when if he's a man the same as that man is a man, he doesn't need any president, he doesn't need any Congress, he doesn't need any Supreme Court, he doesn't need anybody but himself to bring about that which is his, if he is a man?"

Baldwin took a different view. "Malcolm X wants us to act like men," Baldwin said. Yet for Baldwin, masculinity and heroism were not synonymous with the capacity for violence. "The only thing that really arms anybody, when the chips are down, is how closely, how thoroughly, he can relate to himself and deal with the world, yes, as a man. . . . This is one of the standards that has to be revised. I don't think that a warrior is necessarily a man."

Once an advocate of racial separatism, Malcolm ultimately broke from Elijah Muhammad, and a 1964 pilgrimage to Mecca was a turning point. "I have eaten from the same plate, drank from the same glass, slept on the same bed or rug, while praying to the same God . . . with fellow-Muslims whose skin was the whitest of white, whose eyes were the bluest of blue, and whose hair was the blondest of blond—yet it was the first time in my life that I didn't see them as 'white' men," Malcolm wrote from Saudi Arabia. "I could look into their faces and see that these didn't regard themselves as 'white.' "

Mecca was enlightening; America, on the other hand, was about to burn. In New York City in the summer of 1964, on the eve of a threatened "stall-in" at the World's Fair, the journalist and historian Theodore H. White, a pillar of the Eastern Establishment, had a conversation with a leading African American writer. "He quivered in anticipatory ecstasy: tomorrow, when the stall-in took place, Martin Luther King would be through; so would Jim Farmer of CORE; so would Roy Wilkins; so would all the other Negro leaders who made the bridge of contact between white and black," White recalled. "The whites had broken the social contract between men; the United States owed the Negroes for three hundred years of unpaid labor as slaves; the reparations bill was going to be presented tomorrow; New York would be paralyzed. It was too bad that white people might be killed— but if that was the way it had to be, it had to be. . . . He respected me, he said ('I have respect for you, White')—but it was obvious that if I had to be shot, he would merely add regret to his respect."

Riots roiled the nation that summer. In New York, the fatal police shooting of a fifteen-year-old African American, James Powell, set off waves of violence. Officials claimed Powell had been wielding a knife and refused to heed a warning; other witnesses said the young man was unarmed. When protesters marched on a Harlem police precinct, *The New York Times* reported, "they were confronted by a wall of policemen. Bottles and bricks began to rain down from the rooftops; the policemen put on steel helmets and fired their revolvers into the darkness, aiming over the heads of the missile throwers. When a police captain told the Negroes to go home, a voice from the crowd screamed, 'We are home, baby!' . . . Mobs—numbering now in the hundreds—swarmed through the streets. The barrage of bottles and bricks grew heavier; so did the police gunfire. So began a week of wild disorders."

"What did your husband die for?" a reporter asked Rita Schwerner, the widow of one of the Neshoba County martyrs.

"That, I would imagine," she replied, "is up to the people of the United States."

To J. Edgar Hoover's Federal Bureau of Investigation, the people of the United States were forever at risk of falling prey to Communism, the prevailing ideology of the Soviet Union, America's existential rival in the Cold War. Beginning in 1950, Senator Joseph R. McCarthy had presided over a four-year reign of terror. "I just want you to know," McCarthy told reporters, "that I've got a pailful of shit and I'm going to use it where it does me the most good." McCarthy fell from

The FBI's J. Edgar Hoover conducted a year-long campaign to undermine, discredit, and disrupt the civil rights movement. Under his direction, the bureau actively worked to portray the movement as a front for Communism. "No holds were barred," an FBI official told Congress in 1975.

power after being censured by the Senate in 1954, but for many years afterward, as director of the FBI, Hoover continued to conduct campaigns of espionage and harassment.

The civil rights movement was a prominent and perennial target of the FBI's. An FBI informant had told agents that the SNCC of Freedom Summer was an "organization based on anarchy and left wing infiltration"—which was just the kind of thing Hoover, who believed Communism omnipresent, loved to hear. "No holds were barred," an FBI official testified to Congress in 1975. The bureau saw its work against the movement in general and against Martin Luther King in particular as "war." The aim was clear. As the Senate committee investigating intelligence abuses chaired by Senator Frank Church in the 1970s found, the FBI spent much of the 1960s on "an intensive campaign to 'neutralize'" King "as an effective civil-rights leader" and to "'completely discredit'" him and his advisers. The bureau sent King an audiotape of the minister in hotel rooms engaging in extramarital sex. The goal was "to destroy King's marriage," and the FBI included an anonymous note that King believed suggested that he commit suicide unless he wanted the recording leaked to the public. After the March on Washington, the bureau's Domestic Intelligence Division wrote internally that King's "demagogic speech" had made him "the most dangerous and effective Negro leader in the country." Later, in early 1968, the FBI worried that King was "a potential 'messiah' who could 'unify and electrify' the 'black nationalist movement.'" According to the Church committee, "In short, a non-violent man was to be secretly attacked and destroyed as insurance against his abandoning non-violence."

In a Wednesday, April 22, 1964, story headlined "Hoover Says Reds Exploit Negroes: F.B.I. Chief Asserts Party Infiltrates Rights Drive," *The New York Times* reported that Hoover had told Congress that "Communist influence does exist in the Negro movement and it is this influence which is vitally important." The problem was that the facts failed to support Hoover's conclusion. "Based on all available information from the F.B.I. and other sources," Attorney General Robert Kennedy said in mid-1963, "we have no evidence that any of the top leaders of the major civil rights groups are Communists, or Communist controlled. It is natural and inevitable that . . . Communists have made efforts to infiltrate the civil rights groups and to exploit the current racial situation. In view of the real injustices that exist and the resentments against them, these efforts have been remarkably unsuccessful."

Hoover and his men were undeterred—and RFK himself authorized wiretaps on King. A central focus of concern in these years was King adviser Stanley Levison, whom the FBI had long believed to be a Communist. King was repeatedly warned to distance himself from Levison, and he eventually did—at Levison's instigation. (President Kennedy himself advised the break in a private conversation with King in the Rose Garden of the White House.)

Sex and race drove the bureau's long struggle against the movement. To Hoover, King's private life was a source of fascination, even obsession. On one memorandum, Hoover wrote that King was a "tom cat with obsessive degenerate sexual urges." William C. Sullivan, who had served as the FBI's assistant director, recalled that "behind it all was the racial bias, the dislike of Negroes, the dislike of the civil rights movement. . . . I do not think [Hoover] could rise above that."

King audaciously challenged the powerful Hoover publicly, announcing the SCLC was "unalterably opposed to the misguided philosophy of communism" and adding that "it would be encouraging to us if Mr. Hoover and the FBI would be as diligent in apprehending those responsible for bombing churches and killing little children as they are in seeking out alleged communist infiltration in the civil rights movement."

The FBI had opened a large file on SNCC to investigate what the bureau referred to as "Communist Infiltration of Student Non-Violent Coordinating Committee." Special agents across the nation were ordered to "remain alert and report any information indicating any current CP [Communist Party] members are engaging in considerable activities of SNCC or the CP is issuing any instructions aimed at infiltrating, dominating, and/or controlling SNCC."

It was thin gruel. SNCC used the National Lawyers Guild for some legal work, a group that the FBI long—and unsuccessfully—investigated for subversion. As Lewis put it, "No matter who attacked us on this issue, we weren't about to be budged. This was a battle for civil liberties as well as civil rights, and we were as committed to one as we were to the other. . . . If you were willing to work with us for the cause of civil rights, then you were welcome. We did not care about your politics."

In Los Angeles in late 1963, at a Bill of Rights rally, the bureau reported that Lewis had said that "if being called a Communist means freedom and equal rights for Negroes and minority races he would be glad to be called a Communist." In another part of the FBI files on SNCC, a source told the bureau that Lewis had "spent three days in 1963 with JAMES E. JACKSON, editor of 'The Worker,' and JACKSON wrote a pamphlet about it." An admitted leader of the American Communist Party, Jackson was a bold social reformer who had founded the Southern Negro Youth Congress in the mid-1930s, a forerunner of SNCC. Indicted during the McCarthy era for advocating the violent overthrow of the government, Jackson dropped out of sight for several years in the 1950s. He reemerged and was found guilty of conspiracy under the 1940 Smith Act. His conviction was overturned in 1958 after a Supreme Court ruling extended free speech protections. At the time he met Lewis, Jackson was editor of the successor newspaper to the Communists' *Daily Worker*.

Lewis wasn't interested in a Communist revolution. He was interested in a new American one. Did Lewis ever consider becoming a Communist? "Never," he recalled. "Ever. Ever." Jackson was a radical, and Lewis was all about radical reform—just not the kind of reform that would have ripped up the Constitution as part of some kind of Communist conspiracy. The FBI wasn't very good at detecting such nuances; the bureau also reported that "when JOHN LEWIS was in Cairo, Illinois, in 1962, he was just a young Baptist minister with no

political ideas, but he has gotten very close to the Communist Party."
He hadn't, but accuracy wasn't a factor in the bureau's intelligence
gathering. Anything could wind up in the files—and did. "My attitude
was we didn't need Communists to tell us that segregation was wrong,"
Lewis recalled.

The nation was making a crucial decision that summer as Congress
debated the Kennedy-Johnson civil rights bill. LBJ had deployed
all his formidable legislative skills to get the law through to final passage. In the Senate, white Southern Democrats took a last stand.
"This is no longer a battle of the heart for them—they simply have to
die in the trenches; that's what they were sent here for," Senator Hubert H. Humphrey said of his colleagues from the Old Confederacy.
"They're old and they haven't any recruits. They know it—one of
them said to me, 'You simply have to overwhelm us.' And so we have
to beat them to a pulp. No one can make peace. They have to be destroyed." After a fifty-seven-day filibuster and eighty-three days of
debate on a measure supported by both the president and by the Republican leader in the Senate, Everett Dirksen, the bill was approved
by the Senate in the early evening hours of Friday, June 19.

The legislation went to President Johnson for his signature on

*President Johnson confers with Dr. King at the White House. Their complicated
relationship would grow increasingly contentious as King spoke out against the Vietnam
War more and more forcefully.*

LBJ hands King a pen during the signing of the Civil Rights Act on Thursday, July 2, 1964. Lewis was in the Mississippi Delta, still participating in Freedom Summer. "We felt glad," Lewis recalled, "but not joyous."

Thursday, July 2, 1964. John Lewis and so many students had gone into the streets and segregated establishments of the South to seek change, and now there would be change. Public accommodations could no longer be governed by the color line; the federal government was given new powers to fight discrimination in education and employment. The law, Johnson told the nation, "does not restrict the freedom of any American, so long as he respects the rights of others. It does not give special treatment to any citizen. It does say the only limit to a man's hope for happiness, and for the future of his children, shall be his own ability. It does say that . . . those who are equal before God shall now also be equal in the polling booths, in the classrooms, in the factories, and in hotels, restaurants, movie theaters, and other places that provide service to the public." Discrimination on the basis of color, the president said, must end: "Our Constitution, the foundation of our Republic, forbids it. The principles of our freedom forbid it. Morality forbids it. And the law I will sign tonight forbids it." The signing took place in the East Room of the White House. King was there, standing near Johnson, who handed him one of the pens used to bring the law into being.

Though invited, Lewis had chosen not to go to Washington for the occasion. He remained in Greenwood, in the Mississippi Delta, working with Freedom Summer volunteers. "This was where I wanted to be, not on some stage someplace," he recalled. The signing was good news, of course: It just seemed more remote than real. "We felt glad, but not joyous. There was no sense of celebration. We were still in the middle of a war down there, a campaign that was just beginning. The news from Washington felt as if it were coming from another country, from a very distant place." And when he did visit the comfortable chambers of power in Washington, he was acutely aware of the chasm between the world of presidents and of power and the world he knew in the South. In mid-August, Lewis joined an unannounced meeting with President Johnson, Philip Randolph, James Farmer, and Roy Wilkins at the White House. "The White House press secretary, George E. Reedy, said there was no discussion of any political matters . . . ," *The New York Times* reported. "He said the meeting was devoted to problems of law and order in race relations."

Political matters were to dominate the rest of August. One of Freedom Summer's missions—one led in part by Ella Baker—had been the creation of the Mississippi Freedom Democratic Party (MFDP), an integrated alternative to the segregated Mississippi Democratic delegation headed to Atlantic City, New Jersey, for the 1964 Democratic National Convention. Sixty-eight delegates—sixty-four of them black—traveled north to petition the Democratic Party to allow them seats and standing at the convention. The MFDP delegation checked into the Gem Motel in Atlantic City and went to work. The MFDP argument was simple: How could the party of Kennedy and Johnson, the party of the Civil Rights Act, take the all-white delegation sent by a segregated state party and fail to honor an integrated delegation elected by those who had been systematically disenfranchised?

Atlantic City was not to be the place for fair and open debate. The FBI had bugged the MFDP and SNCC as well as King's and Bayard

Rustin's Atlantic City hotel rooms, and the fruits of the eavesdropping were shared with the White House as the days unfolded. A few weeks before Atlantic City, LBJ aide Walter Jenkins had asked FBI deputy director Cartha "Deke" DeLoach to investigate the sixty-eight delegates as well as monitor Lewis and SNCC, King and the SCLC, and James Farmer and CORE during the convention. "The President's men . . . did everything they could to steer the decision their way—including spying," Lewis recalled. "They knew the strategies and decisions being formed on our side even as they were taking shape." After dining with the president at the White House on the eve of the convention, Senator Richard Russell of Georgia wrote in his diary, "Hoover has apparently been turned loose and is tapping everything." Of LBJ's not-very-convincing laments that the FBI reports were keeping him up too late, Russell wrote, "He loved it."

The decision about seating formally lay with the Democrats' credentials committee chaired by former Pennsylvania governor David Lawrence. On Saturday, August 22, in a televised hearing, Fannie Lou

Fannie Lou Hamer of the Mississippi Freedom Democratic Party testifies in Atlantic City, urging the seating of an integrated delegation.

Hamer, an African American sharecropper from Sunflower County, Mississippi, testified before the panel. "I don't like being a celebrity," Hamer told reporters. "I just like being a person who's treated like a human being." Hamer credited the young people of SNCC with bringing her into the broader conversation. "Nobody never come out into the country and talked to real farmers and things . . . because this is the next thing this country has done: it divided us into classes, and if you hadn't arrived at a certain level, you wasn't treated no better by the blacks than you was by the whites," she recalled. "And it was these kids what broke a lot of this down. They treated us like we were special and we loved 'em. . . . We didn't feel uneasy about our language might not be right or something. We just felt like we could talk to 'em. We trusted 'em, and I can tell the world those kids done their share in Mississippi."

In Atlantic City, Lewis watched on a closed-circuit television in a room in the Boardwalk Hall convention center as Hamer told her story:

Mr. Chairman, and to the Credentials Committee, my name is Mrs. Fannie Lou Hamer, and I live at 626 East Lafayette Street, Ruleville, Mississippi, Sunflower County, the home of Senator James O. Eastland, and Senator Stennis.

It was the 31st of August in 1962 that eighteen of us traveled twenty-six miles to the county courthouse in Indianola to try to register to become first-class citizens.

We was met in Indianola by policemen, Highway Patrolmen, and they only allowed two of us in to take the literacy test at the time. After we had taken this test and started back to Ruleville, we was held up by the City Police and the State Highway Patrolmen and carried back to Indianola where the bus driver was charged that day with driving a bus the wrong color.

After we paid the fine among us, we continued on to Ruleville, and Reverend Jeff Sunny carried me four miles in the rural area where I had worked as a timekeeper and sharecropper for eighteen years. I was met there by my children, who told me that the plantation owner was angry because I had gone down to try to register.

After they told me, my husband came, and said the plantation owner was raising Cain because I had tried to register. Before he quit talking the plantation owner came and said, "Fannie Lou, do you know—did Pap tell you what I said?"

And I said, "Yes, sir."

He said, "Well, I mean that." He said, "If you don't go down and withdraw your registration, you will have to leave." Said, "Then if you go down and withdraw," said, "you still might have to go because we are not ready for that in Mississippi."

And I addressed him and told him and said, "I didn't try to register for you. I tried to register for myself."

I had to leave that same night.

Hamer shifted her narrative to the early summer of 1963, when she was arrested in Winona, Mississippi; she had been riding home from a voter registration workshop. In jail she overheard officers beating another woman who had been taken into custody.

After I was placed in the cell I began to hear sounds of licks and screams, I could hear the sounds of licks and horrible screams [from a nearby cell]. And I could hear somebody say, "Can you say, 'yes, sir,' nigger? Can you say 'yes, sir'?"

And they would say other horrible names.

[The woman being attacked] would say, "Yes, I can say 'yes, sir.'"

"So, well, say it."

She said, "I don't know you well enough."

They beat her, I don't know how long. And after a while she began to pray, and asked God to have mercy on those people.

And it wasn't too long before three white men came to my cell. One of these men was a State Highway Patrolman and he asked me where I was from. I told him Ruleville and he said, "We are going to check this."

They left my cell and it wasn't too long before they came back. He said, "You are from Ruleville all right," and he used a curse word. And he said, "We are going to make you wish you was dead."

I was carried out of that cell into another cell where they had two Negro prisoners. The State Highway Patrolmen ordered the first Negro to take the blackjack.

The first Negro prisoner ordered me, by orders from the State Highway Patrolman, for me to lay down on a bunk bed on my face.

I laid on my face and the first Negro began to beat. I was beat by the first Negro until he was exhausted. I was holding my hands behind me at that time on my left side, because I suffered from polio when I was six years old.

After the first Negro had beat until he was exhausted, the State Highway Patrolman ordered the second Negro to take the blackjack.

The second Negro began to beat and I began to work my feet, and the State Highway Patrolman ordered the first Negro who had beat me to sit on my feet—to keep me from working my feet. I began to scream and one white man got up and began to beat me in my head and tell me to hush.

One white man—my dress had worked up high—he walked over and pulled my dress—I pulled my dress down and he pulled my dress back up. . . .

All of this is on account of we want to register, to become first-class citizens. And if the Freedom Democratic Party is not seated now, I question America. Is this America, the land of the free and the home of the brave, where we have to sleep with our telephones off the hooks because our lives be threatened daily, because we want to live as decent human beings, in America?

To Lewis, the testimony was everything it needed to be—moving, frank, and true. "It was a stunning moment," he recalled. "So dramatic. So riveting." Lyndon Johnson agreed—and manufactured a quick appearance on television to force the networks to cut away from the compelling Hamer. The vital presidential business that suddenly required the attention of the nation? A briefing on a White House session with Democratic governors. But the battle was already joined, and LBJ had to make a decision: Where would he land? On the side of the integrated delegation, or with the segregated Mississippi regulars? The rest of the South—the rest of the whole of white America—was watching. If the Mississippi regulars were replaced, John Connally, the governor of Texas, told the president, "the impression around the country is going to be that they just got kicked out because the niggers wanted them kicked out."

The term "backlash," connoting white anxieties about the movement, had become popular in America that summer. Fred Shuttlesworth had used the word in 1961 in the *Pittsburgh Courier* when he noted that blacks were vulnerable to "the severe backlash of venom poured out by those who still believe in segregation more than life itself." George Wallace's success in several presidential primaries in 1964—Wisconsin, Indiana, and Maryland—offered tangible evidence of national white resentment. The Republican Party's nomination of Barry Goldwater, who had voted against the Civil Rights Act, gave the forces of reaction a vehicle if they chose to use it.

Johnson was hearing dire reports from what he feared might become Goldwater country. "The so-called backlash . . . does actually exist," Tennessee governor Buford Ellington wrote the president in August 1964. "People holding jobs with industry and government are afraid they are going to be forced out of jobs to make room for people who are not qualified either by training or experience . . . that white people will be discriminated against in future employment. . . . I find this exists in every state. . . . There is a feeling that law violators are not being apprehended and convicted while they continue to destroy life and property. . . . Any effort that can be made on the part of the Federal government to change a pattern of Negro thinking that accuses the police of 'brutality' for the slightest enforcement of law should be made."

The civil rights and labor lawyer Joseph L. Rauh, Jr., was representing the MFDP and had worked with Lewis in Mississippi that summer. The president assigned Hubert Humphrey, who was to become the vice presidential nominee, and labor leader Walter Reuther to work Rauh over. "He wanted to get me away from what looked like trouble for him and for the convention," Rauh recalled of Johnson. "So first he'd have Hubert call me, trying to get me out, and then Walter would call. This was before the convention, and it got to be a joke around my office. The girls would answer the phone and say to me, 'It's the other one calling.'"

As Rauh recalled it, Reuther raised the stakes the highest: "Walter said, 'I've been talking to the president and we have agreed that if you go through with this—with trying to seat these people—we're going to lose the election.' I said, 'Are you serious? I mean, Goldwater has been nominated. How can you lose it?' He said, 'We both think the backlash is so tremendous that we're going to lose the election if you go through with this. You can't possibly win [the question of seating the MFDP], but if you should win, the pictures of all the black delegates going in to replace the white is going to add to the backlash, and we are convinced Goldwater will be president.'"

The alienation of Southern and border states over race was a far-fetched but real fear of Johnson's as he prepared to face Goldwater. "Now there's not a damn vote that we get by seating these folks [the MFDP]," LBJ told Reuther. "What we want to do is elect some Congressmen to keep 'em from repealing [the Civil Rights Act]. And who's seated at this convention don't amount to a damn. Only reason I would let [the segregated delegation from] Mississippi come in is because I don't want to run off fourteen border states, like Oklahoma and Kentucky."

In a call with Humphrey, Johnson was even more explicit. "And . . . your labor union people . . . are upset," the president said. "Think that nigra's going to get his job. . . . They think a nigra's going to move next door to them. . . . So this is an extremely dangerous election. Now the thing that makes it more dangerous than anything else is—I am telling you, if I know anything I know this—if we mess with that group of Negroes [the MFDP] that were elected to nothing . . . and throw out the Governor and elected officials of the state—if we mess with them, we will lose fifteen states without even campaigning." He grew emotional. "Try to see if the Negroes don't realize that they've got the President, they'll have the Vice President, they've got the law, they'll have the government for four years. . . . Why in the living hell do they want to hand—*shovel*—Goldwater fifteen states?"

The segregationist Richard Russell—of all people—tried to assuage Johnson's worries. "It ain't going to hurt you any in the country to get run over [by the MFDP]," the senator told LBJ. "It would hurt your pride like hell, I know, but it isn't going to hurt you politically."

"I would think that they'd say that hell, the Negroes have got more power in the Democratic party than the President has," Johnson replied, "and the damned nigras are taking it over—and to hell with the Democratic party."

"It would increase the backlash a little bit," Russell admitted. "No question about that—whatever the backlash is. But this is August. It's over two months before the election." It was an odd moment in the evolving politics of identity. The Georgia delegation was integrated, and on the Sunday before the convention opened, the group had supper together. "Whoever thought—we got fifteen Nigrahs here and seven Jews and everybody's having a good time," one white delegate remarked in wonderment.

Russell was being sensible, but Johnson could not be calmed. "Hell, the Northerners are . . . upset about this," the president told Reuther. "They call me and wire me, Walter . . . that the Negroes have taken over the country. They're running the White House. They're running the Democratic party. And it's not Mississippi and Alabama. . . . You're catching hell from Michigan, Ohio, Philadelphia, and New York! . . . They [the MFDP] don't understand that nearly every white man in this country would be frightened if he thought the Negroes were gonna take him over."

As Humphrey, Reuther, Rauh, and others sought a compromise on the MFDP, a proposed deal emerged: The MFDP would get two "at large" seats on the floor and all future delegations would be integrated. Andrew Young, who worked for King's SCLC, urged the adoption of the agreement, but Lewis and many others balked. "We've shed too much blood," Lewis told Young. "We've come much too far to back down now." To the veterans of Freedom Summer, only weeks away from having buried Schwerner, Goodman, and Chaney, the accommodation of white supremacy on the floor of the Democratic National Convention was odious.

On Tuesday, August 25, 1964, a frustrated Johnson had reached his limit. A floor fight over race, a divided party—he couldn't take it. He privately considered a radical move: dropping out of the presidential campaign altogether. "The times require leadership about which there is no doubt and a voice that men of all parties and sections and color can follow," he wrote in a draft statement of withdrawal. "I've learned, after trying very hard, that I am not that voice or that leader." Lady Bird was distraught; his aides were in chaos; no one knew what would happen. "I do not remember hours I ever found harder," Mrs. Johnson told her diary.

Then Walter Reuther called. The president's negotiators thought they'd found a way to avoid a calamitous showdown, calming the other states with the gesture of two at-large delegates while keeping the Mississippi regulars in place. King and others urged the MFDP delegates to take the compromise, but only a handful of the delegates were willing to consider it. By the time the group voted on the question, the decision was unanimous: No deal.

The MFDP was heartbroken, and the all-white Mississippi delegation left the convention anyway after refusing to sign a pledge of loyalty to LBJ. When the MFDP attempted a nonviolent sit-in on the floor of the Boardwalk Arena, they were escorted out by security. Then, rather than seating the MFDP once the white delegation had bolted, the Democrats removed the Mississippi chairs from the floor. "And so they stood there in that vacant space, this tiny group of men

Empty seats on the floor of the Democratic convention. The all-white regular delegation left in protest, and the national party chose not to seat the largely black MFDP for fear of alienating white voters. To Lewis, the system in which he'd put much faith had failed.

and women, forlorn and abandoned," Lewis recalled, "watching silently as Lyndon Johnson was nominated for president by acclamation and Hubert Humphrey was announced as the Democratic Party's vice presidential candidate." On Thursday morning, August 27, the day Lyndon Johnson was to accept the presidential nomination for a full term, Lewis and the MFDP pilgrims left Atlantic City.

The 1964 Democratic convention has largely faded from the popular memory. The politically minded often recall that year's Republican gathering, at San Francisco's Cow Palace, where the Goldwater delegates jeered the moderate New York governor Nelson Rockefeller a few days before Goldwater declared, "I would remind you that extremism in the defense of liberty is no vice . . . [and] moderation in the pursuit of justice is no virtue." San Francisco signaled a rightward move in the Republican Party away from the temperate conservatism of Eisenhower. The tone of the GOP convention was such that Jackie Robinson, until that point a loyal Republican, remarked that being black at the Cow Palace that week gave him "a better understanding of how it must have felt to be a Jew in Hitler's Germany."

Nothing about the politics of 1964, however, mattered more to John Lewis, then or later, than what happened at the Democratic convention on the Jersey Shore. "As far as I'm concerned," Lewis recalled, Atlantic City "was the turning point of the civil rights movement. I'm absolutely convinced of that. Until then, despite every setback and disappointment and obstacle we had faced over the years, the belief still prevailed that the system would work, the system would listen, the system would respond. Now, for the first time, we had made our way to the very center of the system. We had played by the rules, done everything we were supposed to do, had played the game exactly as required, had arrived at the doorstep and found the door slammed in our face."

And their government had actively sought to undermine them through the FBI-run political espionage. As the Church Committee later wrote, "The most important single issue for President Johnson at the Atlantic City convention was the seating challenge of the Mississippi Freedom Democratic Party to the regular Mississippi delegation. From the electronic surveillance of King and SNCC, the White House was able to obtain the most intimate details of the plans of individuals supporting the MFDP's challenge, unrelated to the possibility of violent demonstrations."

Faith in President Johnson was a chancy thing. Lewis saw him do so much good—and so much bad. As American military engagement in Vietnam escalated in 1964–65, Lewis closely monitored the disproportionate toll the war was taking on African American soldiers. As he recalled, African Americans accounted for 25 percent of the U.S. deaths in the war during 1965 despite only making up about ten percent of the American population. "By late 1965," Lewis recalled, "America's front lines in Vietnam were so filled with black men . . . that the soldiers called it Soulville."

His own draft status was subject to prolonged debate. At age twenty-one, he sought to be classified as a conscientious objector (CO). "My personal philosophy of nonviolence gave me no other choice," Lewis recalled. "I remember trying to explain this to my draft board in Pike County, which was a panel of men, all Methodists or Baptists, all white. When I began telling them about the history and philosophy of nonviolence, they had no idea what I was talking about." They denied his request, as did the state draft board. Only after a federal review that took until 1965 was Lewis granted his CO status (called 1-O)—becoming, he was told, "the first black man in the history of the state of Alabama to be classified a conscientious objector."

Lewis signed an antiwar statement, the "Declaration of Conscience Against the War in Vietnam," in the spring of 1965, and SNCC came out against the war early the following year. "I felt we had a moral obligation here, a mandate," Lewis recalled, "that we couldn't talk about what was going on in Mississippi and Alabama and south Georgia and not relate to and identify with the people who were being sent over to Vietnam, as well as the people, American and Vietnamese alike, who were being destroyed there." A copy of a popular poster hung in the SNCC offices: NO VIETNAMESE EVER CALLED ME NIGGER.

The SNCC position was clear and controversial. In a press conference in January 1966, Lewis announced, "We are in sympathy with, and support, the men in this country who are unwilling to respond to a military draft which would compel them to contribute their lives to United States aggression in Vietnam in the name of 'freedom' we find so false in this country." Washington was listening, and it didn't like what it was hearing. "And almost overnight," he recalled in his memoir, "I received a notice from my draft board informing me that my status . . . had now been changed from 1-O to 4-F. I was 'morally unfit' for service, they explained, because of my long record of arrests." The story was actually more complicated than Lewis remembered it in his book. After the antiwar statement, the government had declared him 1-A, or "available for service." Lewis then reached out to Robert Kennedy and to the Justice Department's Burke Marshall for help. The 4-F classification was the result.

The hypocrisy of an America fighting for liberty abroad while tolerating white supremacy at home informed the movement in these years. "It seemed extremely contradictory to me," Lewis recalled, "for President Johnson to be sending tens of thousands of troops to fight this war in Vietnam to 'protect the rights' of the people of South Vietnam at the same time as the rights of black people across the nation continued to be violated without protection."

Lewis knew the lesson of the Psalmist: "Put not your trust in princes." His trust was in the Lord and in the people. But he was tired. Freedom Summer, Atlantic City, the growing war—as he put it, firecrackers burn fast. He wanted to be a pilot light, and burn steadily.

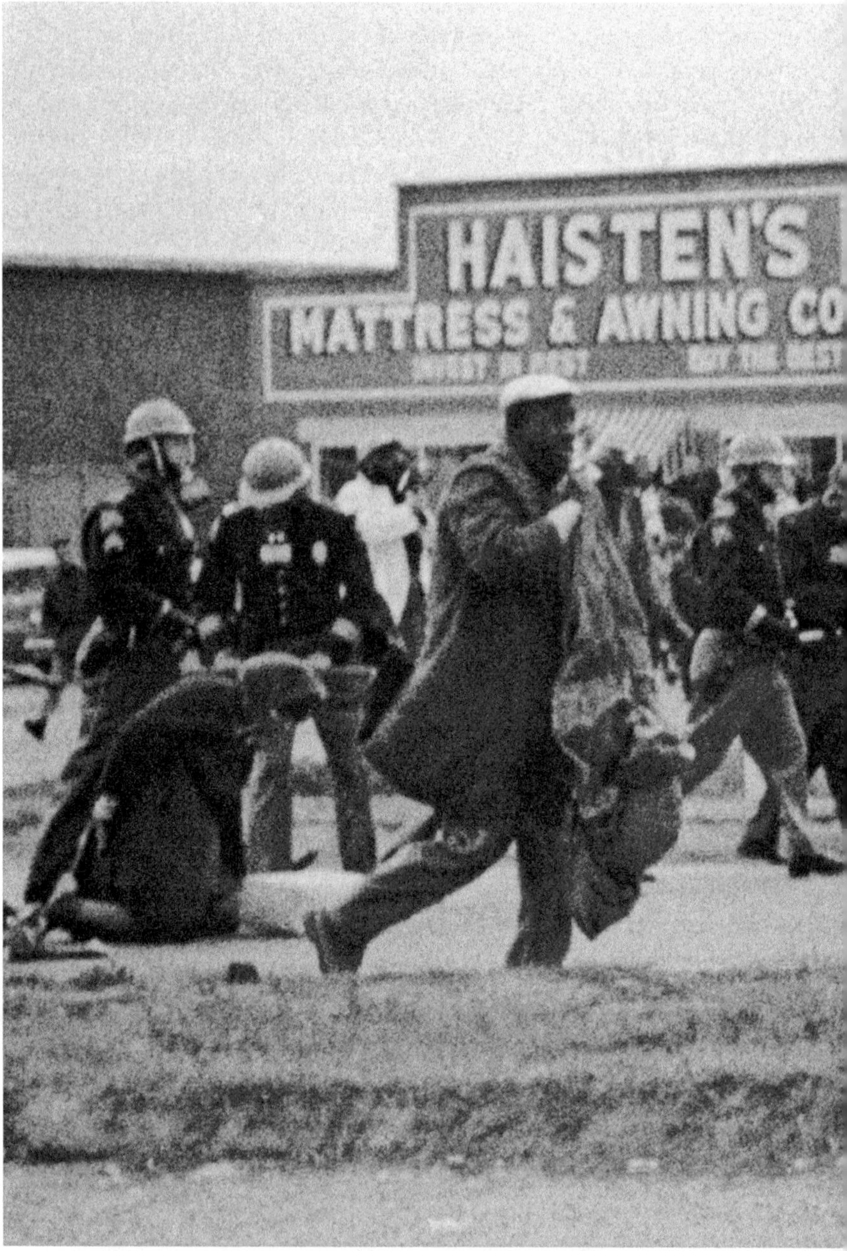
HAISTEN'S
MATTRESS & AWNING CO

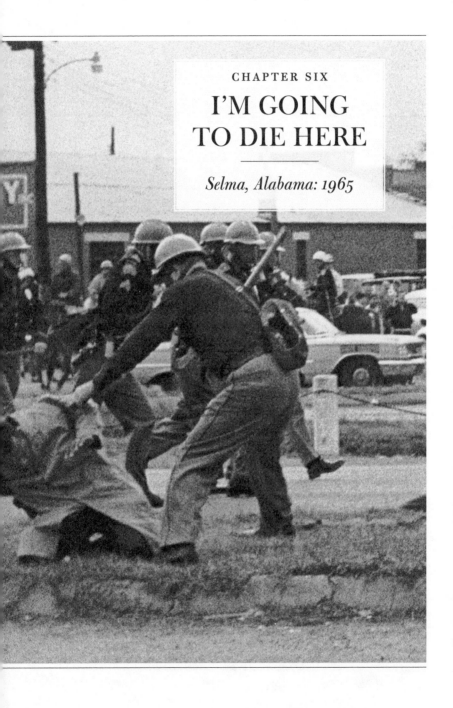

I'M GOING TO DIE HERE

Selma, Alabama: 1965

PREVIOUS PAGES: *Lewis under assault by police and possemen at the foot of the Edmund Pettus Bridge, Sunday, March 7, 1965.*

Selma, the bridge, was a test of the belief that love was
stronger than hate. And it is. Much stronger. So much
stronger.

—JOHN LEWIS

Now, John, you've got to go back and get all those folks
registered. You've got to go back and get those boys
by the *balls*.

—LYNDON B. JOHNSON, to Lewis on the day of the
signing of the Voting Rights Act of 1965

L EWIS NEEDED A RESPITE, and Harry Belafonte had an idea. The
entertainer, a supporter of both SCLC and of SNCC, had raised
a great deal of money to support Freedom Summer. On a visit to
the Delta, he was struck by what he saw. "What impressed me was the
exhaustion of the young people who were carrying the burden of the
movement," Belafonte recalled. In a study of the veterans of Freedom
Summer, the Harvard psychiatrist Robert Coles found symptoms of
" 'battle fatigue.' ... They indicate exhaustion, weariness, despair,
frustration and rage. They mark a crisis in the lives of those youths
who experience them, and also one in the cities which experience the
results, translated into action, of such symptoms." Belafonte had been
talking with Sékou Touré, the president of the African nation of
Guinea. Touré was interested in bringing young Americans over to
learn what he could about the movement. Belafonte suggested that
Lewis lead a SNCC delegation to Africa. "I thought they needed to
see Africa, and to teach, to learn, and, frankly, to rest," Belafonte recalled. "John was mesmerized by the experience." He was indeed. The
journey was a revelation. "For the first time, you saw a group of black
men and women in charge," Lewis recalled. In the American South,
the students had been fighting for one man, one vote; in Africa, "We
saw people making it real, making it happen."

The most memorable part of the trip came in Nairobi, at the New

Harry Belafonte, Andrew Young, and Lewis have a word together on the final day of the Selma-to-Montgomery march. Belafonte was a close adviser to Dr. King and a stalwart supporter of the movement.

Stanley Hotel, where Lewis unexpectedly came across Malcolm X. To Harlem militants, Malcolm had praised Fannie Lou Hamer, saying, "Y'all brothers always rapping about how bad you are. All that talk. Well, this little lady here's bad. She can teach you—all of us—about courage and struggle." Malcolm, Lewis believed, was "moving towards that point of creating an interracial democracy . . . moving away from the idea and the philosophy of a separate society, a separate community."

They spent a few days together talking things over. "Always sit with your back to the wall so you can look out and see who is watching you," Malcolm advised Lewis. "He told us over and over again during our conversations to keep fighting, don't give up," Lewis recalled. "He said, 'You know this is an ongoing struggle. Be prepared for the worst, but keep it up, keep fighting. People are changing, there are people supporting you all over the world.'" He was generous about Lewis's struggles. "Malcolm saw SNCC young people, the young black and white students . . . as being something like guerrilla warriors," Lewis recalled. "They were out there on the cutting edge. He kept saying . . . 'If they don't listen to you, then they will have to deal with us.'"

For a time, the journey gave Lewis's rhetoric a more global tone. "The destiny of Afro-Americans is inseparable from that of our black

"If they don't listen to you," Malcolm X told Lewis during a conversation in Nairobi, "then they will have to deal with us."

brothers in Africa," he said when he returned. "It matters not whether it is in Angola, Mozambique, South-west Africa, or Mississippi, Alabama, Georgia, and Harlem, U.S.A. The struggle is the same.... It is a struggle against a vicious and evil system that is controlled and kept in order for and by a few white men throughout the world." To Stokely Carmichael, the statement was remarkable. "Hey, after a long talk with Malcolm, even John Lewis had come back from Africa sounding like a Pan-Africanist revolutionary."

Lewis was a revolutionary, but at heart he was an American one. The vision of an integrated world guided him still. Impressed by Lewis's rhetoric of aggression—language that put him closer to "Black Power" than to "Freedom Now"—Carmichael had said, "Go, John," but Lewis soon reverted to his mean, which Carmichael dismissed as "that mystical 'beloved community redeemed by suffering'" worldview.

After Freedom Summer and after Atlantic City, Lewis "was devastated, but I was not despondent. I refused to let myself become bitter. I've always refused to do that. I can get angry—I have gotten angry many, many times in my life—but I never let my anger overwhelm me.... When I first got involved in the movement as a teenager, I recognized that this struggle was going to be long, hard and tedious,

A key leader in Selma and in Dallas County, Amelia Boynton, who, like Lewis, was tear-gassed and beaten on Bloody Sunday, was instrumental in creating the conditions for the Selma-to-Montgomery march.

and that I would have to pace myself and be patient where necessary, while continuing to push and push and push, no matter what." His patient pushing would be critical as attention moved to Selma, Alabama, the seat of Dallas County, about ninety miles from Troy.

The ground there had been prepared by figures such as Amelia Boynton, an activist and businesswoman who had a sign in her office that read A VOTELESS PEOPLE IS A HOPELESS PEOPLE. Bernard La-Fayette described Mrs. Boynton as "tall and regal with a perpetual smile yet a manner of quiet defiance." A leader of the Dallas County Voters League, she was a determined woman, and her work created the conditions for the epic events that were to take place in and around Selma. "People need to learn how to stand up for their rights," Mrs. Boynton would say. "No one's going to give you anything, you must demand it."

July 6, 1964, had been a "Freedom Monday" in Selma, a day for black Alabamans to attempt to register to vote. Like Birmingham, the city was proving a perfect foil for the movement. "On first entering Selma," Stokely Carmichael recalled, "my distinct impression was that I sho nuff was back in antebellum Dixie.... Visually, it seemed to

Dallas County Sheriff Jim Clark (center) was an unrepentant and uncompromising force, often wearing a button with a straightforward message: "Never." To Lewis, Clark once said, "You're the lowest form of humanity."

exist in its own time cocoon, a time warp. Eerie." Lewis had been there that July day, and Sheriff Jim Clark had had enough.

"John Lewis," Clark told him in front of the courthouse, "you are nothing but an outside agitator. You're the lowest form of humanity."

"Sheriff, I may be an agitator," Lewis replied, "but I'm not an outsider. . . . And we are going to stay here until these people are allowed to register and vote." With that, Lewis was arrested.

James G. Clark, Jr., was a generation younger than Bull Connor, but he shared the same uncompromising racial worldview. A cattle raiser in Dallas County, Clark was appointed sheriff in 1955 by his friend Governor James "Big Jim" Folsom. Clark carried a pistol, a billy club, and a cattle prod around his waist. On his lapel he sported a pin with a simple pledge: "Never." Described as a "fleshy-faced bear of a man who stood six-foot-2 and weighed 220 pounds," Clark believed the demonstrators were seeking not equality but "black supremacy." The sheriff once broke a finger in his own hand after punching the Reverend C. T. Vivian in the face, and he never repented. "Basically, I'd do the same thing today if I had to do it all over again," Clark told *The Montgomery Advertiser* in 2006. Lewis recalled, "I think he was just a

George Lincoln Rockwell of the American Nazi Party descended on the South to defend segregation. With a "hate bus" at the time of the Freedom Rides and demonstrations in Selma, Rockwell and his swastika-wearing supporters sought to rally sentiment for white supremacy.

man full of hate, full of hate. He never said he was sorry. Never did. Never did."

On Monday, January 18, 1965, Lewis was in Selma to demonstrate for voter registration. The battlefield was crowded. George Lincoln Rockwell, the leader of the American Nazi Party, had come south to take a stand for white power. Rockwell's storm troopers knew the territory from 1961, when they had driven a "hate bus" during the Freedom Rides. Now, almost four years later, Malcolm X sent Rockwell a telegram warning that if the Nazis' "present racist agitation against our people there in Alabama causes physical harm to Reverend King or any other black Americans who are only attempting to enjoy their rights as free human beings . . . you and your Ku Klux Klan friends will be met with maximum physical retaliation from those of us who are not handcuffed by the disarming philosophy of nonviolence, and who believe in asserting our right of self-defense—by any means necessary."

Malcolm himself made a trip to Selma, unsubtly telling reporters, "I think that the people in this part of the world would do well to listen to Dr. Martin Luther King and give him what he's asking for and give it to him fast, before some other factions come along and try to do it another way."

Sheriff Clark didn't care. During one peaceful demonstration he and his deputies forced 160 teenagers and children to run two miles, beating and cattle-prodding them along the way. One boy, Lewis recalled, was clubbed in the mouth. Another, a nine-year-old, had been forced to make the run barefoot. "I thought I had seen everything," Lewis recalled, "but this was disgusting." He drafted a statement for the press: "Sheriff Jim Clark proved today beyond a shadow of a doubt that he is basically no different from a Gestapo officer during the Fascist slaughter of the Jews. . . . This is but one more example of the inhuman, animal-like treatment of the Negro people of Selma, Alabama. This nation has always come to the aid of people in foreign lands who are gripped by a reign of tyranny. Can this nation do less for the people of Selma?"

Events cascaded. King came to town and was physically attacked by an organizer for the white National States Rights Party, Jimmy George Robinson, in the lobby of the Hotel Albert. King was integrating the hotel on Broad Street when Robinson, wearing a khaki paramilitary uniform, approached him at the registration desk. "You're Martin Luther King," Robinson said, punching King in the face and trying to kick him in the groin.

Lewis, who was with King, did something out of character. "I've never been in a fight in my life," he recalled. "I've been hit—many, many times—but I've never hit back. At that moment, though, something shot up in me, something protective, something instinctive, and I jumped in and put a bear hug on the man. I wasn't even thinking about whether he might have a weapon or anything like that. It was just a visceral reaction. . . . Maybe it was because Dr. King meant so much to me, I don't know, but that moment pushed me as close as I've ever been to the limits of my nonviolent commitments. It made me realize there *were* limits, which was a humbling reminder of how human we all are."

Later that day, Clark assaulted Amelia Boynton during a nonviolent demonstration at the county courthouse. The sheriff, Lewis recalled, was "manhandling her, really shoving and roughing her up." Clark "grabbed her by the back of her collar and pushed her roughly and swiftly for half a block into a patrol car," *The New York Times* reported; King called it "one of the most brutal and unlawful acts I have seen an officer commit."

In mid-February, former Mississippi governor Ross Barnett attended the annual White Citizens' Council membership dinner at

The end of Jim Crow, former Mississippi governor Ross Barnett said, could mean the end of civilization. "The secret purpose of our enemies," Barnett told a White Citizens' Council dinner in Selma, "is to diffuse our blood, confuse our minds and degrade our character."

the National Guard Armory in Dallas County. Guests paid $1.50 for a plate of barbecued chicken; the crowd, SNCC's *Student Voice* newspaper reported, "was made up of middle class business people, professionals and well to do farmers, with their wives and children." A former mayor of Selma, Chris Heinz, introduced Barnett. "We have arrived at a point when all white people must stand up and be counted," Heinz said. In his remarks, Barnett called the resistance to arms. "The secret purpose of our enemies is to diffuse our blood, confuse our minds and degrade our character," he said, "that we may not be able to stand against the wiles of the devil."

Four days earlier, a state trooper had shot Jimmie Lee Jackson, a young veteran, in the stomach. Jackson had been trying to help his mother, who was being accosted by a group of whites in a café in nearby Marion, Alabama, after they had left a voting rights meeting at Zion Methodist Church. The shooting came amid a night of beatings in the streets outside the church; an NBC reporter, Richard Valeriani, suffered a head wound. "They . . . shot the lights out, and they beat people at random," Albert Turner, the SCLC field secretary in Alabama, recalled. "They didn't have to be marching. All you had to do was be black. And they hospitaled probably fifteen or twenty folks.

And they just was intending to kill somebody as an example"—and Jimmie Jackson was that somebody. "He was not what you would call a leader or nothing of that nature," Turner said. "He was just a person who attended the meetings. . . . But about this time everybody was active. . . . This was one of the prime reasons for the massacre. Because too many people were getting the message, and a lot of black folks who hadn't never rebelled against the system at all had decided that it was time to rebel against the system."

Jimmie Lee Jackson died eight days later. "A lot of people had been beaten and hurt and jailed" in the campaign at Selma, Lewis recalled. "But no one had died. Not until now."

On a rain-soaked procession from Zion Methodist to bury Jackson, Lewis and James Bevel were walking together when Bevel had a flash of inspiration. They should, Bevel mused, "take Jimmie Lee's body to Montgomery," Lewis recalled. "Walk the entire fifty-four miles from Selma and lay this young man's casket on the capitol steps"—the steps where Jefferson Davis and George Wallace had stood. "Confront the governor. Confront the state of Alabama. Give them something they couldn't turn their heads away from."

That wouldn't happen, but a march would. "We are going to bring a voting bill into being in the streets of Selma," King said. "President Johnson has a mandate from the American people. He must go out and get a voting bill this time that will end the necessity for any more voting bills."

Internal movement politics were difficult. Many in SNCC saw a Selma-to-Montgomery march as a grandstanding play by King and his Southern Christian Leadership Conference, a dangerous move that put lives at risk with little chance of reward. In a marathon meeting at Frazier's café in Atlanta, SNCC's leadership thought a march designed to force more legislation was pointless—the democratic process, many felt, had failed them at Atlantic City and, after all, didn't the Civil Rights Act of 1964 include voting protections? Nobody was enforcing those. SNCC's Jack Minnis, for one, thought it "illusory to the point of fatuity to suppose that any purpose we avow would be served by trying to get still another voting bill passed by Congress." Taylor Branch captured the debate well: "Such skepticism about government was the dominant new mood within SNCC, making Lewis too earnest and steadfast by contrast—too much like King—and the religious optimism of his nonviolence had worn too thin to invite another beating in Selma."

Lewis thought the debate missed the larger point—and to him the larger point was that tribulation was a necessary precursor to the Beloved Community. There could be no crown without the cross, no Easter without Good Friday. That's the way things were. "If these people want to march, I'm going to march with them," he told the skeptics within SNCC. "You decide what you want to do, but I'm going to march." To Bernard LaFayette, Lewis's resolve was impressive. "John went against his own constituency, his own group, because he thought it was the right thing to do," LaFayette recalled. "He said he would march as John Lewis, not as the chairman of SNCC. His conscience was more important to him than the power struggles, I guess you would call it, that could happen in the movement."

George Wallace marshaled the opposition. On Saturday, March 6, the governor declared that there could be no march on U.S. Highway 80—the main road between Selma and Montgomery—and authorized his state troopers "to use whatever measures are necessary to prevent a march." In afteryears, Wallace would say he was trying to protect the marchers, as he put it, in case "some man of hatred might get in the woods there and shoot someone with a rifle."

On Sunday, March 7, a long line of marchers gathered at Brown Chapel AME Church. King was back in Atlanta for Sunday services; Lewis and Hosea Williams led the column of demonstrators; ambulances brought up the rear. Volunteer doctors and nurses had already set up a field medical unit next to the church. Ready to be arrested, Lewis carried two books, an apple and an orange, and a toothbrush and toothpaste in his backpack. One of the books was Columbia University historian Richard Hofstadter's *The American Political Tradition,* which included this quotation from the abolitionist Wendell Phillips: "I must educate, arouse, and mature a public opinion. . . . This I do by frankly and candidly criticizing its present policy. . . . My criticism is not, like that of the traitor presses, meant to paralyze the administration, but to goad it to more activity and vigor." That was Lewis's mission.

The forces he was about to meet on Highway 80 were well described, too, in Hofstadter's first pages, which quoted the Revolutionary-era general Henry Knox. The nation's first secretary of war, Knox had said that men were not angels but were in fact "men—actual men, possessing all the turbulent passions belonging to that animal."

N o one in Lewis's column expected to make it to Montgomery. In the face of Wallace's order, however, they felt they had no choice but to proceed. "Like everyone around me, I was basically playing it by ear," Lewis recalled. "None of us had thought much further ahead than that afternoon. Anything that happened beyond that—if we were allowed to go on, if this march did indeed go all the way to Montgomery—we figured we would take care of as we went along. The main thing was that we *do* it, that we march."

And they did. According to FBI reports of the day, marchers finished up a meeting at Brown Chapel at 2:18 P.M. Central. At that time, about 625 people ("practically all of whom were Negroes," assistant FBI director Al Rosen wrote in an internal memorandum) silently walked from Sylvan Street to Alabama Avenue to the Pettus Bridge, named for a Confederate general who had served as a grand dragon of the Ku Klux Klan. At the crest of the bridge, Lewis looked out and saw what he remembered later as a sea of blue. State troopers under Colonel Al Lingo and a posse of deputies under Jim Clark were lined across Highway 80. "I saw in front of us a solid wall of state troopers, standing shoulder to shoulder," Amelia Boynton recalled. White spectators, some waving Confederate battle flags, watched from outside the Glass House Restaurant, the Chick-N-Treat Drive-In, the Kayo gasoline station, and Lehman's Pontiac dealership. Reporters and cameramen stood ready.

Lewis and Williams looked at the armed ranks, and then glanced down at the river. "John, can you swim?" Williams asked.

"No," Lewis replied. "What about you?"

"A little," Williams said.

"Well, there's a lot of water down there," Lewis said. "We cannot jump. We're going to have to keep marching."

"*This is an unlawful assembly,*" Major John Cloud announced as the marchers reached the bottom of the bridge, face-to-face with the lawmen. It was 2:52 P.M. "*Your march is not conducive to the public safety. You are ordered to disperse and go back to your church or to your homes.*"

Williams asked if they might have a word with Major Cloud.

"There is no word to be had," Cloud replied. The two then repeated the exchange, to the same effect, which was none.

And so the two corps of Americans stood, staring, in the middling hours of afternoon.

At this moment on Highway 80, in the Deep South of a Cold War America unchanged in so many ways from Civil War America, John Lewis's life reached a kind of crescendo. He was still so young—he had turned twenty-five two weeks before—and yet there on that strip of road he was like a martyr or a prophet of old. For all the complexities of race and identity and power and love and hate, for all the dreams fulfilled and dreams deferred, for all the panoply and pain of history, this much, at least, was simple at that hour and that place in Selma: The forces of good were pitted against the forces of evil. The marchers were asking a nation to live up to its word that all were created equal, and the nation, in the form of those troopers and deputies and demonstrators, was saying, as Sheriff Clark's lapel pin put it, "Never."

History isn't always like this. In fact, it's rarely like this. We impose order on the disorder of the past, weaving together multiple strands, disparate events, muddled motives—what William James called reality's "blooming, buzzing confusion." With Selma, however, the narrative need not be neatened. The facts speak for themselves.

Facing Major Cloud, Lewis drew on the lessons learned under Jim Lawson. "I wasn't about to turn around," Lewis recalled. "We were there. We were not going to run. . . . We could have gone forward, marching right into the teeth of those troopers. But that would have been too aggressive, I thought, too provocative. God knew what might have happened if we had done that. These people were ready to be arrested, but I didn't want anyone to get hurt."

The wind riffling his tan trench coat, Lewis pondered what to do. "We couldn't go forward," he recalled. "We couldn't go back. There was only one option left that I could see." He would not fight—not with a weapon of this world, but with a weapon of the world he was seeking to bring into being.

"We should kneel and pray," Lewis said to a nodding Williams.

They wouldn't have time. A moment had passed since Cloud had issued his final warning. "You saw these men putting on their gas masks," Lewis said. Now he heard Cloud's voice pierce the air.

"*Troopers,*" the major cried, "*advance!*"

Within seconds—to Lewis it seemed instantaneous—the wave of blue struck. He remembered the enormity, the totality, of the reaction of his attackers. "The troopers and possemen swept forward as one, like a human wave, a blur of blue shirts and billy clubs and bullwhips," Lewis recalled. "We had no chance to turn and retreat." The pain was to be endured. There was no help for it.

"They came toward us, and Hosea said, 'John, they're going to gas us,'" Lewis recalled. "They came with all types of force, beating us with nightsticks, trampling us with horses. I was the first person to be hit. My feet, my legs went from under me. I was knocked down." Charles Mauldin, a seventeen-year-old who was in the third row of the column, heard the blow. "I'll never forget the sound of the billy club hitting John's head," Mauldin recalled. "It made this sickening, harsh *thwack.*"

The first canister of tear gas had little effect on the column. The troopers then ignited twenty more, which had a great deal of effect. "This quantity of tear gas," an FBI agent clinically remarked, "immediately dispersed the marchers."

Trapped between asphalt and his uniformed attackers, inhaling tear gas and reeling from the billy club blow to his head, Lewis felt everything dimming. He vomited and was struck a second time when he tried to get up.

He could hear screams and slurs and the clop-clop-clop of the troopers' horses. His skull fractured, his vision blurred, Lewis believed the end had come. "People are going to die here," he said to himself. "*I'm* going to die here." Yet for Lewis there was no sense of panic, no gasping, no thrashing, no *fear*. He was at peace.

"At the moment when I was hit on the bridge and began to fall," Lewis recalled, "I really thought it was my last protest, my last march. I thought I saw death, and I thought, 'It's OK, it's all right'—I am doing what I am supposed to do."

It was war. "From observation," FBI Special Agent Joseph M. Conley reported, "it appeared the nightsticks were used by most of the Troopers and Posse as a matter of first recourse, and in general were used indiscriminately." There had been no "waiting for any acts of resistance" before attacking, another agent, Daniel D. Doyle, wrote. "Both women and men," Doyle added, "were struck with nightsticks."

"I'll never forget the sound of the billy club hitting John's head," Charles Mauldin, who stood near Lewis, recalled. "It made this sickening, harsh thwack." As an FBI agent on the scene reported, there had been no "waiting for any acts of resistance" by the Alabama authorities before they attacked the nonviolent marchers.

One girl, about fourteen, ran across the highway. "A Posse member," an FBI agent noted, "saw the girl and gave chase on his horse" and swung at the fleeing marcher "several times with his nightstick." At least six white men who weren't part of the law enforcement corps "attacked and repeatedly struck individual Negroes who had become separated from the crowd"; a black man was forced to the ground and assaulted "with a rubber-covered cable with a metal clamp attached to one end." To Charles Mauldin, who was choking on tear gas, there could be only one explanation. "They were trying to provoke us, I think, into doing something violent, into hitting back. But we didn't." Amelia Boynton was also gassed and beaten.

The journalists on hand watched in horror. "Suddenly the clubs started swinging," *Time* magazine wrote. "From the sidelines, white townspeople raised their voices in cheers and whoops. Joined now by the possemen and deputies, the patrolmen waded into the screaming mob. The marchers retreated for 75 yards, stopped to catch their breath. Still the troopers advanced. Now came the sound of canisters being fired. A Negro screamed: 'Tear gas!' Within seconds the highway was swirling with white and yellow clouds of smoke, raging with the cries of men. Choking, bleeding, the Negroes fled in all directions while the whites pursued them. The mounted men uncoiled bull whips and lashed out viciously as the horses' hoofs trampled the fallen. 'O.K., nigger!' snarled a posseman, flailing away at a running Negro woman. 'You wanted to march—now march!'"

Lewis struggled back to consciousness. "I was bleeding badly," he recalled. "My head was now exploding with pain. That brief, sweet sense of just wanting to lie there was gone. I needed to get up. I'd faded out for I don't know how long, but now I was tuned back in."

The journey back to Brown Chapel was a blur. Parts of the posse gave chase. One Clark deputy had manufactured a cudgel by putting barbed wire around a rubber hose. Others had whips. Mounted possemen rode up the steps of the church; Charles Mauldin worried they might ride into the sanctuary itself.

Seeking safety, the fleeing marchers filled the church, which was, Lewis recalled, "awash with sounds of groaning and weeping. And singing and crying. Mothers shouting out for their children. Children screaming for their mothers and brothers and sisters. So much confusion and fear and anger all erupting at the same time." On a telephone line to SNCC headquarters in Atlanta, Lewis said, "I've never seen anything like it in my life. They are shooting gas, acid. One very old lady I know has a broken arm." At an impromptu mass meeting in the sanctuary, Lewis, bloodied and dirty, with a fractured skull and what one SNCC worker described as a "small hole in his head," told the frightened congregation, "I don't understand how President Johnson can send troops to Vietnam and cannot send troops to Selma, Alabama, to protect the citizens who want to register to vote in America." He was seeing double as he spoke; the pain was enveloping.

The meeting, which Stokely Carmichael said resembled "a wake in a MASH unit," was pitched. "If it has to be a path of blood," James Bevel said, "it is going to be established that Negroes have the right to walk on the highways of Alabama."

Worth Long, who had served as a medic in the air force, realized Lewis might have a concussion. Time was short. Traumatic head injuries could lead to catastrophic clots of blood in the brain. In the parsonage behind the church, Long improvised a stretcher by putting Lewis in a high-backed chair and securing him with strips from a tablecloth (it might have been a sheet, Long recalled). Long asked another SNCC activist, Willie C. Robertson, to help carry Lewis out into the street, where a bread truck with two big back doors was waiting. Long went out first and approached the mounted possemen, calmed the lead horse, and, as Mauldin heard it, drew on his old military vernacular. "We have a soldier who's down," Mauldin heard Long say. "We have to get him to the hospital." It worked. Strapped in the chair, Lewis was allowed through the police cordon, was loaded into the bread truck, and was taken to Good Samaritan, a few blocks away.

When he arrived at the hospital, Lewis was struck by the ambient scent of the tear gas from the clothes of the victims. Forty-eight marchers were treated at the hospital that day; thirteen of them, including Lewis, were admitted. (Another eight were treated at the local Burwell Infirmary, most for the effects of the tear gas.) Sixteen-year-old Jeanette Howard of Marion, Alabama, had been kicked in the head by a horse. Twenty-six-year-old Margaret Clay Brooks of Jones, Alabama, had a laceration of the head, loosened top teeth, and a possibly fractured skull.

Dr. Isabel Dumont diagnosed Lewis with a severe concussion and a fractured skull. He was attended to, given painkillers, and put to bed in the hospital. He was asleep by ten P.M.

Lewis drifted off as images of the Alabama attack ran that evening on national television; ABC broke into the broadcast premiere of *Judgment at Nuremberg* to show the footage. Watching the film of the assault, the writer George B. Leonard, who was in San Francisco, observed, "With the cameras rather far removed from the action and the skies partly overcast everything that happened took on the quality of an old newsreel. Yet this very quality, vague and half silhouetted, gave the scene the vehemence and immediacy of a dream. . . . A shrill cry of terror, unlike any sound that had passed through a TV set, rose up as the troopers lumbered forward, stumbling sometimes on fallen bodies. The scene cut to charging horses, their hoofs flashing over the fallen. Another quick cut: a cloud of tear gas billowed over the highway. Periodically the top of a helmeted head emerged from the cloud, followed by a club on the upswing."

Leonard's wife could not watch. "I can't look any more," she said, in tears. In an editorial, *The Washington Post* deplored the violence at the bridge. "The news from Selma, Alabama, where police beat and mauled and gassed unarmed, helpless and unoffending citizens," the capital newspaper said, "will shock and alarm the whole nation."

On Monday, March 8, two FBI special agents, Daniel Doyle and John H. Lupton, came to Good Samaritan to take a statement from Lewis about what would come to be known as Bloody Sunday. Over four pages, he related the chronology of the march and detailed the attacks at the bridge. For their records—how the FBI loved records—the agents noted that the John Robert Lewis of Monday, March 8, 1965, was five foot five and half, weighed 156 pounds, and had brown eyes. And he was clear about his commitment to nonviolence. "At no time during the above described incident," he told the FBI, "did I assault or in any way interfere with a law enforcement officer."

Lewis was restless as he recuperated. "Maybe it was the drugs, but I had visions of someone slipping into the room and doing something to me," he recalled. "I felt vulnerable, helpless."

He was, though, the furthest thing from helpless. From the White

House down, the broader world was reacting to the circumstances that Lewis had helped create at the Pettus Bridge. "Lyndon lives in a cloud of troubles, with few rays of light," Lady Bird Johnson told her diary on Sunday night. "Now it is the Selma situation . . . and the cauldron is boiling."

Fred Gray, King's lawyer from Montgomery, was asked over to Selma to file a lawsuit for a resumption of the march. Calling for an influx of "clergy of all faiths" to join the protesters and "testify to the fact that the struggle in Selma is for the survival of democracy everywhere in our land," King himself arrived in Selma on Monday, March 8. To comply with a federal order that had temporarily halted the march on Highway 80, he led a partial march to the bridge. (Beforehand, outside Brown Chapel, King prayed by bullhorn: "Almighty God, thou hast called us to walk for freedom, even as thou did the children of Israel.") A hearing later that week before Judge Johnson— Lewis testified in the courtroom—lifted the injunction against the marchers. A white Unitarian minister, James Reeb, died after being beaten outside a Klan hangout, the Silver Moon Café. Meanwhile, cries for a voting rights bill increased, and President Johnson found himself trying to manage the calls for legislation, the plans for a renewed march from Selma to Montgomery—and George Wallace. "If I just send in federal troops with their big black boots, it will look like Reconstruction all over again," Johnson said privately. "I will lose every moderate, not just in Alabama but all over the South. Most southern people don't like this violence. They know deep in their hearts that things are going to change. . . . But not if it looks like the Civil War all over again!"

Wallace came to the White House on Saturday, March 13, 1965. The president seated the governor on a couch in the Oval Office and then positioned himself in a taller rocking chair. "I saw a nervous, aggressive man," Johnson recalled, "a rough, shrewd politician who had managed to touch the deepest chords of pride as well as prejudice among his people."

"Why don't you just desegregate all your schools?" Johnson asked. "You and I go out there in front of those television cameras right now, and you announce you've decided to desegregate every school in Alabama."

"Oh, Mr. President, I can't do that," Wallace said. "You know, the schools have got school boards. They're locally run. I haven't got the political power to do that."

"Don't you shit me, George Wallace," Johnson said. Later in the meeting, the president pressed a larger question.

"George, why are you doing this?" Johnson asked. "You came into office a liberal—you spent all your life trying to do things for the poor. Now, why are you working on this? Why are you off on this Negro thing? You ought to be down there calling for help for Aunt Susie in the nursing home."

"Now, listen, George, don't think about 1968," Johnson said. "Think about 1988. You and me, we'll be dead and gone then, George. . . . What do you want left after you, when you die? Do you want a great big marble monument that reads, 'George Wallace—He Built.' Or do you want a little piece of scrawny pine board lying across that harsh caliche soil that reads, 'George Wallace—He Hated.'"

Under pressure, the governor ultimately consented to ask for federal help to maintain order when the march resumed. "Hell, if I'd stayed in there much longer," Wallace remarked, "he'd have had me coming out for civil rights."

The White House speechwriter Richard Goodwin drafted LBJ's address to Congress on voting rights for Monday, March 15. The text drew deeply on religious themes. Johnson read the pages as they came out of Goodwin's typewriter. "The biblical imagery is part of the American tradition, no matter what your personal beliefs are," Goodwin recalled. "The Old Testament, the New Testament, it is all woven into who we are, Christian, Jew, or whatever. Religious metaphors and religious language form a kind of common bond in America—you can think of it either in literal or literary terms. Even if you are basically secular, the ideals and principles that come out of religion are essentially what we all should share: what is the right thing to do, what is just, what is fair. Most Americans believe there is a higher power at work, whether they call it God or not, and I was trying to frame the civil rights question in terms of what was right, what was just, what was fair—and that was, to me at least, and certainly to Johnson, partly religious."

On that Monday evening, the president stood in the chamber of the House of Representatives. "I speak tonight for the dignity of man and the destiny of democracy," he said. "I urge every member of both parties, Americans of all religions and of all colors, from every section of this country, to join me in that cause." He went on:

> At times history and fate meet at a single time in a single place to shape a turning point in man's unending search for freedom. So it was at Lexington and Concord. So it was a century ago at Appomattox. So it was last week in Selma, Alabama. . . .
>
> In our time we have come to live with moments of great crisis. Our lives have been marked with debate about great issues; issues of war and peace, issues of prosperity and depression. But rarely in any time does an issue lay bare the secret heart of America itself. Rarely are we met with a challenge, not to our growth or abundance, our welfare or our security, but rather to the values and the purposes and the meaning of our beloved Nation.
>
> The issue of equal rights for American Negroes is such an issue. And should we defeat every enemy, should we double our wealth and conquer the stars, and still be unequal to this issue, then we will have failed as a people and as a nation.
>
> For with a country as with a person, "What is a man profited, if he shall gain the whole world, and lose his own soul?"

The evocation of scripture—Johnson was quoting the words of Jesus from the Gospel of Saint Matthew—resonated, and the lawmakers applauded for the first time since the president had begun to speak. Johnson went on:

> There is no Negro problem. There is no Southern problem. There is no Northern problem. There is only an American problem. And we are met here tonight as Americans—not as Democrats or Republicans—we are met here as Americans to solve that problem.
>
> This was the first nation in the history of the world to be founded with a purpose. The great phrases of that purpose still sound in every American heart, North and South: "All men are created equal"—"government by consent of the governed"— "give me liberty or give me death." Well, those are not just clever words, or those are not just empty theories. . . .
>
> Many of the issues of civil rights are very complex and most

difficult. But about this there can and should be no argument. Every American citizen must have an equal right to vote....

Yet the harsh fact is that in many places in this country men and women are kept from voting simply because they are Negroes.

Every device of which human ingenuity is capable has been used to deny this right. The Negro citizen may go to register only to be told that the day is wrong, or the hour is late, or the official in charge is absent. And if he persists, and if he manages to present himself to the registrar, he may be disqualified because he did not spell out his middle name or because he abbreviated a word on the application.

And if he manages to fill out an application he is given a test. The registrar is the sole judge of whether he passes this test. He may be asked to recite the entire Constitution, or explain the most complex provisions of State law. And even a college degree cannot be used to prove that he can read and write.

For the fact is that the only way to pass these barriers is to show a white skin....

What happened in Selma is part of a far larger movement which reaches into every section and State of America. It is the

"I'm just following along trying to do what's right," Johnson told King by telephone after the president's address to the nation on Monday, March 15, 1965. King and Lewis had tuned in together at the home of Richie Jean and Sullivan Jackson, on Lapsley Avenue in Selma.

effort of American Negroes to secure for themselves the full blessings of American life.

Their cause must be our cause too. Because it is not just Negroes, but really it is all of us, who must overcome the crippling legacy of bigotry and injustice.

And we shall overcome.

Lewis and King watched the address together in the Lapsley Avenue home of Dr. Sullivan Jackson, a Selma dentist, and of his wife, Richie Jean. "I looked at Dr. King and tears came down his face," Lewis recalled, "and we all cried a little." King called Johnson afterward. "It is ironic, Mr. President," King said, "that after a century, a southern white President would help lead the way toward the salvation of the Negro."

"Thank you, Reverend," Johnson said. "You're the leader who is making it all possible. I'm just following along trying to do what's right."

The march went on. On Sunday, March 21, 1965, Lewis and thousands of others set out from Selma for Montgomery. Lewis marched the whole way, but his injuries were such that he was driven back to Selma each night instead of camping out along the fifty-four-mile route. He walked seven miles the first day; sixteen the second; eleven the third; sixteen the fourth; and six on the fifth and final day. Phyllis Cunningham, a nurse who was with SNCC and the Medical Committee for Human Rights, drove a VW van up and down Highway 80, bandaging bloody feet and giving exhausted marchers the occasional break.

Arriving at the state capitol, Lewis and others spoke, opening for a final speech by King. "Once more the method of nonviolent resistance was unsheathed from its scabbard, and once again an entire community was mobilized to confront the adversary," King said. "And again the brutality of a dying order shrieks across the land. Yet, Selma, Alabama, became a shining moment in the conscience of man. If the worst in American life lurked in its dark streets, the best of American instincts arose passionately from across the nation to overcome it." Total victory, tragically, was elusive. A white SCLC activist from

Michigan, Viola Gregg Liuzzo, was shot to death by Klansmen on Highway 80 on the evening of the final speeches in Montgomery.

It is difficult to overstate Selma's significance. It was true, as Johnson told the Congress and the nation, that the small Southern city had joined Lexington and Concord and Appomattox as a sacred place where the nation's story had taken a decisive turn. But what sets Selma apart—what sets Lewis's years of contributions during the movement apart—is that Selma became Selma not because of a conventional clash of forces but because the conventions of history were turned upside down. Lexington and Concord featured armed combatants; Appomattox is shorthand for the end of a civil war that claimed about three quarters of a million lives. Selma changed hearts and minds when Americans watched the brutal forces of the visible world meet the forces of an invisible one, and the clubs and horses and tear gas were, in the end, no match for love and grace and nonviolence.

Change in America most often comes when the powerless attract the attention of the powerful. From a pragmatic perspective, that process is perennial, with fits and starts, advances and retreats, good days and bleak ones. In such a view—and it was one shared by many of the American Founders—history is contingent, a succession of compromises and improvisations, world without end. To Lewis, though, history was terminal—and it will end not in despair and dust but in hope and harmony, with the coming of the Beloved Community. To him, then, politics was not an end but a means to bring about a world in which, in the words of the prophet Micah, every man shall dwell under his own vine and fig tree and no one shall make him afraid.

But politics was important, and Lewis was not entirely otherworldly. He appreciated political reality; he just wanted to bend it in the direction of the gospel rather than accepting it as he found it. His goal remained an interracial democracy, not a confederation of color.

The mechanics of bringing that vision to fruition was on President Johnson's mind when he invited Lewis, along with several others, to a private meeting in the study off the Oval Office on the morning of Friday, August 6. The president had successfully fought for the legislation he'd proposed in March, and the bill explicitly eliminated many of the traditional barriers to registration, including the weaponized literacy tests, and authorized federal enforcement. Sitting in an easy

Lewis, third from left, in a private meeting with LBJ in the president's small study off the Oval Office, Friday, August 6, 1965—the day of the signing of the Voting Rights Act. Lewis's openness to working with the White House would create tensions with many in SNCC who wanted to go further, faster.

chair with an ottoman, Johnson held forth for twenty minutes. "I'm going to sign this act," he said, leaning back and pitching forward as the mood struck him. "Now, John, you've got to go back and get all those folks registered. You've got to go back and get those boys by the *balls*. Just like a bull gets on a top of a cow. You've got to get 'em by the balls and you've got to *squeeze*, squeeze 'em till they *hurt*." ("I'd heard Lyndon Johnson enjoyed talking in graphic, down-home terms," Lewis recalled, "but I wasn't quite prepared for all those bulls and balls." The president was, in Lewis's dry recollection, "plain and open.")

A few hours later Lewis stood in the Capitol as the president signed the Voting Rights Act. "Three and a half centuries ago the first Negroes arrived at Jamestown," Johnson said. "They did not arrive in brave ships in search of a home for freedom. They did not mingle fear and joy, in expectation that in this New World anything would be possible to a man strong enough to reach for it. They came in darkness and they came in chains. And today we strike away the last major shackle of those fierce and ancient bonds. Today the Negro story and the American story fuse and blend." Lewis, along with King, stood nearby. Johnson gave them pens from the signing—a token of thanks for their roles in bringing an American tragedy out of the shadows.

As far as Lewis was concerned, however, the work could only stop with the coming of the Kingdom, of the Beloved Community. To him, harmony and justice were closer to hand after Selma but were still out of reach for too many. He left Washington for the South, arriving in Americus, Georgia, where county officials were insisting on segregated voter-registration lines. So it was that he was in police custody within forty-eight hours of conferring personally with the president of the United States.

He'd been to the mountaintop. Selma had changed America; he had talked things over with the president; he was a national figure. Yet here he was, back in jail, back among the least of these. And he was at peace. "Along the way I had what I call an executive session with myself," Lewis recalled. "I said, 'I'm not going to hate. I'm not going to become bitter. I'm not going to live a hostile life. I'm going to treat my fellow human being as a human being.' So when I was being beaten on the Freedom Rides or in a march, I never hated. I respected the dignity and the worth of that person. Because we all are human and we must be human toward each other and love each other."

Lewis's Christian vision was at once inexhaustible and exhausting. Many of his SNCC colleagues were tiring of insistent nonviolence and of what some, like Stokely Carmichael, dismissed as the King-Lewis Sunday school piety and sermonizing. "Just about everyone in the organization, including me, liked John personally," Carmichael recalled. "*Personally*, what was there not to like? John was a regular guy, uncomplicated, friendly, and brave, always willing to put his body on the line. He'd certainly taken his licks. I'll never forget Paul Dietrich, fellow Freedom Rider . . . saying after the March on Washington, 'Wow, this is the first time I've seen John without a bandage on his head.' Yeah, the brother had certainly paid some heavy dues."

Lewis understood. He didn't like it, but he understood. "We're only flesh," he said two years after Bloody Sunday. "I could understand people not wanting to be beaten anymore. The body gets tired. You put out so much energy and you saw such little gain. Black capacity to believe white would really open his heart, open his life to nonviolent appeal, was running out."

CHAPTER SEVEN

THIS COUNTRY
DON'T RUN ON LOVE

New York, Memphis, Los Angeles: 1966–68

Black power is the demand to organize around the question of blackness. We are oppressed for only one reason: because we are black.

—Stokely Carmichael

The problem we faced now was not something so visible or easily identifiable as a Bull Connor blocking our way. Now we needed to deal with the subtler and much more complex issues of attaining economic and political power.

—John Lewis

He had seen it coming. In a May 1965 piece for the *New York Herald Tribune* headlined WE MARCH FOR US . . . AND FOR YOU, Lewis offered a reply to an important question: What happens after voting rights? "Where lack of jobs, intolerable housing, police brutality, and other frustrating conditions exist, it is possible that violence and massive street demonstrations may develop. . . . Reality now is what happens in the streets . . . of Negro communities, north and south, where fear and deprivation form an integral part of daily life. If the government cannot answer our questions, and help us to solve some of these problems, I can only see many long, hot summers ahead."

Events quickly proved him right. In the Watts section of Los Angeles on Wednesday, August 11, 1965, chaos broke out after a white policeman pulled over a black man on suspicion of drunk driving at the corner of Avalon Boulevard and Imperial Highway. By the time the stop was over, the officer, with additional police who had rushed to the scene, had arrested the driver, his brother, and their mother. A crowd that would eventually grow to an estimated 1,000 people had begun hurling rocks and bottles at the white authorities. The police had wielded shotguns to control the gathering masses. "How is it possible?" Lyndon Johnson wondered to his aide Jack Valenti. "After all we've accomplished. How could it be?"

It could be—and it was—because of poverty, police overreach, and a dearth of hope. The historian and theologian Vincent Harding, an associate of King's, noted the sea change. "In a sense, the rounding off of the classic southern phase of the movement in Selma that spring and the summertime explosion in black Los Angeles (as well as in places like Chicago and Philadelphia) proved to mark a turning point," Harding observed. "From there on, the growing attention, energies, and action of the black freedom movement were geared toward the North, toward the cities, toward the problems of political powerlessness, economic exploitation . . . and explosive, sometimes cathartic rage."

Lewis understood the basic question. "Now that we had secured our bedrock, fundamental rights—the rights of access and accommodation and the right to vote—the movement was moving into a new phase, a far stickier and more complex stage of gaining equal footing in this society," he recalled after Selma. "The problem we faced now was not something so visible or easily identifiable as a Bull Connor blocking our way. Now we needed to deal with the subtler and much more complex issues of attaining economic and political power, of dealing with attitudes and actions held deep inside people and institutions that, now that they were forced to let us through the door, could still keep the rewards inside those doors out of our reach."

In movement circles, the Jim Lawson curriculum of the Bible, Thoreau, Niebuhr, Gandhi, and King was being displaced by a 1961 account of the independence struggle in Algiers, Frantz Fanon's *The Wretched of the Earth.* "Get this into your head: if violence were only a thing of the future, if exploitation and oppression never existed on earth, perhaps displays of nonviolence might relieve the conflict," Jean-Paul Sartre wrote in a preface to Fanon's book. "But if the entire regime, even your nonviolent thoughts, is governed by a thousand-year-old oppression, your passiveness serves no other purpose but to put you on the side of the oppressors."

The Fanon message was distilled for popular use in a single phrase, a term that Richard Wright had used as a title for a 1954 book: *Black Power.* For nearly a decade, from the time of the Montgomery bus boycott in 1955 through Selma in 1965, nonviolence had prevailed as the movement's guiding ethos, but there was always dissent. Rising racial consciousness had informed the Black Muslim phenomenon, shaped Malcolm X, and was influencing many African Americans—young and old. Malcolm was gone now, the victim of assassination in the Audubon Ballroom in Harlem on Sunday, February 21, 1965—Lewis's twenty-fifth birthday. "I had my differences with him, of course, but there was no question that he had come to articulate better than anyone else on the scene—including Dr. King—the bitterness and frustration of black Americans," recalled Lewis, who went to New York for Malcolm's funeral.

That bitterness and that frustration was casting significant doubt on the viability of nonviolence. If one definition of insanity was to repeat the same actions over and over again only to see the same results, the thinking went, then wasn't it insane to keep seeking justice and redress from a white power structure that only grudgingly, and only after much violence, gave up even an inch of ground—inches that it could presumably then take back at will or on a whim? "If we are to proceed toward true liberation," a SNCC paper said in the spring of 1966, "we must cut ourselves off from white people. We must form our own institutions, credit unions, co-ops, political parties, write our own histories." During the Selma crisis of 1965, James Forman had

Stokely Carmichael speaks to the concluding rally of the Meredith March Against Fear in Jackson, Mississippi, in June 1966. Carmichael had just recently defeated Lewis for the chairmanship of SNCC at Kingston Springs, Tennessee, and was becoming the central spokesman for "Black Power."

said, "This problem goes to the very *bottom* of the United States, and you know, I said it today and I'll say it again. If we can't sit at the table, let's knock the *fuckin'* legs off!" By 1966, there were voices within SNCC arguing that "white participation, as practiced in the past, is now obsolete."

Stokely Carmichael, while disagreeing with the prospect of a white purge, wanted a new future for SNCC. "Mr. Carmichael," *The New York Times* reported, "does not advocate violence but neither does he believe in turning the other cheek." In an interview with *Newsweek*, Carmichael said, "Coalition's no good. Cause what happens when a bunch of Negroes joins in with a bunch of whites? They get absorbed, that's what." In *Stokely: A Life*, the historian Peniel E. Joseph wrote: "Although today largely forgotten, Stokely Carmichael remains one of the protean figures of the twentieth century: a revolutionary who passionately believed in self-defense and armed rebellion even as he revered [Martin Luther King]; a gifted intellectual who dealt in emotions as well as words and ideas; and an activist whose radical political vision remained anchored by a deep sense of history."

To many white Americans, Black Power connoted chaos and subversion, bloody revolution and burning cities. In the charged and complicated spheres of identity, politics, philosophy, and power in America, though, racism was not situational but systemic. In that context, the appeal of Black Power was understandable. Like Malcolm X and like King (who was becoming increasingly vocal about the need for systemic economic and political reform), Carmichael was searching for ways forward. Lewis's way was different, and he'd remain committed to his vision of the Beloved Community. If others wanted to take a different route—and they clearly did—then so be it. But Lewis would confront his nation's enduring racism by the lights that had brought him this far.

"I think it was a feeling in SNCC on the part of some of the people like Stokely and others," Lewis recalled of 1966, "that they needed someone who would maybe not be so nonviolent, someone who would be 'blacker,' in a sense." To him, the change in climate was lamentable but comprehensible.

In 1965, in Lowndes County, Alabama, which neighbored Selma's Dallas County, Carmichael and others created a new political party, the Lowndes County Freedom Organization. Its emblem: a black

A sample ballot produced by the Lowndes County, Alabama, Freedom Organization, whose emblem was a black panther. "No one ever talked about 'white power,'" Stokely Carmichael remarked, "because power in this country is white."

panther. "Lowndes was a truly totalitarian society—the epitome of the tight, insulated police state," Carmichael recalled in a book co-authored in 1967 with Charles V. Hamilton, *Black Power: The Politics of Liberation in America.* "SNCC people felt that if they could help crack Lowndes, other areas—with less brutal reputations—would be easier to organize. This might be considered a kind of SNCC Domino Theory." It was, Carmichael said, "as ludicrous for Negroes to join [the Democratic Party] as it would have been for Jews to join the Nazi Party in the 1930s."

With his gift for the powerful image and memorable phrase, Carmichael was building a case for radical action that did not depend on the cooperation of whites in the way the 1955–65 movement had. "When the Lowndes County Freedom Organization chose the black panther as its symbol," Carmichael said, "it was christened by the press 'the Black Panther Party'—but the Alabama Democratic Party, whose symbol is a rooster, has never been called the White Cock Party. No one ever talked about 'white power' because power in this country *is* white."

The end of Jim Crow and the passage of voting rights was only the beginning—and it was a vastly overdue beginning at that. Poverty, Vietnam, police brutality, and all the manifestations of systemic racism: These things couldn't be cured by the nonviolent sit-ins and marches of yesteryear. The violence in Watts, Harlem, Chicago, and elsewhere, Carmichael told readers of *The New York Review of Books* in September 1966, came in part because "each time the people in those cities saw Martin Luther King get slapped, they became angry; when they saw four little black girls bombed to death, they were angrier; and when nothing happened, they were steaming. We had nothing to offer that they could see, except to go out and be beaten again. We helped to build their frustration."

On a tour in the North, Carmichael spoke to an audience in Harlem. A seventeen-year-old, Clarissa Williams, opened for him. "We intend to be the generation that says, Friends, we do not have a dream, we do *not* have a dream, we have a plan."

"Hit 'em hard, sister," Carmichael murmured happily.

Then Carmichael rose. "His style dazzles," Bernard Weinraub, writing for *Esquire* in 1967, observed. "He shakes his head as he begins speaking and his body appears to tremble. His voice, at least in the North, is lilting and Jamaican. His hands move effortlessly. His tone—and the audience loves it—is cool and very hip. No Martin Luther King We Shall Overcome oratory."

Carmichael's words were sharp. "Brothers and Sisters, a hell of a lot of us are gonna be shot and it ain't just gonna be in South Vietnam," he said. "We've got to move to a position *in this country* where we're not afraid to say that any man who has been selling us rotten meat for high prices should have had his store bombed fifteen years ago. We have got to move to a position where we will control our *own* destiny. We have got to move to a position where we will have black people represent *us* to achieve *our* needs. This country don't run on love, Brothers, it's run on power and we ain't got none."

He was speaking in a former theater and used the setting to make a vivid point. "Well, I used to come here on Saturday afternoon when I was a little boy and we used to see Tarzan here and all of us would yell like crazy when Tarzan beat up our black brothers," Carmichael said. "Well, you know Tarzan is on television now and from here on in I'm rooting for that black man to beat the hell out of Tarzan." The crowd roared its approval.

Carmichael mused about his father. "He believed genuinely in the great American Dream," Carmichael told Bernard Weinraub. "And because he believed in it he was just squashed. Squashed! He worked himself to death in this country and he died the same way he started: poor and black. . . . My old man would Tom. He was such a good old Joe, but he would *Tom*. And he was a very religious cat too—he was head deacon of the church and he was so honest, so very, very honest. He never realized people lied or cheated or were bad. He couldn't conceive of it. He just prayed and worked. Man, did he work. . . . He just thought that if you worked hard and prayed hard this country would take care of you."

Carmichael and others within SNCC appear to have viewed Lewis in rather the same way. Though Lewis had vocally opposed the war in Vietnam, he had marched in Selma when SNCC had chosen not to. He'd been open to meeting with the Johnson White House—to the fury of those in SNCC who had lost faith in government—and he had not supported the Black Panther effort in Lowndes County. "I have always been a believer in a strong two-party system," Lewis recalled. The MFDP "was open to all people. The Black Panthers, on the other hand, were segregated."

Matters came to a head at a SNCC conference at a wooded retreat center in Kingston Springs, Tennessee, in May 1966. "What I remember was he wasn't representing us," SNCC's Fay Bellamy recalled. "He may have represented SCLC. Or Dr. King. Maybe he was representing himself. But he sure wasn't representing us. He wasn't paying attention to what the organization was doing. Wasn't participating on projects, wasn't doing the job a chairman should. He was making speeches, fronting in the press, but . . . every time LBJ called, he'd rush his clothes into the cleaners and be on the next plane to Washington. You had to wonder where his head really was."

Lewis was out of tune with his own organization. It was, he recalled, "almost like a coup. People were saying that we need someone who will stand up to Lyndon Johnson, we need someone who will stand up to Martin Luther King, Jr." To Carmichael, the Lewis gospel was wrong for the moment. "I don't go along with this garbage that you can't hate, you gotta love," Carmichael said. "I don't go along with that at all. Man, you *can,* you *do* hate."

Lewis was reelected chairman in an initial round of voting, but there was a second balloting, which resulted in what Lewis called his "de-election." Even the leading voice on having a second election, Worth Long, admired Lewis extravagantly. "John was the most courageous person that I have ever worked with in the movement," Long recalled to the historian Clayborne Carson. "John would not just follow you into the lion's den, he would lead you into it." Long simply believed that the seasons had changed and that SNCC needed leadership more in sync with what Carson called "the increasingly militant mood of the staff."

And of the era. "It was very disappointing, after going to jail 40 times, being beaten on the Freedom Ride in '61, and almost facing death during the attempted march from Selma to Montgomery in 1965, to be challenged and unseated, to be reelected and de-elected the same evening," Lewis recalled. "It was a personal loss." As ever, though, he would persevere. "I made a decision that it didn't matter what happened—I would continue to advocate the philosophy and the discipline of nonviolence, that I believed in the interracial democracy, that I believed in black and white people working together." Kingston Springs was only thirty miles or so from "the Holy Hill" at American Baptist, but the two worlds—the ABT of 1957 and the SNCC conference of 1966—were growing apart.

The tensions that had played out privately at Kingston Springs would be on public display in Mississippi within the month. In the first week of June 1966, James Meredith, who had integrated the University of Mississippi in 1962, announced a 220-mile solo march across the state. He was wounded in a shotgun assault, and a call went out for other civil rights figures to take up the march. King, Carmichael, and others came into the state, along with armies of journalists.

In Greenwood, Mississippi, on Friday, June 17, Carmichael took the stage at a rally. He'd been arrested for pitching a tent at a black high school but had been released, and he was primed for a passionate performance. Though King was there, too, Carmichael stirred the crowd the most. "This is the twenty-seventh time I have been arrested—and I ain't going to jail no more!" he cried, his fist raised. "The only way we gonna stop them white men from whuppin' us is to take over. We been saying freedom for six years and we ain't got nothin'. What we gonna start saying now is 'Black Power!'"

"BLACK POWER!" the crowd cried back. Willie Ricks, a Chattanooga, Tennessee–raised SNCC activist, jumped on the stage to press the advantage.

"What do you want?" Ricks asked the rally.

"BLACK POWER!"

"What do you want?"

"BLACK POWER!"

"What do you want?"

"BLACK POWER! BLACK POWER! BLACK POWER!"

In a filmed joint interview amid the Meredith March, NBC's Frank McGee stood between King and Carmichael, asking about the future of the movement as the three made their way down a road.

"Mr. Carmichael," McGee asked, "are you as committed to the nonviolent approach as Dr. King is?"

"No, I'm not."

"Why aren't you?"

"Well, I just don't see it as a way of life," Carmichael said. "I never have. I grew up in the slums of New York and I learned there that the only way that one survived was to use his fists. . . . For me, it's always been a tactic and never a way of life."

"Could you comment on that, Dr. King?" McGee asked, turning to his right.

"The Negro has an opportunity to inject morality in the veins of our civilization," King said, "and for this reason I will continue to preach nonviolence."

Lewis agreed with King, and he was uncomfortable with the cries of "Black Power!" "The way I had always understood the phrase, it had more to do with self-reliance than with black supremacy, though that distinction was hard to see, especially through the fire and spit with which Stokely and some of the others tended to deliver their message," Lewis recalled. "The way he was using it, I thought it tended to create a schism, both within the movement itself and between the races. It drove people apart rather than brought them together."

On Friday, June 24, in Canton, Mississippi, Meredith marchers had been rousted and beaten by Mississippi state troopers at a campground—as at Bloody Sunday, there was tear gas—and Lewis, still a member of SNCC, though no longer chairman, was on hand.

"Fellow freedom fighters," he said. "The whole man must say no nonviolently, his entire Christian spirit must say no to this evil and vicious system."

No one wanted to hear it. "Even as he spoke, listeners sloshed away," Paul Good wrote in *The New York Times Magazine*. "The speaker's credentials were in order, but his time was out of joint. He spoke the old words of militant love, but the spiritual heart of the movement that for years had sent crusaders up and down American roads, trusting in love, was broken and Lewis had become that most expendable commodity, a former leader. It was not so much that he was losing his audience; the audience was already lost."

For Lewis, it was the end of a chapter. "That night in Canton I felt like the uninvited guest," he told Good the next year. "It's hard to accept when something is over even though you know things have to change. In the beginning, with the sit-ins and Freedom Rides, things were much simpler. Or we thought they were. People just had to offer their bodies for their beliefs and it seemed like that would be enough, but it wasn't. By the time of Canton nobody knew what would be enough to make America right, and the atmosphere was very complicated, very negative."

Nobody knew what would be enough to make America right. Here a deeply disappointed Lewis was acknowledging the complications of the journey toward justice. His heart and mind were committed to bearing nonviolent witness in search of an interracial America, and he was long wounded by Carmichael's victory at Kingston Springs. Yet he understood why people were frustrated by the pace of change. Progress was slow—too slow—and many white Americans were too comfortable with their own hegemony to consider opening themselves to the implications of the gospel.

National coverage of Lewis's falling-out with SNCC over Black Power was rooted in a white perspective. White Power had been acceptable since Jamestown. Now even the hint of Black Power was denounced as un-American. Citing the *Times* headline LEWIS QUITS S.N.C.C.; SHUNS BLACK POWER, Good observed, "The headline's partial truths fitted the rationale of a white society that had tolerated racial injustice for a century, yet denounced 'black power' in a day. At the same time, some in the society were paying sentimental homage to the good old days when Negroes faced fire hoses and police dogs with beatific smiles. Moderates lamented. If only Carmichael hadn't raised his raucous voice or Dr. King had stuck to nonviolence in the South instead of messing with Chicago housing or Vietnam. The rationale comforted Americans who had never been black, since it subtly shifted blame from oppressor to oppressed. Lewis, it followed, was a victim of his own kind."

On Friday, July 22, 1966, Lewis packed up his belongings at the SNCC offices in Atlanta. "It hurt," he recalled. "It hurt to leave my family, so many good brothers and sisters with whom I had shared so much. My ego was hurt as well. My feelings were hurt. I felt abandoned, cast out."

Thus began what was, for Lewis, his version of the oldest of biblical stories: that of exile. Adam and Eve were cast out of the garden; Abraham, Joseph, Moses, Elijah, David, Jesus, Paul, and John the Divine were all forced at times into the wilderness, away from friends and from the familiar, as were the people of Israel as a whole. "How," the psalmist asks, "shall we sing the Lord's song in a strange land?"

Lewis would have to find his own answer to that ancient query. Going home to Pike County wasn't an option. "My family had never really been connected to or understood my involvement in the movement," he recalled. "To them, it was as if I was living in a foreign country." He was given a job with the Field Foundation, headquartered in New York City, and caught a train north, into a kind of wilderness. He was overwhelmed with loneliness, with uncertainty. Not doubt; he kept his faith. But, as he'd said after Selma, a body gets tired. He was

In exile in New York after leaving SNCC, Lewis went to Riverside Church to hear Dr. King speak out on Vietnam in the spring of 1967. "It was about what we were doing in Vietnam," Lewis recalled, "but beyond that it was about what we were doing on this earth."

only twenty-six, but he had been buffeted by his sense of the Spirit of History for most of that quarter century. The impulse that had led him and his little cousin Della Mae to conspire to build a bus out of pine had shaped him for so long. He'd faced violence and the prospect of death again and again; suffered behind bars; seen double after beatings. He needed some time.

Once ranging widely over the South, from hotspot to hotspot and headline to headline, his world shrank. He rented a tiny apartment on West Twenty-first Street, in Chelsea, and would ride the subway to the foundation's offices at 250 Park Avenue. After work, he'd open a beer—always just one—and read the papers (the *Times,* the *New York Post,* and the *Amsterdam News*) or letters from Julian Bond back in Atlanta.

On Tuesday, April 4, 1967, he went up to Riverside Church to hear King give a major speech on the Vietnam War. "There is at the outset a very obvious and almost facile connection between the war in Vietnam and the struggle I and others have been waging in America," King said. "A few years ago there was a shining moment in that struggle. It seemed as if there was a real promise of hope for the poor, both black and white, through the poverty program. There were experiments, hopes, new beginnings. Then came the buildup in Vietnam, and I watched this program broken and eviscerated as if it were some idle political plaything of a society gone mad on war. And I knew that America would never invest the necessary funds or energies in rehabilitation of its poor so long as adventures like Vietnam continued to draw men and skills and money like some demonic, destructive suction tube. So I was increasingly compelled to see the war as an enemy of the poor and to attack it as such."

Lewis was struck afresh by King's insights and oratory. "I had heard Dr. King speak many, many times, and I had no doubt that this speech was his finest," Lewis recalled. "It was deep, comprehensive, thoughtful and courageous. It was about what we were doing in Vietnam, but beyond that it was about what we were doing on this *earth.*" Even as he was dwelling in a kind of exile, regathering his strength, Lewis held fast to an Augustinian sense of the movement of history. "I still believed, in the face of so much that seemed to be falling apart," he recalled, "that slowly, inexorably, in ways I might not be able to recognize or figure out, we were continuing to move in the direction we should, toward something better."

That faith would be sorely tested in 1968. He returned to Atlanta to work for the Southern Regional Council. During Lewis's 1967–68 wilderness period, James Bevel had tried to talk him into coming to work for King's SCLC. "But there was no way I would ever consider that," Lewis recalled. "I had been the national chair of a major organization. I'll admit it—it was a matter of pride, to a large degree.... How would I have looked if I returned as an Alabama field secretary for the SCLC? That would have been too much for me to take." Instead he completed his degree at Fisk by writing a paper on the civil rights movement and the church, an exposition of his understanding of the Social Gospel. "My central thesis was that the movement essentially amounted to a religious phenomenon," he recalled. "It was church-based, church-sanctioned.... The church, in a very real way, was the major gateway for the movement.... By giving its blessing to movement organizers, the church leadership opened the door to its membership, who may not have known or understood at first what we were about but who had complete faith in what their church elders told them."

In Atlanta, Bernard LaFayette and Xernona Clayton, another Lewis friend, had a thought: Lewis should meet an engaging, well-educated young woman from Los Angeles, Lillian Miles, who was working with Julian Bond's mother at Atlanta University. They set up a New Year's Eve dinner party; when a guest criticized King, Lillian defended Lewis's hero with gusto. "I was extremely impressed," Lewis recalled. "She not only had feelings about this, but she knew her facts as well." Lewis was interested, as was Lillian. "I was attracted to him before I knew him," Lillian recalled. "Every day and every night on the news was something about what was happening in the civil rights movement, so I felt like I knew him."

As he wryly recalled, Lewis made his move by hosting a birthday party for himself at his bachelor apartment. He'd splurged on a new record turntable, chips, dip, and beer, and had turned his hand to making barbecued chicken wings—the only arrow in his culinary quiver. Lillian arrived with Xernona Clayton, and Lewis was dazzled. Lillian wore a green minidress bedecked with peace symbols; she later admitted to Lewis that she had wanted "to impress me that night as much as I wanted to impress her." Where he was serious minded, she was serious minded *and* pragmatic, a powerful partner who played a significant role in his political career as a strategist and organizer. They married at Ebenezer in Atlanta just before Christmas 1968; Daddy King performed the service. In 1976 they would adopt a son, John-Miles Lewis.

The wedding was a bright spot in what had otherwise been the bloodiest and most tragic of years. On Saturday, March 16, 1968, Senator Robert Kennedy of New York announced a primary challenge to President Johnson, who was vulnerable amid the war in Vietnam. "I do not run for the presidency merely to oppose any man but to propose new policies," Kennedy said. "I run because I am convinced that this country is on a perilous course and because I have such strong feelings about what must be done, and I feel that I'm obliged to do all that I can. I run to seek new policies—policies to end the bloodshed in Vietnam and in our cities, policies to close the gaps that now exist between black and white, between rich and poor, between young and old, in this country and around the rest of the world."

For all their disagreements in the early years of the 1960s, Lewis and Kennedy now saw the world in a similar light. "The America Bobby Kennedy envisioned," Lewis recalled, "sounded much like the Beloved Community I believed in." When he heard RFK's announcement on television, he sent off a telegram: If I can be of help, let me know.

He could, and RFK did. Lewis became a Kennedy lieutenant in those rushed months, organizing the black vote. "He is the one guy who can bring people together," Lewis told a reporter, and Lewis was soon deployed to Indianapolis for the state's Democratic primary. On Sunday, March 31—the same day Martin Luther King preached the Sunday sermon at Washington National Cathedral—President Johnson withdrew from the race; now the Democratic campaign was between Kennedy, Vice President Hubert Humphrey, and Minnesota senator Eugene McCarthy. Indiana would be a crucial first test of the new political calculus.

As the afternoon of Thursday, April 4, faded, Lewis was in inner-city Indianapolis, awaiting his candidate's arrival. A big rally was in

James Lawson and Dr. King arrive at the Lorraine Motel in Memphis on Wednesday, April 3, 1968. King was shot to death the next day on that same balcony. Hearing the news, Lewis was devastated. "I was obliterated, blown beyond any sensations whatever," he recalled. "I was numb. Frozen."

the works. "The weather was brisk, overcast, but a large crowd had turned out, a good crowd, about a thousand people, almost all of them black, all of them upbeat, eager and excited to hear the man who might well be the next president of the United States," Lewis recalled. It was a moment of promise and of possibility: Kennedy was preaching the King-Lewis gospel of an interracial democracy, of a rising tide lifting all boats, of one nation, not competing tribes of race and class.

Then he heard the news. A Kennedy advance man, Walter Sheridan, was the messenger. "John," he said, "we just got word that Dr. King has been shot in Memphis."

Lewis went blank. King had been in Memphis to support a strike by sanitation workers; his main focus of late had been plans for the Poor People's Campaign, a massive demonstration in Washington in pursuit of economic justice. He was determined to attack the root causes of desperation. "And I contend that the cry of 'black power' is, at bottom, a reaction to the reluctance of white power to make the kind of changes necessary to make justice a reality for the Negro," King had said in September 1966. "I think that we've got to see that a riot is the language of the unheard. And, what is it that America has failed to hear? It has failed to hear that the economic plight of the Negro poor has worsened over the last few years."

In 1967, he had published a book, *Where Do We Go from Here: Chaos or Community?*, which, among other topics, advocated a guaranteed minimum income. From war and peace to jobs and housing, King was intent on ameliorating the plight of the poor, of bringing the Beloved Community closer to realization. "The nation is sick, trouble is in the land, confusion all around . . . ," King said on the night before he died. "But I know, somehow, that only when it is dark enough can you see the stars. . . . Something is happening in our world. The masses of people are rising up. And wherever they are assembled today . . . the cry is always the same: 'We want to be free.'" Systemic social justice was crucial. "In the human rights revolution, if something isn't done and done in a hurry to bring the colored peoples of the world out of their long years of poverty, their long years of hurt and neglect, the whole world is doomed."

Now he was gone. For Lewis, the grief was consuming, paralyzing, unspeakable. He had "no feeling," he recalled. "No thoughts. No words. I was obliterated, blown beyond any sensations whatsoever. I was numb. Frozen. Stunned stock-still, inside and out. I just stood there, not moving, not thinking, as the cold Indiana wind stirred the dirt around my feet."

En route to the rally, Robert Kennedy learned what had happened from R. W. Apple, Jr., of *The New York Times*. "His eyes went blank," Apple recalled to the RFK biographer Evan Thomas.

There was debate on the ground about what to do before Kennedy arrived. Should they cancel the rally? A veteran of violence and mass meetings, of pitched emotion and heartbreak, Lewis said no— Kennedy's place, he believed, was here. "Somebody has to speak to these people," Lewis remarked to the other campaign officials. "You can't have a crowd like this come, and something like this happen, and send them home without anything at all. Kennedy has to speak, for his own sake and for the sake of these people."

Sitting in a car awaiting the candidate, Lewis spoke to Kennedy on a two-way radio. "I'm sorry, John," Kennedy said. "You've lost a leader. *We've* lost a leader."

Shortly thereafter, wearing a trench coat of President Kennedy's, RFK broke the news to the crowd. "In this difficult day, in this difficult time for the United States, it is perhaps well to ask what kind of nation we are and what direction we want to move in," Kennedy said. He continued:

> For those of you who are black—considering the evidence there evidently is that there were white people who were responsible—you can be filled with bitterness, with hatred, and a desire for revenge. We can move in that direction as a country, in great polarization—black people amongst black, white people amongst white, filled with hatred toward one another.
>
> Or we can make an effort, as Martin Luther King did, to understand and to comprehend, and replace that violence, that stain of bloodshed that has spread across our land, with an effort to understand with compassion and love. . . .
>
> We've had difficult times in the past. We will have difficult times in the future. It is not the end of violence. It is not the end of lawlessness. It is not the end of disorder.
>
> But the vast majority of white people and the vast majority of black people in this country want to live together, want to improve the quality of our life, and want justice for all human beings who abide in our land.
>
> Let us dedicate ourselves to what the Greeks wrote so many years ago: to tame the savageness of man and to make gentle the life of this world.
>
> Let us dedicate ourselves to that, and say a prayer for our country, and for our people.

Coretta Scott King holds her youngest daughter, Bernice, then five, during funeral services for Dr. King at Ebenezer Baptist Church in Atlanta five days after he was assassinated.

Lewis heard the old notes of the movement in Kennedy's extemporaneous remarks, the rhythms of love, the cadences of compassion. In Atlanta, Lewis escorted Ethel and Robert Kennedy into Ebenezer Church to view King's open

To Lewis, Robert Kennedy was a man at once comfortable with power and conversant with the language of the Beloved Community. Lewis was in a fifth-floor suite at the Ambassador Hotel in Los Angeles when RFK, who had just given a victory speech after the California primary, was assassinated.

casket. It was late, the middle of the night; the sanctuary was illuminated by candlelight. The Kennedys made the sign of the cross; Lewis's mind ranged widely, and deeply. "Dr. King was my friend, my brother, my leader," he recalled. "He was the man, the one who opened my eyes to the world. From the time I was fifteen until the day he died—for almost half my life—he was the person who, more than any other, continued to influence my life, who made me who I was. He made me who I *am*."

At least, he reflected as they buried King in the Atlanta spring, the world still had Robert Kennedy.

They won Indiana; as *Newsweek* wrote, "In a painful era of racial polarization in the U.S.," Kennedy "managed to bridge the chasm separating the gut elements of the traditional Democratic coalition. He swept the Negro vote while at the same time piling up big leads among backlashy white workingmen—the same group that whistled Dixie for Alabama's George Wallace in the primary four years ago." Things were looking good, if not certain. Even after a win in the California primary in early June, the battle at the Democratic National Convention in Chicago would be fraught. And then came the gunshots in the kitchen of the Ambassador Hotel in Los Angeles. Now Robert Kennedy was dying.

Lewis was there, a part of the Kennedy retinue that had stayed upstairs in a fifth-floor suite. Watching the images of the shooting—yet *another* shooting—he fell to the floor. "I was crying, sobbing, heaving as if something had been busted open inside," Lewis recalled. "I sat on the floor, dazed, rocking back and forth . . . saying one word out loud, over and over again.

"*'Why? Why? Why?'*"

"Like Moses," Obama said of John Lewis and the movement generation, "they challenged Pharaoh." The forty-fourth president awarded Lewis the Presidential Medal of Freedom in 2011.

AGAINST THE RULERS OF THE DARKNESS

What can we do? We have to try, we have to seek, we have
to speak up. America can be saved.

—JOHN LEWIS

FORTY YEARS LATER, he was standing where King had stood. Set
thirteen steps above the nave of Washington National Cathedral, the stone Canterbury Pulpit looms ten feet high; its panels
depict scenes from the story of the English Bible, including an image
of King John and the nobles at Runnymede, signing the Magna Carta,
a turning point in the flow of power from the rulers to the ruled. As
Lewis arranged his notes before him on this Sunday, March 30, 2008,
four decades after King had done the same thing in the same place, he
looked up and took in the sweeping church, the rows of the flags of
the fifty states and territories hanging high, the light streaming in the
stained glass and through the great rose window on the far west wall.
He was there to preach—not to chickens, but to a congregation gathered in the capital city where he had now served as a member of Congress for more than two decades.

On this Sunday morning, Lewis reminded his listeners of the text
King had preached on that distant day in 1968. The lesson had come
from Revelation: "And I, John, saw the Holy City, new Jerusalem,
coming down from God out of heaven, prepared as a bride adorned
for her husband. And I heard a great voice out of heaven saying, 'Behold, the tabernacle of God is with men.'"

Not with *God,* but with *men.* "When I recall this sermon that Martin Luther King gave from this great pulpit 40 years ago, when I think
about what Gandhi was saying more than 100 years ago and what
those who are pressing for peace, for environmental justice, for uni-

versal health care and human dignity are saying today, I believe that they are saying what John said and they are telling us that the tabernacle of God is with us," Lewis said. "They are saying that it is our responsibility; it is our duty; it is our job to create the tabernacle here on earth. We are the children of God and as people of faith we are called to actualize the fruits of the Spirit to make them real in our nation, in our government, and in our own lives."

Looking back on the King years, Lewis evoked the old vision anew. "We truly believed that through the discipline and nonviolence, through the power of peace and the power of love, that we could transform this nation into something Martin Luther King, Jr., called a Beloved Community," Lewis said. "This was our conscious goal. We worked, we struggled, and we suffered to make that dream a reality. Consider those two words: *Beloved Community.* 'Beloved' meaning not hateful, not violent, not uncaring, not unkind, and 'Community' meaning not separated, not polarized, not locked in struggle; the Beloved Community is an all-inclusive world society based on simple justice, the values, the dignity, and the worth of every human being, and that is the Kingdom of God." He alluded to Saint Paul's Epistle to the Ephesians, a mission text among the disciples of the movement he had known: "For we wrestle not against flesh and blood, but against principalities, against powers, against the rulers of the darkness of this world."

He knew of what he spoke. The movement of which Lewis had been an integral part had done more to change America for the better than any single domestic undertaking since the Civil War, joining emancipation and women's suffrage as brilliant chapters in an uneven yet unfolding national story. As a young man—little more than a child, really—he had contended against evil with everything he had. And he had prevailed. As always in human affairs, the question was: What now? Was Lewis a relic of a bygone age, a comfortable emblem of lost days, a heroic figure from a vanished world? Or did the truth he had intuited in Troy, the worldview he had formulated in Jim Lawson's workshops in Nashville, the scars he bore from Rock Hill, Montgomery, and Selma—could these things illuminate life in America in the twenty-first century?

Lewis believed so. "If Martin Luther King, Jr., were here today, he would still be saying we are all in this together," he said. "Maybe, just maybe he would say to us today that our forefathers and our fore-mothers all came here in a different ship to this land, to this great country, but we are all now in the same boat. Maybe in a different ship, but we are all now in the same boat. He would be saying that it doesn't matter whether we are black or white or Hispanic or Asian American or Native American, whether we are Democrats or Republicans or independent, that we are one people. We are one house. We are one family. It doesn't matter, we have to find a way to live together. We have to find a way to understand each other. We have to find a way to make peace with each other."

So easy to say, so easy to quote. But there's nothing harder to do, nothing harder to put into action, nothing harder to translate from sentiment to substance, than the message Lewis preached that Sunday. "I have a deep sense of restlessness," Lewis told the author in 2020. "I wish I could say more, do more, to save us, to press on." Yet he tried.

After the murders of King and Robert Kennedy, Lewis and Lillian began their married lives in Atlanta. "I don't have any doubt that we lost something with the deaths of those two leaders that year—in the wake of the death five years earlier of John Kennedy—that as a nation we will never recover," Lewis recalled. "Call it innocence or trust. . . . But still, we do what we can." For him, the sphere of action soon moved from the streets to the corridors of elected power. "Ever since I became involved in Bobby Kennedy's campaign, I'd been con-vinced that politics was the road we must now take to achieve the goals we had pursued until then through direct action," Lewis recalled. "Now that the primary purpose of those years of action—securing the right to vote—had been achieved, it was time to show black Ameri-cans in the South not only that they could select their representatives but that it was possible to *become* those representatives."

He lost a congressional race in 1977—the seat had opened up after the incumbent, Andrew Young, had resigned to become Jimmy Cart-er's ambassador to the United Nations—but he won a seat on the Atlanta City Council in 1981. Five years later, he and Julian Bond squared off for the U.S. House of Representatives. Bond was hand-some and charismatic. Lewis remained Lewis: serene and at times plodding. "Throughout my years in the movement . . . people had always underestimated me," Lewis recalled. "With my background—the poor farm boy from the woods—and my personality—so unassuming and steady—people tended to assume I was soft, pliable, that I could be bent to their needs." If they thought that, they should have checked in with Sheriff Jim Clark.

The 1986 congressional campaign was brutal. A battle between old friends and comrades, the contest was between the polished Bond, who had hosted *Saturday Night Live* and been named one of *Cosmopolitan*'s ten sexiest men, and the far less glamorous Lewis, who didn't mind making the contrasts between them clear. In the movement days, Lewis said, Bond "worked for me. He got out press releases, sent telegrams. I was on the front lines in Montgomery, Birmingham, Mississippi. He stayed back in Atlanta. I'm not saying this in a negative way. He did a good job." Lest anyone miss the point, though, Lewis chose another image to underscore his argument in an interview with *The Washington Post*'s Art Harris: "He's a tail-light rather than a head-light." Rumors swirled about Bond's alleged drug use—it was the cocaine-fueled eighties—and Lewis pointedly said he was happy to take a drug test. (Bond declined.) In the end, buoyed by large margins among the district's minority of white voters, Lewis won.

Congress would consume the rest of his days. "It was another step, serving in the Congress of the United States," Lewis said. "A step down a very long road. The results are harder to see, but the work goes on. When people say, and they sometimes do, that things aren't better now than they were in the sixties, I say, 'Come and walk in my shoes.' We are a better people now in spite of everything. In the final analysis, we're good, we're decent. Yes, we still have miles to go, but that's what a journey is, that's what a march is: Putting one foot in front of the other."

Did he miss the clarity of the movement? "I do, I do," he said. "The movement was real. The movement was clear. There was nothing ambiguous about what we wanted, nothing uncertain about WHITE ONLY and COLORED ONLY signs. A sign—a society—saying, 'You have to go here, you can't go there.' Our job was to 'Make it plain,' which was the advice Daddy King used to give Dr. King when Dr. King was preaching. Daddy King believed you had to make the gospel totally clear, and he thought his son sometimes took things too high, too abstract, talking about theology and quoting these wonderful thinkers. 'Make it plain, son,' Daddy King would say. And that is what we tried to do in the movement: Make it plain."

Lewis was the most reliable of Democratic votes in the House of Representatives through the administrations of Ronald Reagan, George H. W. Bush, Bill Clinton, George W. Bush, Barack Obama, and Donald Trump. His years in Congress were not as overtly remarkable as his years in the movement, but his was an unusual House career. He was arrested five times as a member of Congress—twice at the embassy of South Africa to protest apartheid, twice at the embassy of Sudan to protest the genocide in Darfur, and once at the U.S. Capitol to call for immigration reform. Always mindful of voting rights, Lewis refused to attend the inauguration of George W. Bush in 2001 as a protest against voting irregularities in Florida and the Supreme Court's intervention in the election—*Bush v. Gore* had stopped a recount in Florida, giving Bush the presidency over Al Gore, who won the national popular vote. Yet Lewis then worked with both President Bush and Laura Bush as part of a long effort to build the National Museum of African American History and Culture on the Washington Mall. After a massacre at an Orlando nightclub—only one of a number of mass shootings in the country—Lewis led a 2016 sit-in on the floor of the House to try to force the then-Republican majority to bring a gun-reform bill to a vote. "We have been too quiet for too long," Lewis said. "There comes a time when you have to say something. You have to make a little noise. You have to move your feet. This is the time. How many more mothers? How many more fathers need to shed tears of grief before we do something? Give us a vote. Let us vote. We came here to do our job. We came here to work." He sponsored the Emmett Till Unsolved Civil Rights Crime Act, empowering prosecutors to pursue racially motivated killings committed before 1979.

Lewis was devoted to preserving and passing on the lessons of the 1950s and '60s. As a teenager he had read a comic-book rendering of the bus boycott, *Martin Luther King and the Montgomery Story;* nearly sixty years later, from 2013 to 2016, Lewis published *March,* a popular trilogy of graphic novels on the movement. The third volume won the National Book Award for young people's literature on the same 2016

"A young person should be speaking out for what is fair, what is just, what is right,"
Lewis said fifty-five years after Selma. "Speak out for those who have been left out and
left behind."

evening Ibram X. Kendi was recognized for *Stamped from the Beginning: The Definitive History of Racist Ideas in America,* and Colson Whitehead was honored for the novel *The Underground Railroad.* The ceremony took place only days after Donald Trump had won the presidency, and National Public Radio asked Lewis about the election. "The past week has made me feel like I'm living my life all over again—that we have to fight some of the same fights," Lewis said. "To see some of the bigotry, the hate, I think there are forces that want to take us back."

Horrified by the rise of Trump (whose inaugural he also skipped), Lewis was eloquent during the debates over impeaching the forty-fifth president. In calling for the inquiry, Lewis said, "Sometimes I am afraid to go to sleep for fear that I will wake up and our democracy will be gone and never return." On the day of the House vote, he spoke passionately. "This is a sad day," he said on the floor in late 2019. "This is not a day of joy. Our nation is founded on the principle that we don't have kings. We have presidents, and the Constitution is our compass. When you see something that is not right, not just, not fair, you have a moral obligation to say something, to do something." In closing, Lewis declared, "We have a mission, and we have a mandate to be on the right side of history."

In the late spring of 2020, police in Minneapolis killed George

Floyd, provoking global outrage. Lewis wept when he saw the video of a white officer kneeling on Floyd's neck for eight minutes and forty-six seconds. Carrying a cane, the ailing Lewis toured the large Black Lives Matter mural commissioned by Washington mayor Muriel Bowser, who joined him for the early morning visit on 16th Street NW, across from the White House. "It's very moving. Very moving. Impressive," Lewis told reporters. "I think the people in D.C. and around the nation are sending a mightily powerful and strong message to the rest of the world that we *will* get there."

But *how* do we get there in the face of systemic racism? After Floyd's death, former president Barack Obama hosted a virtual town meeting that included Lewis, who drew on his own experience to offer some measure of hope. The victories over segregation in the South were not foreordained, and battles won can seem less daunting than they actually were. To Lewis, witness and determination brought the country forward—not forward to the Promised Land, not yet, but still forward. He believed this generation could do the same. "To see all of the young people," Lewis said, "all of the young men, not just men of color but black, white, Latino, Asian American, Native American, all of the young women, standing up, speaking up, being prepared to march—they're going to help redeem the soul of America, and save our country, and maybe help save the planet."

Obama got it: The lesson of Lewis was that sustained personal witness to injustice, borne in the public arena where opinions are shaped, laws enacted, and reality changed, is vital. "John's tough, but he's kind of a little dude," Obama remarked fondly at the town hall. "You would not know that that young man could awaken a nation. And that's an example of the power that we each have."

For a long time Lewis was a kind of living monument. The Princeton historian Sean Wilentz profiled him as "The Last Integrationist" in *The New Republic* in the mid-1990s; Obama embraced Lewis on the inaugural platform just moments before the president-elect took the oath of office to become the first African American president of the United States on Tuesday, January 20, 2009.

Lewis had not supported Obama at first. Out of loyalty to a long-time ally and friend, Lewis had endorsed Senator Hillary Rodham Clinton of New York, whom he'd known through her work with Marian Wright Edelman at the Children's Defense Fund in the 1970s. Obama's success in the 2008 primaries, especially among African American voters in districts like Lewis's, changed the congressman's thinking. "Something is happening in America," Lewis said in announcing his reversal. "There is a movement, there is a spirit, there is an enthusiasm in the hearts and minds of the American people that I have not seen in a long time, since the candidacy of Robert Kennedy. The people are pressing for a new day in American politics, and I think they see Senator Barack Obama as a symbol of that change. . . . I want to be on the side of the people, on the side of the spirit of history."

The decision also had its practical aspects. There was talk in African American circles that Lewis wasn't in sync with the flow of politics in the new century—and a primary opponent filed to challenge Lewis in Atlanta. "I understand he's been under tremendous pressure," Hillary Clinton said at the time. "He's been my friend. He will always be my friend." Looking back in 2020, Clinton said, "It was just too hard for John, and I totally understood that. It was a very difficult decision." In the Clinton-Obama primary, the struggle for women's equality and advancement and the struggle for African American equality and advancement were in tension with one another. "That was a historic contest, and many people were torn," Clinton recalled. In 2016, Lewis was back by her side. "He's saintly, but he's also a fighter, a warrior for peace and justice," Clinton recalled. "He's given his heart, his mind, his soul, and his body for the Beloved Community. He's never wavered on the big things."

At a Bloody Sunday commemoration at Brown Chapel in 2007, as Obama was beginning his run for the presidency, the young Illinois senator had addressed an audience that included Lewis and many of the marchers of old. Obama mentioned a letter he'd received from the Reverend Otis Moss, Jr., of Cleveland, Ohio. The senator was facing questions about whether he was too much of a young man in a hurry, but the Reverend Moss turned to scripture to reassure him. "He said, 'If there's some folks out there who are questioning whether or not you should run, just tell them to look at the story of Joshua, because you're part of the Joshua generation.'" At Canaan's edge, after forty years in the wilderness, Moses was not fated to reach the Promised

Land. It would be Joshua, his successor, who would lead Israel forward. John Lewis was a Moses; Obama was a Joshua. "We're in the presence today of giants whose shoulders we stand on," Obama said, "people who battled, not just on behalf of African Americans but on behalf of all of America; that battled for America's soul, that shed blood, that endured taunts and torment and in some cases gave the full measure of their devotion." Obama went on, "Like Moses, they challenged Pharaoh, the princes, the powers who said that some are at the top and others are at the bottom, and that's how it's always going to be."

But it wasn't going to always be that way. "I'm here because somebody marched," Obama said. "I'm here because you all sacrificed for me. I stand on the shoulders of giants. I thank the Moses generation; but we've got to remember, now, that Joshua still had a job to do. . . . We're going to leave it to the Joshua generation to make sure it happens. There are still battles that need to be fought; some rivers that need to be crossed."

He came back to Selma as president of the United States. "We do a disservice to the cause of justice by intimating that bias and discrimination are immutable, that racial division is inherent to America," Obama said at Selma in 2015. "If you think nothing's changed in the past 50 years, ask somebody who lived through the Selma or Chicago or Los Angeles of the 1950s. Ask the female CEO who once might have been assigned to the secretarial pool if nothing's changed. Ask your gay friend if it's easier to be out and proud in America now than it was thirty years ago. To deny this progress, this hard-won progress— our progress—would be to rob us of our own agency, our own capacity, our responsibility to do what we can to make America better."

Hailing Lewis, who led the "mighty march," Obama concluded, "Our job's easier because somebody already got us through that first mile. Somebody already got us over that bridge. When it feels the road is too hard, when the torch we've been passed feels too heavy, we will remember these early travelers, and draw strength from their example, and hold firmly the words of the prophet Isaiah: 'Those who hope in the Lord will renew their strength. They will soar on wings like eagles. They will run and not grow weary. They will walk and not be faint.'"

The scripture captured it all. "It was religion that got us on the buses for the Freedom Rides," Lewis recalled. "We were in Selma that day because of our faith."

At the beginning of the third decade of the twenty-first century, a moment when right-wing populism and white nationalism appear resurgent, Lewis's life and message remain powerfully relevant. It is true that his vision has been somewhat out of fashion at least since 1966, when he lost the chairmanship of SNCC at Kingston Springs. And yet Lewis's unyielding embrace of nonviolence and pursuit of the Beloved Community echoes still.

Those echoes are heard in an America of recent vintage. In many ways the nation is a product of 1965. There was the Voting Rights Act, and October '65 brought the Immigration and Nationality Act, which abolished national quotas and opened the way for the tides of immigration that will help bring the proportion of white Americans below 50 percent of the population by 2045. Other Great Society programs—federal aid to education, the creation of Medicare and Medicaid—expanded the role of government and, along with the civil and voting rights measures, helped lead to a conservative reaction. As early as the midterms of 1966, Ronald Reagan won the governorship of California, and the Republicans picked up forty-seven seats in the U.S. House and three in the Senate. "I think we can claim a mandate from the people; that if any backlash was present, it was a backlash against the Great Society," Governor-elect Reagan wrote a Republican congressman a month after the midterms. The GOP gains foreshadowed Richard Nixon's 1968 victory over Hubert Humphrey and George Wallace (who carried five Southern states and 13.5 percent of the popular vote on a segregationist third-party ticket).

Action and reaction; push and pull: American politics is cyclical and changeable. The movement that culminated in the middle of the 1960s had been at least a century in the making, if not longer. Viewed historically, the remarkable thing is not the persistence of injustice, but that Lewis and his comrades were able to do as much as they did in the pursuit of justice in the face of overwhelming, and violent, opposition. Asked what someone who is the age now that he was when, at nineteen and twenty years old, he set out to desegregate Nashville,

Lewis replied, "A young person should be speaking out for what is fair, what is just, what is right. Speak out for those who have been left out and left behind. That is how the movement goes on."

Go on it must. The problems that disproportionately affect people of color in America are profound. The end of Jim Crow laws did not end systemic poverty, limited opportunity, discrimination, disparities in health outcomes and environmental conditions, barriers to voting, the incidence of violence, deadly encounters with law enforcement—the list is long. Reparations for slavery and segregation are perhaps the most tangled yet urgent question in the politics of race, and Lewis was, at the end, open to that conversation. "I think there should be some way to recognize the sufferings of African Americans and the neglect of the rights of African Americans," he told the author in May 2020. "We have come a distance, but not the full distance. I'm not sure what form it should take—whether it should be silver and gold, dollars, or what exactly. But we should find ways to make people a little more whole."

John Lewis's life is a reminder that progress, however limited, is possible, and that religiously inspired witness and action can help bring about such progress. "The saintly character," William James argued, "is the character for which spiritual emotions are the habitual center of the personal energy." To James, the first test of such a character was a "feeling of being in a wider life than that of this world's selfish little interests; and a conviction, not merely intellectual, . . . of the existence of an Ideal Power." Lewis did not doubt that Ideal Power, and the Christian story to which he gave his heart and his mind and his spirit commands us to open our arms, not to clench our fists. To give, not to take. To see, not to look away.

It can be easy to consign the philosophy of nonviolence to history. And it's easy to dismiss warm words about John Lewis as gauzy and sentimental. But before waving his story off as a Sunday school lesson, consider this: Did his life have consequence? Do we live in a better or a worse nation because of him? If the answer to the latter is that the America of today, for all its injustices, is more just than it was when, in the winter of 1959–60, Lewis walked out of ABT's Griggs Hall on the hill overlooking the Cumberland River in Nashville and decided to take a stand by sitting in, then his story should be told as long as the

Republic endures—and beyond, for if the Republic were to fall, it might well rise again if enough of us were to conduct ourselves as the sons and daughters of the civil rights movement did.

This is not a fairy tale. This is history. And history honors the marchers at Selma, not the mounted possemen; the children of Birmingham, not Bull Connor. In a survey conducted by Gallup at the turn of the millennium, the American public ranked the 1964 Civil Rights Act as the fifth most important event of the twentieth century, outranked only by World War II, women's suffrage, the Holocaust, and the dropping of the atomic bomb on Hiroshima. The civil rights legislation was seen as more significant than World War I, the landing of men on the moon, the assassination of President Kennedy, the fall of the Berlin Wall, and the Great Depression. The Voting Rights Act empowered African American voters throughout the South, bringing millions of previously excluded people into full citizenship. Black elected officials, particularly at the local level, became commonplace in the Old Confederacy; in Dallas County, Alabama, for example, Jim Clark was defeated for reelection as sheriff in 1966. He'd published a ghostwritten memoir. Its title: *The Jim Clark Story: I Saw Selma Raped.* Jim Clark would turn to selling mobile homes. John Lewis would go on to Congress.

They both made history. The question for Americans is what kind of history we want people to make—the kind Jim Clark made, or the kind John Lewis made. Individual decisions, individual dispositions of heart and of mind, matter enormously, even if change often feels out of reach. "It is not so much the powerful leaders that determine our destiny," Eleanor Roosevelt, who once dreamed of sitting in and marching with the students of the South, wrote, "as the much more powerful influence of the combined voice of the people themselves." Reason enough to listen to John Lewis's singular voice once more.

He is telling the old story. In a sunlit conference room on Capitol Hill in the early autumn of 2019, Lewis is, in memory, back in Selma, back on the bridge, back in front of the blue line of troopers and possemen. He is imagining the tear gas and the nightsticks and the clop-clop-clop of the cavalry on the concrete. Reaching the point in his narrative where he is lying, bloodied, and prepared to die, Lewis's voice catches. "But I didn't want to die," he says. "I wanted to live. And somehow, and some way, I lived."

He pauses, unable to go on. Tears come to his eyes. He asks for a moment. "I thought I would make it through" the interview, Lewis says, apologizing. "I'm embarrassed to be crying. This just happens sometimes. To relive that day."

He reaches for a handkerchief. "I'm embarrassed to cry," he repeats. Gathering himself, he takes the long view. "It's okay. . . . It's all right. Sometimes it's good for the soul."

In the twilight, images of the movement would come to him in his sleep. "Oh, God, yes, I dream about those days," Lewis said shortly before he succumbed to cancer and died at home in Atlanta on Friday, July 17, 2020. "I dream of marching, of singing. I hear the music of the movement in my dreams, and the sounds of our feet on the pavement, one after another. I don't have nightmares—I don't relive the beatings in my dreams, at least not that I ever remember. I'm not sure why. Maybe in my mind the good forces are always at work. There is a power of the mind to believe and think on the higher drama of it, the higher things of it, the light, not the dark. We truly believed that we were on God's side, and in spite of everything—the beatings, the bombings, the burnings—God's truth would prevail. Sometimes I'll dream of a march, of moving forward, of light and warmth and happiness. And then I'll wake up and think, 'Oh, that was just a dream.' But you have to believe that it can be real, that it can be more than a dream."

Lewis tours Black Lives Matter Plaza, across from the White House and Lafayette Park, in Washington, D.C., June 2020.

AFTERWORD
By John Lewis

I CAME OF AGE in a segregated America. The message of the civil rights movement was straightforward, and it was a message grounded in hope: We are one people; we are one family; we all live in the same house—the American house, the world house. As Martin Luther King, Jr., taught us, whenever and wherever we saw injustice, we had a moral obligation to say something, to do something, to speak up and speak out. We might get arrested, we might be thrown in jail, we might be beaten, we might be left bloody, or we might be left for dead. But we couldn't stop.

It became a way of life for many young people. The first time I got arrested demonstrating—it was in Nashville, Tennessee, sixty years ago—for speaking up and speaking out against segregation and racial discrimination, I felt free. I felt liberated. I felt as if I had crossed over. It made me a stronger and better person. And eventually, because of the civil rights movement, America became stronger and better.

We must now rededicate ourselves to the ideas and to the actions that accomplished so much good when I was a young man, when the students of the American South helped lead the way, when justice was denied and too many dreams were deferred.

We won the battles of the 1960s. But the war for justice, the war to make America both great and good, goes on. We the People are not a united people right now. We rarely are, but our divisions and our tribalism are especially acute. Many Americans have lost faith in the idea that what binds us together is more important than what separates us. Now as before, we have to choose, as Dr. King once put it, between community and chaos.

We chose community once, in the 1960s, and I believe we can choose community once more. While our problems may seem less clear-cut than the segregated signs of Jim Crow and the obstructionism of voting registrars, the means by which America redeemed part of her soul then can guide us now. When you see something you believe is unfair or unjust, you have to say so.

Silence is not the answer. So much of what makes America truly great is hanging in the balance—our openness to immigrants, our treatment of the poor, our protection of a free and fair right to vote, our care of the climate, our expansion of economic opportunity, our attitude toward our political foes. Fear is abroad in the land, and we must gather the forces of hope and march once more.

The spirit of Dr. King lives with us. The civil rights movement brought about a nonviolent revolution—a revolution in values, a revolution in ideas. The soul force of this movement enabled America to find its moral compass.

I have long believed—I have long preached—that our nation's moral compass comes from God, it is of God, and it is seen through God. And God so loved the world that he gave us the countless men and women who lost their homes and their jobs for the right to vote. God gave us the children of freedom who lost their lives in a bombing in Birmingham and the three young men who were killed in Mississippi. But above all else God gave us courage—the power to believe that what I call the Spirit of History behind us is stronger than the terror of hatred in front of us. That is what I believed then. And I believe it now.

How to march forward? We all can study our history and thus learn what has worked in the past and therefore might just work in the present and in the future. We all can be trained to find our way or to get in the way. The teaching of individuals like James Lawson, Gandhi, and Dr. King lift us. They move us, and they tell us over and over again if another person can do just that, if another generation can get in the way or get in what I call good trouble, necessary trouble, I, too, can do something. I, too, can get in trouble for the greater good.

In the 1960s, the forces of the civil rights movement sensitized and educated a nation. I remember Attorney General Robert Kennedy saying to us on one occasion, "We now understand."

That was the power of the way of peace, the way of love, the way of nonviolence. By appealing to the conscience of the nation, we could say to elected officials, and to the larger American community, "We *can* change. We *can* help create the Beloved Community. We *can* help redeem the soul of America and lift America, lift our country, lift our people to higher heights." That's what the movement did. And if the movement could do it in the face of Bull Connor and Jim Clark, we can do it again now, however difficult the struggle may seem.

There are forces today in America trying to divide people along racial lines. There are forces today that are still preaching hate and division. There are forces today that want us to return to the old ways, to lose ground, to take our eyes off the prize. It makes me sad, for we don't want to go back. We want to go forward and create one community—one America.

The journey begins with faith—faith in the dignity and the worth of every human being. That is an idea with roots in scripture and in the canon of America, in Genesis and in the Declaration of Independence. The journey is sustained by persistence—persistence in the pressing of the justice of the cause. And the journey is informed by hope—hope that someday, in some way, our restless souls will bring heaven and earth together, and God will wipe away every tear.

I think there's something brewing in America that's going to bring people closer and closer together. Adversity can breed unity; hatred can give way to love. We need a leadership of love now, a strong leadership to lift us, to transport us, to remind us that God's truth is marching on. We can do it. We must do it. We have to go forward as one people, one family, one house. I believe in it. I believe we can do it.

Within all of us there is the spark of the divine that helps us and moves us. This force is part of our DNA. Maybe it's planted by God Almighty, and we have to use it for good, to be the best we can be.

We've come too far, we've made too much progress as a people, to stand still or to slip back. When I was growing up there was a song that people would sing in the church:

I'm so glad trouble don't last always
O my Lord, O my Lord . . .

You have to believe that. You have to believe it. It's all going to work out.

Author's Note and Acknowledgments

———————

THE ROOM WAS CROWDED, the hum of Election Night gossip rising. On the evening of Tuesday, November 24, 1992, the voters of Georgia had gone to the polls in a runoff to choose a U.S. senator in the aftermath of Bill Clinton's defeat of President George H. W. Bush. The incumbent, Democrat Wyche Fowler, faced a Republican challenger, Paul Coverdell, and the leading Democratic lights in the state were gathering in an Atlanta hotel to follow the close-run results. Senator Fowler was upstairs, huddled with advisers and allies. It was still early, and one barometer of power on such a night is not ubiquity but elusiveness. In traditional terms, the more important a figure is when the votes are being counted, the less one sees of them. The politically astute maintain their mystique by remaining out of sight, presumably consumed with opaque but essential tasks, like an ancient priest, communing with the gods in an inner sanctum while the common folk stand outside, waiting.

John Lewis, however, stood among the people. He was with his wife, Lillian Miles Lewis, greeting his fellow Georgia Democrats and keeping an eye on the televised returns. He didn't need to be seen as powerful; his status was secure, his standing unassailable. That evening, I was there as a reporter for *The Chattanooga Times,* my hometown newspaper. During a brief exchange, I asked Lewis, who had just won his fourth term as a member of Congress from an Atlanta congressional district, what it was like to have traveled as far as he had—from being beaten for asking for the right to vote to being hailed as a hero of human rights.

"We have come so far," he answered in his deep, slow, preacherly voice. "All of us, all of us in the South, in America. So far. And we have so far to go. The way of the civil rights movement was the way of love, of respect, of the dignity of every person. Not just black, not just white, not just male, not just female, but every person."

But that was then—a moment of clarity, of intensity, of drama. How do you keep that up when there aren't Bull Connors around, no WHITE ONLY signs? It's so much harder, isn't it?

With a steady gaze, he replied, "We marched for what the Reverend Martin Luther King, Jr."—Lewis said the full name, almost as an incantation—"called 'the Beloved Community.' He wanted to make love real, to give the gospel some *legs*—and he taught us that we have to use not only voices but there comes a time when you have to use your *feet*. And *that* march, the march for love, *that* march doesn't end."

In the ensuing years, I spent time with Lewis in Washington, New York City, Nashville, Sewanee, Montgomery, Birmingham, and Selma. We also occasionally spoke by telephone, usually after a major news event or on the marking of an important civil rights anniversary. Sometimes we held formal interviews; on other occasions we simply conversed. I drew on these exchanges, as well as interviews in 2020, for this book.

This is not a full-scale biography. It is, rather, an appreciative account of the major moments of Lewis's life in the movement, of the theological understanding he brought to the struggle, and of the utility of that vision as America enters the third decade of the twenty-first century amid division and fear.

Lewis generously made himself available to me for this project, and as readers will see, I am indebted to his remarkable autobiography, published in 1998, *Walking with the Wind*. The British historian J. H. Plumb once observed that Winston Churchill's histories of World War II left posterity to "move down the broad avenues which he drove through war's confusion and complexity." So, too, with Lewis's book, co-authored with Michael D'Orso. The diplomat Dean Acheson remarked that no man comes out second-best in his own memorandum of conversation. The same might be said of one's own memoir, but the book Lewis and D'Orso wrote is candid, reflective, affecting, and enduring. I quote from it often in these pages to understand how a sharecropper's son played a pivotal role in bringing a great nation to moral account.

The middle of March 1965 marks a high point in American life, an hour of hope in the long and still-unfolding struggle to achieve true and equal justice for all. President Lyndon B. Johnson, soon to be undone by the war in Vietnam, went to Congress eight days after John Lewis and others had led a peaceful march in Selma that was viciously and violently broken up by white authorities. In his speech that night, Johnson invoked the anthem of the movement. "There cannot be anyone alive who knows the names of all the children who carried us and Mr. Johnson to the place where he stood last night," the New York columnist Murray Kempton wrote of LBJ's "We Shall Overcome" address.

That was true. But we know one of their names: John Robert Lewis.

I am indebted to Michael Collins and Brenda Jones, who have long served Congressman Lewis with grace and distinction, for their assistance and kindnesses. Joan Mooney of the Faith & Politics Institute was unfailingly helpful. I am grateful, too, to Michael D'Orso, the coauthor of Lewis's 1998 memoir.

Historians, journalists, and scholars with interests in these matters have long been guides, especially Eddie Glaude, Jr.; Annette Gordon-Reed; Peniel Joseph; Taylor Branch; David Remnick; John Huey; Michael Eric Dyson; David J. Garrow; Charles Peters; Nicholas Lemann; Vern E. Smith; David Halberstam; Karl Fleming, Dick Kopper, John Popham; John Seigenthaler, Sr.; and John Egerton. And I look forward to David Greenberg's work-in-progress, a full-scale Lewis biography; it will doubtless be essential reading. I am perennially grateful to Paul Neely and to the late Ruth Sulzberger Holmberg of *The Chattanooga Times*. My friends Evan Thomas and Michael Beschloss were, as ever, stalwart and gracious. Both read early pages and improved them with their wisdom, as did my friend and editor Porscha Burke.

Jonathan L. Walton, Dean of the School of Divinity, Presidential Chair of Religion and Society, and Dean of Wait Chapel at Wake Forest University, was an invaluable and generous reader of the manuscript. Annette Gordon-Reed and Eddie Glaude were also kind to advise me on the pages. I am, of course, solely responsible for the results.

For kindnesses large and small, my thanks to Allida Black, the founding editor of the Eleanor Roosevelt Papers; Andy Brennan; Dave DiBenedetto of *Garden & Gun*; Clay Risen of *The New York Times*;

John Seigenthaler, Jr.; Zach Johnson; Harold Ford, Jr.; Amanda Urban; Jonathan Karp; Rachel Adler; Barbara DiVittorio; Freddy Ford; Nick Merrill; Michelle Smith; Evan Rosenblum, who handled text permissions; Carol Poticny, who did her characteristically excellent job of photo research; and Jeff Flannery, head of the Library of Congress Manuscript Reading Room. Peter Kunhardt, George Kunhardt, Teddy Kunhardt, and Katie Davison shared unused footage from their documentary *The Soul of America* with me, as well as supporting materials from their award-winning film *King in the Wilderness.* At Vanderbilt University, Nicholas S. Zeppos, Susan Wente, John Geer, Alan Wiseman, David Lewis, Josh Clinton, and John S. Beasley II are wonderful colleagues. Michael E. Shepherd researched and produced the appendix on public opinion about the civil rights movement; he is a preternaturally wise political scientist. At *Time* and *Newsweek,* I learned much from Rick Smith, Maynard Parker, Mark Whitaker, Ann McDaniel, Howard Fineman, Rick Stengel, Nancy Gibbs, Michael Duffy, and Edward Felsenthal.

At Random House, my longtime home, I am grateful to Gina Centrello, Kate Medina, Noa Shapiro, Andy Ward, Avideh Bashirrad, Benjamin Dreyer, Rebecca Berlant, the long-suffering but always gracious Dennis Ambrose, Sandra Sjursen, Richard Elman, Paolo Pepe, Carole Lowenstein, Simon Sullivan, Maria Braeckel, Michelle Jasmine, Susan Corcoran, Barbara Fillon, Katie Tull, and Matthew Martin.

I am fortunate beyond words to work with Michael Hill, Margaret Shannon, Jack Bales, and Merrill Fabry, all of whom are the best at what they do.

And as always, my deepest and most enduring thanks—and, more important, love—to Keith, Mary, Maggie, and Sam.

Appendix

THE PUBLIC AND THE ELECTORATE BEFORE, DURING, AND AFTER THE CIVIL RIGHTS MOVEMENT

The author is indebted to Michael E. Shepherd of Vanderbilt University for the data and analysis in this appendix.

Civil Rights Events

Throughout the 1950s and 1960s, the Gallup and Harris organizations surveyed respondents (most of whom were white) to gauge opinions about the civil rights movement that unfolded from the *Brown v. Board of Education* decision in 1954 through the passages of the Civil Rights Act of 1964 and the Voting Rights Act of 1965.

EVENT/MILESTONE (DATE OF SURVEY)	APPROVE / FAVORABLE OPINION	DISAPPROVE/ UNFAVORABLE
Brown v. BOE (1954)	55%	40%
Freedom Riders/Rides (1961)	22%	61%
March on Washington (1965)	23%	60%
Civil Rights Act (1966)	58%	31%

Source: Survey data from the Gallup and Harris organizations. Accessed via "Public Opinion Polls on Civil Rights Movement, 1961–1969." Civil Rights Movement Archive, CRMVET.org. https://www.crmvet.org/docs/60s_crm_public-opinion.pdf.

In March 1965, Gallup also asked, "In the recent showdown in Selma, Alabama over Negro voting rights, have you tended to side more with the civil rights groups or with the State of Alabama?" Less than half of respondents (48 percent) sided with civil rights activists. Twenty-one percent sided with the state of Alabama and 31 percent reported supporting neither or were not sure who they sided with.

White Attitudes Toward Protest and Demonstrations

At various points throughout the 1960s, Gallup and Harris asked Americans (again, mostly white and sometimes exclusively white samples) whether protests and demonstrations were helping the cause for racial equality.

Question	Fielded	% Has Hurt	% Has Helped
Do you think "sit-ins" at lunch counters, "freedom buses," and other demonstrations by Negroes will hurt or help the Negro's chances of being integrated in the South? [Gallup]	May 1961	57%	28%
Do you think mass demonstrations by Negroes are more likely to help or more likely to hurt the Negro's cause for racial equality? [Gallup]	June 1963	60%	27%
Do you think mass demonstrations by Negroes are more likely to help or more likely to hurt the Negro's cause for racial equality? [Gallup]	May 1964	74%	16%
Now I want to ask you about the riots by Negroes in New York, Rochester and Jersey City. Do you think Negroes helped their cause, hurt it by these demonstrations, or won't it make much difference one way or the other? [Harris]	August 1964	87%	2%

| Do you feel demonstrations by Negroes have helped more or hurt more the advancement of Negro rights? [Harris] | July 1965 | 45% | 36% |
| All in all, do you feel the demonstrations by Negroes on civil rights have helped more or hurt more in the advancement of Negro rights? [Harris] | October 1966 | 85% | 15% |

Source: Survey data from the Gallup and Harris organizations. Accessed via "Public Opinion Polls on Civil Rights Movement, 1961–1969." Civil Rights Movement Archive, CRMVET.org. https://www.crmvet.org/docs/60s_crm_public-opinion.pdf.

From June through August 1969, Gallup surveyed 1,300 American men (black and white), asking, "On the whole, would you say that most negro/black/colored protesters are trying to be helpful, or that they are looking for trouble, or they aren't one way or the other?" Forty-five percent of men claimed that most African American protesters were "just looking for trouble."

Harris Race Polls for Newsweek

The Harris survey organization also ran a series of polls focusing specifically on matters of race and civil rights. Some of these surveys were fielded in partnership with *Newsweek*. The toplines of these surveys were also published in a series of articles by Hazel Erskine in *Public Opinion Quarterly*.

SHOULD THE LAW GUARANTEE NEGROES EQUAL RIGHTS TO WHITE PEOPLE IN . . . ?	% OF ALL WHITES	% OF SOUTHERN WHITES
Voting rights	95%	92%
Uses of buses and trains	91%	80%
Getting good housing	85%	81%
Job opportunities	80%	62%

Using restaurants	79%	49%
Integrating schools	75%	43%

Source: Harris Poll for *Newsweek,* October 1963. Only whites interviewed.

In partnership with *Newsweek,* Harris also asked whites to place themselves in the position of African Americans and give their opinions about justifiable action as an African American. Harris asked, "If you were in the Negro's position, do you think you would be justified to . . . ?" Southern and non-southern whites alike expressed strong opposition to many of the demonstrations and protest actions of the civil rights movement, even when asked to explicitly consider the perspective of African Americans.

	WHITE DISAPPROVAL	SOUTHERN WHITE DISAPPROVAL
Lie down in front of trucks at construction sites to protest hiring discrimination	91%	94%
Sit-ins at lunch counters	67%	84%
Go to jail in protest of discrimination	56%	75%
Boycott businesses who commit hiring discrimination	55%	66%

Source: Harris Poll for *Newsweek,* October 1963. Only whites interviewed.

African American Attitudes During the Civil Rights Movement

Below are topline results from a May 1969 survey of African Americans fielded by Gallup about black experiences and attitudes related to the movement. While the data show that small groups of African Americans actually participated in demonstrations or protests, nearly half of African Americans said they would if asked. Moreover, African

Americans expressed considerably more optimism about the effectiveness of protests and demonstrations than whites.

IN THE CAUSE OF NEGRO RIGHTS, HAVE YOU PERSONALLY OR HAS ANY MEMBER OF YOUR FAMILY ...	DONE	NOT DONE
Taken part in a sit-in?	11%	89%
Marched in a demonstration?	19%	81%

Source: Survey data from the Gallup organization. Accessed via "Public Opinion Polls on Civil Rights Movement, 1961–1969." Civil Rights Movement Archive, CRMVET.org. https://www.crmvet.org/docs/60s_crm_public-opinion.pdf.

IF YOU WERE ASKED, WOULD YOU ...	WOULD	WOULD NOT
Take part in a sit-in?	41%	38%
March in a demonstration?	46%	38%
Picket a store?	42%	40%

Source: Survey data from the Gallup organization. Accessed via "Public Opinion Polls on Civil Rights Movement, 1961–1969." Civil Rights Movement Archive, CRMVET.org. https://www.crmvet.org/docs/60s_crm_public-opinion.pdf.

QUESTION	% HAS HURT (IS HURTING)	% HAS HELPED (IS HELPING)
Do you think activities of these kinds (sit-ins, demonstrations, picketing a store, stop buying at a store, going to jail) have helped Negroes or hurt them in their effort to win their rights?	14%	70%
In your opinion, are Negro college students who get involved in these demonstrations (on college campuses) helping or hurting the Negro cause?	32%	40%

Do you think the methods the civil   10%   74%
rights leaders use, like marches,
picketing, and demonstrations, are
helping or hurting the cause?

Source: Survey data from the Gallup organization. Accessed via "Public Opinion Polls on Civil Rights Movement, 1961–1969." Civil Rights Movement Archive, CRMVET.org. https://www.crmvet.org/docs/60s_crm_public-opinion.pdf.

Attitudes About the Civil Rights Movement at the Turn of the Twenty-first Century

Decades later, Americans came to agree that the movement was one of the key moments in American history. At the end of the twentieth century, Gallup asked respondents to rate the most important events of the previous 100 years from a list of 18 possibilities. The civil rights movement ranked fifth.

Event and Rank	% Saying "One of Most Important Events"
World War II	71%
Women gaining the right to vote	66%
Atomic bomb dropping, Hiroshima	66%
The Holocaust	65%
Passage of the Civil Rights Act (1964)	58%
World War I	53%
Landing on the moon	50%
Assassination of JFK	50%
Fall of the Berlin Wall	48%
The Great Depression	48%

Source: Newport, Frank, David W. Moore, and Lydia Saad. "The Most Important Events of the Century from the Viewpoint of the People" (1999). https://news.gallup.com/poll/3427/most-important-events-century-from-viewpoint-people.aspx.

Changes in the Electorate After the Civil Rights Movement

The Voting Rights and Immigration and Nationality acts of 1965 produced sizable changes in the racial composition of the electorates both of the South and of the broader United States.

Signed in 1965 by President Lyndon Johnson, the Voting Rights Act extended federal protections and increased federal monitoring of state/local elections, especially in the South, to help end discrimination in election administration and curtail illicit practices that had long prevented many African Americans from voting freely in the South. The data is from the U.S. Commission on Civil Rights. Pre-VRA statistics represent the numbers reported by the Southern states at various points in 1964. The post-VRA statistics represent totals reported by the same states in 1967.

Two patterns emerge from these data. First, the VRA clearly had a massive impact on black registration in the South. In every Southern state, nonwhite (which at that point was almost entirely African American) registration leapt after the Voting Rights Act. Second, as Professor Adriane Fresh at Duke University has documented, the VRA increased white registration and overall turnout as well, suggesting that the VRA produced a backlash effect, potentially further dividing the South (and the country) along racial lines. Professor Fresh's estimates are consistent with data from the USCCR. The table below provides information on the changes in the percentage of white and nonwhite voters registered in the former states of the Confederacy (minus Texas, which lacks sufficient data for comparison). In every state, large increases in black and white registration are clear. Looking across the South, the data show that the VRA likely increased nonwhite registration in Southern states by as little as 2 percentage points (Tennessee) to as much as 50 percentage point in particular states (Mississippi).

STATE	CHANGE IN NONWHITE REGISTRATION (1964–1967)	CHANGE IN WHITE REGISTRATION (1964–1967)
Alabama	+ 32.3%	+ 20.4%
Arkansas	+22.4%	+6.9%
Florida	+12.6%	+6.6%
Georgia	+25.2%	+17.7%
Louisiana	+27.3%	+12.6%
Mississippi	+53.1%	+21.6%
North Carolina	+4.5%	-13.8%**
South Carolina	+13.9%	+6.0%
Tennessee	+2.0%	+8.6%
Virginia	+17.3%	+1.8%

Notes: Calculations based on data from United States Commission on Civil Rights. An Assessment of Minority Voting Rights Access in the United States (2018). Accessed April 23, 2020. https://www.usccr.gov/pubs/2018/Minority_Voting_Access_2018.pdf. Calculations by Michael E. Shepherd. **North Carolina appears to have purged or removed significant white "deadwood" from the voter rolls during this period.

To assess the long-run impact of the VRA before the 2006 VRA reauthorization vote, the USCCR collected information on changes in voter registration rates and black–white registration gaps for a handful of Southern states, this time in 2004. Below is a re-created version of the original USCCR data.

STATE	1965 BLACK-WHITE REGISTRATION GAP	2004 BLACK-WHITE REGISTRATION GAP
Alabama	49.9%	0.9%
Georgia	35.2%	-0.7%

Louisiana	48.9%	4.0%
Mississippi	63.2%	-3.8%
South Carolina	38.4%	3.3%
Virginia	22.8%	10.8%

Source: Calculations based on data from United States Commission on Civil Rights. An Assessment of Minority Voting Rights Access in the United States (2018). Accessed April 23, 2020. https://www.usccr.gov/pubs/2018/Minority_Voting_Access_2018.pdf. Calculations by Michael E. Shepherd.

A separate way of analyzing the long-run impact of the VRA is to look at the percentages of African Americans of voting age who were registered to vote at the time the VRA was reauthorized in 2006. In most Southern states, roughly 70 percent of African Americans were registered to vote in 2004, up from averages of as low as 6 percent in Mississippi in 1965.

STATE	PROPORTION OF VOTING-AGE AFRICAN AMERICANS REGISTERED TO VOTE IN 2004
Alabama	72.9%
Georgia	64.2%
Louisiana	71.1%
Mississippi	76.1%
South Carolina	71.1%
Virginia	57.4%

Source: Calculations based on data from United States Commission on Civil Rights. An Assessment of Minority Voting Rights Access in the United States (2018). Accessed April 23, 2020. https://www.usccr.gov/pubs/2018/Minority_Voting_Access_2018.pdf. Calculations by Michael E. Shepherd.

Electorate Changes Following the 1965 Immigration and Nationality Act

The most obvious empirical impacts of the 1965 INA on the American electorate were in the change in the share of immigrants from

Asian and Latin American countries relative to European ones and in the total number of immigrants entering the United States. Estimates suggest that immigration from Asian countries increased by as much as 400 percent following the INA. In total, 18 million legal immigrants arrived between 1965 and 1995, amounting to an increase of over 300 percent from the 1935–1965 time period. In the 1950s, more than 50 percent of immigrants were of European descent and 6 percent were of Asian descent. In the 1990s, only 16 percent were of European descent and 31 percent were of Asian descent. Following the INA, nearly 23 percent of legal immigrants until 2000 came from Mexico specifically. These changes to the demographic makeup of the country were also met with changes to the Voting Rights Act. In 1975, Congress expanded the VRA to include new protections for individuals immigrating from these areas. For example, Congress created the bilingual election administration requirements, which eased the process of registering to vote and voting for non-English speakers.

It is difficult to compare today's electorate to the 1960 electorate, due to limited data on Asian and Hispanic Americans. Data on Asian Americans are particularly scarce. As a result, the census often historically would often lump Asian Americans into a category of "other." While a sizable proportion of the individuals included in this "other" category are Asian Americans, we cannot be sure that these numbers are exactly reflective of the experiences of Asian Americans. With this large caveat aside, reasonable comparisons of the changes in the electorate over time are possible beginning in 1980. The most visible changes have been the increasing share of the electorate comprising black, Hispanic, and "other" voters. White voters made up 87 percent of the voting electorate in 1980, a number that fell to 73 percent in 2016.

Group	Percent of Voting Electorate Comprised by Racial Group (1980)	Percent of Voting Electorate Comprised by Racial Group (2016)
Black	8.9%	11.9%
Hispanic	2.6%	9.2%

"Other"	1.0%	5.5%
White	87.6%	73.3%

Source: File, Thom. "Characteristics of Voters in the Presidential Election of 2016." US Census (2018). https://www.census.gov/content/dam/Census/library/publications/2018/demo/P20-582.pdf.

Source Notes

Overture

3 "WE WERE BEATEN" John Robert Lewis (hereinafter JRL), remarks on Edmund Pettus Bridge, March 8, 2020, author observation.

3 HIS STEPS WERE Author observation.

3 HE LED HIS FELLOW PILGRIMS Ibid.

4 "IF THE YOUNG PEOPLE" Author interview with JRL.

4 "PEOPLE COME UP TO ME" Ibid.

4 SURROUNDED BY CIVIL RIGHTS VETERANS Author observation.

4 NEARLY IMPOSSIBLE TO FIND JRL, transcripts of interviews from PBS documentary series *Eyes on the Prize,* produced by Henry Hampton, Henry Hampton Collection, Film and Media Archive, Washington University, St. Louis, Missouri.

4 "IT IS GOOD TO BE" JRL, remarks on Edmund Pettus Bridge, March 8, 2020, author observation.

4 HIS TEACHER IN NONVIOLENCE See, for instance, Kent Wong, Ana Luz González, and James M. Lawson, Jr., eds., *Nonviolence and Social Movements: The Teachings of Rev. James M. Lawson, Jr.* (Los Angeles, 2016); Michael K. Honey, *Love and Solidarity: James M. Lawson and Nonviolence in the Search for Workers' Rights,* Bullfrog Films, 2019; Karuna Mantena, "Showdown for Nonviolence: The Theory and Practice of Nonviolent Politics," in *To Shape a New World: Essays on the Political Philosophy of Martin Luther King, Jr.,* ed. Tommie Shelby and Brandon M. Terry (Cambridge, Mass., 2018), 78–101.

4 "IS FULL OF" Tertullian, *Ad Martyras (To the Martyrs),* trans. S. Thelwall, in *Ante-Nicene Fathers,* ed. Alexander Roberts, James Donaldson, and A. Cleveland Coxe, vol. 3 (Buffalo, N.Y., 1885), revised and edited for New Advent by Kevin Knight, http://www.newadvent.org/fathers/0323.htm.

5 BROKE INTO A HYMN Edmund Pettus Bridge, March 8, 2020, author observation.

5 "GOD BLESS YOU" Ibid.

5 "GET 'EM!" John Lewis with Michael D'Orso, *Walking with the Wind: A Memoir of the Movement* (New York, 1998), 340. Hereinafter cited as WWTW. For Selma, see also, for instance, Charles A. Bonner, *Tip of the Arrow: A Study in Leadership* (Conneaut Lake, Pa., 2020); Taylor Branch, *At Canaan's Edge: America in the King Years 1965–68* (New York, 2006), 6–202; Clayborne Carson, *In Struggle: SNCC and the Black Awakening of the 1960s* (Cambridge, Mass., 1981), 157–62; Charles E. Fager, *Selma 1965: The March That Changed the South* (New York, 1974); David J. Garrow,

Protest at Selma: Martin Luther King. Jr., and the Voting Rights Act of 1965 (New Haven, Conn., 1978); Garrow, *Bearing the Cross: Martin Luther King, Jr., and the Southern Christian Leadership Conference* (New York, 1986); Bernard LaFayette, Jr., and Kathryn Lee Johnson, *In Peace and Freedom: My Journey in Selma* (Lexington, Ky., 2013); Robert A. Pratt, *Selma's Bloody Sunday: Protest, Voting Rights, and the Struggle for Racial Equality* (Baltimore, 2017); Andrew Young, *An Easy Burden: The Civil Rights Movement and the Transformation of America* (Waco, Texas, 2008), 336–74. The FBI file on Selma is also illuminating: See FBI file 44–28492, section 1, serials 1–42, Alabama (1965) 3/7 Selma to Montgomery March, Edmund Pettus Bridge, National Archives (NAID 7634471).

5–6 "INJECTED SOMETHING VERY" Author interview with JRL.

6 "REDEMPTION—REDEMPTION IS" Ibid.

6 "IN THE FINAL ANALYSIS" Ibid.

6 A COMPLEX CONCEPT See, for instance, Richard Kieckhefer and George D. Bond, eds., *Sainthood: Its Manifestations in World Religions* (Berkeley, Calif., 1988); Stephen Wilson, *Saints and Their Cults: Studies in Religious Sociology, Folklore, and History* (Cambridge, 1983); Simon Yarrow, *The Saints: A Short History* (Oxford, 2016); Kenneth L. Woodward, *Making Saints: How the Catholic Church Determines Who Becomes a Saint, Who Doesn't, and Why* (New York, 1990).

6 SAINTHOOD IS DERIVED Richard Kieckhefer, "Imitators of Christ: Sainthood in the Christian Tradition" in Kieckhefer and Bond, *Sainthood,* 2–4. In a discussion of "Sanctity, A Sign of Revelation," a 1967 essay by René Latourelle, Kieckhefer described sainthood in the sense I mean when applying it to Lewis. As Kieckhefer wrote:

> For [Latourelle], the saint is an extraordinary person who exerts extraordinary attraction and impact on others, but it is not necessary that this bearer of holiness be a canonized saint or an obvious candidate for canonization. The force of example is central to Latourelle's argument, not the power of intercession. He sees sanctity as a "sign of revelation," a manifestation of divine presence, but it is virtuous conduct rather than miracles that show this presence. If the saint differs from other Christians, it is evidently a difference of degree rather than of kind. The holiness of the saint can be shared, and ideally *must* be shared, by broader communities. The otherness of the saint may persist *de facto* but not *de jure*. (Ibid., 38)

See also René Latourelle, "Sanctity, a Sign of Revelation," *Theology Digest* 15 [1967], 41–46.

7 "TOILED AND FOUGHT" Lesbia Scott, "I Sing a Song of the Saints of God," https://hymnary.org/text/i_sing_a_song_of_the_saints_of_god.

7 "THE TRAGEDY OF MAN" Alden Whitman, "Reinhold Niebuhr Is Dead; Protestant Theologian, 78," *NYT*, June 2, 1971.

8 "THE ARC OF THE MORAL UNIVERSE" Martin Luther King, Jr., "Remaining Awake Through a Great Revolution," March 31, 1968, National Cathedral, Washington, D.C., *King Encyclopedia,* Martin Luther King, Jr., Research and Education Institute, Stanford University, https://kinginstitute.stanford.edu/king-papers/publications/knock-midnight-inspiration-great-sermons-reverend-martin-luther-king-jr-10. http://kingencyclopedia.stanford.edu/encyclopedia/documentsentry/doc_remaining_awake_through_a_great_revolution.1.html. See also Paul E. Teed, *A Revolutionary Conscience: Theodore Parker and Antebellum America* (Lanham, Md., 2012), 169. The full quotation of Parker's:

Look at the facts of the world. You see a continual and progressive triumph of the right. I do not pretend to understand the moral universe; the arc is a long one, and my eye reaches but little ways; I cannot calculate the curve and complete the figure by the experience of sight; I can divine it by conscience. And from what I see I am sure it bends towards justice. Things refuse to be mismanaged long. Jefferson trembled when he thought of slavery and remembered that God is just. Ere long all America will tremble. (*The Works of Theodore Parker: Sermons of Religion,* ed. Samuel A. Eliot [Boston, 1908], 64)

8 "THE FINEST TASK OF" Whitman, "Reinhold Niebuhr Is Dead," *NYT.*

8 "HEAVEN AND EARTH" *WWTW,* 78.

8 IN DECEMBER 1975, IN A STORY "Saints Among Us," *Time,* December 29, 1975.

8 "IS HEAVY WITH MEANINGS" Ibid.

9 "A SAINT HAS TO BE" Ibid.

9 "HE WAS HUMAN" Author interview with Diane Nash.

9 "*TIME* MAGAZINE CALLED" Vincent Coppola, "The Parable of Julian Bond and John Lewis," *Atlanta Magazine,* March 1, 1990.

10 "NEXT TO HOLY SCRIPTURE" Kieckhefer, "Imitators of Christ: Sainthood in the Christian Tradition" in *Sainthood,* eds. Kieckhefer and Bond, 7.

10 "I WOULD SAY YES" Author interview with James Lawson.

10 FOR MANY AMERICANS For this section, I drew in part on my essay "Why Religion Is the Best Hope Against Trump," *NYT,* February 25, 2020.

10 "ALL MEN," HOMER WROTE Homer, *The Odyssey,* trans. Robert Fagles (New York, 1996), 109.

11 "IN AGES OF FAITH" Robert A. Nisbet, *History of the Idea of Progress* (New York, 1980), 354–55.

11 THE STORY OF THE CIVIL RIGHTS MOVEMENT See, for instance, Michael K. Honey, *To the Promised Land: Martin Luther King and the Fight for Economic Justice* (New York, 2018); Shelby and Terry, *To Shape a New World;* Peniel E. Joseph, *Waiting 'Til the Midnight Hour: A Narrative History of Black Power in America* (New York, 2006); Joseph, *The Sword and the Shield: The Revolutionary Lives of Malcolm X and Martin Luther King, Jr.* (New York, 2020); Joseph, *Stokely: A Life* (New York, 2014).

11 "WE CANNOT ATTAIN TO" Robert Louis Wilken, *The Christians as the Romans Saw Them* (New Haven, Conn., 1984), 163.

12 "THE MORE I THOUGHT ABOUT" Martin Luther King, Jr., *A Testament of Hope: The Essential Writings and Speeches of Martin Luther King, Jr.,* ed. James Melvin Washington (San Francisco, 2003), 36.

12 "WE SAY WE ARE" Lewis, *Across That Bridge,* 206.

12 "THE EDUCATION OF THE HUMAN RACE" Nisbet, *History of the Idea of Progress,* 61.

13 "HE HAD A REMARKABLE DEGREE" Author interview with Diane Nash.

13 THE BELOVED COMMUNITY See, for instance, *WWTW,* 71–89; Willis Jenkins and Jennifer M. McBride, eds., *Bonhoeffer and King: Their Legacies and Import for Christian Social Thought* (Minneapolis, 2010); Michael G. Long, ed., *Christian Peace and Nonviolence: A Documentary History* (Maryknoll, N.Y., 2011); Charles Marsh, *The Beloved Community: How Faith Shapes Social Justice, from the Civil Rights Movement to Today* (New York, 2005); Patrick Parr, *The Seminarian: Martin Luther King Jr. Comes of Age* (Chicago, 2018); J. Deotis Roberts, *Bonhoeffer and King: Speaking Truth to Power* (Louisville, Ky., 2005); Josiah Royce, *The Problem of Christianity* (Washington, D.C., 2001); Gary Herstein, "The Roycean Roots of the Beloved Community," *Pluralist*

4, no. 2 (2009), 91–107; Rufus Burrow, Jr., "The Beloved Community: Martin Luther King, Jr., and Josiah Royce," *Encounter* 73, no. 1 (2012), 37–64; Cornel West, "The Religious Foundations of the Thought of Martin Luther King, Jr.," in *We Shall Overcome: Martin Luther King, Jr., and the Black Freedom Struggle,* ed. Peter J. Albert and Ronald Hoffman (New York, 1990); Kenneth L. Smith and Ira G. Zepp, *Search for the Beloved Community: The Thinking of Martin Luther King, Jr.* (Valley Forge, Pa., 1998); Michele Moody-Adams, "The Path of Conscientious Citizenship" in Shelby and Terry, *To Shape a New World,* 269–89.

13 "NOTHING LESS THAN" *WWTW*, 78.

14 "SOMETIMES I HEAR" "Transcript: Rep. John Lewis's Speech on 50th Anniversary of the March on Washington," *WP*, August 28, 2013.

14 "THERE WAS NEVER ANY QUESTION" Author interview with Bernard LaFayette, Jr.

14 "WE TOOK A LITTLE WALK" JRL, remarks on Edmund Pettus Bridge, March 8, 2020, author observation. On the legacy and complexities of the civil rights movement in general, see, for instance, Vincent Harding, *Hope and History: Why We Must Share the Story of the Movement* (New York, 2010); Michael Eric Dyson, *I May Not Get There with You: The True Martin Luther King, Jr.* (New York, 2000); Dyson, *April 4, 1968: Martin Luther King, Jr.'s Death and How It Changed America* (New York, 2008); David L. Chappell, *A Stone of Hope: Prophetic Religion and the Death of Jim Crow* (Chapel Hill, N.C., 2004); Chappell, *Waking from the Dream: The Struggle for Civil Rights in the Shadow of Martin Luther King, Jr.* (New York, 2014); Martin Luther King, Jr., *The Radical King,* ed. Cornel West (Boston, 2015); Adam Fairclough, *To Redeem the Soul of America: The Southern Christian Leadership Conference and Martin Luther King, Jr.* (Athens, Ga., 1987); Jacquelyn Dowd Hall, "The Long Civil Rights Movement and the Political Uses of the Past," *Journal of American History* 91, no. 4 (March 2005), 1233–63.

15 "WE LOVE YOU" JRL, remarks on Edmund Pettus Bridge, Sunday, March 8, 2020, author observation.

15 "I—I LOVE YOU" Ibid.

CHAPTER ONE: *A Hard Life, a Serious Life*

19 "WORK AND PUT" *WWTW*, 14.

19 "COSTLY GRACE" Dietrich Bonhoeffer, *The Cost of Discipleship* (New York, 2018), 45.

19 FOR JOHN LEWIS Ibid., 11–13; 23–24; Henry Louis Gates, Jr., *Finding Your Roots: The Official Companion to the PBS Series* (Chapel Hill, N.C., 2014), 22–33; author interviews with JRL. "Growing up, I did not have to imagine what slavery had been like," Lewis recalled. "I only had to look at my great-grandfather, Frank Carter. For he *was* a slave—or had been." Author interview with JRL.

19 WHOM LEWIS CALLED "GRANDPAPA" Author interview with JRL.

19 THE FAMILY HAS LONG BELIEVED Gates, *Finding Your Roots,* 25; author interview with JRL.

19 WERE NOW FREE "The Emancipation Proclamation," January 1, 1863, National Archives, https://www.archives.gov/exhibits/featured-documents/emancipation -proclamation.

19 "WITHIN THE UNITED STATES" "13th Amendment to the Constitution: Abolition of Slavery," https://www.archives.gov/historical-docs/13th-amendment.

19 THE "NEW BIRTH" Abraham Lincoln, "The Gettysburg Address," November 19, 1863, http://www.abrahamlincolnonline.org/lincoln/speeches/gettysburg.htm.

19 WITHIN EIGHT MONTHS Julie Novkov, "Segregation (Jim Crow)," *Encyclopedia of*

Alabama, http://www.encyclopediaofalabama.org/article/h-1248. See also William Warren Rogers, Robert David Ward, Leah Rawls Atkins, and Wayne Flynt, *Alabama: The History of a Deep South State* (Tuscaloosa, Ala., 2018), 221–375, which covers Reconstruction through the state's constitution of 1901.

19 IN 1866, THE FEDERAL GOVERNMENT Novkov, "Segregation (Jim Crow)," *Encyclopedia of Alabama.*

20 THE REACTIONARY BLACK CODE Ibid. See also Rogers, Ward, Atkins, and Flynt, *Alabama,* 250–52.

20 THE KU KLUX KLAN WAS FOUNDED Rogers, Ward, Atkins, and Flynt, *Alabama,* 250–52.

20 EDMUND PETTUS WAS A GRAND DRAGON Errin Whack, "Who Was Edmund Pettus?" *Smithsonian Magazine,* March 7, 2015, https://www.smithsonianmag.com /history/who-was-edmund-pettus-180954501/.

20 ALABAMA HAD REVERTED Novkov, "Segregation (Jim Crow)," *Encyclopedia of Alabama.* See also Rogers, Ward, Atkins, and Flynt, *Alabama,* 343–54.

20 FRANK CARTER LEASED HIS LAND WWTW, 12–13.

20 DILIGENT, RESOURCEFUL, AND DETERMINED Ibid., 13. "It wasn't just his business sense that helped Frank Carter rise to a level of relative success among his neighbors," Lewis recalled. "He could also flat-out *work.* Frank Carter was known throughout the county as a man who could outplow and outpick any man or woman around. He was good and he was fast, not only behind a plow but also with a ledger book." Ibid.

20 "HE COULDN'T READ" Ibid.

20 "HE WOULD SIT" Gates, *Finding Your Roots,* 25.

20 IT WAS THERE WWTW, 14.

20 WHO HAD BEEN BORN Gates, *Finding Your Roots,* 24.

20 EDDIE'S MOTHER, LULA WWTW, 14.

20 WILLIE MAE AND EDDIE Ibid., 14–15.

20 BORN IN A SHOTGUN SHACK WWTW, 15; Gates, *Finding Your Roots,* 22.

20 A COLD WEDNESDAY "The Weather," *The Troy Messenger,* February 21, 1940.

21 SAW HEADLINES ABOUT *The Montgomery Advertiser,* February 21, 1940.

21 CLOSER TO HOME "Man Said to Be from Troy Dies in Suicide Fall," "Fiddling Contest in Troy Next Saturday Night," *The Troy Messenger,* February 21, 1940.

21 "THOUGHT FOR THE DAY" *The Troy Messenger,* February 21, 1940. The verse is found in 1 Peter 4:12 (KJV).

21 JESSE THORNTON, A TWENTY-SIX-YEAR-OLD Charles A. J. McPherson, "The Jesse Thornton Lynching," container 11:B97, file folder no. 9, NAACP Records, Library of Congress, Washington, D.C.; Janette Ekanem, "Injustice Unveiled: The Lynching of Jesse Thornton," Civil Rights and Restorative Justice Clinic, Northeastern University School of Law, 2013, https://repository.library.northeastern .edu/downloads/neu:m040dr115?datastream_id=content.

22 THORNTON'S BODY WAS FOUND *The Luverne Journal,* July 3, 1940.

22 "THE CAUSE OF" Ibid.

22 "THESE LYNCHINGS ARE" McPherson, "Jesse Thornton Lynching."

22 ON THE EVENING OF SUNDAY, SEPTEMBER 3, 1944 For the story of Mrs. Taylor's case, I am indebted to Danielle L. McGuire, *At the Dark End of the Street: Black Women, Rape, and Resistance—A New History of the Civil Rights Movement from Rosa Parks to the Rise of Black Power* (New York, 2010), and the 2017 documentary directed by Nancy Buirski, "The Rape of Recy Taylor." As Robert Corbitt, Mrs. Taylor's brother, says in the film, "Those young boys felt like they can do it and get away

with it. . . . The reason so many people got away with it [was] they felt that the black woman's body didn't belong to her."

22   "WE KNOW THAT" Jon Meacham, ed., *Voices in Our Blood: America's Best on the Civil Rights Movement* (New York, 2001), 19.

23   "THERE WAS A LITTLE GATE" Author interview with JRL.

23   HIS FAMILY CALLED HIM "ROBERT" *WWTW,* 9.

23   "JOHN" DID NOT BECOME Author interview with JRL.

23   "PETER, AND UPON THIS ROCK" Matthew 16:18 (KJV).

23   "CHANGE, AS I LEARNED" *WWTW,* 9.

23   HIS FATHER, EDDIE Ibid., 12–17.

23   "A FIGURE LIKE" Ibid., 17.

23   HE ALWAYS REMEMBERED Ibid., 10.

23   YET HE ALSO RECOILED Ibid.

24   LATER IN LIFE Ibid.

24   "WORKING FOR NOTHING" Ibid., 24.

24   IT PROPELLED HER Ibid., 11. As Lewis recalled, "To understand the spirit that brought thousands of people just like me to those spotlighted stages of protests and marches, I am convinced it is necessary to understand the spirit that carried people like my mother—simple people, everyday people, good, honest, hard-working people—through lives that never made headlines but were the well-spring for the lives that did." Ibid.

25   LEWIS'S FATHER WAS JRL transcripts, *Eyes on the Prize,* Henry Hampton Collection.

25   HALF A MILE *WWTW,* 17.

25   THE SELLER WAS Ibid., 18.

25   "IT WAS GOOD" Ibid.

25   THE FAMILY RAISED JRL transcripts, *Eyes on the Prize,* Henry Hampton Collection.

25   LEWIS RECALLED Author interview with JRL.

25   THE HOUSE WAS *WWTW,* 18–19.

25   PAGES FROM SEARS Ibid., 19.

25   BUT, LEWIS REMEMBERED Ibid.

25   THE FIREPLACE IN Ibid., 18.

25   "IN THE WINTER" Ibid., 19.

25   "THAT'S AN INDICATION" Ibid., 21.

25   DUNN'S CHAPEL AME Ibid.

25   DRESSED CAREFULLY IN Ibid.

26   THE SERVICES FOLLOWED Ibid., 22–23. When it came time to recall those long-ago Sunday prayers as Lewis wrote his memoirs in the closing years of the twentieth century, he reconstructed a typical one:

> This morning, our heavenly Father, it's once more and again that we come before You with knee bent and body bowed in humble submission, thanking You for last night's slumber and this morning's rising, finding that our bed was not our cooling board and our last night's cover was not our winding sheet. Our bodies *was* not wrapped up in the clay of the grave and the four walls of our *room* was not the walls of our *grave.* We stopped right here to say thank You and that You *abled* us to look out our *winder* and see Your darling sun rise in the east and make its way across the blue and settle behind the western hills. Thank You, Lord.
>
> We thank You, Lord, that the fowl of the air are Thine, the fish that

swim the mighty deep are Thine, and the cattle of the hills. We thank You
for putting food on our table, shoes on our feet and a place to lay my head.
Lord, if we haven't been too mean, we ask forgiveness of our sins that they
will not rise against us in the world or the next.

Sweet Jesus, when we come to the end of life's journey, give our souls a
resting place somewhere in Your kingdom where we can praise Your name
forever, where every day will be Sunday and Sabbath will have no end.
This is Your servant's prayer in Jesus' name. Amen. (Ibid., 23)

26 THEN CAME THE SERMON Ibid., 23.

26 LEWIS REMEMBERED SEEING Ibid., 17; author interview with JRL.

26 GIVEN A BIBLE WWTW, 27.

26 "WE HAD A" JRL transcripts, *Eyes on the Prize,* Henry Hampton Collection.

27 BUT NOT QUITE WWTW, 27–28.

27 "THE LITTLE THING" Ibid., 28.

28 "I DON'T THINK" Ibid., 26.

28 AFTER LEWIS WORKED Ibid., 30; author interview with JRL.

28 "NOBODY," HE'D SAY WWTW, 31. "Even a six-year-old could tell that this share-cropper's life was nothing but a bottomless pit," Lewis recalled. "I watched my father sink deeper and deeper into debt, and it broke my heart. More than that, it made me angry. There was no way to get ahead with this kind of farming. The best you could do was do it well enough to *keep* doing it." Ibid.

28 SCHOOL SOON JOINED Ibid., 32–33. "I was there with so many cousins, and it was just a great place to learn," he recalled. Author interview with JRL.

28 THERE WAS A BIG WWTW, 33.

28 THOUGHT IT "MAJESTIC" Ibid.

28 "PUBLIC SPEAKING, OR" Ibid., 33–34.

28 HE WAS DELIGHTED Ibid., 34.

28 AFTER SIXTH GRADE Ibid., 40–41.

28 THEIR BUSES WERE BATTERED JRL transcripts, *Eyes on the Prize,* Henry Hampton Collection.

28 THE ROADS OVER WHICH Ibid.

28 WERE "LEFT LITERALLY" Ibid.

28 "WE SAW THE SIGNS" Ibid. As Lewis recalled, "I became resentful of the signs and all the visible evidence of segregation and racial discrimination." Ibid.

29 "FROM MY EARLIEST" Lewis, *Across That Bridge,* 95.

29 "ONE EVER FEELS" W.E.B. Du Bois, *The Souls of Black Folk* (Mineola, N.Y., 1994), 2–3.

29 "VERY SLEEK, VERY" WWTW, 40.

30 "IT IS CLEAR" "Segregation Ruled Unequal, and Therefore Unconstitutional," American Psychological Association, https://www.apa.org/research/action/segregation.

30 "SEGREGATION OF WHITE" Ibid.

30 "AS INFERIOR" Lewis, *Across That Bridge,* 97; author interview with JRL.

30 THE TWO "GRABBED" WWTW, 38.

30 IT WAS 1951 WWTW, 38–40; author interview with JRL.

30 "IT WAS ANOTHER WORLD" Author interview with JRL.

30 THE CAR RIDE WWTW, 38.

31 "FRIED CHICKEN" Ibid.

31 "ON *BOTH* SIDES" Ibid., 39.

31 "She was beautiful" Ibid., 43; author interview with JRL.

32 At the all-white public library Author interview with JRL.

32 "I wanted to" Lewis, *Across That Bridge,* 98.

32 The unanimous opinion *Brown v. Board of Education of Topeka,* Opinion; May 17, 1954; Records of the Supreme Court of the United States; Record Group 267; National Archives.

32 Alabama leaders to *The Montgomery Advertiser,* May 18, 1954.

32 "Alabama's segregation system" Ibid.

32 "More and more" Ibid.

32 The coverage *The Troy Messenger,* May 18, 1954.

32 "While the Supreme Court" "Freedom of Choice Approach May Mitigate Segregation Decision," *The Troy Messenger,* May 18, 1954.

33 "Every day after" Lewis, *Across That Bridge,* 98–99.

33 The preacher at Macedonia *WWTW,* 44.

33 "It seemed to me" Ibid., 45. Lewis added, "My thoughts on this subject weren't too sophisticated or developed—I was only fourteen—but they were earnest, and they were in my head almost all the time." Ibid.

33 "In most ways" Ibid., 63.

33 Lewis first encountered Author interview with JRL.

33 The big, bulky *WWTW,* 17–18.

33 "You have a" Martin Luther King., Jr., "Paul's Letter to the American Christians," Dexter Avenue Baptist Church, November 4, 1956, https://kinginstitute.stanford.edu/king-papers/publications/knock-midnight-inspiration-great-sermons-reverend-martin-luther-king-jr-1. See also Jonathan L. Walton, "Dignity as a Weapon of Love" in Shelby and Terry, *To Shape a New World,* 339–48. As Walton wrote, King was "an original thinker who championed grand ideals. Like those of the ancient Palestinian teacher Jesus, King's moral ideals and visions of a just society were often characterized as the kingdom of God. King was, first and foremost, a Christian preacher. Nevertheless, no one can ever accuse him of being so heavenly minded as to render his thoughts no earthly good." Ibid., 341.

34 "I understand that" King, "Paul's Letter to the American Christians."

34 "was not concerned" JRL transcripts, *Eyes on the Prize,* Henry Hampton Collection.

34 "In your struggle for justice" King, "Paul's Letter to the American Christians."

35 "When I heard" Lewis, *Across That Bridge,* 80.

35 "a Moses, using" Carson, *In Struggle,* 21.

35 Rauschenbusch published Julian Gotobed, incorporating material submitted by Michelle Charles, "Walter Rauschenbusch (1861–1918)," Boston Collaborative Encyclopedia of Western Theology, http://people.bu.edu/wwildman/bce/rauschenbusch.htm. See also Christopher H. Evans, *The Kingdom Is Always but Coming: A Life of Walter Rauschenbusch* (Grand Rapids, Mich., 2004).

35 King read the book King, *Testament of Hope,* 37.

35 Lewis came to it *WWTW,* 65.

35 asked which thinker had been Author interview with JRL.

35 "In a few" Walter Rauschenbusch, *Christianity and the Social Crisis* (New York, 1916), xv.

35 In a moving Ibid., 44–92.

35 "Whoever uncouples the" Ibid., 48–49.

35 "The gospel at" King, *Testament of Hope,* 37–38.

36 To Rauschenbusch's way Rauschenbusch, *Christianity and the Social Crisis,* 50–51.

36 When John was Ibid., 50.

36 "The voice of him" Luke 3:1–6; Isaiah 40:3–5 (KJV).

36 "I couldn't accept" *WWTW,* 47.

37 of "heightened awareness" George Bush with Victor Gold, *Looking Forward* (New York, 1987), 31.

37 "It was a" Ibid.

37 Or from Mississippi *WWTW,* 46–47.

37 Emmett Till was Ibid. See also "Mississippi to Sift Negro Boy's Slaying," *NYT,* September 2, 1955; "Murder Most Foul," *NYT,* September 11, 1955; "White Asks Inquiry in Boy's Killing," *WP,* September 2, 1955; "Delta Slaying Probed," *The Christian Science Monitor,* September 2, 1955.

37 Till was beaten *WWTW,* 46.

37 allegedly making overtures See, for instance, Jason Parham, "Emmett Till's Murder: What Really Happened That Day in the Store?" *NYT,* January 27, 2017; Richard Penez-Pena, "Woman Linked to 1955 Emmett Till Murder Tells Historian Her Claims Were False," *NYT,* January 27, 2017; Timothy B. Tyson, *The Blood of Emmett Till* (New York, 2017).

37 "The body," *Time* reported "The Law: Trial by Jury," *Time,* October 3, 1955.

37 Moses Wright, Till's *WWTW,* 46–47. See also "Mississippi: The Accused," *Newsweek,* September 19, 1955; "The Law: Trial by Jury," *Time,* October 3, 1955.

37 "I remember that" Author interview with JRL.

38 The killing stayed Ibid.

38 "I was fifteen" *WWTW,* 47; author interview with JRL.

38 Rosa Parks was Frank Adams with Myles Horton, *Unearthing Seeds of Fire: The Idea of Highlander* (Winston-Salem, N.C., 1975), 148–51; Martin Luther King, Jr., *Stride Toward Freedom: The Montgomery Story* (New York, 1958), 30–40; Taylor Branch, *Parting the Waters: America in the King Years, 1954–63* (New York, 1988), 132–33.

38 Inculcated in nonviolent Branch, *Parting the Waters,* 130.

38 "We are here" Ibid., 138–41.

39 "I can still" *WWTW,* 48.

39 He read accounts in JRL transcripts, *Eyes on the Prize,* Henry Hampton Collection.

39 The newspaper was *WWTW,* 50–51. See also Wayne Phillips, "Tuscaloosa: A Tense Drama Unfolds," *NYT,* February 26, 1956.

39 A native of Kerri Lee Alexander, "Autherine Lucy," National Women's History Museum, Washington, D.C., https://www.womenshistory.org/education-resources/biographies/autherine-lucy. See also "Alabama Storm Center: Autherine Juanita Lucy," *NYT,* February 9, 1956.

39 After prolonged litigation Alexander, "Autherine Lucy," National Women's History Museum; "First in Alabama," *Time,* February 13, 1956.

39 Angry whites quickly "Welcome for Miss Lucy," *Newsweek,* February 20, 1956; "Miss Lucy v. Alabama," *NYT,* February 12, 1956. See also "Alabama Authorities Were Too Late—with Too Little," *The New Republic,* February 20, 1956; Wayne Phillips, "Dean Is Critical of Miss Lucy's Bid," *NYT,* February 23, 1956.

39 "A cross had" "Welcome for Miss Lucy," *Newsweek,* February 20, 1956.

40 The crowd chanted "Alabama's Scandal," *Time,* February 20, 1956.

40 was pelted with Ibid.

40 university trustees voted Ben Price, "Miss Lucy Expelled by Alabama U.," *WP,* March 2, 1956; "Text of Alabama Resolution," *NYT,* March 2, 1956; "Segre-

gation Victory?" *Newsweek*, March 12, 1956; "Round Two in Alabama," *Time*, March 12, 1956.

40 LEWIS PREACHED HIS *WWTW*, 51; author interview with JRL.

41 SHOT TO DEATH "Negro Leader Slain in Georgia Dispute," *NYT*, February 19, 1956. The story ran on the front page of the *Times*.

41 A VOTING RIGHTS Ibid.

41 BREWER WAS SHOT Ibid.

41 A GRAND JURY "Freed in Negro Death," *NYT*, March 1, 1956; "Jury Refuses In-dictment in Negro Slaying," *WP*, March 1, 1956.

41 DESCRIBING THE EPISODE *WWTW*, 51–52.

41 KIDNAPPED AND MURDERED Adam Nossiter, "Widow Inherits a Confession to a 36-Year-Old Hate Crime," *NYT*, September 4, 1993; Paige Eugenia Young, "Un-known Martyr: The Murder of Willie Edwards, Jr., and Civil Rights Violence in Montgomery, Alabama" (master's thesis, University of Georgia, 2003).

41 HIS DREAM WAS *WWTW*, 53.

42 A TINY INSTITUTION See Ruth Marie Powell, *Lights and Shadows: The Story of the American Baptist Theological Seminary, 1924–64* (Nashville, 1964), for a history of the school.

43 WAS TUITION FREE *WWTW*, 53.

43 "IT'S NOT HARD" Ibid., 9.

43 "WHEN I'D COME" Paul Good, "Odyssey of a Man—And a Movement," *NYT*, June 25, 1967.

43 "WHOEVER COMES TO ME" Luke 14:25–27 (CEB).

43 IN GREEK, THE WORD https://bibleapps.com/greek/3404.htm.

43 "COSTLY GRACE IS" Dietrich Bonhoeffer, *The Cost of Discipleship* (New York, 2018), 45.

43 "HIS WRITING, HIS THINKING" Author interview with JRL.

43 WITH $100—A GIFT *WWTW*, 54.

43 HIS FATHER TOOK Ibid.

CHAPTER TWO: *The Spirit of History*

47 "THE UNIVERSE OF" *WWTW*, 63.

47 "HOWEVER LARGE THE" Reinhold Niebuhr, *Major Works on Religion and Politics*, ed. Elisabeth Sifton (New York, 2015), 333.

47 "BY GOING TO" JRL transcripts, *Eyes on the Prize*, Henry Hampton Collection.

47 THE CAMPUS WAS *WWTW*, 58–59; author observation; "American Baptist Theo-logical Seminary Historic District," National Register of Historic Places Pro-gram, National Park Service, https://www.nps.gov/nr/feature/places/13000399.htm.

47 A SEVEN-DOLLAR CAB *WWTW*, 59.

47 THERE WERE ABOUT Ibid.

47 "THE HOLY HILL" Ibid., 58.

47 GRIGGS HALL "American Baptist Theological Seminary Historic District," Na-tional Register of Historic Places Program, National Park Service, https://www.nps.gov/nr/feature/places/13000399.htm. The building was named for Sutton E. Griggs (1872–1933). See, for instance, Finnie D. Coleman, *Sutton E. Griggs and the Struggle Against White Supremacy* (Knoxville, Tenn., 2007).

47 IN ROOM 202 *WWTW*, 60.

47 THE PRIMARY ACTIVITY Ibid., 61. "It was the center of our existence from the moment we awoke," Lewis recalled. Ibid.

47 IN EXCHANGE FOR Ibid., 62. See also "Congressman John Lewis: An American Saint," *The Journal of Blacks in Higher Education* 21 (Autumn 1998), 42.

47 "JOHN ALWAYS HAD A KIND OF" Author interview with Bernard LaFayette, Jr.

48 LATE NIGHTS WOULD BE Ibid.

48 "WE WERE SMALL" Ibid.

48 ONE SPRING, AROUND Ibid.

48 "SO MANY OF US" Ibid.

48 IN CHARGE OF "CLOWNING" Ibid.

48 THE ABT STUDENTS LISTENED *WWTW,* 64–65.

48 "LEWIS," BEVEL SAID Ibid., 65.

48 "THE AMERICAN [BAPTIST]" Mark Newman, *Getting Right with God: Southern Baptists and Desegregation, 1945–1995* (Tuscaloosa, Ala., 2001), 134.

48 "I THINK WE NEED" *WWTW,* 65.

49 "JOHN," ANOTHER STUDENT Ibid.

49 "BE ASHAMED TO" Paula A. Treichler, "Metaphor and Institutional Crisis: The Near-Death Experience of Antioch College" in *Making the University Matter,* ed. Barbie Zelizer (New York, 2011), 123. See also Clayborne Carson, *Martin's Dream: My Journey and the Legacy of Martin Luther King Jr.* (New York, 2013), 200–201.

49 DEAN OF STUDENTS Powell, *Lights and Shadows,* 3.

49 "SEEMED SO COMPLETELY" *WWTW,* 63.

49 "PROFESSOR POWELL WOULD" Ibid. Lewis recalled, "Now I saw philosophical and theological underpinnings for what I'd sensed and deeply felt all my life—that there was a contradiction between what was and what ought to be." Ibid.

49 "IT WAS AT THIS TIME" Ibid., 64. He went on:

> It is the essence of the moral force of the universe, and at certain points in life, in the flow of human existence and circumstances, this force, this spirit, finds you or selects you, it chases you down, and you have no choice; you must allow yourself to be used, to be guided by this force and to carry out what must be done. To me, that concept of surrender, of giving yourself over to something inexorable, something so much larger than yourself, is the basis of what we call faith. And it is the first and most crucial step toward opening yourself to the Spirit of History.
>
> This opening of the self, this alignment with Fate, has nothing to do with ego or self-gratification. On the contrary, it's an absolutely selfless thing. If the self is involved, the process is interrupted. Something is in the way. The self, even a *sense* of the self, must be totally removed in order to allow this spirit in. It is a process of giving over one's very being to whatever role history chooses for you. Ibid.

49 U.S. TROOPS RING *The Tennessean,* September 25, 1957.

49 LEWIS PRAYED FOR *WWTW,* 66.

49 JOINED A YOUTH JRL transcripts, *Eyes on the Prize,* Henry Hampton Collection.

49 EXPLORED ORGANIZING Ibid.

49–50 THE SCHOOL'S PRESIDENT, DR. MAYNARD P. TURNER, JR., *WWTW,* 66.

50 "WE DIDN'T SUCCEED" JRL transcripts, *Eyes on the Prize,* Henry Hampton Collection.

50 THE ANSWER CAME *WWTW,* 66–67.

50 HE LOVED HIS Ibid., 66. "I didn't particularly want to go to Troy State," Lewis wrote. "I was happy at ABT." Ibid.

50 AT CHRISTMAS 1957 Ibid., 67. On Martin Luther King, Jr., in general, see, for instance, Branch, *Parting the Waters*; Branch, *Pillar of Fire: America in the King Years, 1963–65* (New York, 1998); Branch, *At Canaan's Edge*; Garrow, *Bearing the Cross*; David Levering Lewis, *King: A Biography* (Urbana, Ill., 1978); Vincent Harding, *Martin Luther King: The Inconvenient Hero* (Maryknoll, N.Y., 1996); Thomas F. Jackson, *From Civil Rights to Human Rights: Martin Luther King, Jr., and the Struggle for Economic Justice* (Philadelphia, 2007); Walton, "Dignity as a Weapon of Love" in Shelby and Terry, *To Shape a New World*, 339–48.

51 "I WAS OVERWHELMED" WWTW, 67.

51 "DESTINY IS NOT" William Jennings Bryan and Mary Baird Bryan, *Speeches of William Jennings Bryan, Revised and Arranged by Himself* (New York, 1909), 11.

51 LEWIS RODE A GREYHOUND WWTW, 67.

51 THE LAWYER GREETED Ibid., 67–68; author interview with Fred Gray.

51 "ARE YOU THE BOY FROM TROY?" Author interview with JRL.

51 "I WAS MESMERIZED" WWTW, 68.

51 "WHO IS THIS" Ibid.

51 THE TWO MINISTERS Ibid.

51 "THEY TALKED AND TALKED" Author interview with Fred Gray.

51 "YOU KNOW, JOHN" WWTW, 68.

51 "IF YOU REALLY" Ibid., 69.

51 "THE PRESSURE THAT WHITE PEOPLE" Author interview with Fred Gray.

52 "HE TOLD ME" WWTW, 69.

52 "TOTAL DARKNESS SWALLOWED" Ibid.

52 LEWIS'S PARENTS TRIED Ibid., 69–70.

52 IN THE END Ibid., 69–70; author interview with JRL.

52 "I WAS HEARTBROKEN" WWTW, 70.

52 "THAT WAS A HARD LETTER" Ibid.

52 "THERE WERE GIRLS" Ibid., 62.

52 JOHNSON HAD MOVED Obituary of Helen Jean Johnson Wakefield, December 14, 2019, http://albertsonsmortuary.com/helen-jean-johnson-wakefield/.

52 "WE SPENT A LOT OF TIME TOGETHER" Ibid.

52 "I WAS MORE" WWTW, 62.

53 HIS FIRST BEER Author interview with JRL.

53 DIDN'T LEARN TO DRIVE Ibid.; see also WWTW, 49–50.

53 CAME ALIVE ON THE DANCE FLOOR WWTW, 270–72.

53 "JOHN'S SMILE—IT'S VERY GENUINE" Author interview with Diane Nash.

53 IN THE FALL WWTW, 73.

53 KING . . . WAS ASSAULTED Ibid.; Branch, *Parting the Waters*, 243–45.

53 A SEVEN-INCH IVORY-HANDLED LETTER OPENER Nikita Stewart, "'I've Been to the Mountaintop': Dr. King's Last Sermon Annotated," *NYT*, April 2, 2018. See also Hugh Pearson, *When Harlem Nearly Killed King: The 1958 Stabbing of Dr. Martin Luther King, Jr.* (New York, 2002).

53 "THAT'S ALL RIGHT" Branch, *Parting the Waters*, 244.

53 "AND THAT BLADE" Stewart, "'I've Been to the Mountaintop,'" *NYT*.

53 A UNITED PRESS INTERNATIONAL Ibid.

53 WITH KING RECOVERING WWTW, 73.

53 DESCRIBING A JANUARY "King's Home Bombed," January 30, 1956, https://king institute.stanford.edu/encyclopedia/kings-home-bombed.

53 SHE HAD "FOUND THERE WAS" "U.S. Should Lead Way, Says Mrs. King in Talk Here," *The Tennessean,* October 20, 1958.

53–54 "STEAL AWAY TO JESUS" "Steal Away to Jesus," https://www.negrospirituals.com /songs/steal_away_to_jesus.htm.

54 "WATCHING CORETTA SCOTT KING" *WWTW,* 73.

54 HE WAS A REGULAR Ibid., 73–74; JRL transcripts, *Eyes on the Prize,* Henry Hampton Collection.

54 THE REVEREND KELLY MILLER SMITH *WWTW,* 73–74; author interview with JRL; David E. Sumner, "Kelly Miller Smith Sr.," *Tennessee Encyclopedia,* https://ten nesseeencyclopedia.net/entries/kelly-miller-smith-sr/; Leila A. Meier, "'A Different Kind of Prophet': The Role of Kelly Miller Smith in the Nashville Civil Rights Movement, 1955–1960" (master's thesis, Vanderbilt University, 1991).

54 A WHITE-RUN FIRST BAPTIST Bobby L. Lovett, "First Baptist Church, Capitol Hill, Nashville," *Tennessee Encyclopedia,* https://tennesseeencyclopedia.net/entries /first-baptist-church-capitol-hill-nashville/; "Our History: First Baptist Church, Capitol Hill, 1865–" https://www.firstbaptistcapitolhill.org/our-history/.

54 "HE TRULY HONORS" Bobby L. Lovett, *The African-American History of Nashville, Tennessee, 1780–1930: Elites and Dilemmas* (Fayetteville, Ark., 1999), 33.

54 THEY FORMED THEIR OWN Lovett, "First Baptist Church, Capitol Hill, Nashville," *Tennessee Encyclopedia.*

54 "NASHVILLE, AT THE TIME" JRL transcripts, *Eyes on the Prize,* Henry Hampton Collection.

54 "SINCE INTEGRATION AND SEGREGATION" Powell, *Lights and Shadows,* 93.

55 ONE EARLY AUTUMN *WWTW,* 74–75.

55 JAMES MORRIS LAWSON Author interview with JRL.

55 THE FELLOWSHIP OF RECONCILIATION Michael L. Westmoreland-White, "A Brief History of the Fellowship of Reconciliation," https://levellers.wordpress .com/2009/11/08/a-brief-history-of-the-fellowship-of-reconciliation/.

55 "NONVIOLENT REVOLUTION IS" Clayborne Carson, David J. Garrow, Gerald Gill, Vincent Harding, Darlene Clark Hine, eds., *The Eyes on the Prize: Civil Rights Reader; Documents, Speeches, and Firsthand Accounts from the Black Freedom Struggle, 1954–1990* (New York, 1991), 130–31. On nonviolence in general, see also Sharon Erickson Nepstad, *Nonviolent Struggle: Theories, Strategies, and Dynamics* (New York, 2015).

56 "MY LEADER, MY TEACHER" Author observation.

56 BORN IN UNIONTOWN Author interview with James Lawson. For background details on Lawson, see *WWTW,* 75; Transcript of interview of James M. Lawson, Jr., conducted by Robert Penn Warren, March 17, 1964, for his book *Who Speaks for the Negro?* The Digital Archive Collection, Robert Penn Warren Center for the Humanities, Vanderbilt University; "Lawson, James M.," https://kinginsti tute.stanford.edu/encyclopedia/lawson-james-m; "What Makes Lawson's Role Unique?" James Lawson Institute, https://jameslawsoninstitute.org/history/; Theo Emery, "Activist Ousted From Vanderbilt Is Back, as a Teacher," *NYT,* October 4, 2006; Ray Waddle, "Days of Thunder: The Lawson Affair," *Vanderbilt Magazine,* Winter 2002.

56 "JIM CAME SOUTH" JRL interview for documentary film *The Soul of America,* HBO/ Kundhardt Films, 2019.

56 "IT WAS THE SERMON ON THE MOUNT" King, *Testament of Hope,* 16.

56 "CHRIST FURNISHED THE SPIRIT" Ibid., 38. See also, for instance, Wong, Gonzalez, and Lawson, *Nonviolence and Social Movements;* and Sudarshan Kapur, *Raising Up a Prophet: The African-American Encounter with Gandhi* (Boston, 1992).

56   KING HAD ENCOUNTERED "Johnson, Mordecai Wyatt," https://kinginstitute
.stanford.edu/encyclopedia/johnson-mordecai-wyatt. See also Mary King, *Mahatma Gandhi and Martin Luther King, Jr.: The Power of Nonviolent Action* (Paris, 1999),
and Martha C. Nussbaum, "From Anger to Love: Self-Purification and Political
Resistance" in Shelby and Terry, *To Shape a New World,* 105–26.

56   IN A TALK   Martin Luther King, Jr., "Six Talks in Outline," 1949, https://kingin
stitute.stanford.edu/king-papers/documents/six-talks-outline.

56   THE GANDHIAN EXAMPLE   See, for instance, Kapur, *Raising Up a Prophet: The African-
American Encounter with Gandhi;* "Thurman Howard," https://kinginstitute.stanford
.edu/encyclopedia/thurman-howard; "Who Is Howard Thurman?" The Howard Thurman Center for Common Ground, Boston University, https://www.bu
.edu/thurman/about-us/who-is-howard-thurman/.

57   ARGUING FOR THE LIBERATING POWER   Howard Thurman, *Jesus and the Disinherited*
(New York, 1949).

57   A BOOK THAT KING TURNED TO   "Thurman, Howard," https://kinginstitute.stan
ford.edu/encyclopedia/thurman-howard.

57   JIM LAWSON'S TASK   WWTW, 75–76.

57   "JOHN LEWIS OUGHT TO BE"   Author interview with James Lawson.

57   "HE HAS WRITTEN"   Ibid.

57   BRIGHT, ENGAGING, BRAVE   WWTW, 83–86; author interviews with JRL, Bernard
LaFayette, Jr., and Diane Nash. See also Diane Nash, "Inside the Sit-ins and
Freedom Rides: Testimony of a Southern Student," in *The New Negro,* ed. Mathew
H. Ahmann (Notre Dame, Ind., 1961), 43–60.

57   SHE'D COMPETED IN   David Halberstam, *The Children* (New York, 1998), 145.

57   NASH HAD TRANSFERRED   Carson, *In Struggle,* 21.

57   "SEGREGATION WAS DEHUMANIZING"   Author interview with Diane Nash.

57   "IT WAS JOHN LEWIS"   Author interview with Bernard LaFayette, Jr.

58   "ALSO I HEARD THE"   Isaiah 6:8 (KJV).

58   LAWSON'S TUESDAY NIGHT WORKSHOPS   WWTW, 76.

58   "IT CHANGED MY LIFE"   JRL interview for the documentary *The Soul of America.*

58   "WE STUDIED THE WHOLE IDEA"   Ibid.

59   THEY READ HENRY DAVID THOREAU   WWTW, 76. Another critical document was
a republished version of Krishnalal Shridharani, *War Without Violence: A Study of
Gandhi's Method and Its Accomplishments* (New York, 1939). The Fellowship of Reconciliation created the pamphlet, which was widely read in reform circles.

59   "UNJUST LAWS EXIST"   Henry David Thoreau, *Civil Disobedience and Other Essays*
(Mineola, N.Y., 2012), 7.

59   "IS A DEMOCRACY"   Ibid., 18.

60   IN NIEBUHR'S 1932 BOOK   For Niebuhr's influence on the movement, see, for instance, Branch, *Parting the Waters,* 69–104.

60   NONVIOLENCE, THOUGH, OFFERED   Niebuhr, *Major Works,* 334.

60   "IT IS HOPELESS"   Ibid., 332.

60   "A PARTICULARLY STRATEGIC"   Ibid.

60   "THERE IS NO PROBLEM"   Ibid., 334–35.

60   FOUNDED AT AN APRIL 1960 CONFERENCE   Carson, *In Struggle,* 19–30. For SNCC
in general, see also Julian Bond, *Race Man: Selected Works, 1960–2015,* ed. Michael G.
Long (San Francisco, 2020); J. Todd Moye, *Ella Baker: Community Organizer of the
Civil Rights Movement* (Lanham, Md., 2013); Barbara Ransby, *Ella Baker and the Black
Freedom Movement: A Radical Democratic Vision* (Chapel Hill, N.C., 2005); Charles E.
Cobb, Jr., *This Nonviolent Stuff'll Get You Killed: How Guns Made the Civil Rights Movement*

Possible (Durham, N.C., 2015); James Forman, *The Making of Black Revolutionaries* (Seattle, 1985); Halberstam, *The Children*; Wesley C. Hogan, *Many Minds, One Heart: SNCC's Dream for a New America* (Chapel Hill, N.C., 2007); Faith S. Holsaert, Martha Prescod Norman Noonan, Judy Richardson, Betty Garman Robinson, Jean Smith Young, and Dorothy M. Zellner, eds., *Hands on the Freedom Plow: Personal Accounts by Women in SNCC* (Urbana, Ill., 2010); Andrew B. Lewis, *The Shadows of Youth: The Remarkable Journey of the Civil Rights Generation* (New York, 2009); Robert Moses and Charles E. Cobb, Jr., *Radical Equations: Civil Rights from Mississippi to the Algebra Project* (Boston, 2002); Cleveland Sellers with Robert Terrell, *The River of No Return: The Autobiography of a Black Militant and the Life and Death of SNCC* (New York, 1973); Howard Zinn, *SNCC: The New Abolitionists* (Boston, 1964). For the FBI's investigative files on SNCC, see Student Non-Violent Coordinating Committee (SNCC), FBI file 100–439190, parts 1–14, National Archives.

60 A DESCENDANT OF SLAVES See, for instance, Ransby, *Ella Baker and the Black Freedom Movement: A Radical Democratic Vision*; "Ella Baker," https://snccdigital.org/people /ella-baker/; C. Gerald Fraser, "Ella Baker, Organizer for Groups in Civil-Rights Movement in South," *NYT*, December 17, 1986; *WWTW*, 83–84, 107–08.

60 A COMMON REALITY OF THE DAY See, for instance, Shatema Threadcraft and Brandon M. Terry, "Gender Trouble: Manhood, Inclusion, and Justice" in Shelby and Terry, *To Shape a New World*, 205–35; *WWTW*, 84–85. See also, for instance, Holsaert et al., eds., *Hands on the Freedom Plow: Personal Accounts by Women in SNCC*; Bettye Collier-Thomas and V. P. Franklin, eds., *Sisters in the Struggle: African American Women in the Civil Rights-Black Power Movement* (New York, 2001); McGuire, *At the Dark End of the Road*.

60 "YOU DIDN'T SEE ME" Fraser, "Ella Baker," *NYT*.

61 KNOWN AS "FUNDI" Ibid.

61 ONE WHO HANDS DOWN Ibid.

61 "MADE IT CRYSTAL CLEAR" Ella Baker, "Bigger Than a Hamburger," *The Southern Patriot*, May 1960, https://www.crmvet.org/docs/sncc2.htm.

62 "WE AFFIRM" Carson, *In Struggle*, 23–24. See also "Philosophy," *The Student Voice*, June 1960, in *The Student Voice, 1960–1965: Periodical of the Student Nonviolent Coordinating Committee*, ed. Clayborne Carson (Westport, Conn., 1990), 2.

62 "WE ARE TALKING" *WWTW*, 77.

63 "I ALWAYS CONSIDER" John Adams, "Fragmentary Draft of a Dissertation on Canon and Feudal Law, February 1765," Founders Online, National Archives, https://founders.archives.gov/documents/Adams/01–01–02–0009–0002 –0001.

63 A "MARCH OF CIVILIZATION" Thomas Jefferson to William Ludlow, September 6, 1824, Founders Online, National Archives, https://founders.archives.gov /documents/Jefferson/98–01–02–4523.

63 KNEW "OF NO SOIL" Frederick Douglass in *Let Nobody Turn Us Around: Voices of Resistance, Reform, and Renewal*, ed. Manning Marable and Leith Mullings (Lanham, Md., 2003), 101. See also David W. Blight, *Frederick Douglass: Prophet of Freedom* (New York, 2018), and Frederick Douglass, *Autobiographies*, ed. Henry Louis Gates, Jr. (New York, 1994).

63 WORKING FROM A PHRASE OF For Royce and his influence on the movement, see, for instance, Herstein, "The Roycean Roots of the Beloved Community," *Pluralist* 4, no. 2 (Summer 2009), 91–107; Burrow, "The Beloved Community: Martin Luther King, Jr., and Josiah Royce," *Encounter* 73, no. 1 (Fall 2012), 37–64.

63 HAS "MADE LOVE" Smith and Zepp, *Search for the Beloved Community*, 142.

63   "THE DREAM"   Ibid., 138.

64   IT WAS CALLED   See, for instance, Myles Horton with Judith Kohl and Herbert Kohl, *The Long Haul: An Autobiography* (New York, 1998); Frank Adams with Myles Horton, *Unearthing Seeds of Fire: The Idea of Highlander* (Winston-Salem, N.C., 1975); Myles Horton and Paulo Freire, *We Make the Road by Walking: Conversations on Education and Social Change,* ed. Brenda Bell, John Gaventa, and John Peters (Philadelphia, 1990).

64   NORMAN THOMAS AND NIEBUHR   Horton, *Long Haul,* 61–62.

65   "YOU CAN HITCH"   Ibid., epigraph.

65   AS A CHILD   Ibid., 7.

65   HORTON CREATED ONE   Ibid., 185.

65   "IT LOOKED LIKE"   Young, *An Easy Burden,* 130.

65   "HIGHLANDER'S VERSION OF THE COCKTAIL HOUR"   Ibid.

65   IN 1955, BEFORE   Horton, *Long Haul,* 149–50; Branch, *Parting the Waters,* 130.

65   MARTIN LUTHER KING   Horton, *Long Haul,* 118–19.

65   PETE SEEGER CAME   Ibid., 158. On the history of "We Shall Overcome," see, for instance, Victor V. Bobetsky, ed., *We Shall Overcome: Essays on a Great American Song* (Lanham, Md., 2015); Pete Seeger, *Pete Seeger in His Own Words,* ed. Rob Rosenthal and Sam Rosenthal (Boulder, Colo., 2012), 116–18, 193–94; Allan W. Winkler, "We Shall Overcome," *American Heritage* 62, no. 5 (Fall 2017).

65   ELEANOR ROOSEVELT CAME   Horton, *Long Haul,* 188.

65   JOHN LEWIS CAME   WWTW, 80–82.

65   "I THINK THAT"   Horton, *Long Haul,* 184.

66   THE PERSON WHO MOST IMPRESSED LEWIS   Katherine Mellen Brown, *Freedom's Teacher: A Life of Septima Clark* (Chapel Hill, N.C., 2009); Cynthia Stokes Brown, ed., *Ready from Within: A First Person Narrative: Septima Clark and the Civil Rights Movement* (Navarro, Calif., 1986); WWTW, 80–81; "Septima Clark," https://snccdigital.org/people/septima-clark/; "Clark, Septima Poinsette," https://kinginstitute.stanford.edu/encyclopedia/clark-septima-poinsette.

66   "HER SPECIALTY WAS"   WWTW, 80–81.

66   "DAY BY DAY"   "Citizenship Schools Class Workbook, Georgia [1962]," https://www.crmvet.org/docs/cit_schools_ga_workbook62.pdf.

66   "HE SHOWED US"   WWTW, 85.

67   THE STORE'S MOTTO   "Looking Back: The Harvey Family and Their Department Stores," *The Tennessean,* June 17, 2016.

67   THE SEGREGATED MONKEY BAR   WWTW, 87.

67   MUCH OF NASHVILLE'S ATTENTION   "Snow and Cold Fail to Deter Football Fans: Freezing Predicted as Crowds Prepare for Vandy-Vol Game," *The Tennessean,* November 28, 1959.

67   VANDERBILT WOULD WIN   https://utsports.com/sports/football/schedule/1959.

67   "I CAME TO TOWN"   Sarah Taylor, "Early Shoppers Fill City, Stores," *The Tennessean,* November 28, 1959.

67   "A SOLID MASS OF CARS"   Ibid.

67   BRAVING COLD TEMPERATURES   "Cloudy, Cold," *The Tennessean,* November 28, 1959.

67   IT HAD SNOWED OVERNIGHT   "Snow and Cold Fail to Deter Football Fans," *The Tennessean,* November 28, 1959.

67   WALKED INTO HARVEY'S   WWTW, 87. On the sit-ins, see also Linda T. Wynn, "The Dawning of a New Day: The Nashville Sit-Ins, February 13–May 10, 1960," *Tennessee Historical Quarterly* 50, no. 1 (1991), 42–54.

67   "I WAS NERVOUS"   WWTW, 87.

67 THE MISSISSIPPI-BORN Ibid., 86.

67 "I'M SORRY" Ibid., 87.

68 "MAY WE SPEAK" Ibid.

68 THE WAITRESS WAS Ibid.

68 "IT IS OUR" Ibid., 88–89.

68 THE TEST HAD BEEN JRL transcripts, *Eyes on the Prize,* Henry Hampton Collection.

68 "I CAME BACK" Ibid., 88.

68 THE NEXT WEEKEND WWTW, 88–89.

68 LEWIS BORROWED HIS Ibid., 92.

68 THAT FOUR FRESHMEN Ibid., 91–92.

68 QUIET SIT-INS Ibid., 92; Wynn, "Dawning of a New Day," THQ.

68 A TELEPHONE CALL JRL transcripts, *Eyes on the Prize,* Henry Hampton Collection.

68 HUNDREDS OF STUDENTS For the sit-ins, see WWTW, 92–111.

68 THEY MARCHED QUIETLY JRL transcripts, *Eyes on the Prize,* Henry Hampton Collection.

68 "WE TOOK OUR" Ibid.

69 COLD BUT SUNNY "Sunny, Cold," *The Tennessean,* February 27, 1959.

69 IN THE MORNING WWTW, 98–99.

69 "HE SAID THAT" JRL transcripts, *Eyes on the Prize,* Henry Hampton Collection.

70 "GO HOME, NIGGER!" WWTW, 99.

70 THE WHITE TOUGHS Ibid.; JRL transcripts, *Eyes on the Prize,* Henry Hampton Collection.

70 "WHAT'S THE MATTER?" WWTW, 99.

70 LEWIS WAS HIT Ibid.

70 THERE WAS PULLING Ibid.; JRL transcripts, *Eyes on the Prize,* Henry Hampton Collection.

70 SOME BURNED THE STUDENTS JRL transcripts, *Eyes on the Prize,* Henry Hampton Collection.

70 A YOUNG REPORTER David Halberstam, "A Good City Gone Ugly," *The Reporter,* March 30, 1960.

70 "AS THE YOUNG" WWTW, 100.

70 THE STUDENTS MET JRL transcripts, *Eyes on the Prize,* Henry Hampton Collection.

70 "THAT WAS THE FIRST TIME" Ibid.

70 "THAT PADDY WAGON" WWTW, 100–101.

71 "IT WOULD NOT" Powell, *Lights and Shadows,* 93.

71 "THEY THREW US Ibid., 93–94.

71 IN THE NASHVILLE JAIL WWTW, 101–2.

71 Z. ALEXANDER LOOBY JRL transcripts, *Eyes on the Prize,* Henry Hampton Collection.

71 A CHOICE OF WWTW, 103.

71 THIRTY-THREE AND ONE-THIRD Wynn, "Dawning of a New Day," THQ, 47.

71 THREE THOUSAND PEOPLE "Negroes Throng Sitdown Trials," *NYT,* March 1, 1960; "Three Students Fined in Nashville Sitdown," *WP,* March 1, 1960. See also Harrison E. Salisbury, "Negro Cleric Sets Nonviolent Aims," *NYT,* March 2, 1960.

71 COURT OFFICERS USED A LOUDSPEAKER "Negroes Throng Sitdown Trials," *NYT,* March 1, 1960.

72 "WE FEEL THAT" WWTW, 103.

72 "WE'RE GOING TO FILL" "Rights Protests Spreading; Russell Charges Incitement," *WP,* February 28, 1960.

72 IN A COMPANION PIECE Robert C. Albright, "Senator Sees Aim to Influence Legislation," *WP,* February 28, 1960.

72 THE CITY'S MAYOR, BEN WEST, ARRANGED *WWTW,* 103.

72 "A NEGRO MINISTER CALLED TODAY" Salisbury, "Negro Cleric Sets Nonviolent Aims," *NYT.*

72 A LIST OF INSTRUCTIONS Ibid.; *WWTW,* 98; author interview with JRL.

73 SOON A FULL ECONOMIC BOYCOTT *WWTW,* 105–6.

73 ATTACKERS HURLED DYNAMITE Ibid., 109.

73 LEWIS GOT THE NEWS Ibid., 108–9.

73 THEY QUICKLY DECIDED JRL transcripts, *Eyes on the Prize,* Henry Hampton Collection.

73 WITHIN HOURS, ABOUT Ibid.

73 WOULD THE MAYOR USE *WWTW,* 110.

73 WAS EXPELLED BY Waddle, "The Lawson Affair," *Vanderbilt Magazine.* Eventually Lawson, who finished his studies at Boston University, would contribute financially to the Divinity School and return to Vanderbilt to teach. The university is also now home to his papers. I am indebted to John Beasley for his guidance on these points.

73 "CUT OFF THE HEAD" *WWTW,* 104.

74 "THERE IS MORE POWER" *Eyes on the Prize Civil Rights Reader,* 113–14.

74 "I WONDER FOR" James Baldwin, "They Can't Turn Back," in *Reporting Civil Rights,* eds. Clayborne Carson, David J. Garrow, Bill Kovach, Carol Polsgrove (New York, 2003), 1:485.

74 "AMERICANS KEEP WONDERING" Ibid., 493.

74 "THE LUNCH COUNTER" Claude Sitton, "Negro Sitdowns Stir Fear of Wider Unrest in South," *NYT,* February 15, 1960.

74 "JUST AS THE SUPREME COURT" Dan Wakefield, "Eye of the Storm," *Reporting Civil Rights,* 1:473.

75 LINKED THE STUDENTS Louis E. Lomax, "The Negro Revolt Against 'The Negro Leaders,'" *Harper's,* June 1960.

75 "THE STUDENTS SAT" Ibid.

75 KING HAD ARRIVED *WWTW,* 110–11.

75 "GOING INTO THE MOVEMENT" Author interview with JRL.

76 HE COULDN'T BREATHE *WWTW,* 121–23; author interview with JRL; Garry Fullerton, "Water, Insect Spray Fail to Stop Sit-in," *The Tennessean,* November 11, 1960; Branch, *Parting the Waters,* 379–80.

76 AT ABOUT TWO-THIRTY THAT AFTERNOON Fullerton, "Water, Insect Spray Fail to Stop Sit-in," *The Tennessean.*

76 "THEY TOLD US" Ibid.

76 THE STUDENTS WOULDN'T GET UP Ibid.

76 "IT WAS JUST" Ibid.

76 LEWIS AND BEVEL WENT OVER Ibid.

76 "HE TOLD US" Ibid.

76 LEWIS AND BEVEL REFUSED TO LEAVE *WWTW,* 122.

76 BEVEL BEGAN TO PREACH Ibid.

76 "AND WHOEVER FALLETH" Daniel 3:6; this quotation is the language as Lewis recalled it. *WWTW,* 122.

76 "THEN NEBUCHADNEZZAR SPAKE" Daniel 3:28 (KJV).

77 "WE WERE BOTH" *WWTW,* 122.

77 THEN THE CITY FIRE DEPARTMENT Ibid., 122–23.

77–78 "That could have" Author interview with JRL.

78 He marked his WWTW, 127.

78 "standing in" Ibid., 124–27.

78 *Swiss Family Robinson* *The Tennessean*, February 21, 1961.

78 the "Showplace of" Ibid.

78 There was more bloodshed WWTW, 124–26.

79 "I listened to the debate" Ibid., 126–27.

79 Thurgood Marshall, the NAACP counsel Ibid., 107.

79 "It's a waste" Ibid.

80 "The SNCC people" Horton, *Long Haul*, 187. In telling the story of Nashville, it became something of a commonplace to say that the sit-ins and the successive battles against Jim Crow were like Isaiah's vision of the coming of a Messiah: "The wolf also shall dwell with the lamb, and the leopard shall lie down with the kid; and the calf and the young lion and the fatling together; and a little child shall lead them." Isaiah 11:6 (KJV).

It's a poetic image—among the most poetic and moving in the Bible—but to think of Lewis as an innocent toddler minimizes the courage, both moral and physical, it took for him to travel the path he took. Like Jesus on the eve of the Passion, Lewis grasped that pain and heartbreak and tragedy were at hand, but such was the Father's will, and it was the Father's will that must be done.

These were resilient people. Bernard LaFayette, for one, was in a terrible car accident with two other ABT students in the mountains of Tennessee one night. In a fog, the car had run off a dangerous curve, threaded stands of trees, flipped, and come to rest in a hog pen. ("I was eye to eye with a hog, and they were absolutely shocked," LaFayette recalled. "I could see their eyes go up.") Everyone survived, and the three refused to ride to the hospital in either an ambulance or a police car. "We walked the whole way, preaching and singing and praying out loud," LaFayette recalled. "We knew we had survived for a purpose. So when the movement came, we had no fear, because we had already passed through fear." Author interview with Bernard LaFayette, Jr.

80 "The nonviolent movement" Author interview with Diane Nash.

80 would come into Ibid.

80 "People would show up" Ibid.

CHAPTER THREE: *Soul Force*

85 "This is the most important" WWTW, 129.

85 Lewis first read about WWTW, 128; "Freedom Ride," *The Student Voice*, March 1961, in Carson, *The Student Voice 1960–1965*, 41.

85 was to be "a dramatic move" Ibid.

85 Interested parties were to write Ibid.

85 The previous December Raymond Arsenault, *Freedom Riders: 1961 and the Struggle for Racial Justice* (New York, 2006), 93.

85 Lewis had been WWTW, 89; Arsenault, *Freedom Riders*, 105–6.

85 Afterward, the two Arsenault, *Freedom Riders*, 106; WWTW, 127–28.

86 "Though appreciative of" Arsenault, *Freedom Riders*, 106.

86 "I couldn't believe" WWTW, 128.

86 "At this time" Arsenault, *Freedom Riders*, 105. See also WWTW, 129, and Freedom Rider application, John R. Lewis, section 456, reel 44, Congress of Racial Equality Papers.

86 HE'D HAD TO POSTPONE *WWTW,* 127, 129.

87 THE TEXT FOR Ibid., 127; author interview with JRL.

87 "THINK NOT THAT I AM COME" Matthew 10:34 (KJV).

87 "THE SWORD WAS NOT" Author interview with JRL.

87 HE'D NEVER BEEN "Transcript: Rep. John Lewis's Speech on 50th Anniversary of the March on Washington," *WP,* August 28, 2013.

87 ON SUNDAY, APRIL 30 Arsenault, *Freedom Riders,* 106; *WWTW,* 131.

87 WOULD "SIT AT" Howell Raines, *My Soul Is Rested: Movement Days in the Deep South* (New York, 1977), 110–11.

87 WENT OUT TO DINNER Arsenault, *Freedom Riders,* 108; *WWTW,* 135.

87 LEWIS HAD NEVER *WWTW,* 135; JRL transcripts, *Eyes on the Prize,* Henry Hampton Collection.

87 A FEW OTHERS WERE AT DINNER Stokely Carmichael with Ekwueme Michael Thelwell, *Ready for Revolution: The Life and Struggles of Stokely Carmichael (Kwame Ture)* (New York, 2003), 182.

87 BORN IN TRINIDAD IN 1941 Michael T. Kaufman, "Stokely Carmichael, Rights Leader Who Coined 'Black Power,' Dies at 57," *NYT,* November 16, 1998.

88 "WHEN I FIRST HEARD ABOUT" Ibid. The recollection came from an interview with Gordon Parks in *Life* magazine in 1967.

88 CHARMING AND ELOQUENT Kaufman, "Stokely Carmichael, Rights Leader," *NYT,* November 16, 1998.

88 "THAT EVENING WAS" Carmichael with Thelwell, *Ready for Revolution,* 182.

88 "IN ANY SANE" Ibid., 178.

88 *THE WASHINGTON POST* HEADLINE Arsenault, *Freedom Riders,* 111; Elsie Carper, "Pilgrimage Off on Racial Test," *WP,* May 5, 1961.

88 "WE HAD BEEN TOLD" JRL transcripts, *Eyes on the Prize,* Henry Hampton Collection.

88 IN AN ASSOCIATED PRESS STORY "Mixed Group's Tour to Challenge Segregation, Montgomery Included," *The Montgomery Advertiser,* May 5, 1961. RFK had been told of the Freedom Rides beforehand, but apparently forgot. Arsenault, *Freedom Riders,* 110–11; Evan Thomas, *Robert Kennedy: His Life* (New York, 2000), 128.

88 THE RIDERS HAD PACKED Arsenault, *Freedom Riders,* 112; *WWTW,* 135; author interview with JRL.

88 "CHRISTIAN NONVIOLENCE IS" Long, *Christian Peace and Nonviolence,* 208. Merton also wrote:

> It is not out for the conversion of the wicked to the ideas of the good, but for the healing and reconciliation of man with himself, man the person and man the human family. The nonviolent resister is not fighting simply for "his" truth or for "his" pure conscience, or for the right that is on "his side." On the contrary, both his strength and his weakness come from the fact that he is fighting for *the* truth, common to him and to the adversary, *the* right which is objective and universal. He is fighting for *everybody.* . . . For the Christian the basis of nonviolence is the Gospel message of salvation for all and the Kingdom of God to which *all* are summoned. . . . The saving grace of God in the Lord Jesus is proclaimed to man existentially in the love, the openness, the simplicity, the humility, and the self-sacrifice of Christians. (Ibid.)

88 THE RIDERS HAD SUNG "CORE Group Maps Tour of Protest," *The Chattanooga Times,* May 5, 1961.

89 A WHITE PACIFIST JRL transcripts, *Eyes on the Prize,* Henry Hampton Collection.

89 A Harvard-educated Quaker Randy Kennedy, "Albert Bigelow, 87, Pacifist Who Tried to Halt Nuclear Tests," *NYT,* October 8, 1993.

89 They rolled on *WWTW,* 137; JRL transcripts, *Eyes on the Prize,* Henry Hampton Collection; Arsenault, *Freedom Riders,* 120–21.

89 A barber, Grady H. Williams Bill Hughes, "'Freedom Riders' Hit a Snag in Charlotte, First in Dixie," *The Charlotte News,* May 9, 1961; "CORE Tester Gets Big Test," *Rocky Mount Telegram,* May 9, 1961.

89 The judge, citing Arsenault, *Freedom Riders,* 121.

89 "Life is not" Ibid., 119.

89 A dominant force Michael S. Reynolds, "York County," *South Carolina Encyclopedia,* http://www.scencyclopedia.org/sce/entries/york-county/; Federal Writers Project, *South Carolina: A Guide to the Palmetto State* (New York, 1941), 254; Francis B. Simkins, "The Ku Klux Klan in South Carolina, 1868–1871, *The Journal of Negro History* 4 (1927), 606–47.

89 "Grand Wizard of the Invisible Empire" Allen W. Trelease, *White Terror: The Ku Klux Klan Conspiracy and Southern Reconstruction* (Baton Rouge, 1971), 14–16.

89 "a time of terror" Federal Writers Project, *South Carolina,* 254.

89 President Grant declared Reynolds, "York County," *South Carolina Encyclopedia.* See also Jean Edward Smith, *Grant* (New York, 2001), 543–48.

90 The sit-in movement *WWTW,* 137. To show support, Diane Nash and other SNCC activists had come over to Rock Hill and taken part in a "jail-in." Ibid.

90 In that period "Klansman on Parade," *NYT,* March 1, 1960.

90 an anonymous bomb threat Ibid.

90 "I was once" Andrew Dys, "Years After Racial Strife in Rock Hill, 2 Whites Apologize to 5 Blacks," *The Herald* (Rock Hill, S.C.), January 24, 2009.

90 An admitted Ku Klux Klansman Dys, "I Need to Tell Some People I Am Sorry," *The Herald* (Rock Hill, S.C.), January 24, 2009.

90 "marched against integration" Ibid.

90 Bigelow and Lewis got off "Biracial Unit Tells of Beating in South," *NYT,* May 11, 1961; JRL transcripts, *Eyes on the Prize,* Henry Hampton Collection; Branch, *Parting the Waters,* 415–16.

90 were smoking cigarettes *WWTW,* 137.

90 Lewis remembered their Ibid.

90 "Other side, nigger" Ibid.

90 "I have a" Ibid.

90 "Shit on that" Ibid., 138.

90 "beat us and" JRL transcripts, *Eyes on the Prize,* Henry Hampton Collection.

90 Repeatedly struck in *WWTW,* 138.

90 the taste of Ibid.

91 "My fists" Dys, "I Need to Tell Some People I Am Sorry," *The Herald.*

91 A Rock Hill policeman watched *WWTW,* 138.

91 "woozy and feeling" Ibid.

91 "We're not here" Lewis, *Across That Bridge,* 191.

91 "No child is born in hate" Ibid., 193.

91 The Rock Hill police captain "Biracial Unit Tells of Beating in South," *NYT,* May 11, 1961.

91 he refused to leave Arsenault, *Freedom Riders,* 122.

91 bandaged up *WWTW,* 139.

91 he'd applied JRL transcripts, *Eyes on the Prize,* Henry Hampton Collection; *WWTW,* 139.

91 THE COMMITTEE TELEGRAMMED HIM *WWTW*, 139.

91 (THE QUAKERS HAD) Ibid.

91 LEWIS CAUGHT A FLIGHT Ibid.

91 HE WAS THRILLED Ibid., 140.

91 HE'D GO TO CHURCH Author interview with JRL.

91 THE CITY'S THEATERS HAD *WWTW*, 140.

91 LEWIS WOULD JOIN Author interview with JRL.

91 NASHVILLE WAS LOVELY *WWTW*, 140; Branch, *Parting the Waters*, 424–25.

91 IT WAS SUNNY "High in the 80s," *The Tennessean*, May 14, 1961.

92 JAMES BEVEL WAS PREACHING *WWTW*, 140.

92 "I FELT SHOCK" Ibid.

92 THE BUS HAD ARRIVED Ibid., 140–41; "Bi-Racial Buses Attacked, Riders Beaten in Alabama," *NYT*, May 15, 1961; Arsenault, *Freedom Riders*, 143.

92 BUT THE BACK TIRES *WWTW*, 141.

93 "THE BUS JUST" JRL transcripts, *Eyes on the Prize*, Henry Hampton Collection.

93 THE KLANSMEN ROARED UP *WWTW*, 141.

93 "BURN THEM ALIVE!" Arsenault, *Freedom Riders*, 145.

93 "OH MY GOD" Ibid., 144.

93 IN THE CHAOS Ibid.; "Bi-Racial Buses Attacked," *NYT*.

94 THE FREEDOM RIDERS' TRAILWAYS BUS JRL transcripts, *Eyes on the Prize*, Henry Hampton Collection; *WWTW*, 142–43; Arsenault, *Freedom Riders*, 149–61.

94 "ONE PASSENGER WAS" Arsenault, *Freedom Riders*, 165; *WWTW*, 142. *The New York Times* also cited Smith's report. "Eyewitness Account: Smith of C.B.S. Says 'Toughs' Used Pipes on Victims," *NYT*, May 15, 1961. For Smith's account, see Howard K. Smith, *Events Leading Up to My Death: The Life of a Twentieth-Century Reporter* (New York, 1996), 268–76.

94 THERE WAS LAWLESSNESS Arsenault, *Freedom Riders*, 165.

94 "NOBODY NEEDS TO" Arthur M. Schlesinger, Jr., *A Thousand Days: John F. Kennedy in the White House* (Boston, 1965), 931.

94 JFK HAD SIGNALED HIS SYMPATHY The details of this episode are drawn from Harris Wofford, *Of Kennedys and Kings: Making Sense of the Sixties* (Pittsburgh, Pa., 1992), 11–28; Theodore H. White, *The Making of the President 1960* (New York, 1961), 351–53, and Schlesinger, *Thousand Days*, 73–74. For the view from Nixon's camp, see White, *Making of the President 1960*, 344–45, and Richard M. Nixon, *Six Crises* (New York, 1962), 362–63.

94 HAD BEEN ARRESTED White, *Making of the President 1960*, 351.

94 CORETTA KING, WHO WAS Ibid.

94 "THEY ARE GOING TO" Wofford, *Of Kennedys and Kings*, 11.

94 HARRIS WOFFORD, A NOTRE DAME White, *Making of the President 1960*, 351.

94 WOULD JFK CALL Ibid.

94 SHRIVER CALLED THE CANDIDATE Ibid., 351–52.

94 "WHY DON'T YOU" Wofford, *Of Kennedys and Kings*, 18.

95 "THAT'S A GOOD IDEA" Ibid., 18–19. See also Schlesinger, *Thousand Days*, 74.

95 "I KNOW THIS MUST BE" Wofford, *Of Kennedys and Kings*, 19.

95 ROBERT KENNEDY WAS INITIALLY Schlesinger, *Thousand Days*, 74.

95 "YOU BOMB THROWERS" Ibid. See also Wofford, *Of Kennedys and Kings*, 19–20.

95 THEN ROBERT KENNEDY THOUGHT AGAIN Schlesinger, *Thousand Days*, 74; Wofford, *Of Kennedys and Kings*, 21–22. As John Seigenthaler recalled it, RFK explained his call to the judge this way: "It just burned me up. . . . It grilled me. The more I thought about the injustice of it, the more I thought what a son of a bitch the

judge was. I made it clear to him that it was not a political call; that I am a lawyer, one who believes in the right of all defendants to make bond. . . . I felt it was disgraceful." Wofford, *Of Kennedys and Kings,* 21.

95 KING WAS SOON RELEASED Schlesinger, *Thousand Days,* 74.

95 RFK BRIEFED LYNDON B. JOHNSON Ibid.

95 "TELL JACK THAT WE'LL RIDE" Ibid.

95 THE MANEUVERS PAID OFF Ibid.; White, *Making of the President 1960,* 352–53.

95 HAD ENDORSED RICHARD NIXON White, *Making of the President 1960,* 352. King's father had "told newspapermen that he never thought he could vote for a Catholic but that the call to his daughter-in-law had changed his mind. 'Imagine Martin Luther King having a bigot for a father,' [John] Kennedy said—then added quizzically, 'Well, we all have fathers, don't we?' " Schlesinger, *Thousand Days,* 74.

95 "BECAUSE THIS MAN" White, *Making of the President 1960,* 352. See also Wofford, *Of Kennedys and Kings,* 23.

95 FLYERS HERALDING THE KENNEDY-KING EPISODE Wofford, *Of Kennedys and Kings,* 23–25.

95 IN SUCH A CLOSE-RUN ELECTION Ibid., 25–27; White, *Making of the President 1960,* 352–53.

95 "HISTORIANS OF THE TWENTY-FIRST CENTURY" Schlesinger, *Thousand Days,* 924.

95 "THE ANSWER TO" Ibid.

96 "IT IS NOT" Ibid.

96 "BY SUCH MEANS" Ibid.

96 HIS HANDS TREMBLED Thomas, *Robert Kennedy,* 127. See also Arsenault, *Freedom Riders,* 129.

96 "FROM THE CONGO" Robert F. Kennedy, "Law Day Address at the University of Georgia Law School," May 6, 1961, https://www.americanrhetoric.com/speeches /rfkgeorgialawschool.htm.

96 "WE ARE MAINTAINING" Ibid.

96 ELEANOR ROOSEVELT WAS WORKING Allida M. Black, *Casting Her Own Shadow: Eleanor Roosevelt and the Shaping of Postwar Liberalism* (New York, 1996), 127.

97 "I HAD THE MOST WONDERFUL DREAM" Ibid.

97 "TELL THEM TO" Thomas, *Robert Kennedy,* 129.

97 JAMES FARMER WAS THINKING Arsenault, *Freedom Riders,* 166–67.

97 "THE CITIZENS OF THE STATE" Ibid., 170.

97 DECIDED TO SEND AN EMISSARY John Seigenthaler Oral History, April 2, 2012, John Seigenthaler Papers, Special Collections Library, Vanderbilt University, Nashville, Tennessee. See also Arsenault, *Freedom Riders,* 173.

97 "FLY DOWN IMMEDIATELY" Seigenthaler Oral History, April 2, 2012, Vanderbilt.

97 SEIGENTHALER GRABBED SOME CLOTHES Ibid.

97 FOR HARRIED HOURS Arsenault, *Freedom Riders,* 168–76, 617.

97 AT 10:38 P.M. ON MONDAY Ibid., 175.

97 "I THOUGHT I WAS" Seigenthaler Oral History, April 2, 2012, Vanderbilt.

97 DURING MEETINGS *WWTW,* 143–45; Arsenault, *Freedom Riders,* 179–87.

98 "DON'T COME," THEY WERE TOLD Nash, "Inside the Sit-ins and Freedom Rides," in Ahmann, *New Negro,* 53.

98 "MOB VIOLENCE," NASH SAID Ibid.

98 "RETREAT IS ONE THING" *WWTW,* 143.

98 IN NEW ORLEANS Seigenthaler Oral History, April 2, 2012, Vanderbilt.

98 "WHO THE HELL" Ibid.

98 "BOB, SHE'S A YOUNG STUDENT" Ibid.

98 "WELL, SHE'S SENDING" Ibid.

98 SEIGENTHALER TRACKED NASH DOWN Ibid.

98 "OF COURSE WE CAN'T [STOP NOW]" Ibid.

98 "SHE WAS PREACHING TO ME" Ibid.

99 "THE ADULTS DID NOT" Author interview with Bernard LaFayette, Jr.

99 ON WEDNESDAY, MAY 17, 1961 *WWTW*, 145.

99 AT THE BIRMINGHAM CITY LIMITS Ibid., 147.

99 ONCE THERE, THE POLICE Ibid.

99 AN ANGRY CROWD GATHERED Ibid., 147–48.

99 THE DRIVER SCHEDULED Ibid.; William A. Nunnelly, *Bull Connor* (Tuscaloosa, 1991), 102.

99 "I HAD SEEN" Author interview with JRL.

99 BORN IN 1897 Nunnelly, *Bull Connor*, 9.

99 AND NEVER FINISHED HIGH SCHOOL Ibid., 10.

99 AS A RADIO SPORTSCASTER Ibid., 11–12.

100 IN 1934, "PARTLY FOR" Ibid., 12.

100 HE WAS A DEVOTED DEFENDER Ibid., 30.

100 A DECADE LATER Ibid., 31–32.

100 "IT IS PART" Ibid., 32.

100 AT THE NATIONAL CONVENTION Ibid., 34.

100 CONNOR WHO WELCOMED THE Ibid. For an illuminating account of the Dixiecrat convention in Birmingham, see John M. Coski, *The Confederate Battle Flag: America's Most Embattled Emblem* (Cambridge, Mass., 2005), 98–109.

100 "I WANT TO TELL YOU" Jack Bass and Marilyn W. Thompson, *Strom: The Complicated Personal and Political Life of Strom Thurmond* (New York, 2005), 117.

101 "BULL IS THE LAW" Harrison E. Salisbury, "Fear and Hatred Grip Birmingham," *NYT,* April 8, 1960.

101 "BALL PARKS AND TAXICABS" Ibid.

101 IN A PIECE ENTITLED Nunnelly, *Bull Connor,* 5; Salisbury, "Fear and Hatred Grip Birmingham," *NYT.* For Birmingham's reaction, see "Connor Blasts N.Y. Times Story," *The Birmingham News,* April 15, 1960; "N.Y. Times Continues Attack," *The Birmingham News,* April 15, 1960; "A Grave Disservice," *The Birmingham News,* April 15, 1960.

102 TO A MEETING OF THE Bud Gordon, "Negroes Want Supremacy, Not Equality, Connor Says," *The Birmingham News,* April 15, 1960.

102 "I DON'T NEED" Ibid.

102 "THEY WANT TO" Ibid.

102 "DAILY ENCOURAGING MORE" Ibid.

102 "I'LL TELL YOU" Ibid.; Nunnelly, *Bull Connor,* 89.

102 "YES, WE ARE" Gordon, "Negroes Want Supremacy." *The Birmingham News,* April 15, 1960.

102 TWO WEEKS BEFORE Nunnelly, *Bull Connor,* 92.

102 "BY GOLLY," HE SAID Ibid.

103 "WE ARE NOT" Ibid., 101.

103 IT WAS THE FIRST TIME *WWTW*, 148–49.

103 "WERE BEING TAKEN" JRL transcripts, *Eyes on the Prize,* Henry Hampton Collection.

103 AS A "DUNGEON" *WWTW*, 149.

103 WENT ON A HUNGER STRIKE JRL transcripts, *Eyes on the Prize,* Henry Hampton Collection. "We refused to eat anything," Lewis recalled, "refused to drink any water." Ibid.

103 THEY SANG FREEDOM SONGS Author interview with JRL.

103 THAT EVENING, THE NATION Diane McWhorter, *Carry Me Home: Birmingham, Alabama—The Climactic Battle of the Civil Rights Revolution* (New York, 2001), 223–44. See also Smith, *Events Leading Up to My Death,* 272–76.

103 "AFTER TEN MINUTES" McWhorter, *Carry Me Home,* 224.

103 "WITNESSING THE SAVAGE BEATINGS" Smith, *Events Leading Up to My Death,* 272.

103 SMITH WOULD LOSE HIS JOB Herbert Mitgang, "Howard K. Smith: TV History," WP, April 16, 1996.

103 BY ELEVEN-THIRTY P.M. Arsenault, *Freedom Riders,* 197.

104 "YOU PEOPLE CAME" Ibid.

104 "WE DIDN'T GO" JRL transcripts, *Eyes on the Prize,* Henry Hampton Collection.

104 LEWIS RODE IN THE CAR Author interview with JRL.

104 "HE TRIED BEING FRIENDLY" WWTW, 149.

104 ONE OF THE RIDERS Ibid.

104 HAPPY TO, CONNOR REPLIED Ibid.; Nunnelly, *Bull Connor,* 102.

104 ABOUT 120 MILES Arsenault, *Freedom Riders,* 198.

105 "THIS IS WHERE" Ibid.

105 THE POLICE LEFT Ibid.

105 "WE WERE FRIGHTENED" JRL transcripts, *Eyes on the Prize,* Henry Hampton Collection.

105 WHAT THEY DID KNOW Author interview with JRL.

105 "A BUS WILL" JRL transcripts, *Eyes on the Prize,* Henry Hampton Collection.

105 THE SMALL GROUP SET OFF Ibid.; WWTW, 150–51; Raines, *My Soul Is Rested,* 118–19.

105 "WHAT DO YOU" JRL transcripts, *Eyes on the Prize,* Henry Hampton Collection; author interview with JRL.

105 ANOTHER OF DIANE NASH'S CALLS Carmichael with Thelwell, *Ready for Revolution,* 186–87.

106 BACK IN ALABAMA WWTW, 151–52.

106 IT WAS THE LARGEST CROWD Ibid., 152.

106 FOR EIGHTEEN HOURS Arsenault, *Freedom Riders,* 202–8.

106 "NO BUS DRIVER" JRL transcripts, *Eyes on the Prize,* Henry Hampton Collection.

106 THE SCHEDULED WHITE DRIVER Loory, "Reporter Tails 'Freedom' Bus, Caught in Riot," *Reporting Civil Rights,* 1:578.

106 "I HAVE ONLY" JRL transcripts, *Eyes on the Prize,* Henry Hampton Collection.

106 WORKING FROM WASHINGTON Thomas, *Robert Kennedy,* 128–32.

106 PREVAILED ON CAVERNO Loory, "Reporter Tails 'Freedom' Bus," *Reporting Civil Rights,* 1:578; Raines, *My Soul Is Rested,* 119–20.

106 AT LAST, AT EIGHT-THIRTY Loory, "Reporter Tails 'Freedom' Bus," *Reporting Civil Rights,* 1:574.

106 AS THEY REACHED Ibid.

106 "NOT SINCE RECONSTRUCTION" Dan Wakefield, "Eye of the Storm," *Reporting Civil Rights,* 1:455.

106 TO LAUGHS AND APPLAUSE Ibid.

106 "SPRING IS HERE" Ibid.

107 "AT THE BUS STATION" JRL transcripts, *Eyes on the Prize,* Henry Hampton Collection.

107 THE GOAL OF THE JOURNEY Loory, "Reporter Tails 'Freedom' Bus," *Reporting Civil Rights,* 1:575.

107 "WE JUST GOT" Ibid.

107 "GET THOSE NIGGERS!" Ibid.

107 "The moment we" JRL transcripts, *Eyes on the Prize,* Henry Hampton Collection.

107 "Do not run" *WWTW,* 155.

107 Lewis was struck Ibid., 156.

107 "I could feel" Ibid.

107 John Seigenthaler arrived Ibid., 156–57; Arsenault, *Freedom Riders,* 213–15.

107 Seigenthaler was out Arsenault, *Freedom Riders,* 215.

107 "Oh, there are" Arthur M. Schlesinger, Jr., *Robert Kennedy and His Times* (Boston, 1978), 309.

107 "I literally thought" JRL transcripts, *Eyes on the Prize,* Henry Hampton Collection.

107 After he regained consciousness *WWTW,* 157.

107 reading an injunction against "entry" Ibid.

108 "I hardly listened" Ibid.

108 "I was sickened" Calvin Trillin, "Back on the Bus," *The New Yorker,* July 18, 2011.

108 the congregation cooled off Kempton, "Tear Gas and Hymns," *Reporting Civil Rights,* 1:580.

108 Lewis remembered joining *WWTW,* 158–62.

108 "This is a" Kempton, "Tear Gas and Hymns," *Reporting Civil Rights,* 1:581.

108 There were Confederate flags *WWTW,* 159–60.

108 a brick crashing Ibid., 160.

108 In Abernathy's basement office Ibid., 158–60.

108 "John, John" Schlesinger, *Thousand Days,* 936.

108 RFK had arranged Thomas, *Robert Kennedy,* 130.

108–09 "I wonder which" Ibid.

109 "seemed a home" Kempton, "Tear Gas and Hymns," *Reporting Civil Rights,* 1:580.

109 "had become a" Ibid.

109 "Fear not" *WWTW,* 161.

109 "As long as" Thomas, *Robert Kennedy,* 130.

109 But it wasn't Ibid.

109 The congregation sang Kempton, "Tear Gas and Hymns," *Reporting Civil Rights,* 1:583.

110 The National Guard arrived *WWTW,* 161.

110 "Their rifles were" Ibid.

110 "So now we" Ibid.

110 "Out on the pavement" Kempton, "Tear Gas and Hymns," *Reporting Civil Rights,* 1:584.

110 Lewis was taken *WWTW,* 162.

110 home of Dr. Richard Harris Ibid. See also "Rep. John Lewis on the Death of Vera Harris," September 12, 2019, https://johnlewis.house.gov/media-center/press-releases/rep-john-lewis-death-mrs-vera-harris.

110 Harris served the *WWTW,* 162.

110 wired a warning Arsenault, *Freedom Riders,* 251.

111 "A mob asks no questions" "Statement by the Honorable Robert F. Kennedy, Attorney General of the United States, May 24, 1961," https://www.justice.gov/sites/default/files/ag/legacy/2011/01/20/05-24-1961b.pdf.

111 "We've been cooling" *WWTW,* 175.

111 "the first time" Branch, *Parting the Waters,* 475.

111 "Freedom Riders must" Arsenault, *Freedom Riders,* 253–54.

111 "I'd never been" *WWTW,* 166.

III "AT THE OUTSKIRTS" Frank Holloway, "A Deep South Tourist," *Reporting Civil Rights*, 1:602.

III ONCE ASKED Theodore H. White, *The Making of the President 1964* (New York, 1965), 175.

III AT THE JACKSON, MISSISSIPPI, BUS STATION *WWTW,* 167.

III CONVICTED OF BREACHING THE PEACE Arsenault, *Freedom Riders*, 284–86.

III HE SPENT A *WWTW,* 167.

III BRETHREN WERE HERDED Ibid., 168.

III TO PARCHMAN FARM Ibid.; Branch, *Parting the Waters*, 483–85; Arsenault, *Freedom Riders*, 325–42. For a history of Parchman, see David M. Oshinsky, *"Worse Than Slavery": Parchman Farm and the Ordeal of Jim Crow Justice* (New York, 1996).

III "DESTINATION DOOM" Arsenault, *Freedom Riders*, 325; Oshinsky, *"Worse Than Slavery,"* I. The quotation comes from Faulkner's *The Mansion*.

112 "WE HAVE BAD" Branch, *Parting the Waters*, 483.

112 PARCHMAN'S SUPERINTENDENT, FRED JONES *WWTW,* 168.

112 THE GUARDS WIELDED Ibid.

112 STRETCHED FARTHER THAN Author interview with JRL.

112 "SING YOUR GODDAMNED" Ibid.

112 "PARCHMAN WAS NOT" Ibid.

112 "WE WERE LED" *WWTW,* 169–70.

112 HE WROTE THE Branch, *Parting the Waters*, 485.

112 "THE PEOPLE WHO WERE" Author interview with JRL.

113 EACH FREEDOM RIDER WAS ASSIGNED Author interview with Bernard LaFayette, Jr.

113 "WE DID A LOT" Author interview with JRL.

113 BERNARD LAFAYETTE REMEMBERED Author interview with Bernard LaFayette, Jr.

113 THEY WERE CONSCIOUS Ibid.

113 "ABOUT MIDNIGHT" See Acts 16:22–26 (NIV).

114 "PAUL AND SILAS BOUND IN JAIL" Author interview with JRL.

114 "IT WAS LIKE" Ibid.

115 KING MET THEM Branch, *Parting the Waters*, 489.

115 "WE WILL WEAR YOU DOWN" Ibid.

115 "DO TO US" Wakefield, "Eye of the Storm," *Reporting Civil Rights*, 1:477.

115 "A YEAR OF THE VICTORY" Schlesinger, *Thousand Days*, 957.

115 "I WAS HUNGRY" *WWTW,* 182–84.

CHAPTER FOUR: *In the Image of God and Democracy*

119 "ALTOGETHER, IT WAS" *N.B.C. White Paper: The Nashville Sit-in Story,* NBC News, December 20, 1960.

119 "NIGGUHS HATE WHITES" Marshall Frady, *Wallace* (New York, 1968), 14.

119 IN A CONCERTED CAMPAIGN For accounts of Birmingham, see, for instance, Branch, *Parting the Waters*, 673–802; Garrow, *Bearing the Cross*, 231–87; McWhorter, *Carry Me Home*, 303–454; Raines, *My Soul Is Rested*, 139–85; Forman, *Making of Black Revolutionaries*, 311–16.

119 THE HOSES THAT CONNOR Claude Sitton, "Rioting Negroes Routed by Police at Birmingham," *NYT,* May 8, 1963.

119 "BRICKS WERE TORN" Len Holt, "Eyewitness: The Police Terror at Birmingham," *Reporting Civil Rights*, 1:799.

119 FRED SHUTTLESWORTH WAS TAKEN AWAY Ibid.

119   "I waited a week" Sitton, "Rioting Negroes Routed by Police at Birmingham," *NYT,* May 8, 1963.

119   One African American father Raymond R. Coffey, "Waiting in the Rain at the Birmingham Jail," *Reporting Civil Rights,* 1:802.

119   "And as it" Ted Widmer, ed., *Listening In: The Secret White House Recordings of John F. Kennedy* (New York, 2012), 111–13. See also Michael Beschloss, *Presidential Courage: Brave Leaders and How They Changed America, 1789–1989* (New York, 2007), 262–64.

120   "I am not asking" Schlesinger, *Thousand Days,* 959.

120   In a television documentary *NBC White Paper: Sit-In,* NBC News, December 20, 1960.

120   "one of the networks" Jack Gould, "TV: Study of Sit-Ins; 'N.B.C. White Paper' on Nashville Issue Is an Exciting Social Document," *NYT,* December 21, 1960.

120   the young people *WWTW,* 196.

120   In the documentary The ensuing details are drawn from *NBC White Paper: Sit-in,* NBC News.

123   would cut out images *WWTW,* 197–98.

123   "Snarling German shepherds" Ibid., 197.

123   "I hope that" Schlesinger, *Thousand Days,* 959.

123   "This nigger has" Ibid.

123   "In his broadest" "Dr. King Denounces President on Rights," *NYT,* June 10, 1963.

123   "We were like" White, *Making of the President 1964,* 180.

124   Over that weekend Tom Wicker, "Kennedy Appeals for Local Action on Race Problem," *NYT,* June 10, 1963.

124   The same edition Claude Sitton, "Alabama Guardsmen in Tuscaloosa as Wallace Plans to Defy U.S. Court," *NYT,* June 10, 1963.

124   Inside the paper "Klan Meeting in Alabama," *NYT,* June 10, 1963.

124   "It is clear" Wicker, "Kennedy Appeals for Local Action on Race Problem," *NYT.*

125   "In my opinion" Sitton, "Alabama Guardsmen in Tuscaloosa as Wallace Plans to Defy U.S. Court," *NYT.*

125   "You know, we just can't" Frady, *Wallace,* 141. I drew on my portrait of Wallace in *The Soul of America: The Battle for Our Better Angels* (New York, 2018), 218–20, for this account. See also Stephan Lesher, *George Wallace: American Populist* (Reading, Mass., 1994).

125   He veered between Lesher, *George Wallace,* 79, 125–26.

125   "He had a genuine aversion" Frady, *Wallace,* 130.

126   "John Patterson out-nigguhed" Ibid., 127.

126   (Wallace denied this) Lesher, *George Wallace,* 128–29.

126   "He used to be" Frady, *Wallace,* 141.

126   "a low-down" Ibid., 133.

126   "The crowd liked" Ibid., 137–38.

126   "In the name of" "Inaugural Address of Governor George Wallace," Alabama Department of Archives and History, http://digital.archives.alabama.gov/cdm/ref/collection/voices/id/2952.

127   Wallace made a show Frady, *Wallace,* 170–71; Branch, *Parting the Waters,* 821–22.

127   In anticipation Frady, *Wallace,* 154.

127   "You think it" Ibid., 157.

127   "Well, I think" Ibid.

127 "No one can deny" Schlesinger, *Thousand Days,* 964.

127 He had not given much Theodore C. Sorensen, *Kennedy* (New York, 1965), 494–95.

127 The president did in fact Beschloss, *Presidential Courage,* 270.

127 "Now the time has come" Ibid., 495.

128 Late that night Claude Sitton, "N.A.A.C.P. Leader Slain in Jackson; Protests Mount," *NYT,* June 13, 1963.

128 After parking his Ibid.

128 Cries of "Daddy!" Ibid.

128 Evers, thirty-seven, was Ibid.

128 "It was hard" *WWTW,* 199.

129 He was elected chairman "Lewis Elected as SNCC Chairman," *The Student Voice,* August 1963, in Carson, *The Student Voice 1960–1965,* 69; author interview with JRL.

129 "Lewis, 23, has been arrested" "Lewis Elected as SNCC Chairman," *The Student Voice,* August 1963, in Carson, *The Student Voice 1960–1965,* 69.

129 Lewis stood in *WWTW,* 201.

129 "Again, as I" Ibid.

129 6 Raymond Street NW *The Student Voice,* August 1963, in Carson, *The Student Voice 1960–1965,* 69.

129 "It was sparsely" *WWTW,* 269.

130 "I'm not impetuous" Ibid., 42.

130 "During that period" Author interview with JRL.

130 "She'd be in the kitchen" Author interview with Mae Lewis Tyner.

130 "Bob's going to be" Ibid.

130 "My father was supportive" Author interview with JRL.

130 "Some of the deepest" *WWTW,* 269.

131 "One of the guys" Ibid., 270–71.

131 "Make it," Lewis later explained Ibid., 272.

131 "And she was right" Ibid.

131 "What a terrible business" Schlesinger, *Thousand Days,* 966.

131 "Yes," JFK replied Ibid.

131 "The purpose and avowed object" "Reconstruction: Hon. Thaddeus Stevens on the Great Topic of the Hour. An Address Delivered to the Citizens of Lancaster, Sept. 6, 1865," *NYT,* September 10, 1865.

131 slavery as the "corner-stone" Alexander H. Stephens, " 'Corner Stone' Speech," https://teachingamericanhistory.org/library/document/cornerstone-speech/.

132 white supremacy "has not been" Edward Alfred Pollard, *The Lost Cause Regained* (New York, 1868), 13. See also Meacham, *Soul of America,* 51–69.

132 the "true hope" Pollard, *Lost Cause Regained,* 14.

132 "White men alone" Eric Foner, *Reconstruction: America's Unfinished Revolution* (New York, 2014), 180.

132 "No independent government" Ibid.

132 this was "probably" Ibid.

132 "The white race" John Marshall Harlan, "Judge Harlan's Dissent," http://chnm.gmu.edu/courses/nclc375/harlan.html. See also Meacham, *Soul of America,* 68–69, 305, and Eric Foner, *Forever Free: The Story of Emancipation and Reconstruction* (New York, 2005), 207–8.

132 "Criticism, analysis, detachment" Dan Wakefield, "Eye of the Storm," *Reporting Civil Rights,* 1:458.

132 the Citizens' Councils in the South See, for instance, Stephanie R. Rolph,

Resisting Equality: The Citizens' Council, 1954–1989 (Baton Rouge, La., 2018), for an illuminating study of the Citizens' Councils and their role in—and relation to—American conservatism.

132 FOUNDED IN THE MISSISSIPPI DELTA Ibid., 13–68.

133 IN HER NOVEL Harper Lee, *Go Set a Watchman* (New York, 2015); Michiko Kakutani, "Harper Lee's 'Go Set a Watchman' Gives Atticus Finch a Dark Side," *NYT*, July 10, 2015.

133 "BORN AND BRED IN THE SOUTH" Lee, *Go Set a Watchman*, 108.

133 PRISON OFFICIALS AT PARCHMAN Author interview with JRL.

133 ENTITLED *RACE AND REASON* Robert Mcg. Thomas, Jr., "Carleton Putnam Dies at 96; Led Delta and Wrote on Race," *NYT*, March 16, 1998.

133 "THE WHOLE MATTER" Carleton Putnam, *Race and Reason: A Yankee View* (Washington, D.C., 1961). See https://www.jrbooksonline.com/PDFs/Race_and_Reason .pdf.

133 "THERE ARE NO" Schlesinger, *Thousand Days*, 943–44.

133 "I HAVE ALMOST REACHED" Martin Luther King, Jr., "Letter from Birmingham Jail," *Reporting Civil Rights*, 1:784–85.

134 KING CITED JESUS Ibid., 788.

134 PRIVILEGED CLASSES, KING NOTED Ibid., 781.

134 NOT A NEW IDEA *WWTW*, 203.

134 THE DEAN OF CIVIL RIGHTS ACTIVISTS Kenneth S. Davis, *FDR: The War President, 1940–1943* (New York, 2000), 200–206.

134 HOW TO BLAST Ibid., 202.

134 "THE VIRTUE AND RIGHTNESS" Ibid.

134 A LARGE DEMONSTRATION Ibid., 203.

134 IN A DIFFICULT MEETING Ibid., 203-05.

135 BROKERED A COMPROMISE Ibid.

135 AT TEN-THIRTY JFK Daily Schedule, June 22, 1963, John F. Kennedy Presidential Library, Boston.

135 KENNEDY APPEARED PREOCCUPIED *WWTW*, 206.

135 THE PRESIDENT'S AGENDA Ibid.

135 "WE WANT SUCCESS" Schlesinger, *Thousand Days*, 969.

135 "THE NEGROES ARE" Ibid.

135 "IN SPITE OF" JRL transcripts, *Eyes on the Prize*, Henry Hampton Collection.

135 THE CABINET ROOM Branch, *Parting the Waters*, 839.

135 "PRESIDENT KENNEDY'S BODY LANGUAGE" Author interview with JRL. "President Kennedy . . . was a little frightened by it and he was troubled," Lewis recalled in another interview. JRL transcripts, *Eyes on the Prize*, Henry Hampton Collection.

136 "WELL, I WORRY" Author interview with JRL.

136 KING WEIGHED IN Schlesinger, *Thousand Days*, 970.

136 "INCLUDING THE ATTORNEY" Ibid.

136 "I DON'T THINK" Ibid., 970–71.

136 "AN AUDIBLE INTAKE" Ibid., 71.

136 "AFTER ALL, HE" Ibid.

136 "THIS IS A VERY SERIOUS FIGHT" Ibid.

136 AS KENNEDY PREPARED Branch, *Parting the Waters*, 839.

136 "I MAY LOSE" Ibid.

136 SOUGHT TO CONTROL IT Reeves, *President Kennedy*, 580–81.

136 JOHN DOUGLAS, AN ASSISTANT Ibid.

136 STATIONED BEHIND THE MEMORIAL Ibid., 581.

136–37 JOHN REILLY, A JUSTICE DEPARTMENT OFFICIAL I am grateful to Michael Beschloss for this detail. See also Dennis Hevesi, "John R. Reilly, Adviser to Mondale, Is Dead at 80," *NYT*, October 15, 2008.

137 EVERYTHING WAS TO TAKE PLACE Reeves, *President Kennedy*, 581.

137 LEWIS HAD WORKED *WWTW*, 216.

137 "I THOUGHT IT WAS" JRL transcripts, *Eyes on the Prize,* Henry Hampton Collection.

137 THE NIGHT BEFORE Ibid.

137 "WE REALLY ARGUED" Ibid.; *WWTW*, 221–23.

137 ROY WILKINS OF THE NAACP *WWTW*, 225.

137 "MR. WILKINS," LEWIS REPLIED Ibid.

137 THEN RANDOLPH MADE Ibid., 226.

137 "HOW COULD I" Ibid.

137 LEWIS TWEAKED HIS SPEECH For a comparison of speeches as written and as delivered, see Lauren Feeney, "Two Versions of John Lewis' Speech," July 24, 2013, https://billmoyers.com/content/two-versions-of-john-lewis-speech/. See also Forman, *Making of Black Revolutionaries,* 331–37, and *WWTW*, 219–21.

138 ("JOHN," KING HAD) *WWTW*, 225.

138 "I NOW HAVE" "Rep. John Lewis' Speech at the 1963 March on Washington," https://vimeo.com/70657416.

138 HIS AMENDED NOTES IN HAND Ibid. The ensuing details are drawn from viewing the cited footage.

142 "I THINK HE WAS" Author interview with JRL.

142 "UNLIKE POPULAR OPINION" Author interview with Harry Belafonte.

142 IN HIS CLOSING REMARKS Martin Luther King, Jr., "I Have a Dream . . ." National Archives, https://www.archives.gov/files/press/exhibits/dream-speech.pdf; Branch, *Parting the Waters,* 875–83; Clarence B. Jones and Stuart Connelly, *Behind the Dream: The Making of the Speech That Transformed a Nation* (New York, 2011).

142 "HE'S DAMN GOOD" Branch, *Parting the Waters,* 883.

142 "'I HAVE A DREAM'" Reeves, *President Kennedy,* 584.

142 ("HE NODDED AGAIN") Ibid.

142 TO LEWIS, KENNEDY SAID ONLY *WWTW*, 229. "You gave us your blessings," the NAACP's Roy Wilkins told Kennedy. "We think it changed the character of the protests. It was one of the prime factors in turning it into an orderly protest to help our government rather than a protest against our government. I think you'll agree that was psychologically important. And the mood and the attitude of the people there today pleased all of us, without exception." Widmer, *Listening In,* 128.

Wilkins also alluded to the message manifested by the crowd of 250,000. "We think that today's demonstration," he said, "if it did nothing else, showed that people back home, from the small towns, to the big cities, the working people, men who gave up two days' pay, three days' pay, $30, $40, $50, $100, who flew from Los Angeles at three hundred dollars' round trip to come here means that they, not Martin Luther King, or Roy Wilkins, or Whitney Young or Walter Reuther dreamed up this civil rights business." Reeves, *President Kennedy,* 585.

Vice President Johnson offered his thoughts on the legislative battle ahead. "Now there's one thing the President can do, he can plead and lead and persuade and even threaten Congress, but he can't run the Congress," LBJ told the civil rights leaders. "Franklin Roosevelt at the height of his popularity in '37 lost his court plan overwhelmingly, and he only lost two states in the '36 election. I came here during that period. And this President can't get those sixty votes, if he turned this White House upside down, and he preached on television an hour every day, it will just drive some of those men stronger into [opposition]. Maybe the men at this table can do it. But things are going to be pretty hard." (Widmer, *Listening In,* 131)

143   Lewis was obscured *WWTW,* 229.

143   James Forman long urged Ibid., 211.

143   "I've never been" Ibid.

144   Sixty percent of Americans Gallup, August 1963, https://www.crmvet.org/docs/60s_crm_public-opinion.pdf.

144   fully 74 percent Gallup, May 1964, https://www.crmvet.org/docs/60s_crm_public-opinion.pdf.

144   "It's just like" Malcolm X, "Message to the Grass Roots," *Eyes on the Prize Civil Rights Reader,* 248–61.

144   "They told those" *WWTW,* 230.

144   thought King's "peroration" James Reston, "'I Have a Dream . . . ,'" *NYT,* August 29, 1963.

145   "Sometimes you look" White, *Making of the President 1964,* 28.

145   "John," Robert Kennedy *WWTW,* 215.

CHAPTER FIVE: *We Are Going to Make You Wish You Was Dead*

149   "During the past" Walker Percy, *Signposts in a Strange Land* (New York, 1991), 42.

149   "If they want Goldwater" Michael R. Beschloss, *Taking Charge: The Johnson White House Tapes, 1963–1964* (New York, 1997), 526.

149   He was back home *WWTW,* 233.

149   Mrs. Ella C. Demand had just finished "16th Street Baptist Church Bombing (1963)," National Park Service, https://www.nps.gov/articles/16thstreetbaptist.htm; Claude Sitton, "Birmingham Bomb Kills 4 Negro Girls in Church; Riots Flare; 2 Boys Slain," *NYT,* September 16, 1963.

149   "Short of a mass holocaust" Robert E. Baker, "Grief and Fear Shared," *WP,* September 19, 1963.

149   Lewis needed *WWTW,* 233.

150   Otis Carter didn't want Ibid.

150   sixty miles in the other direction Author interview with JRL.

150   "He thought that" Ibid.

150   used a megaphone "Six Dead After Church Bombing: Blast Kills Four Children; Riots Follow; Two Youths Slain; State Reinforces Birmingham Police," *WP,* September 16, 1963.

150   "'The Lord is'" Ibid.

150   "I looked at" *WWTW,* 234. "It was so sad," Lewis recalled. "So dark." Author interview with JRL.

150   The dynamite had blown out "Six Dead After Church Bombing," *WP,* September 16, 1963.

150   "God still has" Martin Luther King, Jr., "Eulogy for the Young Victims of the 16th Street Baptist Church Bombing," September 18, 1963, https://mlkscholars.mit.edu/king-eulogy-1963/.

151   "So many tears" *WWTW,* 234.

151   "There were many" Ibid.

151 "That was always a question" Author interview with JRL.

151 On a television program in New York Branch, *Parting the Waters*, 895–96.

152 Eight days after *WWTW*, 238. See also "SNCC Workers Arrested, Slugged in Selma Vote Drive," *The Student Voice*, August 1963, in Carson, *The Student Voice, 1960–1965*, 71; "Selma Drive for Votes Continues," *The Student Voice*, November 11, 1963, in Carson, *The Student Voice, 1960–1965*, 77, 79.

152 The first and third *WWTW*, 239.

152 Dallas County officials Ibid., 238–39.

152 "I knew what" Ibid., 239.

152 the Selma prison farm Ibid.

152 "Our men's cell" Ibid. Later in 1963, the county sheriff raided the SNCC office and a Freedom House apartment in Selma. The police "completely wrecked it," a SNCC worker said, ripping a telephone from the wall and hurling twenty-one-year-old James Austin against a window. "We've been after you a long time," the sheriff said. "Selma Office Raided," *The Student Voice*, December 30, 1963, in Carson, *The Student Voice, 1960–1965*, 97–98.

152 Lewis was in Nashville *WWTW*, 244.

152 "I felt sick" Ibid.

152 He kept to his schedule Ibid., 245.

152 He called Julian Bond Ibid.

152 "I felt lost" Ibid.

152 He got back Ibid.

153 Alone with his thoughts Ibid.

153 "I felt as if I was" Ibid. For his part, King was not content to watch the proceedings; he flew to Washington and stood in the streets with the masses of mourners. King was more of a practical politician than Lewis was, and when, not long after the assassination, he was asked about the implications of Kennedy's death for the movement, King replied, "I'm convinced that had he lived, there would have been continual delays, and attempts to evade it at every point, and water it down at every point. But I think his memory and the fact that he stood up for this civil rights bill will cause many people to see the necessity for working passionately.... So I do think we have some very hopeful days ahead." Branch, *Parting the Waters*, 922.

On the afternoon of the assassination, King's eight-year-old daughter Yolanda was distraught. "Oh, Daddy," she said, "now we will never get our freedom!" King was reassuring. "Now don't you worry, baby. It's going to be all right." Nick Kotz, *Judgment Days: Lyndon Baines Johnson, Martin Luther King, Jr., and the Laws That Changed America* (Boston, 2005), 9.

153 "He was the first" "Rep. John Lewis on the Legacy of President John F. Kennedy," November 22, 2013, https://johnlewis.house.gov/media-center/press-releases/rep-john-lewis-legacy-president-john-f-kennedy.

153 "I can still" Ibid.

153 "Kennedy could bring" James MacGregor Burns, *John Kennedy: A Political Profile* (New York, 1960), 281.

154 "I had several" *WWTW*, 246.

154 in the midst of a great conversion See, for instance, Kotz, *Judgment Days*, 59–64.

154 "This civil rights program" Theodore H. White, *America in Search of Itself: The Making of the President 1956–1980* (New York, 1982), 109.

154 Though LBJ had declined Kotz, *Judgment Days,* 38, 45.

154 "I wasn't a crusader" Richard N. Goodwin, *Remembering America: A Voice from the Sixties* (Boston, 1988), 316.

155 "We're all Americans" Transcript of LBJ and Theodore Sorensen telephone conversation, June 3, 1963, Collections of the Lyndon B. Johnson Presidential Library.

155 "Lyndon acts as if" William Manchester, *The Glory and the Dream: A Narrative History of America, 1932–1972* (Boston, 1974), 1010.

155 "Now I represent" Goodwin, *Remembering America,* 316.

155 "Well, I'm going to" Kotz, *Judgment Days,* 16.

155 "I think you've" Beschloss, *Taking Charge,* 29–30.

156 In a call with the president Ibid., 37.

156 a previously scheduled conference "Over 300 Attend SNCC Conference," *The Student Voice,* December 9, 1963, in Carson, *The Student Voice, 1960–1965,* 88. See also "Rights Push Continues," *St. Cloud Times,* December 4, 1963. "There is little prospect," the newspaper wrote, "that the subdued and chastened national mood will have any retarding effect on the organized drive for equality in civil rights." Ibid.

156 James Baldwin opened "Over 300 Attend SNCC Conference," in Carson, *The Student Voice, 1960–1965,* 88.

156 Andrew Rankin Memorial Chapel "Baldwin and Rustin to Address SNCC Conference," November 20, 1963, https://www.crmvet.org/docs/pr/631122_sncc_pr_conf.pdf.

156 "Kennedy was killed" "Over 300 Attend SNCC Conference," in Carson, *The Student Voice, 1960–1965,* 88.

156 "When the day comes" Ibid., 90.

156 "We, as students" Ibid. In his memoirs, Lewis recalled: "I thought—I hoped—that the situation itself, the circumstances taking shape in the South, most prominently the campaign we were mounting in Mississippi, would help make some of Johnson's decisions *for* him, that the movement might guide and shape and develop the attitudes and reactions of the man, as it had begun to do with the Kennedy brothers." *WWTW,* 246.

156 "There will be no revolution" *Eyes on the Prize Civil Rights Reader,* 130–31.

157 *"The central front"* Schlesinger, *Thousand Days,* 935.

157 He spent Christmas 1963 "Christmas in Jail," *The Student Voice,* December 23, 1963; "Workers Spend Xmas in Jail," December 30, 1963, in Carson, *The Student Voice, 1960–1965,* 95–99; author interview with JRL.

157 he was also arrested "Nashville Erupts as Protests Begin," *The Student Voice,* May 5, 1964, in Carson, *The Student Voice, 1960–1965,* 143, 146.

157 "Before the Negro people" Bruce Watson, *Freedom Summer: The Savage Season That Made Mississippi Burn and Made America a Democracy* (New York, 2010), 11.

157 The announcement came *The Student Voice,* March 3, 1964, in Carson, *The Student Voice, 1960–1965,* 131.

157 "a summer Peace Corps type" Ibid.

157 a "Freedom Vote" in the state For the Mississippi project, see, for instance, Forman, *Making of Black Revolutionaries,* 371–86; Watson, *Freedom Summer,* 6–8; Lisa Anderson Todd, *For a Voice and the Vote: My Journey with the Mississippi Freedom Democratic Party* (Lexington, Ky., 2014); Carson, *In Struggle,* 96–129.

157 "NAACP" really stood for Merle Miller, *Lyndon: An Oral Biography* (New York, 1980), 478.

157 SNCC SET UP White, *America in Search of Itself,* 104; "Miss. Summer Project Set," *The Student Voice,* March 3, 1964.

157 THE "IRONY OF" *WWTW,* 254.

157 WITH THE HARVARD-EDUCATED BOB MOSES See, for instance, Carson, *In Struggle,* 96–97.

157 IN APRIL 1964 *WWTW,* 253. See also "Editors Hear Report on JFK, Ruby Coverage," *The South Bend Tribune,* April 17, 1964; Vermont C. Royster, "Both Races Confused About Rights," *The Charlotte Observer,* April 25, 1964.

158 TO BURN CROSSES IN SIXTY-FOUR *WWTW,* 254.

158 *THE FREEDOM FIGHTER,* A KKK PUBLICATION "Terror Reigns in Mississippi," *The Student Voice,* May 19, 1964, in Carson, *The Student Voice, 1960–1965,* 147, 149.

158 OTHER GROUPS TOOK SHAPE Ibid.

158 SIGNED A LAW GIVING HIMSELF "Police Enlarged; Whites Organize," *The Student Voice,* May 26, 1964, in Carson, *The Student Voice, 1960–1965,* 151, 153.

158 "MISSISSIPPI IS NOW" Ibid.

158 "NO EX-MISSISSIPPIAN IS" Walker Percy, "Mississippi: The Fallen Paradise," *Harper's,* April 1965.

158 "NO PASSION SO" "Inquiry into the Sublime and Beautiful," pt. 2, sec. 2, in "Terror" from Edmund Burke, *Reflections on the Revolution in France, and Other Writings,* ed. Jesse Norman (New York, 2015), 55.

158 "ONCE THE FINAL" Percy, "Mississippi: The Fallen Paradise," *Harper's.*

158 THREE FREEDOM SUMMER WORKERS *WWTW,* 261–64; Watson, *Freedom Summer,* 71–104. See also "Rights Workers Still Missing," *The Student Voice,* June 30, 1964, in Carson, *The Student Voice, 1960–1965,* 163, 165–66; "Three Murdered Workers Found," *The Student Voice,* August 12, 1964, in Carson, *The Student Voice, 1960–1965,* 183, 186; "Nation Mourns Slain Workers," *The Student Voice,* August 19, 1964, in Carson, *The Student Voice, 1960–1965,* 187

159 HE "WALKED AROUND" *WWTW,* 264–65.

160 BY THE FIRST WEEK OF AUGUST Watson, *Freedom Summer,* 205–6.

160 EACH HAD BEEN SHOT Ibid., 209–10.

160 CHANEY HAD BEEN HORRIBLY BEATEN *WWTW,* 276.

160 LEWIS WAS CRUSHED Ibid., 276–77.

160 "IF YOU GO" Ibid.; see also Watson, *Freedom Summer,* 212–13.

160 WITH A SHOUT Ibid., 213.

160 "ON FRIDAY, AUGUST 7" Ibid., 211.

160 "WE TRULY BELIEVED" Author interview with JRL.

160 "TO ME, 'DOING'" *WWTW,* 277.

160 "YOU HEARD THE TERM" Ibid., 189.

161 "SINCE THE FEDERAL GOVERNMENT" Julian Mayfield, "Challenge to Negro Leadership: The Case of Robert Williams," *Reporting Civil Rights,* 1:552. See also Robert F. Williams, *Negroes with Guns* (New York, 1962).

161 ON SATURDAY, OCTOBER 5, 1957 "Gunfire Report Denied in Klan-Negro Clash," *Louisville Courier-Journal,* October 6, 1957; Mayfield, "Challenge to Negro Leadership," *Reporting Civil Rights,* 1:552, 561–62; Williams, *Negroes with Guns,* 50–58.

161 "IT'S AS IF" Mayfield, "Challenge to Negro Leadership," *Reporting Civil Rights,* 1:562.

161 IN 1962, WILLIAMS PUBLISHED Williams, *Negroes with Guns.*

161 "ON THE OTHER SIDE" Widmer, *Listening In,* 115–16.

162 "WITHIN THE PAST FIVE YEARS" Alex Haley, "An Interview with Malcolm X: A Candid Conversation with the Militant Major-domo of the Black Muslims," *Playboy,* May 1963.

162 THE BLACK MUSLIMS Ibid.

162 SAW BLACKS AS "DIVINE" Gertrude Samuels, "Feud Within the Black Muslims," *NYT*, March 22, 1964.

162 MALCOLM X HAD BEEN BORN See, in general, Malcolm X, *The Autobiography of Malcolm X* (New York, 1965); Joseph, *The Sword and the Shield*; "Malcolm X: Biography," https://www.malcolmx.com/biography/.

162 "WE DON'T DESERVE" Threadcraft and Terry, "Gender Trouble" in Shelby and Terry, *To Shape a New World*, 213.

162 "THE QUESTION WAS NOT" Terry, "Requiem for a Dream" in Shelby and Terry, *To Shape a New World*, 297.

162 "THE USE OF ORDINARY METHODS" Zinn, *SNCC: The New Abolitionists*, 213.

163 HAD CREATED A "THOMPSON TANK" Ibid.

163 "THERE IS ONE POWERFUL JUSTIFICATION" Ibid., 213–14.

163 AN APRIL 1961 DEBATE "1961 Debate Between Malcolm X and James Baldwin," https://www.democracynow.org/2001/2/1/james_baldwin_and_malcolm_x_debate.

163 "I THINK THAT" Ibid.

163 "I DON'T AGREE" Ibid.

163 "THE BLACK MAN" Ibid.

164 "TAKE PEARL HARBOR" Ibid.

164 "WAIT FOR THE SUPREME COURT" Ibid.

164 "MALCOLM X WANTS US" Ibid.

164 "I HAVE EATEN" M. S. Handler, "Malcolm X Pleased By Whites' Attitude on Trip to Mecca," *NYT*, May 8, 1964. On Malcolm's views, see also, for instance, Joseph, *The Sword and the Shield*; "Malcolm X Letters Show His Evolution," *NYT*, March 8, 2002; Nussbaum, "From Anger to Love: Self-Purification and Political Resistance" in Shelby and Terry, *To Shape a New World*, 105–26.

165 "HE QUIVERED IN" White, *Making of the President 1964*, 197.

165 IN NEW YORK, THE FATAL POLICE SHOOTING "'Hot Summer'; Race Riots in North," *NYT*, July 26, 1964.

165 "THEY WERE CONFRONTED" Ibid.

165 "WHAT DID YOUR" Watson, *Freedom Summer*, 208.

165 "THAT, I WOULD" Ibid.

165 TO J. EDGAR HOOVER'S FEDERAL BUREAU OF INVESTIGATION See, for instance, David J. Garrow, *The FBI and Martin Luther King, Jr.: From "Solo" to Memphis* (New York, 1981); Forman, *Making of Black Revolutionaries*; Congress, U.S., Senate Select Committee to Study Governmental Operations with Respect to Intelligence Activities, *Final Report—Book II, Supplementary Detailed Staff Reports on Intelligence Activities and the Rights of Americans*, 94th Cong., 2d sess., 1976, https://www.aarclibrary.org/publib/church/reports/book2/html/ChurchB2_0015a.htm; Senate Select Committee to Study Governmental Operations with Respect to Intelligence Activities, *Final Report—Book III*, https://www.aarclibrary.org/publib/church/reports/book3/html/ChurchB3_0001a.htm.

165 BEGINNING IN 1950 On McCarthy, see, for instance, David M. Oshinsky, *A Conspiracy So Immense: The World of Joe McCarthy* (New York, 2005); Roy Cohn, *McCarthy* (New York, 1968); J. Ronald Oakley, *God's Country: America in the Fifties* (New York, 1986); David Halberstam, *The Fifties* (New York, 1994); Edwin R. Bayley, *Joe McCarthy and the Press* (Madison, Wis., 1981); Richard H. Rovere, *Senator Joe McCarthy* (Berkeley, Calif., 1996).

165 "I JUST WANT YOU TO KNOW" Bayley, *Joe McCarthy and the Press*, 36.

166 THE CIVIL RIGHTS MOVEMENT WAS Senate Select Committee to Study Governmental Operations with Respect to Intelligence Activities, *Final Report—Book II,* 11–12. See also, for instance, idem, *Final Report—Book III; WWTW,* 278–80; Wofford, *Of Kennedys and Kings,* 209–39; Garrow, *FBI and Martin Luther King, Jr.;* Kenneth O'Reilly, *Racial Matters: The FBI's Secret File on Black America, 1960–1972* (New York, 1989); Jeff Woods, *Black Struggle, Red Scare: Segregation and Anti-Communism* (Baton Rouge, La., 2004); Honey, *To the Promised Land,* 66–68, 77–78, 81–87, 170–74.

166 AN FBI INFORMANT "Report of February 4, 1966," SNCC, FBI file 100–439190, parts 1–14, National Archives.

166 "NO HOLDS WERE BARRED" Senate Select Committee to Study Governmental Operations with Respect to Intelligence Activities, *Final Report—Book II,* 11.

166 AS "WAR" Ibid.

166 "AN INTENSIVE CAMPAIGN" Ibid.

166 THE BUREAU SENT KING AN AUDIOTAPE Ibid. See also Beverly Gage, "I Have a [Redacted]," *NYT,* November 16, 2014.

166 AFTER THE MARCH ON WASHINGTON Senate Select Committee to Study Governmental Operations with Respect to Intelligence Activities, *Final Report—Book II,* 11.

166 LATER, IN EARLY 1968 Ibid., 11–12.

166 "IN SHORT, A NON-VIOLENT MAN" Ibid., 12.

167 "COMMUNIST INFLUENCE DOES EXIST" "Hoover Says Reds Exploit Negroes," *NYT,* April 22, 1964.

167 "BASED ON ALL AVAILABLE INFORMATION" Ibid.

167 RFK HIMSELF AUTHORIZED See, for instance, Garrow, *FBI and Martin Luther King, Jr.,* 72–73.

167 A CENTRAL FOCUS OF CONCERN See, for instance, "Levison, Stanley David," https://kinginstitute.stanford.edu/encyclopedia/levison-stanley-david.

167 HAD LONG BELIEVED TO BE A COMMUNIST See, for instance, Garrow, "The FBI and Martin Luther King," *The Atlantic,* July/August 2002.

167 KING WAS REPEATEDLY WARNED Ibid.

167 PRESIDENT KENNEDY HIMSELF Wofford, *Of Kennedys and Kings,* 216–17.

167 SEX AND RACE DROVE See, for instance, ibid., 213; Gage, "I Have a [Redacted]," *NYT.*

167 A "TOM CAT WITH" Gage, "I Have a [Redacted]," *NYT.*

167 "BEHIND IT ALL" Wofford, *Of Kennedys and Kings,* 213.

167 KING AUDACIOUSLY CHALLENGED Ibid., 214.

167 THE FBI HAD OPENED SNCC, FBI file 100–439190, parts 1–14, National Archives.

168 SNCC USED *WWTW,* 278–79.

168 A GROUP THAT THE FBI William Glaberson, "FBI Admits Bit to Disrupt Lawyers Guild," *NYT,* October 13, 1989.

168 "NO MATTER WHO" *WWTW,* 279.

168 IN LOS ANGELES IN LATE 1963 "Report of September 28, 1964," SNCC, FBI file 100–439190, parts 1–14, National Archives. On another occasion, according to the FBI file on SNCC, "LEWIS was asked if he would exclude a person who had admitted being a Communist" and had replied, in the July 11, 1965, edition of *The Atlanta Times,* "Well, see, in the first place, it would be hard, for me, as an individual, as an American citizen, to determine what a Communist is. We do not make any type of security check on people. If people are committed to working

for what we call inter-racial democracy, an open society, we accept them." "Report of February 4, 1966," ibid.

168 LEWIS "HAD SPENT THREE DAYS" "Report of May 28, 1965," ibid.

168 AN ADMITTED LEADER See, for instance, Sara Rzeszutek Haviland, *James and Esther Cooper Jackson: Love and Courage in the Black Freedom Movement* (Lexington, Ky., 2015); David Levering Lewis, Michael H. Nash, and Daniel J. Leab, eds., *Red Activists and Black Freedom: James and Esther Jackson and the Long Civil Rights Movement* (New York, 2010); Dennis Hevesi, "James Jackson, Rights Activist, Dies at 92," *NYT,* September 7, 2007.

168 "NEVER," HE RECALLED Author interview with JRL.

168 "WHEN JOHN LEWIS WAS" "Report of May 28, 1965," SNCC, FBI file 100–439190, parts 1–14, National Archives.

169 "MY ATTITUDE," Lewis recalled Ibid.

169 "THIS IS NO LONGER" White, *Making of the President 1964,* 184.

169 AFTER A FIFTY-SEVEN-DAY FILIBUSTER "Civil Rights Act of 1964," National Park Service, https://www.nps.gov/articles/civil-rights-act.htm.

169 WAS APPROVED BY White, *Making of the President 1964,* 186.

170 THE LEGISLATION WENT "Civil Rights Act (1964)," https://www.ourdocuments.gov/doc.php?flash=false&doc=97.

170 "DOES NOT RESTRICT" "July 2, 1964; Remarks Upon Signing the Civil Rights Bill," https://millercenter.org/the-presidency/presidential-speeches/july-2-1964-remarks-upon-signing-civil-rights-bill.

170 "OUR CONSTITUTION" Ibid.

171 KING WAS THERE Garrow, *Bearing the Cross,* 338–39.

171 HANDED HIM ONE Photograph: "President Johnson shakes hands with the Rev. Martin Luther King after handing him a pen during the signing of the Civil Rights bill into law during a White House ceremony 7/2," Washington, D.C., July 2, 1964, https://www.loc.gov/item/2005681248/.

171 THOUGH INVITED, LEWIS *WWTW,* 274.

171 "THIS WAS WHERE" Ibid.

171 AN UNANNOUNCED MEETING Anthony Lewis, "Democrats Weigh Policy on Seating and Districting," *NYT,* August 20, 1964.

171 ONE OF FREEDOM SUMMER'S MISSIONS *WWTW,* 283–93, tells the story of the Atlantic City convention and MFDP's role. See also Forman, *Making of Black Revolutionaries,* 386–406; Todd, *For a Voice and the Vote;* White, *Making of the President 1964,* 291–96; Nancy Beck Young, *Two Suns of the Southwest: Lyndon Johnson, Barry Goldwater, and the 1964 Battle Between Liberalism and Conservatism* (Lawrence, Kans., 2019), 129–36.

171 LED IN PART BY ELLA BAKER "Baker, Ella Jospehine," https://kinginstitute.stanford.edu/encyclopedia/baker-ella-josephine.

171 THE FBI HAD BUGGED John C. Skipper, *Showdown at the 1964 Democratic Convention: Lyndon Johnson, Mississippi and Civil Rights* (Jefferson, N.C., 2012), 83–95, 177–78.

172 A FEW WEEKS BEFORE. Skipper, *Showdown at the 1964 Democratic National Convention,* 84–85.

172 "THE PRESIDENT'S MEN" *WWTW,* 289–90.

172 AFTER DINING WITH THE PRESIDENT Skipper, *Showdown at the 1964 Democratic National Convention,* 91.

172 OF LBJ'S NOT-VERY-CONVINCING LAMENTS Ibid.

172 THE DECISION ABOUT SEATING *WWTW,* 287. See also Jack Markowitz, "Miss. 'Freedom Party' Poses a Moral Issue," *Philadelphia Daily News,* August 24, 1964; "Floor Fight Looms," *Asheville Citizen-Times,* August 24, 1964.

172 "I DON'T LIKE BEING" Catherine Mackin, "She Steals LBJ's Thunder," *The San Francisco Examiner,* August 26, 1964.

172 "NOBODY EVER COME" Raines, *My Soul Is Rested,* 233.

173 IN ATLANTIC CITY, LEWIS WATCHED *WWTW,* 287.

173 "MR. CHAIRMAN, AND" Fannie Lou Hamer, "Testimony Before the Credentials Committee, Democratic National Convention," August 22, 1964, http://ameri canradioworks.publicradio.org/features/sayitplain/flhamer.html.

174 "AFTER I WAS PLACED" Ibid.

175 "IT WAS A STUNNING MOMENT" *WWTW,* 288. See also Mackin, "She Steals LBJ's Thunder," *The San Francisco Examiner,* August 26, 1964.

175 LYNDON JOHNSON AGREED *WWTW,* 288.

175 A BRIEFING ON A WHITE HOUSE SESSION Skipper, *Showdown at the 1964 Democratic Convention,* 106.

175 "THE IMPRESSION AROUND" Beschloss, *Taking Charge,* 469.

175 THE TERM "BACKLASH" White, *Making of the President 1964,* 245. White wrote that the economics columnist Eliot Janeway had used it to capture "what he feared might happen if automation and economic downturn combined to squeeze factory employment down in the near future. In any competition between Negro and white workingmen for jobs in a shrinking market, Janeway feared that white workers might 'lash back' at Negro competitors." Ibid.

175 "THE SEVERE BACKLASH" F. L. Shuttlesworth, "A Southerner Speaks," *Pittsburgh Courier,* January 21, 1961.

175 GEORGE WALLACE'S SUCCESS White, *Making of the President 1964,* 245.

176 "THE SO-CALLED BACKLASH" Jeremy D. Mayer, "LBJ Fights the White Backlash, Part 2," *Prologue* magazine, Spring 2001.

176 THE PRESIDENT ASSIGNED Miller, *Lyndon: An Oral Biography,* 478.

176 "HE WANTED TO GET ME" Ibid.

176 "WALTER SAID, 'I'VE'" Ibid.

176 "NOW THERE'S NOT" Beschloss, *Taking Charge,* 510–11.

177 "AND . . . YOUR LABOR UNION" Ibid., 515–16.

177 "TRY TO SEE" Ibid., 516.

177 "IT AIN'T GOING" Ibid., 524.

177 "I WOULD THINK" Ibid.

177 "IT WOULD INCREASE" Ibid.

177 "WHOEVER THOUGHT" White, *Making of the President 1964,* 295.

177 "HELL, THE NORTHERNERS" Beschloss, *Taking Charge,* 527.

178 A PROPOSED DEAL *WWTW,* 288–89; Miller, *Lyndon: An Oral Biography,* 478–79; White, *Making of the President 1964,* 293–94; *WWTW,* 288–90.

178 ANDREW YOUNG, WHO WORKED *WWTW,* 289.

178 "WE'VE SHED TOO MUCH" Ibid.

178 A FRUSTRATED JOHNSON Beschloss, *Taking Charge,* 527–34.

178 "THE TIMES REQUIRE" Ibid., 529.

178 "I DO NOT REMEMBER" Ibid., 534.

178 THE PRESIDENT'S NEGOTIATORS Ibid.

178 THE DECISION WAS UNANIMOUS *WWTW,* 290.

178 LEFT THE CONVENTION Tom Wicker, "Mississippi Delegates Withdraw, Rejecting a Seating Compromise; Convention Then Approves Plan," *NYT,* August 26, 1964. See also Michael Lydon, "'We Won at Convention,' Negro Party Declares," *The Boston Globe,* August 30, 1964.

178 WHEN THE MFDP *WWTW,* 290.

178 RATHER THAN SEATING THE MFDP Ibid.

178 "AND SO THEY STOOD THERE" Ibid.

179 ON THURSDAY MORNING Ibid.

179 THAT YEAR'S REPUBLICAN GATHERING See, for instance, White, *Making of the President 1964,* 200–31.

179 "I WOULD REMIND YOU" "Goldwater's 1964 Acceptance Speech," *WP,* https://www.washingtonpost.com/wp-srv/politics/daily/may98/goldwaterspeech.htm.

179 "A BETTER UNDERSTANDING" Michael Beschloss, "Jackie Robinson and Nixon: Life and Death of a Political Friendship," *NYT,* June 6, 2014.

180 "AS FAR AS" *WWTW,* 291.

180 "I'M ABSOLUTELY CONVINCED" Ibid.

180 "THE MOST IMPORTANT SINGLE ISSUE" Skipper, *Showdown at the 1964 Democratic National Convention,* 177.

180 AFRICAN AMERICANS ACCOUNTED FOR *WWTW,* 369.

180 "BY LATE 1965" Ibid.

180 HIS OWN DRAFT STATUS Ibid., 280, 372, 375–76.

180–81 ONLY AFTER A FEDERAL REVIEW Ibid., 280.

181 "THE FIRST BLACK MAN" Ibid., 280.

181 LEWIS SIGNED AN ANTIWAR STATEMENT Ibid., 370–71.

181 "I FELT WE HAD" Ibid., 371–72.

181 A COPY OF A POPULAR POSTER Ibid., 372.

181 IN A PRESS CONFERENCE Ibid., 375.

181 "AND ALMOST OVERNIGHT" Ibid, 376.

181 AFTER THE ANTIWAR STATEMENT Author interview with JRL; O'Reilly, *Racial Matters,* 398–99; Andrew Lewis, *The Shadows of Youth,* 243; United Press International, "Move to Draft Rights Leader," *The Afro-American,* January 22, 1966.

181 LEWIS THEN REACHED OUT Author interview with JRL.

181 THE JUSTICE DEPARTMENT'S BURKE MARSHALL O'Reilly, *Racial Matters,* 398–99.

181 "IT SEEMED EXTREMELY" *WWTW,* 371.

181 "PUT NOT YOUR TRUST" Psalm 146:3 (KJV).

181 FIRECRACKERS BURN FAST Author interview with JRL.

CHAPTER SIX: *I'm Going to Die Here*

185 "SELMA, THE BRIDGE" Author interview with JRL.

185 "NOW, JOHN, YOU'VE GOT TO" *WWTW,* 361.

185 HARRY BELAFONTE HAD AN IDEA Ibid., 293; author interview with Harry Belafonte. See also Forman, *Making of Black Revolutionaries,* 407–11.

185 "WHAT IMPRESSED ME" Author interview with Harry Belafonte.

185 IN A STUDY OF *WWTW,* 281.

185 BELAFONTE HAD BEEN TALKING *WWTW,* 293.

185 "I THOUGHT THEY NEEDED" Author interview with Harry Belafonte.

185 "FOR THE FIRST TIME" JRL transcripts, *Eyes on the Prize,* Henry Hampton Collection.

186 "Y'ALL BROTHERS ALWAYS RAPPING" Carmichael with Thelwell, *Ready for Revolution,* 441.

186 WAS "MOVING TOWARDS THAT POINT" JRL transcripts, *Eyes on the Prize,* Henry Hampton Collection.

186 "ALWAYS SIT WITH" Ibid.

186 "MALCOLM SAW SNCC" Ibid.

186 "The destiny of Afro-Americans" Carmichael with Thelwell, *Ready for Revolution*, 478–79. See also *WWTW*, 299.

187 "Hey, after a long talk" Carmichael with Thelwell, *Ready for Revolution*, 440.

187 Impressed by Lewis's rhetoric Ibid., 478–79.

187 Lewis "was devastated" *WWTW*, 292–93.

188 figures such as Amelia Boynton LaFayette and Johnson, *In Peace and Freedom*, 30–35; *WWTW*, 318; "Amelia Boynton," https://snccdigital.org/people/amelia -boynton/.

188 a sign in her office "Amelia Boynton Robinson," National Park Service, https://www.nps.gov/people/amelia-boynton-robinson.htm.

188 "tall and regal" LaFayette and Johnson, *In Peace and Freedom*, 31.

188 "People need to learn" Ibid.

188 July 6, 1964 *WWTW*, 312.

188 "On first entering" Carmichael with Thelwell, *Ready for Revolution*, 443.

189 "John Lewis," Clark told him *WWTW*, 312.

189 a generation younger Margalit Fox, "Jim Clark, Sheriff Who Enforced Segregation, Dies at 84," *NYT*, June 7, 2007; Alvin Benn, "1960s Selma Sheriff Won't Back Down," *The Montgomery Advertiser*, March 3, 2006.

189 "fleshy-faced bear of a man" Fox, "Jim Clark, Sheriff Who Enforced Segregation," *NYT*.

189 The sheriff once *WWTW*, 327.

189 "Basically, I'd do" Benn, "1960s Selma Sheriff Won't Back Down," *The Montgomery Advertiser*; Fox, "Jim Clark, Sheriff Who Enforced Segregation," *NYT*.

189 "I think he was just" Author interview with JRL.

190 Rockwell's storm troopers knew *WWTW*, 320. See also Frederick J. Simonelli, *American Fuehrer: George Lincoln Rockwell and the American Nazi Party* (Urbana, Ill., 1999), 73–77, 96–106, and "Rockwell, Nazi Group Will Heckle King," *The Sacramento Bee*, January 17, 1965

190 "present racist agitation" Malcolm X, *Malcolm X Speaks*, ed. George Breitman (New York, 1965), 201.

190 "I think that" *WWTW*, 324.

190 During one peaceful demonstration Ibid., 326.

191 forced to make Ibid.

191 "I thought I" Ibid.

191 King came to town Ibid., 320–21; Simonelli, *American Fuehrer*, 76.

191 King was integrating the hotel "King Punched, Kicked in Ala.; Man Arrested," *The Evening Sun* (Baltimore), January 18, 1965.

191 "You're Martin Luther King" *WWTW*, 321.

191 punching King in the face "King Punched, Kicked in Ala.; Man Arrested," *The Evening Sun* (Baltimore). "It was weird," Lewis recalled. "Very spontaneous, as if the man was just seized by some impulse." *WWTW*, 321.

191 "I've never been in a fight" *WWTW*, 321.

191 Clark assaulted Amelia Boynton Ibid.

191 was "manhandling her" Ibid.

191 "grabbed her by the back" Ibid.; "Amelia Boynton Robinson," *The Independent*, August 28, 2015, https://www.independent.co.uk/news/people/amelia-boynton -robinson-civil-rights-activist-who-led-voting-drives-in-the-1960s-and -whose-attack-by-10475548.html; John Herbers, "67 Negroes Jailed in Alabama Drive," *NYT*, January 20, 1965.

191 "one of the most brutal" "Amelia Boynton Robinson," *The Independent*.

191 White Citizens' Council membership dinner "The White Citizens' Council," *The Student Voice,* March 26, 1965, in Carson, *The Student Voice, 1960–1965,* 213.

192 Guests paid $1.50 Ibid.

192 "We have arrived" Ibid.

192 "The secret purpose" Ibid.

192 Four days earlier, a state trooper *WWTW,* 327–28; Garrow, *Protest at Selma,* 61–62; "Jackson, Jimmie Lee," https://kinginstitute.stanford.edu/encyclopedia/jackson-jimmie-lee.

192 The shooting came Garrow, *Protest at Selma,* 61.

192 "They . . . shot the" Raines, *My Soul Is Rested,* 189.

193 "A lot of people" *WWTW,* 329.

193 On a rain-soaked procession Ibid.

193 "take Jimmie Lee's" Ibid.

193 "We are going" Roy Reed, "266 Apply to Vote as Selma Speeds Negro Registration," *NYT,* March 2, 1965.

193 Internal movement politics Branch, *At Canaan's Edge,* 23–43.

193 thought it "illusory" Ibid., 42.

193 "Such skepticism about" Ibid.

194 "If these people" Ibid., 41.

194 "John went against" Author interview with Bernard LaFayette, Jr.

194 George Wallace marshaled Garrow, *Protest at Selma,* 72. See also "No March from Selma, Says Wallace," *The Montgomery Advertiser,* March 7, 1965; "Massive Disorder Averted Here When Officers Intervene," *The Selma Times-Journal,* March 7, 1965; "Selmans Jeer White Group," *The Tennessean,* March 7, 1965.

194 "some man of hatred" George Wallace transcripts, *Eyes on the Prize,* Henry Hampton Collection.

194 King was back in Atlanta *WWTW,* 336–38.

194 Lewis carried two books Ibid., 332; author interview with JRL; Sean Wilentz, "The Last Integrationist: John Lewis's American Odyssey," *The New Republic,* July 1, 1996.

194 "I must educate" Richard Hofstadter, *The American Political Tradition* (New York, 1948), 196–97.

195 "men—actual men" Ibid., 5–6.

195 "Like everyone around" *WWTW,* 337.

195 And they did Branch, *At Canaan's Edge,* 48–54. See also "Selma: Beatings Start the Savage Season," *Life,* March 19, 1965; FBI file 44–28492, section 1, serials 1–42, Alabama (1965) 3/7 Selma to Montgomery March, Edmund Pettus Bridge, National Archives (NAID 7634471).

195 marchers finished up "FBI Memorandum from Al Rosen to Alan Belmont, Subject: Registrar of Voters of Dallas County, Alabama/Voting Discrimination/Civil Rights—Election Law," March 10, 1965, FBI file 44–28492, National Archives (NAID 7634471).

195 the Pettus Bridge Errin Whack, "Who Was Edmund Pettus?" *Smithsonian Magazine,* March 7, 2015, https://www.smithsonianmag.com/history/who-was-edmund-pettus-180954501/.

195 At the crest *WWTW,* 338.

195 State troopers under Ibid., 338–39.

195 "I saw in front of us" "Amelia Boynton," https://snccdigital.org/people/amelia-boynton/.

195 White spectators, some waving Ibid., 339.

195 WATCHED FROM OUTSIDE "FBI Report of Special Agent Joseph M. Conley," March 11, 1965, FBI file 44–28492, National Archives.

195 LEHMAN'S PONTIAC DEALERSHIP "FBI Report of Special Agent Archibald L. Riley," March 11, 1965, FBI file 44–28492, National Archives.

195 REPORTERS AND CAMERAMEN *WWTW*, 339.

195 LEWIS AND WILLIAMS LOOKED Author interview with JRL.

195 *"THIS IS AN UNLAWFUL ASSEMBLY"* *WWTW*, 339.

195 IT WAS 2:52 P.M. "FBI Memorandum from Al Rosen to Alan Belmont, Subject: Registrar of Voters of Dallas County, Alabama/Voting Discrimination/Civil Rights—Election Law," March 10, 1965, FBI file 44–28492, National Archives.

195 *"YOUR MARCH IS NOT"* *WWTW*, 339.

196 "BLOOMING, BUZZING CONFUSION" William James, *The Principles of Psychology: Volume 1* (New York, 1890), 488.

196 "I WASN'T ABOUT" *WWTW*, 339.

196 "WE COULDN'T GO" Ibid., 339–40.

196 "WE SHOULD KNEEL" Ibid., 340.

196 A MOMENT HAD PASSED "FBI Memorandum from Al Rosen to Alan Belmont, Subject: Registrar of Voters of Dallas County, Alabama/Voting Discrimination/Civil Rights—Election Law," March 10, 1965, FBI file 44–28492, National Archives.

196 "YOU SAW THESE" JRL interview for the documentary *The Soul of America*.

196 HE HEARD CLOUD'S VOICE Author interview with JRL.

197 *"TROOPERS," THE MAJOR CRIED* *WWTW*, 340.

197 "THE TROOPERS AND POSSEMEN" Ibid.

197 "I'LL NEVER FORGET" Author interview with Charles Mauldin.

197 THE FIRST CANISTER "FBI Report of Special Agent Joseph M. Conley," March 11, 1965, FBI file 44–28492, National Archives.

197 "THIS QUANTITY OF TEAR GAS" Ibid.

197 LEWIS FELT EVERYTHING DIMMING Author interview with JRL.

197 HE VOMITED "John Robert Lewis Statement to FBI," March 11, 1965, FBI file 44–28492, National Archives. Lewis gave the agents his account on Monday, March 8, 1965. Ibid.

197 WAS STRUCK A SECOND TIME Ibid.

197 "PEOPLE ARE GOING TO DIE" *WWTW*, 340.

197 "AT THE MOMENT" Author interview with JRL.

197 "FROM OBSERVATION" "FBI Report of Special Agent Joseph M. Conley," March 11, 1965, FBI file 44–28492, National Archives.

197 NO "WAITING FOR ANY SIGNS" "FBI Report of Special Agent Daniel D. Doyle," ibid.

199 ONE GIRL, ABOUT FOURTEEN "FBI Report of Special Agent Archibald L. Riley," ibid.

199 AT LEAST SIX "FBI Report of Special Agent Daniel D. Doyle," ibid.

199 ASSAULTED "WITH A RUBBER-COVERED" Ibid.

199 "THEY WERE TRYING" Author interview with Charles Mauldin.

199 "SUDDENLY THE CLUBS" *Time*, March 19, 1965.

199 "I WAS BLEEDING" *WWTW*, 341.

199 THE JOURNEY BACK Ibid., 342.

199 BARBED WIRE AROUND Ibid.

199 MOUNTED POSSEMEN RODE UP Author interview with Charles Mauldin.

199 "AWASH WITH SOUNDS" *WWTW*, 342.

199–200   ON A TELEPHONE LINE Branch, *At Canaan's Edge*, 53.

200   A "SMALL HOLE" Ibid.

200   "I DON'T UNDERSTAND" Author interview with JRL.

200   HE WAS SEEING DOUBLE Ibid. At the church, Lewis told the FBI, "I began to feel severe pain in my head. I, therefore, went next door to the church parsonage where I awaited an ambulance which subsequently took me to Good Samaritan Hospital in Selma." "John Robert Lewis Statement to FBI," March 11, 1965, FBI file 44–28492, National Archives.

200   "A WAKE IN A MASH UNIT" Carmichael with Thelwell, *Ready for Revolution*, 449.

200   "IF IT HAS TO" Associated Press, March 8, 1965.

200   WORTH LONG, WHO HAD SERVED Author interview with Worth Long.

200   TIME WAS SHORT Author interviews with Charles Maudlin and Worth Long.

200   IN THE PARSONAGE Ibid.

200   LONG ASKED ANOTHER Author interview with Worth Long.

200   LONG WENT OUT FIRST Ibid.

200   "WE HAVE A SOLDIER" Author interview with Charles Maudlin.

200   WHEN HE ARRIVED WWTW, 343–44; author interview with JRL.

200   FORTY-EIGHT MARCHERS WERE TREATED "Check of Medical Records and Interviews with Doctors at Medical Facilities: Patients Admitted to Good Samaritan Hospital/Sunday, March 7, 1965, As a Result of Attack on Civil Rights Demonstrators by Alabama State Troopers and Members of Dallas County Posse," FBI file 44–28492, National Archives.

200   (ANOTHER EIGHT WERE TREATED) "FBI Report from Mrs. Annie Bottoms, Burwell Infirmary," ibid.

200   SIXTEEN-YEAR-OLD JEANETTE HOWARD "Check of Medical Records and Interviews with Doctors at Medical Facilities," ibid.

200   TWENTY-SIX-YEAR-OLD MARGARET CLAY BROOKS Ibid.

200   DR. ISABEL DUMONT DIAGNOSED LEWIS Ibid.; WWTW, 343–44.

201   HE WAS ATTENDED TO WWTW, 344.

201   ABC BROKE INTO Fager, *Selma 1965*, 98; WWTW, 344; Branch, *At Canaan's Edge*, 55–56.

201   "WITH THE CAMERAS" *Eyes on the Prize Civil Rights Reader*, 213–14.

201   "I CAN'T LOOK" Ibid., 214.

201   "THE NEWS FROM" "Outrage at Selma," WP, March 9, 1965.

201   ON MONDAY, MARCH 8, TWO FBI SPECIAL AGENTS "John Robert Lewis Statement to FBI," March 11, 1965, FBI file 44–28492, National Archives.

201   FOR THEIR RECORDS Ibid.

201   "AT NO TIME" Ibid.

201   LEWIS WAS RESTLESS WWTW, 345–46.

202   "LYNDON LIVES IN" Lady Bird Johnson, *A White House Diary* (New York, 1970), 247–48.

202   FRED GRAY, KING'S LAWYER Author interview with Fred Gray.

202   CALLING FOR AN INFLUX Branch, *At Canaan's Edge*, 60.

202   A PARTIAL MARCH Ibid., 76–79. "Dr. King's Closed Strategy Session Set the Strategy," *Life*, March 19, 1965.

202   PRAYED BY BULLHORN Branch, *At Canaan's Edge*, 74.

202   A WHITE UNITARIAN MINISTER, JAMES REEB Garrow, *Protest at Selma*, 91, 97.

202   "IF I JUST SEND" Kotz, *Judgment Days*, 303.

202   WALLACE CAME TO THE WHITE HOUSE The ensuing scene is drawn from Kotz, *Judgment Days*, 303–6, and Goodwin, *Remembering America*, 321–24. See also Meacham, *Soul of America*, 239–41, 346–47, from which this account is adapted.

203 JOHNSON READ THE PAGES Author interview with Richard Goodwin. See also Jon Meacham, *American Gospel: God, the Founding Fathers, and the Making of a Nation* (New York, 2006), 195–96.

203 "THE BIBLICAL IMAGERY" Author interview with Richard Goodwin.

203 "I SPEAK TONIGHT" "President Johnson's Special Message to the Congress: The American Promise," March 15, 1965, http://www.LBJLibrary.org/lyndon-baines -johnson/speeches-films/president-johnsons-special-message-to-the-congress -the-american-promise.

204 THE LAWMAKERS APPLAUDED Ibid.

206 LEWIS AND KING WATCHED *WWTW*, 353.

206 IN THE LAPSLEY AVENUE HOME "Jackon, Sullivan, and Richie Jean, House," National Register of Historic Place Program, https://www.nps.gov/nr/feature /places/pdfs/13001033.pdf.

206 "I LOOKED AT" JRL interview for the documentary *The Soul of America*.

206 "IT IS IRONIC" Kotz, *Judgment Days*, 314.

206 LEWIS MARCHED THE WHOLE WAY *WWTW*, 358–59.

206 HE WALKED SEVEN MILES Ibid., 358–60.

206 DROVE A VW VAN Author interview with Phyllis Cunningham.

206 "ONCE MORE THE" Martin Luther King, Jr., "Address at the Conclusion of the Selma to Montgomery March," March 25, 1965, https://kinginstitute.stanford .edu/king-papers/documents/address-conclusion-selma-montgomery-march.

206 A WHITE SCLC ACTIVIST Garrow, *Protest at Selma*, 117.

207 IT IS DIFFICULT TO OVERSTATE See, for instance, William E. Schmidt, "Selma, 20 Years After the Rights March," *NYT*, March 1, 1985; Schmidt, "March for Rights Resounds After 20 Years," *NYT*, March 8, 1985; George Lardner Jr., "Spirit of Selma Resurrected 20 Years Later," *WP*, March 4, 1965; Gay Talese, "Selma 1990: Old Faces and a New Spirit," *NYT*, March 7, 1990; Ronald Smothers, "A Selma March Relives Those First Steps of '65," *NYT*, March 5, 1996; Stuart Miller, "Reliving Selma's 'Bloody Sunday,'" *Newsweek*, March 6, 2015.

208 "I'M GOING TO" JRL interview for the documentary *The Soul of America*.

208 LEANING BACK AND PITCHING FORWARD *WWTW*, 361.

208 "NOW, JOHN, YOU'VE" Ibid.

208 "I'D HEARD LYNDON" Ibid.

208 "PLAIN AND OPEN" JRL interview for the documentary *The Soul of America*.

208 "THREE AND A HALF CENTURIES" "August 6, 1965: Remarks on the Signing of the Voting Rights Act," https://millercenter.org/the-presidency/presidential -speeches/august-6–1965-remarks-signing-voting-rights-act. On the Voting Rights Act in general, see, for instance, Chandler Davidson and Bernard Grofman, eds., *Quiet Revolution in the South: The Impact of the Voting Rights Act, 1965–1990* (Princeton, N.J., 1994), and Garrine P. Laney, *The Voting Rights Act of 1965, as Amended: Its History and Current Issues* (New York, 2008).

209 IN AMERICUS, GEORGIA *WWTW*, 368.

209 "ALONG THE WAY" JRL interview for the documentary *The Soul of America*.

209 "JUST ABOUT EVERYONE" Carmichael with Thelwell, *Ready for Revolution*, 478.

209 "WE'RE ONLY FLESH" Good, "Odyssey of a Man—and a Movement," *NYT*.

CHAPTER SEVEN: *This Country Don't Run on Love*

213 "BLACK POWER IS" Bernard Weinraub, "The Brilliancy of Black," *Esquire*, January 1967.

213   "The problem we faced now" *WWTW*, 364.

213   Lewis offered a reply *WWTW*, 363–64; John Lewis, "SNCC's Lewis: We March for Us . . . And for You," *New York Herald Tribune*, May 23, 1965.

213   In the Watts section Manchester, *Glory and the Dream*, 1062; Kotz, *Judgment Days*, 338–39; "1,000 Riot in L.A.: Police and Motorists Attacked," *Los Angeles Times*, August 12, 1965; "7,000 in New Watts Rioting; National Guard Alerted," *Los Angeles Times*, August 13, 1965; "Riot Spreads, 4 Killed, Guards Called," *Los Angeles Times*, August 14, 1965; "Editorial: Anarchy Must End," *Los Angeles Times*, August 14, 1965; "'Get Whitey,' Scream Blood-Hungry Mobs,'" *Los Angeles Times*, August 14, 1965; "Negro Riots Rage On; Death Toll 25," *Los Angeles Times*, August 15, 1965; "Editorial: A Time for Prayer," *Los Angeles Times*, August 15, 1965; "Riot Toll 30; Outbreak in Long Beach," *Los Angeles Times*, August 16, 1965; "Riot Declared Over but Snipers Still Hit and Run," *Los Angeles Times*, August 17, 1965.

213   "How is it possible" Kotz, *Judgment Days*, 340.

214   "In a sense" *Eyes on the Prize Civil Rights Reader*, 234.

214   "Now that we" *WWTW*, 364.

214   was being displaced Carson, *In Struggle*, 192; *WWTW*, 365.

214   "Get this into your head" Frantz Fanton, *The Wretched of the Earth*, trans. Richard Philcox (New York, 2004), lviii.

214   a term that Richard Wright had used John Feffer, E. Ethelbert Miller, James Miller, Michele L. Simms Burton, and Jerry W. Ward, "Richard Wright on Black Power," June 6, 2008, https://ips-dc.org/richard_wright_on_black_power/.

215   the victim of assassination See, for instance, Manning Marable, *Malcolm X: A Life of Reinvention* (New York, 2011); Josiah Bates, "The Enduring Mystery of Malcolm X's Assassination," *Time*, February 20, 2020.

215   "I had my differences" *WWTW*, 328. Lewis added: "He had begun looking beyond issues of race to issues of class, and those ideas were intriguing and appealing." Ibid.

215   "If we are to proceed" Carson, *In Struggle*, 198.

216   "This problem goes" Branch, *At Canaan's Edge*, 121.

216   "White participation, as practiced" *Eyes on the Prize Civil Rights Reader*, 246.

216   while disagreeing with Carson, *In Struggle*, 199–200.

216   "Mr. Carmichael," *The New York Times* reported Joseph, *Stokely: A Life*, 103. For the original article, see Gene Roberts, "New Leaders and New Course for 'Snick,'" *NYT*, May 22, 1966.

216   In an interview with *Newsweek* Joseph, *Stokely: A Life*, 104. For the original article, see "Growl of the Panther," *Newsweek*, May 30, 1966.

216   "Although today largely forgotten" Joseph, *Stokely: A Life*, xi.

216   To many white Americans See, for instance, Joseph, *Stokely: A Life*; Joseph, *Waiting 'Til the Midnight Hour*; Terry, "Requiem for a Dream" in Shelby and Terry, *To Shape a New World*, 290–324; *WWTW*, 388–89; author interview with JRL.

Black Power must be seen in the context of the stubbornness and the scope of systemic racism in America. Brandon M. Terry has written, "Institutional racism, as [Carmichael and Hamilton] describe it, does not operate primarily through overt acts of racial antipathy perpetrated by discrete individuals, but through the interpenetration of institutions whose resonant and reinforcing actions disproportionately disadvantage predominantly black communities and subject them to various forms of arbitrary power. The *racism*, of institutional racism, they contend, stems from the crucial role played by 'the active and pervasive operation of anti-black attitudes and practices'" Terry, "Requiem for a Dream" in Shelby and Terry, *To Shape a New World*, 316.

216 "I THINK IT" JRL transcripts, *Eyes on the Prize*, Henry Hampton Collection.

216 CREATED A NEW POLITICAL PARTY *Eyes on the Prize Civil Rights Reader*, 262–78.

217 "LOWNDES WAS TRULY" Ibid., 263.

217 "AS LUDICROUS FOR" Carson, *In Struggle*, 200.

217 "WHEN THE LOWNDES" Stokely Carmichael, "'What We Want,'" *The New York Review of Books*, September 22, 1966. "There was this feeling that somehow and some way this movement must be more black-dominated and black-led," Lewis recalled. JRL transcripts, *Eyes on the Prize*, Henry Hampton Collection. For an extended discussion of the debates within SNCC, see, for instance, Forman, *Making of Black Revolutionaries*, 411–47.

218 THE VIOLENCE IN Stokely Carmichael, "What We Want," *The New York Review of Books*, September 22, 1966.

218 "WE INTEND TO" Bernard Weinraub, "Brilliancy of Black," *Esquire*, January 1967.

218 "HIT 'EM HARD" Ibid.

218 "BROTHERS AND SISTERS" Ibid.

218 HE WAS SPEAKING Ibid.

218 "HE BELIEVED GENUINELY" Ibid.

219 "I HAVE ALWAYS BEEN" *WWTW*, 369.

219 IN KINGSTON SPRINGS For accounts of the conference, see Carson, *In Struggle*, 200–206; *WWTW*, 378–86; Forman, *Making of Black Revolutionaries*, 447–56; Carmichael with Thelwell, *Ready for Revolution*, 479–83; Sellers, *River of No Return*, 164–68; "Panther Founder Takes Helm of Student Society," *The Selma Times-Journal*, May 17, 1966; "Black Panther Founder Named SNCC Chairman," *The Jackson Sun*, May 17, 1966; "Militant Civil Rights Leader Named Head of SNCC," *The Greenwood Commonwealth*, May 17, 1966.

219 "WHAT I REMEMBER" Carmichael with Thelwell, *Ready for Revolution*, 481. See also Lewis, *Shadows of Youth*, 192.

219 "ALMOST LIKE A COUP" JRL transcripts, *Eyes on the Prize*, Henry Hampton Collection.

219 "I DON'T GO ALONG" Weinraub, "Brilliancy of Black," *Esquire*.

219 LEWIS WAS REELECTED Carson, *In Struggle*, 202–3.

219 CALLED HIS "DE-ELECTION" Author interview with JRL.

219–20 "JOHN WAS THE MOST COURAGEOUS" Carson, *In Struggle*, 203.

220 LONG SIMPLY BELIEVED Ibid.

220 "IT WAS VERY" JRL transcripts, *Eyes on the Prize*, Henry Hampton Collection. See also Rowland Evans and Robert Novak, "The New Snick," *WP*, May 25, 1966; Nicholas von Hoffman, "SNCC's Old Guard Rides Panther's Tail," *WP*, May 26, 1966; von Hoffman, "King Terms SNCC Ideas 'Unrealistic,'" *WP*, May 30, 1966.

220 "I MADE A DECISION" JRL transcripts, *Eyes on the Prize*, Henry Hampton Collection.

220 IN THE FIRST WEEK OF JUNE Carson, *In Struggle*, 207.

220 "THIS IS THE TWENTY-SEVENTH TIME" *Eyes on the Prize Civil Rights Reader*, 281–82.

221 IN A FILMED JOINT INTERVIEW See footage in *King in the Wilderness*, HBO/Kunhardt Films, 2018.

221 "THE WAY I" *WWTW*, 389.

221 ROUSTED AND BEATEN "Meredith March," SNCC Digital Gateway, https://snccdigital.org/events/meredith-march/.

221 "Fellow Freedom Fighters" Good, "Odyssey of a Man—And a Movement," *NYT.*

222 "That night in" Ibid.

222 he was long wounded Author interview with JRL.

222 Yet he understood why people Ibid.

222 "The headline's partial" Good, "Odyssey of a Man—And a Movement," *NYT.* See also "Lewis Quits S.N.C.C.; Shuns 'Black Power,'" *NYT,* July 1, 1966; "Kennedy Notes a Peril," *NYT,* July 1, 1966; "Civil Rights: Black Power in the Red," *Time,* July 8, 1966; Jack Nelson, "Lewis Explains SNCC Ouster," *WP,* August 1, 1966.

223 "It hurt," he recalled *WWTW,* 391.

223 "How," the psalmist asks Psalm 137:4 (KJV).

223 "My family had" Ibid.

224 He rented a tiny apartment Ibid., 393–96.

224 After work, he'd Ibid., 394.

224 "There is at" Martin Luther King, Jr., "Beyond Vietnam," April 4, 1967, https://kinginstitute.stanford.edu/king-papers/documents/beyond-vietnam. For King's antiwar views and on his broader political philosophy, see, for instance, Honey, *To the Promised Land;* Shelby and Terry, *To Shape a New World;* Jackson, *From Civil Rights to Human Rights.*

224 "I had heard" *WWTW,* 395-96.

224 "I still believed" Ibid.

225 "But there was no way" Ibid., 397.

225 he completed his degree Ibid., 400.

225 Lewis should meet *WWTW,* 401–2.

225 "I was attracted" Michelle E. Shaw, "Lillian Miles Lewis, 73: Wife, Adviser of U.S. Rep. John Lewis," *The Atlanta Journal-Constitution,* December 31, 2012.

225 As he wryly recalled *WWTW,* 402; author interview with JRL.

225 Lillian arrived with *WWTW,* 402.

226 They married Ibid., 425.

226 In 1976 they Ibid., 438.

226 "I do not" Robert F. Kennedy, "Announcement of Candidacy for President," March 16, 1968, http://www.4president.org/Speeches/rfk1968announcement.htm.

226 "The America Bobby Kennedy envisioned" *WWTW,* 403.

226 he sent off a telegram Ibid.

226 "He is the one guy" Ibid.

226 Lewis was in inner-city Indianapolis Ibid., 404.

227 "The weather was" Ibid., 404–5.

227 Then he heard the news Ibid., 404.

227 King had been in Memphis *WWTW,* 402–03.

227 He was determined to attack On King and economic justice generally, see, for instance, Tommie Shelby, "Prisons of the Forgotten: Ghettos and Economic Injustice" in Shelby and Terry, *To Shape a New World,* 187–204; Dyson, *I May Not Get There With You; King, The Radical King,* ed. West.

227 "And I contend" Lily Rothman, "What Martin Luther King, Jr., Really Thought About Riots," *Time,* April 28, 2015.

228 In 1967, he had published Martin Luther King, Jr., *Where Do We Go from Here: Chaos or Community?* (New York, 1967). See also Shelby, "Prisons of the Forgotten," 192–93. King had proposed his economic program in his annual address to

the SCLC in August 1967. See King, "Where Do We Go from Here?: Address Delivered at the Eleventh Annual SCLC Convention," August 16, 1967, https://kinginstitute.stanford.edu/king-papers/documents/where-do-we-go-here-address-delivered-eleventh-annual-sclc-convention.

228 "THE NATION IS SICK" Martin Luther King, Jr., "'I've Been to the Mountaintop,' Address Delivered at Bishop Charles Mason Temple," April 3, 1968, https://kinginstitute.stanford.edu/king-papers/documents/ive-been-mountaintop-address-delivered-bishop-charles-mason-temple.

228 "IN THE HUMAN-RIGHTS REVOLUTION" Ibid.

228 "HIS EYES WENT" Thomas, *Robert Kennedy*, 366.

228 THERE WAS DEBATE *WWTW*, 405.

228 SITTING IN A CAR Ibid., 406.

229 A TRENCH COAT OF PRESIDENT KENNEDY'S Thomas, *Robert Kennedy*, 366.

229 "IN THIS DIFFICULT DAY" *WWTW*, 407.

229 LEWIS ESCORTED ETHEL Thomas, *Robert Kennedy*, 368.

230 IT WAS LATE *WWTW*, 410–11.

230 "DR. KING WAS" Ibid., 412–13.

230 "IN A PAINFUL ERA" *Newsweek*, May 20, 1968.

231 HE FELL TO THE FLOOR *WWTW*, 415.

EPILOGUE: *Against the Rulers of the Darkness*

233 "WHAT CAN WE DO" Author interview with JRL.

233 SET THIRTEEN STEPS I am indebted to Margaret Shannon for the details about the Canterbury Pulpit.

233 THE TEXT KING HAD PREACHED Martin Luther King, Jr., "Remaining Awake Through a Great Revolution," March 31, 1968, Washington National Cathedral.

233 "AND I, JOHN, SAW" Revelation 21:2–3 (KJV).

233 "WHEN I RECALL" John Lewis, "Racial Justice and Reconciliation Week," March 30, 2008, https://cathedral.org/sermons/racial-reconciliation-and-justice-week/.

234 "WE TRULY BELIEVED" Ibid.

234 "FOR WE WRESTLE NOT" Ephesians, 6:12 (KJV).

234 "IF MARTIN LUTHER KING, JR., WERE HERE TODAY" Lewis, "Racial Justice and Reconciliation Week," March 30, 2008.

235 "I HAVE A DEEP SENSE" Author interview with JRL.

235 "I DON'T HAVE ANY DOUBT" *WWTW*, 417.

235 "EVER SINCE I" Ibid., 429.

235 "THROUGHOUT MY YEARS" Ibid., 466.

236 THE 1986 CONGRESSIONAL CAMPAIGN WAS BRUTAL Ibid., 461–79; Lewis, *Shadows of Youth*, 273–84; Art Harris, "Legends in the Cross Fire," *WP*, July 21, 1986; author interview with JRL; Coppola, "The Parable of Julian Bond and John Lewis," *Atlanta Magazine*; "Mr. Lewis' Victory," *WP*, September 8, 1986. For his career in the 1970s and early '80s, see also *WWTW*, 397–437; Gregory S. Kearse, "JOHN LEWIS: He's Still 'On the Case,'" *Ebony*, November 1976; Jacqueline Trescott, "John Lewis: After the Angry Words," *WP*, August 21, 1983.

236 THE POLISHED BOND Harris, "Legends in the Cross Fire," *WP*.

236 BOND "WORKED FOR ME" Ibid.

236 "HE'S A TAIL-LIGHT" Ibid.

236 RUMORS SWIRLED ABOUT *WWTW*, 469–70.

236   BUOYED BY LARGE MARGINS "Mr. Lewis' Victory," WP, September 8, 1986. The schism between Bond and Lewis lasted for many years. In 1999, the historian Taylor Branch, who had known both men since 1968, was asked to help heal the breach by bringing both men to New Orleans to receive honorary degrees from Dillard University. Branch, who was also being honored, managed to pull it off, and the reconciliation dinner was held at Lucky Cheng's, which featured a cross-dressing waitstaff. When Lewis arrived at the table, one of the servers took the opportunity to plop down in the congressman's lap. "We thought it was going to mortify him," Branch recalled, "but he started to laugh and tell jokes. I think he has hidden layers of sophistication. He has to pay a price for his sainthood, but he can be great fun." Author interview with Taylor Branch. Lewis remembered the evening fondly. Author interview with JRL.

236   "IT WAS ANOTHER STEP" Author interview with JRL. See also Laura Parker, "John Lewis: Scarred Survivor Brings Home Lessons of '60s," WP, March 6, 1990. Lewis, *Shadows of Youth*, 295–98, takes a respectful but skeptical view of Lewis's legislative career. "His official congressional biography devotes more space to his accomplishments in SNCC than to his accomplishments in Congress," Andrew Lewis wrote in 2009. "His 1998 autobiography essentially ends with his 1986 election to Congress, barely touching on his career in the House. As much as anyone, he loved reliving the old war stories, and he always found time to address schools or civic groups on the movement. Unfortunately, his invocations seemed more about nostalgia." Andrew Lewis cited an exchange with Atlanta high school students in the early 1990s who pressed him on how they could make a difference in "health care, housing, or education."

John Lewis's answer: "Register and vote. People died to give you the right to vote." As Andrew Lewis saw it, "The very parts of SNCC's history that young people might find useful in dealing with these intractable problems—its youthful impatience, its unwillingness to defer to an older generation, the premium it placed on morality over political expediency—were left uncited by Congressman Lewis." Lewis, *Shadows of Youth*, 296–97.

236   "I DO, I DO" Author interview with JRL.

237   HE WAS ARRESTED William Douglas, "Rep. John Lewis Busted for 45th Time," McClatchy Washington Bureau, October 8, 2013, https://www.mcclatchydc.com/news/politics-government/article24756802.html.

237   LEWIS REFUSED TO ATTEND David M. Jackson, "Attacked by Trump, Lewis Acknowledges He Boycotted Bush Inauguration, Too," USA Today, January 17, 2017.

237   YET LEWIS THEN WORKED WITH Author interview with JRL.

237   AFTER A MASSACRE AT AN ORLANDO NIGHTCLUB Rachael Bade, Heather Caygle and Ben Weyl, "Democrats Stage Sit-in On House Floor to Force Gun Vote," Politico, June 22, 2016, https://www.politico.com/story/2016/06/democrats-stage-sit-in-on-house-floor-to-force-gun-vote-224656.

237   "WE HAVE BEEN TOO QUIET" Ibid.

237   THE EMMETT TILL UNSOLVED CIVIL RIGHTS CRIME ACT See, for instance, "The Attorney General's Seventh Annual Report to Congress Pursuant to the Emmett Till Unsolved Civil Rights Crime Act of 2007 and First Annual Report to Congress Pursuant to the Emmett Till Unsolved Civil Rights Crimes Reauthorization Act of 2016," February 2018, https://www.courthousenews.com/wp-content/uploads/2018/07/TillDOJ.pdf.

237   AS A TEENAGER Author interview with JRL.

237   WON THE NATIONAL BOOK AWARD Colin Dwyer, "Colson Whitehead, Rep. John

Lewis Among National Book Award Winners," National Public Radio, November 16, 2016.

238 "THE PAST WEEK" Ibid.

238 "SOMETIMES I AM AFRAID TO GO TO SLEEP" "Transcript of U.S. Rep. John Lewis' Call for Start of Impeachment," Atlanta Journal-Constitution, September 25, 2019, https://www.ajc.com/news/national/john-lewis-impeachment-delay-would -betray-the-foundation-our-democracy/7xFwexG35boZwZAOH9uvAI/.

238 "THIS IS A SAD DAY" Stephanie Toone, "What John Lewis Said About Impeachment on Vote Day," *Atlanta Journal-Constitution,* December 18, 2019.

239 LEWIS WEPT WHEN HE SAW Author interview with JRL.

239 THE VIDEO OF A WHITE OFFICER https://www.nytimes.com/2020/05/31/us/george -floyd-investigation.html.

239 LEWIS TOURED THE Tia Mitchell, "John Lewis Visits Black Lives Matter Plaza in Washington," *Atlanta Journal-Constitution,* June 7, 2020, https://www.ajc.com/news /state--regional-govt--politics/rep-john-lewis-tours-black-lives-matter-street -mural-with-mayor/3OQuDLWSon8g6v5ywF6YMP/.

239 "TO SEE ALL OF THE YOUNG PEOPLE" MBK Town Hall Alliance Series, June 5, 2020, https://www.obama.org/anguish-and-action/.

239 "JOHN'S TOUGH, BUT" Ibid.

239 LEWIS HAD NOT SUPPORTED See, for instance, "Rep. Lewis Switches to Obama," *Los Angeles Times,* February 28, 2008; Jeff Zeleny, "Black Leader Changes Endorsement to Obama," *NYT,* February 28, 2008.

239 WHOM HE'D KNOWN THROUGH HER WORK Author interviews with JRL and Hillary Rodham Clinton.

240 "SOMETHING IS HAPPENING" "Big Backer Goes from Clinton to Obama," CNN, https://www.cnn.com/2008/POLITICS/02/27/lewis.switch/index.html.

240 THERE WAS TALK Richard T. Cullen and Charles Mahtesian, "HRC's Black Supporters Pressed to Support Obama," *Politico,* February 27, 2008, https://www .politico.com/story/2008/02/hrcs-black-supporters-pressed-to-support-obama -008734.

240 "I UNDERSTAND HE'S BEEN" "Rep. Lewis Switches to Obama," *Los Angeles Times.*

240 "IT WAS JUST TOO HARD" Author interview with Hillary Rodham Clinton.

240 "THAT WAS A HISTORIC CONTEST" Ibid.

240 "HE'S SAINTLY, BUT" Ibid.

240 "HE SAID, 'IF THERE'S SOME FOLKS" Obama, "Selma Voting Rights Commemoration Speech," March 4, 2007.

241 "I'M HERE BECAUSE" Ibid.

241 "WE DO A DISSERVICE" Barack Obama, "Remarks by the President at the 50th Anniversary of the Selma to Montgomery Marches," March 7, 2015, https:// obamawhitehouse.archives.gov/the-press-office/2015/03/07/remarks-president -50th-anniversary-selma-montgomery-marches.

241 THE "MIGHTY MARCH" Ibid.

241 "OUR JOB'S EASIER" Ibid.

242 "IT WAS RELIGION" Author interview with JRL; quoted in Meacham, *American Gospel,* 192.

242 THE IMMIGRATION AND NATIONALITY ACT Joshua Zeitz, *Building the Great Society: Inside Lyndon Johnson's White House* (New York, 2018), 195–97. See also Tom Gjelten, "The Immigration Act That Inadvertently Changed America," *The Atlantic,* October 2, 2015.

242 BELOW 50 PERCENT OF THE POPULATION BY 2045 William H. Frey, "The U.S. Will

Become 'Minority White' in 2045, Census Projects," March 14, 2018, https://
www.brookings.edu/blog/the-avenue/2018/03/14/the-us-will-become
-minority-white-in-2045-census-projects/. See also Frey, *Diversity Explosion: How
New Racial Demographics Are Remaking America* (Washington, D.C., 2018); Hua Hsu,
"The End of White America?" *The Atlantic,* January–February 2009.

242 THE REPUBLICANS PICKED UP Jonathan Darman, *Landslide: LBJ and Ronald Reagan at
the Dawn of a New America* (New York, 2014), 326–40.

242 "I THINK WE CAN" Ibid., 340. The letter was written to Congressman Edward J.
Derwinski of Illinois.

242 WHO CARRIED FIVE SOUTHERN STATES Theodore H. White, *The Making of the President 1968* (New York, 1969), 509–10.

243 "A YOUNG PERSON SHOULD" Author interview with JRL.

243 THE PROBLEMS WHICH DISPROPORTIONATELY AFFECT See, for instance, Janelle
Jones, John Schmitt, and Valerie Wilson, "50 Years After the Kerner Commission," Report of the Economic Policy Institute, February 26, 2018, https://www
.epi.org/publication/50-years-after-the-kerner-commission/.

243 REPARATIONS FOR SLAVERY See, for instance, Ta-Nehisi Coates, "The Case for
Reparations," *The Atlantic,* June 2014.

243 "I THINK THERE SHOULD BE" Author interview with JRL.

243 "THE SAINTLY CHARACTER" William James, *The Varieties of Religious Experience: A
Study in Human Nature* (London, 1910), 271.

243 A "FEELING OF BEING" Ibid., 272.

244 THE AMERICAN PUBLIC RANKED Frank Newport, David W. Moore, and Lydia
Saad, "The Most Important Events of the Century from the Viewpoint of the
People," Gallup, December 6, 1999, https://news.gallup.com/poll/3427/most
-important-events-century-from-viewpoint-people.aspx.

244 THE VOTING RIGHTS ACT EMPOWERED See, for instance, Gavin Wright, *Sharing the
Prize: The Economics of the Civil Rights Revolution in the American South* (Cambridge,
Mass., 2013); James C. Cobb, "The Voting Rights Act at 50: How It Changed the
World," *Time,* August 6, 2015.

244 BLACK ELECTED OFFICIALS U.S. Department of Justice, Civil Rights Division,
Voting Section, "The Effect of the Voting Rights Act," https://epic.org/privacy
/voting/register/intro_c.html. See also, for instance, Anna Brown and Sara
Atske, "Blacks Have Made Gains in U.S. Political Leadership, but Gaps Remain,"
Pew Research Center, January 18, 2019, https://www.pewresearch.org/fact-tank
/2019/01/18/blacks-have-made-gains-in-u-s-political-leadership-but-gaps
-remain/.

244 JIM CLARK WAS DEFEATED Pratt, *Selma's Bloody Sunday,* 121–22. As Fred Shuttlesworth said, "A man can't beat us up in 1964 and 1965 and expect us to vote for
him in 1966." Ibid., 121.

244 HE'D PUBLISHED A GHOSTWRITTEN MEMOIR Benn, "1960s Selma Sheriff Won't
Back Down," *The Montgomery Advertiser.*

244 SELLING MOBILE HOMES "Remembering Jim Clark," *The Selma Times-Journal,* June 5,
2007.

244 "IT IS NOT SO MUCH" Eleanor Roosevelt, *Tomorrow Is Now* (New York, 2012), 10.

244 HE IS TELLING JRL interview for the documentary *The Soul of America,* 2019.

245 "I'M EMBARRASSED TO CRY" Ibid.

245 "IT'S OKAY.... IT'S ALL RIGHT" Ibid.

245 "OH, GOD, YES, I DREAM" Author interview with JRL.

Appendix

260 AT THE END OF THE 20TH CENTURY Frank Newport, David W. Moore, and Lydia Saad, "The Most Important Events of the Century from the Viewpoint of the People" (1999), https://news.gallup.com/poll/3427/most-important-events -century-from-viewpoint-people.aspx.

261 THIS DATA IS FROM U.S. Commission on Civil Rights. An Assessment of Minority Voting Rights Access in the United States (2018), accessed April 23, 2020, https://www.usccr.gov/pubs/2018/Minority_Voting_Access_2018.pdf.

261 THE VRA INCREASED WHITE REGISTRATION Adriane Fresh, "The Effect of Section 5 Coverage on Enfranchisement: Evidence from North Carolina," *The Journal of Politics* 80, no. 2 (2018): 713–18.

264 ESTIMATES SUGGEST THAT U.S. Immigration Since 1965 (2010), https://www .history.com/topics/immigration/us-immigration-since-1965.

Bibliography

Manuscripts and Archival Sources

Brown v. Board of Education of Topeka, Opinion, May 17, 1954. Records of the Supreme Court of the United States, Record Group 267, National Archives, Washington, D.C.

Eyes on the Prize. Transcripts of interviews for the PBS documentary series produced by Henry Hampton. Henry Hampton Collection, Film and Media Archive, Washington University, St. Louis, Mo.

Federal Bureau of Investigation. "FBI File on Selma." FBI file 44-28492, Section 1, Serials 1–42, Alabama. Selma to Montgomery March, March 7, 1965, Edmund Pettus Bridge, NAID 7634471. National Archives, Washington, D.C.

Federal Bureau of Investigation. Investigative files on the Student Nonviolent Coordinating Committee (SNCC). File #100-439190, Parts 1–14. National Archives, Washington, D.C.

Federal Bureau of Investigation. "Southern Christian Leadership Conference," parts 1–14. FBI Records: The Vault. https://vault.fbi.gov/southern-christian-leadership-convention/Southern%20Christian%20Leadership%20Conference%20Part%2001%20of%2014/view.

Johnson, Lyndon B., and Theodore Sorensen. Transcript of telephone conversation, June 3, 1963. Collections of the Lyndon Baines Johnson Library and Museum, Austin, Tex.

Kennedy, John F. Daily Schedule, June 22, 1963. John F. Kennedy Presidential Library and Museum, Boston, Mass.

Lawson, James M., Jr. Transcript of interview conducted by Robert Penn Warren, March 17, 1964, for Warren's book *Who Speaks for the Negro?* (Random House, 1965). The Digital Archive Collection, Robert Penn Warren Center for the Humanities, Vanderbilt University, Nashville, Tenn.

McPherson, Charles A. J. "The Jesse Thornton Lynching," Container 11:B97, file folder #9. National Association for the Advancement of Colored People (NAACP) Records, Library of Congress, Washington, D.C.

Seigenthaler, John. Oral history, April 2, 2012. John Seigenthaler Papers, Special Collections Library, Vanderbilt University, Nashville, Tenn.

Books

Adams, Frank, with Myles Horton. *Unearthing Seeds of Fire: The Idea of Highlander*. Winston-Salem, N.C.: J. F. Blair, 1975.

Adams, John. *The Works of John Adams, Second President of the United States. With a Life of the Author, Notes and Illustrations,* by his grandson Charles Francis Adams. Vol. 6. Boston: Little, Brown, 1851.

Ahmann, Mathew H., ed. *The New Negro.* Notre Dame, Ind.: Fides Publishers, 1961.

Albert, Peter J., and Ronald Hoffman, eds. *We Shall Overcome: Martin Luther King, Jr., and the Black Freedom Struggle.* New York: Pantheon Books in cooperation with the United States Capitol Historical Society, 1990.

Alexander, Michelle. *The New Jim Crow: Mass Incarceration in the Age of Colorblindness.* New York: New Press, 2010.

Alexander, Shawn Leigh. *An Army of Lions: The Civil Rights Struggle Before the NAACP.* Politics and Culture in Modern America. Philadelphia: University of Pennsylvania Press, 2012.

Angelou, Maya. *I Know Why the Caged Bird Sings.* Foreword by Oprah Winfrey. New York: Random House, 2015.

Arsenault, Raymond. *Freedom Riders: 1961 and the Struggle for Racial Justice.* Pivotal Moments in American History. Oxford: Oxford University Press, 2006.

Augustine of Hippo, Saint. *City of God.* Translated by Marcus Dods. New York: Modern Library, 1993.

Baillie, John. *The Belief in Progress.* London: Oxford University Press, 1950.

Baldwin, James. *The Price of the Ticket: Collected Nonfiction, 1948–1985.* New York: St. Martin's/Marek, 1985.

Bass, Jack, and Marilyn W. Thompson. *Strom: The Complicated Personal and Political Life of Strom Thurmond.* New York: PublicAffairs, 2005.

Bayley, Edwin R. *Joe McCarthy and the Press.* Madison: University of Wisconsin Press, 1981.

Bean, Jonathan, ed. *Race and Liberty in America: The Essential Reader.* Lexington: University Press of Kentucky, 2009.

Bellah, Robert N. *The Broken Covenant: American Civil Religion in Time of Trial.* 2nd ed. Chicago: University of Chicago Press, 1992.

———, and Phillip E. Hammond. *Varieties of Civil Religion.* San Francisco: Harper & Row, 1980.

Bennett, David H. *The Party of Fear: From Nativist Movements to the New Right in American History.* 2nd Vintage Books ed., rev. and updated. New York: Vintage Books, 1995.

Beschloss, Michael. *Presidential Courage: Brave Leaders and How They Changed America, 1789–1989.* New York: Simon & Schuster, 2007.

Black, Allida M. *Casting Her Own Shadow: Eleanor Roosevelt and the Shaping of Postwar Liberalism.* New York: Columbia University Press, 1996.

Blackwell, Unita, with JoAnne Prichard Morris. *Barefootin': Life Lessons from the Road to Freedom.* New York: Crown Publishers, 2006.

Blight, David W. *Race and Reunion: The Civil War in American Memory.* Cambridge, Mass.: Harvard University Press, 2002.

Bobetsky, Victor V., ed. *We Shall Overcome: Essays on a Great American Song.* Lanham, Md.: Rowman & Littlefield, 2015.

Bond, Julian. *Race Man: Selected Works, 1960–2015.* Edited by Michael G. Long. San Francisco: City Lights Books, 2020.

Bonhoeffer, Dietrich. *The Cost of Discipleship.* New York: Touchstone, (2018). First published in 1959 as an abridged translation of the author's *Nachfolge,* published in Munich by C. Kaiser in 1937.

Bonner, Charles A. *Tip of the Arrow: A Study in Leadership.* Conneaut Lake, Penn.: Page Publishing, 2020.

Boorstin, Daniel J. *The Genius of American Politics*. 1st Phoenix ed. Charles R. Walgreen Foundation Lectures. Chicago: University of Chicago Press, 1958.

Boritt, Gabor S., ed. *Why the Confederacy Lost*. New York: Oxford University Press, 1992.

Bourke, Joanna. *Fear: A Cultural History*. Emeryville, Calif.: Shoemaker Hoard, 2006.

Bowers, Claude G. *The Tragic Era: The Revolution after Lincoln*. Blue Ribbon Books. Cambridge, Mass.: Houghton Mifflin, 1929.

Branch, Taylor. *At Canaan's Edge: America in the King Years, 1965–68*. New York: Simon & Schuster, 2006.

———. *Parting the Waters: America in the King Years, 1954–63*. New York: Simon & Schuster, 1988.

———. *Pillar of Fire: America in the King Years, 1963–65*. New York: Simon & Schuster, 1998.

Brown, Cynthia Stokes, ed. *Ready from Within: Septima Clark and the Civil Rights Movement*. Navarro, Calif.: Wild Trees Press, 1986.

Bryan, William Jennings. *Speeches of William Jennings Bryan*. Revised and arranged by himself. With a biographical introduction by Mary Baird Bryan, his wife. 2 vols. New York: Funk & Wagnalls, 1909.

Budiansky, Stephen. *The Bloody Shirt: Terror after the Civil War*. New York: Viking, 2008.

Bullard, Sara. *Free at Last: A History of the Civil Rights Movement and Those Who Died in the Struggle*. New York: Oxford University Press, 1993.

Burke, Edmund. *Reflections on the Revolution in France, and Other Writings*. Edited by Jesse Norman. Everyman's Library, no. 365. New York: Alfred A. Knopf, 2015.

Burlingame, Michael. *Abraham Lincoln: A Life*. 2 vols. Baltimore: Johns Hopkins University Press, 2008.

Burns, Edward McNall. *The American Idea of Mission: Concepts of National Purpose and Destiny*. Westport, Conn.: Greenwood Press, 1973.

Burns, James MacGregor. *John Kennedy: A Political Profile*. New York: Harcourt, Brace, 1960.

Bush, George, with Victor Gold. *Looking Forward*. Garden City, N.Y.: Doubleday, 1987.

Carmichael, Stokely, with Ekwueme Michael Thelwell. *Ready for Revolution: The Life and Struggles of Stokely Carmichael (Kwame Ture)*. New York: Scribner, 2003.

Caro, Robert A. *The Years of Lyndon Johnson*. 4 vols. New York: Alfred A. Knopf, 1982–2012.

Carson, Clayborne. *In Struggle: SNCC and the Black Awakening of the 1960s*. Cambridge, Mass.: Harvard University Press, 1981.

———. *Martin's Dream: My Journey and the Legacy of Martin Luther King Jr.* New York: Palgrave Macmillan, 2013.

Carson, Clayborne, et al., eds. *The Eyes on the Prize: Civil Rights Reader; Documents, Speeches, and Firsthand Accounts from the Black Freedom Struggle, 1954–1990*. New York: Penguin Books, 1991.

Carson, Clayborne, et al., eds. *Reporting Civil Rights*. Vol. 1. New York: Library of America, 2003.

Carson, Clayborne, senior editor and director. *The Student Voice, 1960–1965: Periodical of the Student Nonviolent Coordinating Committee*. Compiled by the staff of the Martin Luther King, Jr., Papers Project; sponsored by the Martin Luther King, Jr., Center for Nonviolent Social Change, Inc. in association with Stanford University. Westport, Conn.: Meckler, 1990.

Carter, Hodding. *First Person Rural*. Garden City, N.Y.: Doubleday, 1963.

Cash, W. J. *The Mind of the South*. New York: Alfred A. Knopf, 1941.

Castel, Albert. *The Presidency of Andrew Johnson*. American Presidency Series. Lawrence: Regents Press of Kansas, 1979.

Chalmers, David M. *Hooded Americanism: The History of the Ku Klux Klan.* 3rd ed. Durham: Duke University Press, 1981.

Chappell, David L. *A Stone of Hope: Prophetic Religion and the Death of Jim Crow.* Chapel Hill: University of North Carolina Press, 2004.

———. *Waking from the Dream: The Struggle for Civil Rights in the Shadow of Martin Luther King, Jr.* New York: Random House, 2014.

Charron, Katherine Mellen. *Freedom's Teacher: The Life of Septima Clark.* Chapel Hill: University of North Carolina Press, 2009.

Chernow, Ron. *Grant.* New York: Penguin Press, 2017.

Chester, Lewis, Geoffrey Hodgson, and Bruce Page. *An American Melodrama: The Presidential Campaign of 1968.* New York: Viking Press, 1969.

Coates, Ta-Nehisi. *Between the World and Me.* New York: Spiegel & Grau, 2015.

———. *We Were Eight Years in Power: An American Tragedy.* New York: One World, 2017.

Cobb, Charles E., Jr. *On the Road to Freedom: A Guided Tour of the Civil Rights Trail.* Chapel Hill, N.C.: Algonquin Books of Chapel Hill, 2008.

———. *This Nonviolent Stuff'll Get You Killed: How Guns Made the Civil Rights Movement Possible.* Durham, N.C.: Duke University Press, 2015.

Cohn, Roy. *McCarthy.* New York: New American Library, 1968.

Cohodas, Nadine. *Strom Thurmond and the Politics of Southern Change.* New York: Simon & Schuster, 1993.

Coleman, Finnie D. *Sutton E. Griggs and the Struggle Against White Supremacy.* Knoxville: University of Tennessee Press, 2007.

Collier-Thomas, Bettye, and V. P. Franklin, eds. *Sisters in the Struggle: African American Women in the Civil Rights–Black Power Movement.* New York: New York University Press, 2001.

Cooper, William J., Jr., and John M. McCardell, Jr., eds. *In the Cause of Liberty: How the Civil War Redefined American Ideals.* Baton Rouge: Louisiana State University Press, 2009.

Coski, John M. *The Confederate Battle Flag: America's Most Embattled Emblem.* Cambridge, Mass.: Belknap Press of Harvard University Press, 2005.

Crespino, Joseph. *Strom Thurmond's America.* New York: Hill and Wang, 2012.

Curry, Constance, et al. *Deep in Our Hearts: Nine White Women in the Freedom Movement.* Athens: University of Georgia Press, 2000.

Dallek, Robert. *Flawed Giant: Lyndon Johnson and His Times, 1961–1973.* New York: Oxford University Press, 1998.

Darman, Jonathan. *Landslide: LBJ and Ronald Reagan at the Dawn of a New America.* New York: Random House, 2014.

Davidson, Chandler, and Bernard Grofman, eds. *Quiet Revolution in the South: The Impact of the Voting Rights Act, 1965–1990.* Princeton, N.J.: Princeton University Press, 1994.

Davis, Kenneth S. *FDR, the War President, 1940–1943.* New York: Random House, 2000.

Dierenfield, Bruce J. *The Civil Rights Movement.* Rev. ed. New York: Pearson Longman, 2008.

Dixie, Quinton H., and Peter Eisenstadt. *Visions of a Better World: Howard Thurman's Pilgrimage to India and the Origins of African American Nonviolence.* Boston: Beacon Press, 2011.

Douglass, Frederick. *Douglass: Autobiographies.* Edited by Henry Louis Gates, Jr. New York: Library of America, 1994.

———. *Selected Speeches and Writings.* Edited by Philip S. Foner. Chicago: Lawrence Hill, 1999.

Dozier, Rush W., Jr. *Why We Hate: Understanding, Curbing, and Eliminating Hate in Ourselves and Our World.* Chicago: Contemporary Books, 2002.

Du Bois, W.E.B. *Black Reconstruction in America: An Essay Toward a History of the Part Which*

Black Folk Played in the Attempt to Reconstruct Democracy in America, 1860–1880. Studies in American Negro Life. New York: Atheneum, 1983. First published 1935.

———. *The Souls of Black Folk.* Everyman's Library. New York: Alfred A. Knopf, 1993. First published 1903.

Dyson, Michael Eric. *April 4, 1968: Martin Luther King, Jr.'s Death and How It Changed America.* New York: Basic Civitas Books, 2008.

———. *I May Not Get There with You: The True Martin Luther King, Jr.* New York: Free Press, 2000.

Ebony (Chicago, Illinois). *The White Problem in America.* By the editors of Ebony. First published as a special issue of *Ebony* magazine, August 1965. Chicago: Johnson Publishing, 1966.

Edsall, Thomas Byrne, with Mary D. Edsall. *Chain Reaction: The Impact of Race, Rights, and Taxes on American Politics.* New York. W. W. Norton, 1992.

Egerton, Douglas R. *The Wars of Reconstruction: The Brief, Violent History of America's Most Progressive Era.* New York: Bloomsbury, 2014.

Ellison, Ralph. *Shadow and Act.* New York: Random House, 1964.

Etheridge, Eric. *Breach of Peace: Portraits of the 1961 Mississippi Freedom Riders.* Exp. ed. Nashville, Tenn.: Vanderbilt University Press, 2018.

Evans, Christopher H. *The Kingdom Is Always but Coming: A Life of Walter Rauschenbusch.* Library of Religious Biography. Grand Rapids, Mich.: William B. Eerdmans Pub., 2004.

Fager, Charles E. *Selma 1965: The March That Changed the South.* 2nd edition. Beacon Paperback, no. 695. Boston: Beacon Press, 1985. First published 1974.

Fairclough, Adam. *To Redeem the Soul of America: The Southern Christian Leadership Conference and Martin Luther King, Jr.* Athens: University of Georgia Press, 1987.

Fanon, Frantz. *The Wretched of the Earth.* Translated from the French by Richard Philcox. New York: Grove Press, 2004.

Fleming, Karl. *Son of the Rough South: An Uncivil Memoir.* New York: PublicAffairs, 2005.

Foner, Eric. *Forever Free: The Story of Emancipation and Reconstruction.* New York: Alfred A. Knopf, 2005.

———. *Reconstruction: America's Unfinished Revolution, 1863–1877.* Updated ed. New York: HarperCollins, 2014.

———. *The Second Founding: How the Civil War and Reconstruction Remade the Constitution.* New York: W. W. Norton, 2019.

Forman, James. *The Making of Black Revolutionaries: Illustrated Edition.* Seattle: University of Washington Press, 1997. First published 1972.

Frady, Marshall. *Wallace.* New York: World Publishing, 1968.

Frank, Gerold. *An American Death: The True Story of the Assassination of Dr. Martin Luther King, Jr. and the Greatest Manhunt of Our Time.* Garden City, N.Y.: Doubleday, 1972.

Fraser, James W. *A History of Hope: When Americans Have Dared to Dream of a Better Future.* New York: Palgrave Macmillan, 2002.

Frey, William H. *Diversity Explosion: How New Racial Demographics Are Remaking America.* Washington, D.C.: Brookings Institution Press, 2018.

Garrow, David J. *Bearing the Cross: Martin Luther King, Jr., and the Southern Christian Leadership Conference.* New York: William Morrow, 1986.

———. *The FBI and Martin Luther King, Jr.: From "Solo" to Memphis.* New York. W. W. Norton, 1981.

———. *Protest at Selma: Martin Luther King, Jr., and the Voting Rights Act of 1965.* New Haven: Conn.: Yale University Press, 1978.

Gates, Henry Louis, Jr. *Colored People: A Memoir.* New York: Alfred A. Knopf, 1994.

———. *Finding Your Roots: The Official Companion to the PBS Series.* Chapel Hill: University of North Carolina Press, 2014.

Gerber, David A. *American Immigration: A Very Short Introduction.* Very Short Introductions, no. 274. Oxford: Oxford University Press, 2011.

Gjerde, Jon, ed. *Major Problems in American Immigration and Ethnic History.* Documents and Essays. Major Problems in American History Series. Boston: Houghton Mifflin, 1998.

Goetz, Stewart, and Charles Taliaferro. *A Brief History of the Soul.* Hoboken, N.J.: Wiley-Blackwell, 2011.

Goodwin, Richard N. *Remembering America: A Voice from the Sixties.* Boston: Little, Brown, 1988.

Gordon, Linda. *The Second Coming of the KKK: The Ku Klux Klan of the 1920s and the American Political Tradition.* New York: Liveright Publishing, 2017.

Gordon-Reed, Annette. *Andrew Johnson.* American Presidents Series. New York: Times Books, 2011.

Gorski, Philip. *American Covenant: A History of Civil Religion from the Puritans to the Present.* Princeton, N.J.: Princeton University Press, 2017.

Gray, Fred D. *Bus Ride to Justice: Changing the System by the System: The Life and Works of Fred D. Gray, Preacher, Attorney, Politician.* Montgomery, Ala.: Black Belt Press, 1995.

Greenberg, Cheryl Lynn, ed. *A Circle of Trust: Remembering SNCC.* New Brunswick, N.J.: Rutgers University Press, 1997.

Halberstam, David. *The Children.* New York: Random House, 1998.

———. *The Fifties.* New York: Villard Books, 1993.

Hale, Jon N. *The Freedom Schools: Student Activists in the Mississippi Civil Rights Movement.* New York: Columbia University Press, 2016.

H[amilton], J[oseph] G. de R[oulhac]. "Pollard, Edward Alfred." In *Dictionary of American Biography,* edited by Allen Johnson and Dumas Malone. Vol. 8, 47–48. New York: Charles Scribner's Sons, 1935.

Hamlin, Françoise N. *Crossroads at Clarksdale: The Black Freedom Struggle in the Mississippi Delta After World War II.* Chapel Hill: University of North Carolina Press, 2012.

Harding, Vincent. *Hope and History: Why We Must Share the Story of the Movement.* 2nd ed. Maryknoll, N.Y.: Orbis Books, 2009.

———. *Martin Luther King, the Inconvenient Hero.* Maryknoll, N.Y.: Orbis Books, 1996.

Hartford, Bruce. *The Selma Voting Rights Struggle and the March to Montgomery.* Freedom Now! Series. San Francisco: Westwind Writers, 2014.

Haviland, Sara Rzeszutek. *James and Esther Cooper Jackson: Love and Courage in the Black Freedom Movement.* Lexington: University Press of Kentucky, 2015.

Henry, Aaron, with Constance Curry. *Aaron Henry: The Fire Ever Burning.* Jackson: University Press of Mississippi, 2000.

Historical Statistics of the United States, Colonial Times to 1970. Part 2. Washington, D.C.: U.S. Department of Commerce, Bureau of the Census, 1975.

Hitchcock, William I. *The Age of Eisenhower: America and the World in the 1950s.* New York: Simon & Schuster, 2018.

Hofstadter, Richard. *The American Political Tradition and the Men Who Made It.* New York: Alfred A. Knopf, 1948.

Hogan, Wesley C. *Many Minds, One Heart: SNCC's Dream for a New America.* Chapel Hill: University of North Carolina Press, 2007.

Holsaert, Faith S., Martha Prescod Norman Noonan, Judy Richardson, Betty Garman Robinson, Jean Smith Young, and Dorothy M. Zellner, eds. *Hands on the Freedom Plow: Personal Accounts by Women in SNCC.* Urbana: University of Illinois Press, 2010.

Homer. *The Odyssey.* Translated by Robert Fagles. New York: Viking, 1996.

Honey, Michael K. *To the Promised Land: Martin Luther King and the Fight for Economic Justice.* New York: W. W. Norton, 2018.

Horton, Myles, and Paulo Freire. *We Make the Road by Walking: Conversations on Education and Social Change.* Edited by Brenda Bell, John Gaventa, and John Peters. Philadelphia: Temple University Press, 1990.

Horton, Myles, with Judith Kohl and Herbert Kohl. *The Long Haul: An Autobiography.* New York: Teachers College Press, 1998.

Houck, Davis W., and Dixon, David E., eds. *Rhetoric, Religion and the Civil Rights Movement, 1954–1965.* Studies in Rhetoric and Religion, no. 1. Waco, Tex.: Baylor University Press, 2006.

Humphrey, Hubert H. *The Education of a Public Man: My Life and Politics.* Edited by Norman Sherman. Garden City, N.Y.: Doubleday, 1976.

Jackson, Thomas F. *From Civil Rights to Human Rights: Martin Luther King, Jr., and the Struggle for Economic Justice.* Politics and Culture in Modern America. Philadelphia: University of Pennsylvania Press, 2007.

James, William. *The Principles of Psychology.* Edited by Frederick H. Burkhardt. Vol. 1. Cambridge, Mass.: Harvard University Press, 1981.

———. *The Varieties of Religious Experience: A Study in Human Nature; Being the Gifford Lectures on Natural Religion Delivered at Edinburgh in 1901–1902.* London: Longmans, Green, 1910.

Jenkins, Willis, and Jennifer M. McBride, eds. *Bonhoeffer and King: Their Legacies and Import for Christian Social Thought.* Minneapolis: Fortress Press, 2010.

Johnson, Lady Bird. *A White House Diary.* New York: Holt, Rinehart and Winston, 1970.

Johnson, Lyndon B. *Reaching for Glory: Lyndon Johnson's Secret White House Tapes, 1964–1965.* Edited by Michael R. Beschloss. New York: Simon & Schuster, 2001.

———. *Taking Charge: The Johnson White House Tapes, 1963–1964.* Edited by Michael Beschloss. New York: Simon & Schuster, 1997.

———. *The Vantage Point: Perspectives of the Presidency, 1963–1969.* New York: Holt, Rinehart and Winston, 1971.

Jones, Clarence B., and Stuart Connelly. *Behind the Dream: The Making of the Speech That Transformed a Nation.* New York: Palgrave Macmillan, 2011.

Jones, William P. *The March on Washington: Jobs, Freedom, and the Forgotten History of Civil Rights.* New York: W. W. Norton, 2013.

Joseph, Peniel E. *Stokely: A Life.* New York: Basic Civitas, 2014.

———. *The Sword and the Shield: The Revolutionary Lives of Malcolm X and Martin Luther King Jr.* New York: Basic Books, 2020.

———. *Waiting 'Till the Midnight Hour: A Narrative History of Black Power in America.* New York: Henry Holt, 2006.

Kapur, Sudarshan. *Raising Up a Prophet: The African-American Encounter with Gandhi.* Boston: Beacon Press, 1992.

Kempton, Murray. *America Comes of Middle Age: Columns.* New York: Viking Press, 1963.

Kendi, Ibram X. *Stamped from the Beginning: The Definitive History of Racist Ideas in America.* New York: Nation Books, 2016.

Kennedy, Peggy Wallace, with H. Mark Kennedy. *The Broken Road: George Wallace and a Daughter's Journey to Reconciliation.* New York: Bloomsbury Publishing, 2019.

Kennedy, Stetson. *Jim Crow Guide to the U.S.A.: The Laws, Customs and Etiquette Governing the Conduct of Nonwhites and Other Minorities as Second-Class Citizens.* Tuscaloosa: University of Alabama Press, 2011. First published 1959.

Kieckhefer, Richard, and George D. Bond, eds. *Sainthood: Its Manifestations in World Religions.* Berkeley: University of California Press, 1988.

King, Martin Luther, Jr. *The Papers of Martin Luther King, Jr.* Edited by Clayborne Carson et al. 7 vols. Berkeley: University of California Press, 1992–2014. Vol. 1, *Called to Serve, January 1929–June 1951,* 1992. Vol. 2, *Rediscovering Precious Values, July 1951–November 1955,* 1994. Vol. 3, *Birth of a New Age, December 1955–December 1956,* 1997. Vol. 4, *Symbol of the Movement, January 1957–December 1958,* 2000. Vol. 5, *Threshold of a New Decade, January 1959–December 1960,* 2005. Vol. 6, *Advocate of the Social Gospel, September 1948–March 1963,* 2007. Vol. 7, *To Save the Soul of America, January 1961–August 1962,* 2014.

———. *The Radical King.* Edited by Cornel West. Boston: Beacon Press, 2015.

———. *Stride Toward Freedom: The Montgomery Story.* The King Legacy. Boston: Beacon Press, 2010.

———. *A Testament of Hope: The Essential Writings and Speeches of Martin Luther King, Jr.* Edited by James Melvin Washington. San Francisco: HarperOne, 2003.

King, Mary. *Mahatma Gandhi and Martin Luther King Jr.: The Power of Nonviolent Action.* Cultures of Peace Series. Paris: UNESCO Pub., 1999.

Knight, Louise W. *Jane Addams: Spirit in Action.* New York: W. W. Norton, 2010.

Kotz, Nick. *Judgment Days: Lyndon Baines Johnson, Martin Luther King Jr., and the Laws That Changed America.* Boston: Houghton Mifflin, 2005.

LaFayette, Bernard, Jr., and Kathryn Lee Johnson. *In Peace and Freedom: My Journey in Selma.* Lexington: University Press of Kentucky, 2013.

Lakoff, Sanford A. *Equality in Political Philosophy.* Harvard Political Studies. Cambridge: Harvard University Press, 1964.

Laney, Garrine P. *The Voting Rights Act of 1965, As Amended: Its History and Current Issues.* New York: Nova Science, 2008.

Lee, Harper. *Go Set a Watchman.* New York: Harper, 2015.

———. *To Kill a Mockingbird.* Philadelphia: Lippincott, 1960.

Lesher, Stephan. *George Wallace: American Populist.* Reading, Mass.: Addison-Wesley, 1994.

Leuchtenburg. William E. *The White House Looks South: Franklin D. Roosevelt, Harry S. Truman, Lyndon B. Johnson.* Walter Lynwood Fleming Lectures in Southern History. Baton Rouge: Louisiana State University Press, 2005.

Lewis, Andrew B. *The Shadows of Youth: The Remarkable Journey of the Civil Rights Generation.* New York: Hill and Wang, 2009.

Lewis, David Levering. *King: A Biography.* 2nd ed. Urbana: University of Illinois Press, 1978.

———, Michael Nash, and Daniel J. Leab, eds. *Red Activists and Black Freedom: James and Esther Jackson and the Long Civil Rights Revolution.* New York: Routledge, 2010.

Lewis, John, and Andrew Aydin. *March: Book One.* Art by Nate Powell. Marietta, Ga.: Top Shelf Productions, 2013.

———. *March: Book Three.* Edited by Leigh Walton. Art by Nate Powell. Marietta, Ga., Top Shelf Productions, 2016.

———. *March: Book Two.* Art by Nate Powell. Marietta, Ga., Top Shelf Productions, 2015.

Lewis, John, with Brenda Jones. *Across That Bridge: Life Lessons and a Vision for Change.* New York: Hyperion, 2012.

Lewis, John, with Michael D'Orso. *Walking with the Wind: A Memoir of the Movement.* New York: Simon & Schuster, 1998.

Long, Michael G., ed. *Christian Peace and Nonviolence: A Documentary History.* Maryknoll, N.Y.: Orbis Books, 2011.

Lovett, Bobby L. *The African-American History of Nashville, Tennessee, 1780–1930: Elites and Dilemmas.* Fayetteville: University of Arkansas Press, 1999.

Lyon, Danny. *Memories of the Southern Civil Rights Movement.* The Lyndhurst Series on the

South. Chapel Hill: Published for the Center for Documentary Studies, Duke University, by the University of North Carolina Press, 1992.

Lytle, Andrew Nelson. *Bedford Forrest and His Critter Company*. New York: Minton, Balch, 1931.

MacLean, Nancy. *Behind the Mask of Chivalry: The Making of the Second Ku Klux Klan*. New York: Oxford University Press, 1994.

Maddex, Jack P., Jr. *The Reconstruction of Edward A. Pollard: A Rebel's Conversion to Postbellum Unionism*. James Sprunt Studies in History and Political Science, vol. 54. Chapel Hill: University of North Carolina Press, 1974.

Manchester, William. *The Glory and the Dream: A Narrative History of America, 1932–1972*. Boston: Little, Brown, 1974.

Marable, Manning. *Malcolm X: A Life of Reinvention*. New York: Penguin Group, 2011.

———, and Leith Mullings, eds. *Let Nobody Turn Us Around: Voices of Resistance, Reform, and Renewal: An African American Anthology*. Lanham, Md.: Rowman & Littlefield, 2003.

Marsh, Charles. *The Beloved Community: How Faith Shapes Social Justice, from the Civil Rights Movement to Today*. New York: Basic Books, 2005.

Marshall, James P. *The Mississippi Civil Rights Movement and the Kennedy Administration, 1960–1964: A History in Documents*. Baton Rouge: Louisiana State University Press, 2018.

———. *Student Activism and Civil Rights in Mississippi: Protest Politics and the Struggle for Racial Justice, 1960–1965*. Baton Rouge: Louisiana State University Press, 2013.

Martin, Spider. *Selma 1965. The Photographs of Spider Martin*. Austin: University of Texas Press, 2015.

Marty, Martin E. *The One and the Many: America's Struggle for the Common Good*. Cambridge, Mass.: Harvard University Press, 1997.

Matthews, Chris. *Bobby Kennedy: A Raging Spirit*. New York: Simon & Schuster, 2017.

———. *Kennedy and Nixon: The Rivalry That Shaped Postwar America*. New York: Simon & Schuster, 1996.

McGuire, Danielle L. *At the Dark End of the Street: Black Women, Rape, and Resistance—A New History of the Civil Rights Movement from Rosa Parks to the Rise of Black Power*. New York: Alfred A. Knopf, 2010.

McMahon, Kevin J. *Reconsidering Roosevelt on Race: How the Presidency Paved the Road to Brown*. Chicago: University of Chicago Press, 2004.

McVeigh, Rory. *The Rise of the Ku Klux Klan: Right-Wing Movements and National Politics*. Social Movements, Protest, and Contention, vol. 32. Minneapolis: University of Minnesota Press, 2009.

McWhorter, Diane. *Carry Me Home: Birmingham, Alabama, the Climactic Battle of the Civil Rights Revolution*. New York: Simon & Schuster, 2001.

Meacham, Ellen B. *Delta Epiphany: Robert F. Kennedy in Mississippi*. Jackson: University Press of Mississippi, 2018.

Meacham, Jon. *American Gospel: God, the Founding Fathers, and the Making of a Nation*. New York: Random House, 2006.

———. *Destiny and Power: The American Odyssey of George Herbert Walker Bush*. New York: Random House, 2015.

———. *The Soul of America: The Battle for Our Better Angels*. New York: Random House, 2018.

———, ed. *Voices in Our Blood: America's Best on the Civil Rights Movement*. New York: Random House, 2001.

Merton, Thomas. *Faith and Violence: Christian Teaching and Christian Practice*. Notre Dame, Ind.: University of Notre Dame Press, 1984. First published 1968.

Miller, Merle. *Lyndon, an Oral Biography*. New York: G. P. Putnam's Sons, 1980.

Minter, William, Gail Hovey, and Charles Cobb, Jr., eds. *No Easy Victories: African Liberation and American Activists Over a Half Century, 1950–2000.* Trenton, N.J.: Africa World Press, 2008.

Moody, Anne. *Coming of Age in Mississippi.* New York: Dial Press, 1968.

Moses, Robert, and Charles E. Cobb. *Radical Equations: Civil Rights from Mississippi to the Algebra Project.* Boston: Beacon Press, 2002.

Moye, J. Todd. *Ella Baker: Community Organizer of the Civil Rights Movement.* Lanham, Md.: Rowman & Littlefield, 2013.

———. *Let the People Decide: Black Freedom and White Resistance Movements in Sunflower County, Mississippi, 1945–1986.* Chapel Hill: University of North Carolina Press, 2004.

Myrdal, Gunnar. *An American Dilemma: The Negro Problem and Modern Democracy.* 20th anniversary ed. New York: Harper & Row, 1962.

Nepstad, Sharon Erickson. *Nonviolent Struggle: Theories, Strategies, and Dynamics.* New York: Oxford University Press, 2015.

Newman, Mark. *Getting Right with God: Southern Baptists and Desegregation, 1945–1995.* Tuscaloosa: University of Alabama Press, 2001.

Nichols, David A. *A Matter of Justice: Eisenhower and the Beginning of the Civil Rights Revolution.* New York: Simon & Schuster, 2007.

Niebuhr, Reinhold. *Reinhold Niebuhr: Major Works on Religion and Politics.* Edited by Elisabeth Sifton. New York: Library of America, 2015.

Nisbet, Robert A. *History of the Idea of Progress.* New York: Basic Books, 1980.

———. *Social Change and History: Aspects of the Western Theory of Development.* A Galaxy Book, no. 313. London: Oxford University Press, 1970.

Nixon, Richard M. *Six Crises.* Garden City, N.Y.: Doubleday, 1962.

Novak, Robert D. *The Agony of the G.O.P. 1964.* New York: Macmillan, 1965.

Nunnelley, William A. *Bull Connor.* Tuscaloosa: University of Alabama Press, 1991.

Oakley, J. Ronald. *God's Country: America in the Fifties.* New York: Dembner Books, 1986.

O'Donnell, Lawrence. *Playing with Fire: The 1968 Election and the Transformation of American Politics.* New York: Penguin Press, 2017.

O'Reilly, Kenneth. *Racial Matters: The FBI's Secret File on Black America, 1960–1972.* New York: Free Press, 1989.

Oshinsky, David M. *A Conspiracy So Immense: The World of Joe McCarthy.* Oxford: Oxford University Press, 2005. First published 1983.

———. *Worse Than Slavery: Parchman Farm and the Ordeal of Jim Crow Justice.* New York: Free Press, 1996.

Parker, Theodore. *Sermons of Religion.* Edited by Samuel A. Eliot. Vol. 3 of *Works.* Centenary ed. Boston: American Unitarian Association; Cambridge: University Press, 1908.

———. "Speech at the New England Anti-Slavery Convention in Boston, May 29, 1850." In *Speeches, Addresses, and Occasional Sermons,* vol. 2, 174–208. Boston: W. Crosby and H. P. Nichols, 1852.

Parr, Patrick. *The Seminarian: Martin Luther King Jr. Comes of Age.* Chicago: Lawrence Hill Books, 2018.

Parsons, Elaine Frantz. *Ku-Klux: The Birth of the Klan During Reconstruction.* Chapel Hill: University of North Carolina Press, 2015.

Patterson, James T. *Grand Expectations: The United States, 1945–1974.* The Oxford History of the United States, vol. 10. New York: Oxford University Press, 1996.

Pauley, Garth E. *The Modern Presidency and Civil Rights: Rhetoric on Race from Roosevelt to Nixon.* Presidential Rhetoric Series, no. 3. College Station: Texas A & M University Press, 2001.

Payne, Charles M. *I've Got the Light of Freedom: The Organizing Tradition and the Mississippi Freedom Struggle.* Berkeley: University of California Press, 2007. First published 1995.

Pearson, Hugh. *When Harlem Nearly Killed King: The 1958 Stabbing of Dr. Martin Luther King, Jr.* New York: Seven Stories Press, 2002.

Percy, Walker. *Signposts in a Strange Land.* Edited by Patrick Samway. New York: Farrar, Straus, and Giroux, 1991.

Perlmutter, Philip. *Legacy of Hate: A Short History of Ethnic, Religious, and Racial Prejudice in America.* Armonk, N.Y.: M. E. Sharpe, 1999.

Peters, Charles. *We Do Our Part: Toward a Fairer and More Equal America.* New York: Random House, 2017.

Pollard, Edward A. *The Lost Cause: A New Southern History of the War of the Confederates; Comprising a Full and Authentic Account of the Rise and Progress of the Late Southern Confederacy [. . .].* New York: E. B. Treat, 1866.

———. *The Lost Cause Regained.* New York: G. W. Carleton, 1868.

"Pollard, Edward A." In *The American Annual Cyclopaedia and Register of Important Events of the Year 1872.* Vol. 12, 676. New York: D. Appleton, 1873.

Powell, Ruth Marie. *Lights and Shadows: The Story of the American Baptist Theological Seminary, 1924–1964.* Nashville, Tenn.: n.p., 1965.

Pratt, Robert A. *Selma's Bloody Sunday: Protest, Voting Rights, and the Struggle for Racial Equality.* Witness to History. Baltimore: Johns Hopkins University Press, 2017.

Purdum, Todd S. *An Idea Whose Time Has Come: Two Presidents, Two Parties, and the Battle for the Civil Rights Act of 1964.* New York: Henry Holt, 2014.

Putnam, Carleton. *Race and Reason: A Yankee View.* Washington, D.C.: Public Affairs Press, 1961.

Rable, George C. *But There Was No Peace: The Role of Violence in the Politics of Reconstruction.* Athens: University of Georgia Press, 1984.

Raines, Howell. *My Soul Is Rested: Movement Days in the Deep South Remembered.* New York: Putnam, 1977.

Ransby, Barbara. *Ella Baker and the Black Freedom Movement: A Radical Democratic Vision.* Gender & American Culture. Chapel Hill: University of North Carolina Press, 2005.

Rauschenbusch, Walter. *Christianity and the Social Crisis.* New York: Macmillan, 1916. First published 1907.

Reeves, Richard. *President Kennedy: Profile of Power.* New York: Simon & Schuster, 1993.

Remnick, David. *The Bridge: The Life and Rise of Barack Obama.* New York: Alfred A. Knopf, 2010.

Rice, Arnold S. *The Ku Klux Klan in American Politics.* New York: Haskell House Publishers, 1972.

Risen, Clay. *The Bill of the Century: The Epic Battle for the Civil Rights Act.* New York: Bloomsbury Press, 2014.

Roberts, J. Deotis. *Bonhoeffer and King: Speaking Truth to Power.* Louisville, Ky.: Westminster John Knox Press, 2005.

Robin, Corey. *Fear: The History of a Political Idea.* Oxford: Oxford University Press, 2004.

———. *The Reactionary Mind: Conservatism from Edmund Burke to Sarah Palin.* New York: Oxford University Press, 2011.

Rogers, William Warren, Robert David Ward, Leah Rawls Atkins, and Wayne Flynt. *Alabama: The History of a Deep South State.* Tuscaloosa: University of Alabama Press, 2018.

Rolph, Stephanie R. *Resisting Equality: The Citizens' Council, 1954–1989.* Making the Modern South. Baton Rouge: Louisiana State University Press, 2018.

Roosevelt, Eleanor. *Tomorrow Is Now.* New York: Penguin Books, 2012. First published 1963.

Rovere, Richard H. *Senator Joe McCarthy.* Berkeley: University of California Press, 1996. First published 1959.

Rowan, Carl T. *Go South to Sorrow.* New York: Random House, 1957.

Royce, Josiah. *The Problem of Christianity.* Washington, D.C.: Catholic University of America Press, 2001. First published 1913.

Schlesinger, Arthur M., Jr. *The Cycles of American History.* Boston: Houghton Mifflin, 1986.

———. *The Disuniting of America.* New York: W. W. Norton, 1992.

———. *Journals, 1952–2000.* Edited by Andrew Schlesinger and Stephen C. Schlesinger. New York: Penguin Press, 2007.

———. *A Life in the Twentieth Century: Innocent Beginnings, 1917–1950.* Boston: Houghton Mifflin, 2000.

———. *Robert Kennedy and His Times.* Boston: Houghton Mifflin, 1978.

———. *A Thousand Days: John F. Kennedy in the White House.* Boston: Houghton Mifflin, 1965.

Seeger, Pete. *Pete Seeger: In His Own Words.* Edited by Rob Rosenthal and Sam Rosenthal. Nine Lives Musical Series. Boulder, Col.: Paradigm Publishers, 2012.

Sellers, Cleveland, with Robert Terrell. *The River of No Return: The Autobiography of a Black Militant and the Life and Death of SNCC.* New York: William Morrow, 1973.

Shelby, Tommie, and Brandon M. Terry, eds. *To Shape a New World: Essays on the Political Philosophy of Martin Luther King, Jr.* Cambridge, Mass.: The Belknap Press of Harvard University Press, 2018.

Simonelli, Frederick J. *American Fuehrer: George Lincoln Rockwell and the American Nazi Party.* Urbana: University of Illinois Press, 1999.

Skipper, John C. *Showdown at the 1964 Democratic Convention: Lyndon Johnson, Mississippi and Civil Rights.* Jefferson, N.C.: McFarland, 2012.

Smith, Howard K. *Events Leading Up to My Death: The Life of a Twentieth-Century Reporter.* New York: St. Martin's Press, 1996.

Smith, Kenneth L., and Ira G. Zepp, Jr. *Search for the Beloved Community: The Thinking of Martin Luther King, Jr.* Valley Forge, Penn.: Judson Press, 1998. First published 1974.

Sorensen, Theodore C. *Kennedy.* New York: Harper & Row, 1965.

Sridharani, Krshnalala. *War Without Violence: A Study of Gandhi's Method and Its Accomplishments.* New York: Harcourt, Brace, 1939.

Stewart, John G. *Witness to the Promised Land: Observations on Congress and the Presidency from the Pages of* Christianity & Crisis. Santa Ana, Calif.: Seven Locks Press, 2005.

Sullivan, Patricia. *Lift Every Voice: The NAACP and the Making of the Civil Rights Movement.* New York: New Press, 2009.

Tertullian. *Ad Martyras.* Trans. S. Thelwall. In *Ante-Nicene Fathers: Translations of the Writings of the Fathers Down to A.D. 325,* vol. 3. Edited by Alexander Roberts, James Donaldson, and A. Cleveland Coxe. Buffalo, N.Y.: Christian Literature Publishing Co., 1885.

Thelwell, Michael. *Duties, Pleasures, and Conflicts: Essays in Struggle.* Amherst: University of Massachusetts Press, 1987.

Thomas, Evan. *Robert Kennedy: His Life.* New York: Simon & Schuster, 2000.

Thoreau, Henry David. *Civil Disobedience and Other Essays.* Mineola, N.Y.: Dover Publications, 2012. First published by Dover in 1993.

Thurber, Timothy N. *Republicans and Race: The GOP's Frayed Relationship with African Americans, 1945–1974.* Lawrence: University Press of Kansas, 2013.

Thurman, Howard. *Jesus and the Disinherited.* New York: Abingdon-Cokesbury Press, 1949.

Tocqueville, Alexis de. *Democracy in America.* Edited by J. P. Mayer and translated by

George Lawrence. Garden City, N.Y.: Doubleday, 1969. First published in two volumes in 1835 and 1840.

Todd, Lisa Anderson. *For a Voice and the Vote: My Journey with the Mississippi Freedom Democratic Party*. Lexington: University Press of Kentucky, 2014.

Trelease, Allen W. *White Terror: The Ku Klux Klan Conspiracy and Southern Reconstruction*. New York: Harper & Row, 1971.

Tucker, Richard K. *The Dragon and the Cross: The Rise and Fall of the Ku Klux Klan in Middle America*. Hamden, Conn.: Archon Books, 1991.

Tyson, Timothy B. *The Blood of Emmett Till*. New York: Simon & Schuster, 2017.

Umoja, Akinyele Omowale. *We Will Shoot Back: Armed Resistance in the Mississippi Freedom Movement*. New York: New York University Press, 2013.

United States. Congress. Senate. Select Committee to Study Governmental Operations with Respect to Intelligence Activities. *Final Report of the Select Committee to Study Governmental Operations with Respect to Intelligence Activities, United States Senate: Together with Additional, Supplemental, and Separate Views*. Report, 94th Cong., 2d sess., Senate, no. 94–755. Book 2, *Intelligence Activities and the Rights of Americans*. Book 3, *Supplementary Detailed Staff Reports on Intelligence Activities and the Rights of Americans*. Washington, D.C.: U.S. Government Printing Office, 1976.

Varon, Elizabeth R. *Appomattox: Victory, Defeat, and Freedom at the End of the Civil War*. Oxford: Oxford University Press, 2014.

Visser-Maessen, Laura. *Robert Parris Moses: A Life in Civil Rights and Leadership at the Grassroots*. Chapel Hill: University of North Carolina Press, 2016.

Walker, Alice. *In Search of Our Mothers' Gardens: Womanist Prose*. San Diego: Harcourt Brace Jovanovich, 1983.

Wallach, Jennifer Jensen, and John A. Kirk, eds. *Arsnick: The Student Nonviolent Coordinating Committee in Arkansas*. Fayetteville: University of Arkansas Press, 2011.

Walton, Hanes, Jr., and Robert C. Smith. *American Politics and the African American Quest for Universal Freedom*. New York: Longman, 2000.

Warren, Robert Penn. *The Legacy of the Civil War: Meditations on the Centennial*. New York: Random House, 1961.

———. *Segregation: The Inner Conflict in the South*. New York: Random House, 1956.

Watson, Bruce. *Freedom Summer: The Savage Season That Made Mississippi Burn and Made America a Democracy*. New York: Viking, 2010.

Welty, Eudora. *The Eye of the Story: Selected Essays and Reviews*. New York: Random House, 1978.

White, Theodore H. *America in Search of Itself: The Making of the President, 1956–1980*. A Cornelia and Michael Bessie Book. New York: Harper & Row, 1982.

———. *The Making of the President, 1960*. New York: Atheneum, 1961.

———. *The Making of the President, 1964*. New York: Atheneum, 1965.

———. *The Making of the President, 1968*. New York: Atheneum, 1969.

Whitman, James Q. *Hitler's American Model: The United States and the Making of Nazi Race Law*. Princeton, N.J.: Princeton University Press, 2017.

Whittemore, Katharine, and Gerald Marzorati, eds. *Voices in Black & White: Writings on Race in America from* Harper's *Magazine*. The American Retrospective Series. New York: Franklin Square Press, 1993.

Widmer, Ted, ed. *Listening In: The Secret White House Recordings of John F. Kennedy*. New York: Hyperion, 2012.

Wilken, Robert L. *The Christians as the Romans Saw Them*. New Haven: Yale University Press, 1984.

Williams, Robert F. *Negroes with Guns.* Edited by Marc Schleifer. New York: Marzani & Munsell, 1962.

Wilson, James Southall. "Edward Alfred Pollard." In *Library of Southern Literature,* edited by Edwin A. Alderman, Joel C. Harris, and Charles W. Kent. Vol. 9, 4147–50. Atlanta, Ga.: Martin and Hoyt, 1907.

Wilson, Stephen, ed. *Saints and Their Cults: Studies in Religious Sociology, Folklore, and History.* Cambridge: Cambridge University Press, 1983.

Wofford, Harris. *Of Kennedys and Kings: Making Sense of the Sixties.* New York: Farrar, Straus, Giroux, 1980.

Wong, Kent, Ana Luz González, and James M. Lawson, Jr., eds. *Nonviolence and Social Movements: The Teachings of Rev. James M. Lawson Jr.* Los Angeles: UCLA Center for Labor Research and Education, 2016.

Woods, Jeff. *Black Struggle, Red Scare: Segregation and Anti-Communism in the South, 1948–1968.* Baton Rouge: Louisiana State University Press, 2004.

Woodward, C. Vann. *The Strange Career of Jim Crow.* 3rd rev. ed. New York: Oxford University Press, 1974.

Woodward, Kenneth L. *Making Saints: How the Catholic Church Determines Who Becomes a Saint, Who Doesn't, and Why.* A Touchstone Book. New York: Simon & Schuster, 1990.

Wright, Gavin. *Sharing the Prize: The Economics of the Civil Rights Revolution in the American South.* Cambridge, Mass.: Belknap Press of Harvard University Press, 2013.

Wright, Richard. *12 Million Black Voices: A Folk History of the Negro in the United States.* Photo-direction by Edwin Rosskam. New York: Viking Press, 1941.

X, Malcolm. *The Autobiography of Malcolm X.* New York: Grove Press, 1965.

———. *Malcolm X Speaks: Selected Speeches and Statements.* Edited by George Breitman. New York: Merit Publishers, 1965.

Yarrow, Simon. *The Saints: A Short History.* Oxford: Oxford University Press, 2016.

Young, Andrew. *An Easy Burden: The Civil Rights Movement and the Transformation of America.* Waco, Tex.: Baylor University Press, 2008. First published 1996.

Young, Nancy Beck. *Two Suns of the Southwest: Lyndon Johnson, Barry Goldwater, and the 1964 Battle Between Liberalism and Conservatism.* American Presidential Elections. Lawrence: University Press of Kansas, 2019.

Zeitz, Joshua. *Building the Great Society: Inside Lyndon Johnson's White House.* New York: Viking, 2018.

Zelizer, Barbie, ed. *Making the University Matter.* Shaping Inquiry in Culture, Communication and Media Studies. New York: Routledge, 2011.

Zinn, Howard. *SNCC: The New Abolitionists.* Boston: Beacon Press, 1964.

Articles

Baker, Robert E. "Grief and Fear Shared." *Washington Post,* September 19, 1963.

Burrow, Rufus, Jr. "The Beloved Community: Martin Luther King, Jr. and Josiah Royce." *Encounter* 73, no. 1 (Fall 2012): 37–64.

Carmichael, Stokely. "What We Want." *The New York Review of Books,* September 22, 1966.

Coates, Ta-Nehisi. "The Case for Reparations." *The Atlantic,* June 2014. https://www.theatlantic.com/magazine/archive/2014/06/the-case-for-reparations/361631/.

Cobb, James C. "The Voting Rights Act at 50: How It Changed the World." *Time,* August 6, 2015. https://time.com/3985479/voting-rights-act-1965-results/.

Coles, Robert, and Joseph Brenner. "American Youth in a Social Struggle: The Mississippi Summer Project." *American Journal of Orthopsychiatry* 35, no. 5 (October 1965): 909–26.

"Congressman John Lewis: An American Saint." *The Journal of Blacks in Higher Education* 21 (Autumn 1998): 42–43.

Coppola, Vincent. "The Parable of Julian Bond & John Lewis." *Atlanta,* March 1, 1990. https://www.atlantamagazine.com/great-reads/the-parable-of-julian-bond-john -lewis//.

"Dr. King's Closed Strategy Session Set the Strategy." *Life,* March 19, 1965.

Garrow, David J. "The FBI and Martin Luther King." *The Atlantic,* July / August 2002. https://www.theatlantic.com/magazine/archive/2002/07/the-fbi-and-martin -luther-king/302537/.

Gjelten, Tom. "The Immigration Act That Inadvertently Changed America." *The Atlantic,* October 2, 2015. https://www.theatlantic.com/politics/archive/2015/10/immigration -act-1965/408409/.

Good, Paul. "Odyssey of a Man—and a Movement." *New York Times Magazine,* June 25, 1967.

Halberstam, David. "A Good City Gone Ugly." *The Reporter,* March 31, 1960.

———. "The White Citizens Councils: Respectable Means for Unrespectable Ends." *Commentary,* October 1956.

Haley, Alex. "An Interview with Malcolm X: A Candid Conversation with the Militant Major-Domo of the Black Muslims." *Playboy,* May 1963.

Hall, Jacquelyn Dowd. "The Long Civil Rights Movement and the Political Uses of the Past." *Journal of American History* 91, no. 4 (March 2005): 1233–63.

Hardwick, Elizabeth. "After Watts." *The New York Review of Books,* March 31, 1966.

Harris, Art. "Legends in the Cross Fire." *Washington Post,* July 21, 1986.

Herstein, Gary. "The Roycean Roots of the Beloved Community." *The Pluralist* 4, no. 2 (Summer 2009): 91–107.

"Hoover Says Reds Exploit Negroes." *New York Times,* April 22, 1964.

" 'Hot Summer'; Race Riots in North." *New York Times,* July 26, 1964.

Hsu, Hua. "The End of White America?" *The Atlantic,* January–February 2009. https:// www.theatlantic.com/magazine/archive/2009/01/the-end-of-white-america /307208/.

Hunter-Gault, Charlayne. "Representative." *New Yorker,* April 1, 1967.

Kaufman, Michael T. "Stokely Carmichael, Rights Leader Who Coined 'Black Power,' Dies at 57." *New York Times,* November 16, 1998.

Kearse, Gregory S. "John Lewis: He's Still 'On the Case.'" *Ebony,* November 1976.

Latourelle, Rene. "Sanctity, a Sign of Revelation." *Theology Digest* 15, no. 1 (1967): 41–46.

"The Law: Trial by Jury." *Time,* October 3, 1955.

Lewis, John. "SNCC's Lewis: We March for Us . . . And for You." *New York Herald Tribune,* May 23, 1965.

Lomax, Louis E. "The Negro Revolt Against 'The Negro Leaders.'" *Harper's,* June 1960.

Lydon, Michael. " 'We Won at Convention,' Negro Party Declares." *Boston Globe,* August 30, 1964.

Mackin, Catherine. "She Steals LBJ's Thunder." *San Francisco Examiner,* August 26, 1964.

Mayer, Jeremy D. "LBJ Fights the White Backlash, Part 2." *Prologue Magazine,* Spring 2001.

"Mr. Lewis' Victory." *Washington Post,* September 8, 1986.

"Outrage at Selma." *Washington Post,* March 9, 1965.

Parham, Jason. "Emmett Till's Murder: What Really Happened That Day in the Store?" Review of *The Blood of Emmett Till,* by Timothy B. Tyson. *New York Times,* January 27, 2017.

Penez-Pena, Richard. "Woman Linked to 1955 Emmett Till Murder Tells Historian Her Claims Were False." *New York Times,* January 27, 2017.

Percy, Walker. "Mississippi: The Fallen Paradise." *Harper's,* April 1965.

Remnick, David. "The President's Hero." *New Yorker,* February 2, 2009.

Rustin, Bayard. "From Protest to Politics: The Future of the Civil Rights Movement." *Commentary,* February 1965.

"Saints Among Us: The Work of Mother Teresa." *Time,* December 29, 1975. http://content.time.com/time/subscriber/article/0,33009,945463,00.html.

Shaw, Michelle E. "Lillian Miles Lewis, 73: Wife, Adviser of U.S. Rep. John Lewis." *Atlanta Journal-Constitution,* December 31, 2012.

Simkins, Francis B. "The Ku Klux Klan in South Carolina, 1868–1871." *The Journal of Negro History* 12, no. 4 (October 1927): 606–47.

Sitton, Claude. "Birmingham Bomb Kills 4 Negro Girls in Church; Riots Flare; 2 Boys Slain." *New York Times,* September 16, 1963.

"Six Dead After Church Bombing." *Washington Post,* September 16, 1963.

"Transcript: Rep. John Lewis's Speech on 50th Anniversary of the March on Washington." *Washington Post,* August 28, 2013.

Trescott, Jacqueline. "John Lewis: After the Angry Words." *Washington Post,* August 21, 1983.

Trillin, Calvin. "Back on the Bus." *New Yorker,* July 18, 2011.

———. "State Secrets." *New Yorker,* May 29, 1995.

Waddle, Roy. "Days of Thunder: The Lawson Affair." *Vanderbilt Magazine,* Fall 2002.

Watters, Pat. "Keep on A-Walking, Children." *New American Review,* January 1969.

Weinraub, Bernard. "The Brilliancy of Black." *Esquire,* January 1967. https://classic.esquire.com/article/1967/1/1/the-brilliancy-of-black.

Whack, Errin. "Who Was Edmund Pettus?" *Smithsonian Magazine,* March 7, 2015. https://www.smithsonianmag.com/history/who-was-edmund-pettus-180954501/.

Wicker, Tom. "Mississippi Delegates Withdraw, Rejecting a Seating Compromise; Convention Then Approves Plan." *New York Times,* August 26, 1964.

Wilentz, Sean. "The Last Integrationist: John Lewis's American Odyssey." *The New Republic,* July 1, 1996.

Wynn, Linda T. "The Dawning of a New Day. The Nashville Sit-Ins, February 13–May 10, 1960." *Tennessee Historical Quarterly* 50, no. 1 (Spring 1991): 42–54.

Dissertation and Theses

Meier, Leila A. "'A Different Kind of Prophet': The Role of Kelly Miller Smith in the Nashville Civil Rights Movement, 1955–1960." Master's thesis, Vanderbilt University, 1991.

Rocksborough-Smith, Ian. "Bearing the Seeds of Struggle: *Freedomways* Magazine, Black Leftists, and Continuities in the Freedom Movement." Master's thesis, Simon Fraser University, 2005.

Sumner, David E. "The Local Press and the Nashville Student Movement, 1960." PhD. diss., University of Tennessee, 1989.

Young, Paige Eugenia. "Unknown Martyr: The Murder of Willie Edwards, Jr., and Civil Rights Violence in Montgomery, Alabama." Master's thesis, University of Georgia, 2003.

Documentary Films and Programs

CBS Reports: Who Speaks for Birmingham? Produced by David Lowe, narrated by Howard K. Smith. CBS, May 18, 1961. 60 min.

Eyes on the Prize. Produced by Henry Hampton. Blackside, 1987. 14 parts. http://www.pbs .org/wgbh/americanexperience/films/eyesontheprize/.

King in the Wilderness. Directed by Peter Kunhardt. Kunhardt Films, 2018. 1 hr., 51 min. https://www.kunhardtfilms.com/our-films/king-in-the-wilderness.

Love & Solidarity: James Lawson & Nonviolence in the Search for Workers' Rights. Directed by Michael Honey. Bullfrog Films, 2016. 38 min. http://www.bullfrogfilms.com/catalog /love.html.

NBC White Paper: Sit-In. Produced by Irving Gitlin, narrated by Chet Huntley. NBC, December 20, 1960. 59 min., 45 sec.

The Rape of Recy Taylor. Produced and directed by Nancy Buirski. Augusta Films, 2017. 91 min. https://www.therapeofrecytaylor.com/.

Soul of America. Kunhardt Films, 2020.

Websites

"American Baptist Theological Seminary Historic District." National Register of Historic Places Program, National Park Service. https://www.nps.gov/nr/feature/places /13000399.htm.

Brown, Anna, and Sara Atske. "Blacks Have Made Gains in U.S. Political Leadership, but Gaps Remain." Pew Research Center, January 18, 2019. https://www.pewresearch .org/fact-tank/2019/01/18/blacks-have-made-gains-in-u-s-political-leadership -but-gaps-remain/.

Gotobed, Julian, incorporating material submitted by Michelle Charles. "Walter Rauschenbusch (1861–1918.)" In *Boston Collaborative Encyclopedia of Western Theology*, edited by Wesley Wildman. http://people.bu.edu/wwildman/bce/rauschenbusch .htm.

Johnson, Lyndon Baines. "President Johnson's Special Message to the Congress: The American Promise." LBJ Presidential Library, March 15, 1965, http://www.LBJLibrary .org/lyndon-baines-johnson/speeches-films/president-johnsons-special-message -to-the-congress-the-american-promise.

Jones, Janelle, John Schmitt, and Valerie Wilson. "50 Years After the Kerner Commission." Economic Policy Institute, February 26, 2018. https://www.epi.org/publication /50-years-after-the-kerner-commission/.

Lewis, John. "Racial Reconciliation and Justice Week." Washington National Cathedral, March 30, 2018. https://cathedral.org/sermons/racial-reconciliation-and -justice-week/.

———. "Rep. John Lewis on the Legacy of President John F. Kennedy." Congressman John Lewis, Representing Georgia's 5th District, November 22, 2013. https://john lewis.house.gov/media-center/press-releases/rep-john-lewis-legacy-president -john-f-kennedy.

Newport, Frank, David W. Moore, and Lydia Saad. "The Most Important Events of the Century from the Viewpoint of the People." Gallup, December 6, 1999. https:// news.gallup.com/poll/3427/most-important-events-century-from-viewpoint -people.aspx.

Novkov, Julie. "Segregation (Jim Crow)." Encyclopedia of Alabama. http://www.ency clopediaofalabama.org/article/h-1248.

Obama, Barack. "Remarks by the President at the 50th Anniversary of the Selma to Montgomery Marches." The White House: President Barack Obama, March 7, 2015. https://obamawhitehouse.archives.gov/the-press-office/2015/03/07/remarks -president-50th-anniversary-selma-montgomery-marches.

Reynolds, Michael S. "York County." South Carolina Encyclopedia. http://www.scency clopedia.org/sce/entries/york-county/.

"Segregation Ruled Unequal, and Therefore Unconstitutional." American Psychological Association. https://www.apa.org/research/action/segregation.

United States Department of Justice, Civil Rights Division, Voting Section. "The Effect of the Voting Rights Act." Electronic Privacy Information Center. https://epic .org/privacy/voting/register/intro_c.html.

Author Interviews

Harry Belafonte, Taylor Branch, Hillary Clinton, Phyllis Cunningham, Richard Goodwin, Fred Gray, Bernard LaFayette, Jr., James M. Lawson, John Lewis, Worth Long, Charles Mauldin, Diane Nash, Mae Lewis Tyner.

Illustration List and Credits

downtown Nashville, February 21, 1961. Aiding the students is Rev. James Lawson. © GERALD HOLLY/USA TODAY NETWORK

82–83 A Freedom Rider bus went up in flames when a fire bomb was tossed through a window near Anniston, Alabama. The bus riders were testing bus station segregation in the south and escaped the burning bus to be beaten by a mob, May 14, 1961. ASSOCIATED PRESS

86 Blood-splattered Freedom Riders John Lewis and James Zwerg stand together after being attacked and beaten by pro-segregationists in Montgomery, Alabama, May, 1961. BETTMANN/GETTY IMAGES

92 Passengers on the Freedom Ride take refuge at the First Baptist Church from violence that met them at the Greyhound Bus Station. The church was besieged by a crowd who threatened to set fire to the building, Montgomery, Alabama, May 21, 1961. EXPRESS/PICTORIAL PARADE/ARCHIVE PHOTOS/HULTON ARCHIVE/GETTY IMAGES

93 The Freedom Riders relax, regroup, and heal in a safe house after being rescued from the First Baptist Church, Montgomery, Alabama, May 1961. PAUL SCHUTZER/THE LIFE PICTURE COLLECTION VIA GETTY IMAGES

100 Dixiecrat poster for Strom Thurmond's 1948 presidential campaign. HERITAGE AUCTIONS, HA.COM

101 Southern Democrats, mostly University of Mississippi students, rally for Strom Thurmond's presidential campaign, Birmingham, Alabama, 1948. CQ ROLL CALL VIA GETTY IMAGES

104 Eugene "Bull" Connor, Birmingham commissioner of public safety, 1963. © BOB ADELMAN ESTATE

109 Civil rights leaders hold a news conference announcing that the Freedom Rides will continue. In the foreground is John Lewis, with a bandage on his head, one of the riders who was beaten. Others, left to right: James Farmer, Rev. Ralph Abernathy, and Rev. Martin Luther King, Jr., Montgomery, Alabama, May 23, 1961. ASSOCIATED PRESS

113 A guard observing prisoners at Parchman Prison, Mississippi, 1963. © DANNY LYON/MAGNUM PHOTOS

114 John Lewis mug shots from arrests in Nashville, Tennessee, February 1961 and February 1962. COURTESY OF DAVID STEELE EWING AND NASHVILLE POLICE DEPARTMENT

116–117 John Lewis, chairman of the Student Nonviolent Coordinating Committee, speaks at the March on Washington for Jobs and Freedom, Washington, D.C., August 28, 1963. AFRO AMERICAN NEWSPAPERS/GADO/GETTY IMAGES

120 President John F. Kennedy making his televised speech on civil rights, June 11, 1963. PICTORIAL PRESS LTD /ALAMY STOCK PHOTO

121 (top) Walter Gadsden, 15, is attacked by a police dog during a civil rights demonstration. Gadsden was an onlooker to the protest, Birmingham, Alabama, May 3, 1963. BILL HUDSON/ASSOCIATED PRESS

121 (bottom) Black children being hosed by police and firemen, Birmingham, Alabama, May 3, 1963. COURTESY CSU ARCHIVES/EVERETT COLLECTION

124 Klu Klux Klan members burning a cross north of Tuscaloosa, Alabama, 1963. CLAUDE SITTON/THE NEW YORK TIMES/REDUX

125 Alabama governor George C. Wallace promises "segregation now,

	segregation tomorrow, segregation forever" during his 1963 inaugural address. BETTMANN/GETTY IMAGES
128	James Baldwin and Medgar Evers, Mississippi, 1963. © STEVE SCHAPIRO, COURTESY OF FAHEY/KLEIN GALLERY
146–147	Delegates and stage at the 1964 Democratic National Convention, Atlantic City, New Jersey. EVERETT COLLECTION/ALAMY STOCK PHOTO
149	Carol Denise McNair, 11; Carole Robertson, 14; Addie Mae Collins, 14; and Cynthia Wesley, 14, were killed in the Sixteenth Street Baptist Church bombing on September 15, 1963, shown in these 1963 photos. REX/SHUTTERSTOCK
150	Civil rights activists Jimmy Hicks, Julian Bond, John Lewis, and Jeremiah X stand across the street from a bombed church where four young black girls were killed while attending Sunday school, Birmingham, Alabama, 1963. © DANNY LYON/MAGNUM PHOTOS
159 (top)	The burned station wagon of three missing civil rights workers— Michael Schwerner, Andrew Goodman, and James Earl Chaney— found in a swampy area near Philadelphia, Mississippi, June 24, 1964. JACK THORNELL/ASSOCIATED PRESS
159 (bottom)	FBI missing persons poster displays the photographs of civil rights workers Andrew Goodman, James Earl Chaney, and Michael Henry Schwerner after they disappeared in Mississippi in June 1964. It was later discovered that they were murdered by the Ku Klux Klan. BETTMANN/GETTY IMAGES
161	Robert Franklin Williams and Mabel Williams working on newsletter, Havana, 1963. © 2020 ROBERT CARL COHEN
166	FBI director J. Edgar Hoover, circa 1960. EVERETT COLLECTION
169	President Lyndon Johnson meets with Martin Luther King, Jr., in the Cabinet Room at the White House, Washington, D.C., March 18, 1966. LBJ LIBRARY PHOTO BY YOICHI OKAMOTO
170	President Johnson shakes hands with Martin Luther King, Jr., after signing the Civil Right Act, July 2, 1964. BETTMANN/GETTY IMAGES
172	Fannie Lou Hamer, Mississippi Freedom Democratic Party delegate, Democratic National Convention, Atlantic City, New Jersey, August 22, 1964. GLASSHOUSE IMAGES/ALAMY STOCK PHOTO
179	Empty seats of the Mississippi delegation at the 1964 Democratic National Convention. Led by Fannie Lou Hamer, the Mississippi Freedom Democratic Party challenged the credentials of the all-white and anti–civil rights delegation, Atlantic City, New Jersey, August 24, 1964. EVERETT COLLECTION
182–183	State troopers swing billy clubs to break up a civil rights voting march. John Lewis, chairman of the SNCC, is being beaten, and sustained a fractured skull, Selma, Alabama, March 7, 1965. ASSOCIATED PRESS
186	Harry Belafonte, SCLC leader Andrew Young, and SNCC leader John Lewis during the final day of the Selma-to-Montgomery March for Voting Rights, March 21, 1965. MATT HERRON/TAKE STOCK/ TOPFOTO
187	Malcolm X reading stories about himself in a pile of newspapers, circa 1963. THREE LIONS/HULTON ARCHIVE/GETTY IMAGES

Index

Note: Page numbers in *italics* refer to photographs or their captions.

JON MEACHAM is a Pulitzer Prize–winning presidential historian. A contributing writer for *The New York Times Book Review* and a contributing editor of *Time* magazine, he is the author of the *New York Times* bestsellers *The Hope of Glory, Destiny and Power: The American Odyssey of George Herbert Walker Bush, Thomas Jefferson: The Art of Power, American Lion: Andrew Jackson in the White House, American Gospel,* and *Franklin and Winston.* Meacham is a distinguished visiting professor and holds the Rogers Chair in the American Presidency at Vanderbilt University. He lives with his family in Nashville, Tennessee.